Estonia:

A Ramble Through The Periphery

For Sarah

*Tanto gentile e tanto onesta pare
la donna mia quand'ella altrui saluta
ch'ogne lingua deven tremando muta
e li occhi no l'ardiscon do guardare.*

Dante
Vita Nuova, iv. 2

and to friend and sage, T. Peter Park

Fantagraphics Books, 7563 Lake City Way NE, Seattle, Washington 98115 | Editor: Gavin Lees; Editorial Liaison: Gary Groth; Designer: Alexa Koenings; Photographs: Alexander Theroux and Sarah Son-Theroux; Cover and interior paintings: Sarah Son-Theroux; Associate Publisher: Eric Reynolds; Published by Gary Groth & Kim Thompson | *Estonia: A Ramble Through the Periphery* is copyright © 2011 Alexander Theroux; This edition is copyright © 2011 Fantagraphics Books. All rights reserved. Permission to quote or reproduce material for reviews must be obtained from the author or the publisher. | To receive a free catalogue of books, including those by Mr. Theroux, call 1-800-657-1100 or visit our website at www.fantagraphics.com. | Distributed in the U.S. by W.W. Norton and Company, Inc. (800-233-4830); Distributed in Canada by Canadian Manda Group (800-452-6642 x862); Distributed in the U.K. by Turnaround Distribution (44 (0)20 8829-3002) | ISBN 978-1-60699-465-8 | Printed in China.

"It is clear that the causal nexus is not a nexus at all."

Ludwig Wittgenstein

"If the volume or the tone of the work can lead one to believe that the author is attempting a sum, hasten to point out to him that he is face to face with the opposite attempt, that of an implacable *subtraction*."

Julio Cortázar
Hopscotch

"The noble Phocion…was afraid of applause. For a true man feels that he has quite another office than to tickle or flatter. He is here to bite and to stab and to inflict wounds on self-love and easy, prosperous falsehood, which shall not quickly heal. Demosthenes, when the people hissed him for his ragged and untuneable voice, cried out, 'You are to judge players, indeed, by their sweet voices, but orators by the gravity and power of their sentences.'"

Ralph Waldo Emerson
New England: Genius, Manners, and Customs

Contents

Overture

I will be your guide on this trip, for want of anyone else — this way, if you please. We are not touring a mainstream destination, right off. Graham Greene originally titled his 1954 novel *Our Man in Tallinn*, remember, not *Havana* — I have no doubt he wanted a more recognizable map. Marco Polo did not go to Estonia. Neither did Ibn Battuta, Richard Hakluyt, Bayard Taylor, George Borrow, Joshua Slocum, Somerset Maugham, or for that matter Captain James Cook who traveled the world. Richard Halliburton never went there. Neither did Herodotus or Pigafetta, Burton or Speke, Geoffrey Moorehouse or Bruce Chatwin. Edward S. Aarons' famous fictional globe-trotting detective, Sam Durell, traveled to virtually every country on earth — Hungary, Burma, Ceylon, etc. — but never to Estonia. If it is not the back of beyond, it is just in front of it.

It is a place at such a remove, so to speak, if not an actual outback, that I had a ghastly dream the other night that I was collecting rocks in a Gustave Doré-like quarry there resembling Mars. So, if you will, please think of me as your "man" in this unique and faraway republic. As I say, Estonia is a distant and remote country, with many masks, changing identities, alien habits, altering connotations, idiosyncratic manners. A Baltic hinterland. Eastland. Late a Cold War appendage to the Soviet Union.

When I mentioned to him that I intended to travel to this relatively far-flung location, John Updike playfully inquired of me, "Estonia. Isn't that Finland's baby brother?" Estonia, which is indeed small, is part of that Baltic trisect, along with both Latvia and Lithuania. It is an "unspoiled extension of Scandinavia, with only a residue of Russia," wrote Priit Vesilind in *National Geographic Traveler*. Back in the days of gruesome occupation, not much more than a decade ago, it was but a little piglet to the left of its vast and imposing sow, the Soviet Union, a very tiny part of it, to be sure, the second smallest country in population (1.3 million) and in size, of all the Soviet republics — the smallest republic was actually Armenia with an area of 29,800 square kilometers (Estonia has 45,277 square kilometers) — one of the true runts of the litter. Indeed, T.R. Reid has compared Estonians to "defenseless badgers living beside the den of a giant bear, perpetually on its haunches next door."

Mother Russia, the gigantic, authoritarian overlord which shares land borders with as many as fourteen countries from Norway to North Korea — indeed, the largest country in the world — was always Estonia's psychic or mythic opposite, its Jungian shadow, occupying one-sixth of the earth's land surface and possessing almost every natural resource. If "California is the west coast of Iowa," as writer Joan Didion once cavalierly pronounced, Estonia is something like the back hall or lumber room of Russia. With its population of 143 million, one of the world's largest, Russia ranks right near the top in world industry. It was the first to send a satellite in space. And there, standing — hunkered down — next to it: Estonia. It thuds in visual disproportion much more profoundly than tiny Kuwait to Iraq. One could apply to the Russian/Estonian *politique* what, when summing up the attitude of the Greeks to their neighbors, historian Thucydides wrote: "The strong did what they could; the weak suffered what they must." Size so cruelly predetermines a country's, a people's, fate. So be it.

Maktub. It is written.

Little Estonia. Sancho Panza. Peewee. A collapsing tiny box-set of a republic that is dark as a cave in winter, shit-cold for most of the year, a strange ignored dorp with no ice-free ports, a queer language, curious laws, rummy food, eccentric people, funny money, and a veritable forest of unreadable signs. I will say right off that I was eager to go to Estonia, for who would deny that to wake up to find oneself in any new place is surely one of the major thrills of being alive? When suddenly I awakened to find myself there, so abruptly it seemed to be without explanation, my only thought was: *just splendid: no one ever comes here and that's the delight!* A bit of background is in order. My wife, Sarah, an artist, was awarded a Fulbright Grant there to paint landscapes and wanted my company. I decided to spend the winter and spring, perhaps even longer, to be with her, to do some traveling, and to frog away on a novel which had been on my mind for a decade and which I had already begun. I packed my bags, whistling, and flew east with joy by way of Stockholm. I will add here that immediately upon arrival, landing in Tallinn, I knew I was going to write about the place, seeing with growing conviction, how unique it was. I would make a book of it as surely as Father Robinson in *The Swiss Family Robinson*, with nothing more than the shell of a giant sea-tortoise, contrived to make a wash basin. I brought my imagination with me. There is a fiction in one's head that frames, that forms, that fashions — that encourages — the meeting of facts in reality. A poem is never finished, or so Shelley said, it is abandoned. A country is not merely found, it must be sought.

Over the years I had read many travel books, fascinating accounts particularly of small, out-of-the-way places. I especially enjoyed small, tidy, informative records of remote but intriguing, outré locales of which travel literature abounds. What came to mind were books like W.H. Auden and Louis MacNeice's *Letters from Iceland*, Evelyn Waugh's *Remote People*, Jacques-Henri Bernadin de Saint-Pierre's *Journey to Mauritius*, William Burroughs' *The Yage Letters*, E.E. Cummings' *Eimi: A Journal Through Soviet Russia*, Charles Dickens' *Pictures from Italy*, Henry Miller's *The Colossus of Maroussi*, Maxim Gorky's *American Sketches*, Bayard Taylor's *A Journey to Central Africa; or Life and Landscapes from Egypt to the Negro Kingdom of the White Nile*, Henry James' *A Little Tour in France*, Rebecca West's *Black Lamb and Grey Falcon* — maybe the most thorough travel book ever penned — Doris Lessing's *African Laughter: Four Visits to Zimbabwe*, Julio Cortázar's *Autonauts of the Cosmoroute*, Truman Capote's *The Muses Are Heard*, and, among others, Sacheverell Sitwell's insightful book on postwar Japan, *The Bridge of the Brocade Sash*.

Estonia, frankly, is more than out of the way. It is secluded, unfrequented, a tiny, unlikely outback. As I say, Marco Polo gave it a pass. Columbus sailed nowhere near it. Juan Ponce de Leon wanted to find Bimini, Coronado the Seven Cities of Cibola, Magellan the Philippines. Who sought Estonia? The last full *National Geographic* article to focus on Estonia exclusively and in depth was as far back as December 1939. (I sought a commission from them before I left to write a major article for their magazine, but they never bothered to answer my letter.) Not one of mystery writer Agatha Christie's 66 novels, many set in exotic locations, uses Estonia as a location. In Patricia Schultz's 2003 best-seller *1,000 Places To See Before You Die* — a book 900-plus pages thick — Estonia does not merit a single reference. Look in vain for it in Frederic E. Tyarks' *The Guide to Traveling Around the World by Passenger-Carrying Freighters*, a vade mecum for college students in the 1960s. It is not even mentioned in any of the "How People Live" segments of Charlie Brown's *Fourth Super Book of Questions and Answers*. I doubt that many people will be surprised that there is no Red Michelin Guide for Estonia. As N.Y. Yankee manager Casey Stengel would say, "You can look it up."

It has never predominated, never been a hub, never a circus, in the British sense of being a center. No Olympic Games were ever held there, in winter or summer. No World's Fair or Exposition ever took place in Estonia. No International Horticultural Exposition. No World Summit. No World Council of Religious Leaders ever convened there. Buffalo Bill's Wild West Show toured Europe over the course of four years, intermittently, from 1902 through 1906, visiting such outbacks as Ljubljana, Slovenia; Békéscsaba, Hungary; Bielsko-Biala, Poland; Kikinda, Serbia; and, among other places, Arad, Romania. It never went to to Estonia.

I had flown from Boston to New York, Stockholm to Tallinn, all the while collaborating with my multicolored dreams of where I was going. I landed like a wet nighthawk in a snowstorm, and breezing through, well, customs (a few small rooms, one loud-speaker predictably off-adjustment, and a single uniformed man whose over-sized cap gave him bat-ears) was met at the airport by Sarah who, having gone ahead of me, had been living there alone for some months. We had talked a lot on the telephone intermittently, in flurries of emails, and I knew the protracted winter darkness there had begun to oppress her. The calamity had an almost organized gravity. For a landscape painter? Scoping sites? Needing light? No, she had a distinct point. The remedy? "I take comfort in the light of my computer," she had wistfully emailed me on Christmas Eve, and it almost broke my heart. But she was young and resilient, our plans were big, and in spite of it all we were singing the "Ode to Joy." So there I was, suddenly walking the icy streets and peering up at old wooden houses and living under the pewter skies of *Estland* among an odd bustling crowd of natives, many who seemed sad in repose, extremely buttoned-up, busy in the city with briefcases and downflapped caps, and in other, outlying, rural areas where I took old wheezing buses to see an essentially sober, working, gum-booted population of snub-nosed *untermensch* quizzically holding up hay forks as you passed and seeming to wonder exactly what it was you wanted. I quickly began to wonder why Estonians were so — um, standoffish does not adequately describe the mood. Do you know the condition known as "impression management"? Where certain obliging, often neurotic types, who know what people want, desperately try to give it to them, in order to try to manage the impression one receives of them? I was beginning to see that the Estonian mind was exactly the *opposite!* I knew of course that it was a country with a painful past — a place that for more than half a century was virtually hidden from the world — but I saw, with some regret, that natives still seemed to peer out at one from under shells, even if psychological ones. Look at the country. It is even *shaped* something like a turtle shell!

"Memory is the same as the imagination," wrote Giambattista Vico in *New Science* in 1725. People in Estonia who cannot help but sustain many bad memories — they have been run over by the Nazis and the Communists for over 70 years — cannot now and doubtless will ever relinquish those dark, haunting, and indelible memories. Bad as they were, however, I was told that folks there could always imagine worse. A pessimistic truism is that the Estonian mind only conforms to reality. Czeslaw Milosz suggests in *The Captive Mind* that it is possible that the only real memory we have is the memory of wounds. May one say pessimism has its virtues? It is rank pessimism, after all, that spurs people, being frankly realistic, never mind properly circumspect, to take out insurance against hurricanes and floods, to invest in gold in financial crises, and before marriage to check into prenuptial agreements. In the Bible there is no mention that the sky is blue. Is that not revealing? Perhaps. We thrive on doubt constantly, downsizing our hopes and dreams as we grow older. What child is not set up for black reversals and sharp disappointment? Who has not experienced some form of early reversal, as I did when innocently crossing a neighbor's lawn at the age of seven I was slapped across the face, allowing for a lifetime of such unexpected possibilities? Which of us is not told by some bumptious and overweening parent that he can grow up to be anything he wants, only to find out he cannot manage to get grades above C in high school? So when does it end, if ever? The unlikely is too often the probable. Rainer Maria Rilke met death by picking a rose. To honor a visitor, the Egyptian beauty Nimet Eloui, he gathered some roses from his garden. While doing so, he pricked his hand on a thorn. This small wound failed to heal, grew rapidly worse, soon his entire arm was swollen, and his other arm became affected as well, and so he died. On his gravestone can be seen his coat of arms and two mysterious lines in German as his epitaph:

Rose, oh reiner Widerspruch Lust
Neimandes Schlaf zu sein unter soviel Lidern[1]

An Estonian as a pedlar of positivism is in all instances a walking oxymoron. His recollections are far too extensive, his memory too long, his wounds too recent to put a tingle of optimism in his besieged and beleaguered heart. Memory and imagination, at least in a Viconian sense, are often very much the same. During an occupation, far more than a country is captured — a national soul is possessed. Brutalized. Mortified. Hurt. Made inflexible. Freedom itself, the very idea of it, becomes victim, as well. More than self is lost, a soul harmed. There is the loss of the sense of adventure. Circumspection results. A collective unconscious is left with fears and a terrible rigidity it can never relinquish. Stasis murders. William Gass in "The Doomed in Their Sinking"[2] wisely observed, "[As] authorities 'over' us are removed, as we wobble out on our own, the question of whether to be or not to be arises with real relevance for the first time, since the burden of being is felt most fully by the self-determining self."

Citing a philosophical difference between them, A.N. Whitehead faulted John Dewey for giving too much emphasis in thought on security. "But the vitality of man's mind is in adventure," said Whitehead[3] who even stated beauty came before truth. ("Apart from beauty, truth is neither good nor bad.") Through rigidity, he points out, even the daring of once intrepid pilgrims of the Plymouth Colony "curdled." "The idea was losing its vitality. It had ceased to be adventure. The inheritors of it inherit[ed] the idea without inheriting the fervour." It is for this reason that he opts for the daring, civilizing Greek mind with its stress on aesthetics as contrasted to the less adventurous Egyptians. There is a stasis that inevitability takes over under the stress of insecurity.

Russia, which can still flex its muscles, during the frozen winter of

2008 peevishly went ahead and simply shut off the gas supply to the entire Ukraine over disputes of supplies, prices, and debts. As far back as 420 B.C., Thucydides in his *History of the Peloponnesian War* made the poignant observation: "It is a maxim allowed, that no state can possibly preserve itself free unless it be a match for neighboring powers." He was correct. Estonia which is bite-sized is also pretty much off the standard tourist radar, a low profile piece of Eastern Europe with a benighted tribal people that is keen to but not quite ready to adapt easily to other ways. Train stations are far and few between. Many of those are dark and desolate and in some of the smaller towns seem deserted, and often are, with no ticket agents and no services of any kind. A train leaves from Tallinn to Riga or Vilnius only three times a week. There is no train station in Tartu. No train to Riga or Vilnius leaves from or goes to the town — Estonia's second largest — only a bumpy bus. Some of the country buses are outmoded and can be slow. I remember one old bus we took to Põlva whose ancient motor sounded weakly like the slow unflexing of an open potato-chip bag. You cannot fly anywhere from Tartu. To go to Vilnius in Lithuania by air, you have to take a three-hour bus to Tallinn from Tartu. A bus from Tartu to Vilnius takes 12 hours. You always have to be in the capital city to be able to fly. St. Petersburg and Tallinn are serviced by an overnight train on alternate evenings, and an overnight train runs every evening between Moscow and Tallinn.

Right now European trains cannot reach the railroads of the Baltic states, and the only direction abroad from Tallinn's train station leads to the East, making Estonia, like all the Baltic states, the most isolated part of Europe. A new project being discussed is for "Rail Baltica," linking Finland to Germany, going through Estonia, Latvia, Lithuania, and Poland, but as all countries which had been under the Soviet empire used the Russian rail gauge, 9 cm wider than the European standard, a "gauge battle" is now being fought. Many prefer no change, although it would help the economy. (Income from tourism in the Baltics is ten times less than in Finland, Sweden, and Denmark.) It seemed sadly significant to me. Renegadism explains a lot about Estonia. I saw early that the people did things their own way there, restlessly, under the slate-gray skies there, the cruel winter skies, the soul-flattening, washed-out, blue-green skies that always seem to be the color of dirty ice. "The Baltic, restless, Wehrmacht grey," as Thomas Pynchon wrote in *Gravity's Rainbow*. But I was still looking for the glass half-full. I was traveling with a light heart. I wanted to wash the window-panes, not slubber them. I wanted to write a travel book, not compose what would turn out, by default, to be a grim prison diary.

Poking Around the Periphery

Although Estonia is presently considered a high-technology country, computer-wired and all — citizens were given permission in 2007 to cast ballots by way of the Internet in parliamentary elections, and by parliamentary approval it will become the very first country to allow its citizens to cast their votes by mobile telephone in the next parliamentary election in 2011 — I began slowly to suspect that too much of the country was still local and pretty much a boat-axe culture of potato-sellers and loggers, apiculturists and cabbage-hoers. I took for granted that it was all there in the *Kalevipoeg*, the national epic, which in its legends depicts a rude and rustic world. So was I correct in my smug and self-assured estimate? Not at all. The incontrovertible fact is that Estonia has the third-highest literacy rate in the entire world (99.8), following — yes — Georgia and Cuba, higher than the United States. Its almost unresponsive smallness is what gives it, sadly, the rustification tag. Sparse as Norway, which has the lowest population density in Europe — only 4,300,000 people — Estonia has fewer residents than the present-day Gaza Strip, only a few more people than Mauritania. Estonia's dwindling population-rate which has not quite reached the lower reproductive potential of the California condor[4] poses something of a scandal even to them, and to know that it ranks somewhere near the bottom of the world in terms of world-population is a source of no small awkwardness and, to a large degree, even worry to them. With only 1.3 million inhabitants, Estonia is one of the least populous countries in the European Union.[5] The current fertility rate there is 1.41 children per mother. (Benefits for pregnancy in Estonia include a more-than-generous *16-month paid leave* for the mother-to-be, so eagerly are births welcomed there.) I was often reminded of this in the way that Estonians almost superstitiously love children — to see, to pamper them — even though in a weird paradox they seem to rarely hold them. During the Soviet occupation, the country of Estonia also had the highest rate of emigration than any of the other Soviet republics, with people looking to emigrate at every possibility.

I walked everywhere. I tried, by walking, to observe the people and places. Walking in the electric blue cold always helped me proceed much faster and perhaps more purposefully. Harry Truman on his post-presidential constitutionals — for exercise — always saw to it that the fast pace he kept was precisely 120 steps per minute! I will bet that on a windy Baltic winter day if I did not match him, I came close. I walked past beetfields, through green mists and spoiling fog, walked out at night to outlying highways where it was eerie and soundless until roaring trucks would go past like a herd of Triceratops.

A sense of depletion in the outlying sections of Estonia still sadly maintains. There is a vastness of long woods outside all main cities. Nearly 40% of the country is forested, mainly with pine and birches along the coasts. Cutting down trees and selling lumber is probably the major small industry there, for its forests are vast, its countryside a flat, ongoing sameness.

Food, construction and newly-burgeoning electronic industries are Estonia's most important. The country exports mainly machinery and equipment, wood and paper, textiles, food products, furniture, metals, and chemical products. It also exports 1.562 billion kilowatt hours of electricity annually. The country had a frighteningly high unemployment rate — 14.3% — in 2010. It has a fairly high tax burden, with its VAT (value added tax) of 20%, to make the comparison, even higher than it presently is in the UK. Its border with Russia is the fourth longest in Europe, but, from what I managed to see, little of significance is happening along that eastern march. A visitor looks around to try to find a figure in the carpet. What exactly is there in the country's profile that can be drawn as a way to know them? I felt confounded in the main, for there is in the national personality a guard that is rarely dropped, a methodical indifference that with an almost fatally easy sense of disobligation steadily refuses to invite one in. A want of identity is invariably a topic raised but rarely pursued in essential Estonian conversation. I have always considered it depressingly apposite to this situation, a sort of objective correlative, that in Theodore H. White's *Fire in the Ashes*, a book that specifically addressed the subject of "Europe in mid-century," an astute, thoroughgoing report documenting the Soviet bloc and the merciless stranglehold that it held on so much of Europe for so long, he mentions the country of Estonia *not at all*. The country is not named, not referenced, never alluded to, not once. Neither is Latvia or Lithuania, and that includes the index. So much for postwar value.

I mention technology. Skype, the Internet telephone service, was once strictly an Estonian company. It was the pride of Estonia. It was bought in 2006 by eBay for more than two billion dollars. In May of 2011, however, Microsoft went on to purchase Skype for $8.5 billion in cash, the largest acquisition that Microsoft has ever made, but chump change for the Seattle giant. As I say, Estonia is more than just technologically hip; it is mobile-phone addicted and completely Internet-literate. (In 2010, Estonia got rid of every one of its street telephone booths and canceled the use of telephone cards intended for them. The number of calls made from them had decreased by 30 times over the past 10 years, and they were no longer in demand.) In this small country, Wi-Fi is everywhere. Voting can be done on-line by way of a national identity card. I believe that they have more cell phones in the country, percentage-wise, than does the United States, and there they are used for everything from buying newspapers from a vending machine to selecting numbers in the lottery to ascertaining when the next bus is coming. It is amazing how geekishly "connected" the country is in regard to technology. Identity cards in general are popular entry tools. As a visitor to that country, I had to buy a card in the University of Tartu library just to walk around. I may mention here, however, that Estonia is a highly dependent country in terms of energy and energy production. In recent years many companies have been investing in renewable energy sources. Wind power and interest in it has been increasing steadily in Estonia, and many projects in wind, to capture the robust east wind coming across from Russia, or sinewy west wind relentlessly driving in from the oceans, are being thoroughly developed even as I write. The country, which has no nuclear plant, however, is presently investigating nuclear power and looking to increase its oil shale production.[6]

While technological growth is hugely important for the country, one also hopes that coming out of a long night of relative obscurity Estonia will not become a slave to science at the expense of free-ranging imagination. H.G. Wells' verdict on Lenin was that he was "a dreamer in technology." Lenin's gnomic remark, "Communism is Electrification plus Soviets" surely indicates a blind faith in the machine as savior and agent of socialism. As André Malraux told Bruce Chatwin,

> As the young have discovered, the secret divinity of the twentieth-century is science. But Science is incapable of forming character. The more people talk of human sciences, the less effect human sciences have on man. You know as well as I do that psychoanalysis has never made a man. And the formation of man is his most pressing problem facing humanity.[7]

A Little History

A people closely related to the Finns, Estonians have existed in one form or other in this small postage stamp of land for nearly 11,000 years, since the end of the Ice Age. The very earliest settlements in Estonia began around 8500 B.C. By 6500 B.C. Estonia and neighboring areas of the eastern Baltic Sea coast from southern Finland to northern Lithuania supported the hunting and fishing Mesolithic (European Middle Paleolithic) "Kunda Culture" — over 3,000 years before Egypt's King Cheops built the Great Pyramid around 2700 B.C. Rudimentary life in the peat bogs. Seal-hunting. Bone and antler tools.

Around 4000 B.C., the Kunda Culture gave way to the "Comb-Ceramic" Culture with its distinctive pottery — and possibly the earliest form of the Estonian language. It is not exactly known when Finno-Ugric languages ancestral to modern Finnish, Hungarian, Sami (Laplander), and Estonian were first introduced into the Baltic region from a presumed original homeland near the Volga River and Ural Mountains. Various linguists, however, have suggested dates between 4000 and 2000 B.C. What languages the very earliest ancestors of the Estonians (e.g., the Kunda folk) may have spoken is frankly not known. Could they have spoken something akin to Basque? We know that Finnish was strongly influenced by Swedish over the centuries, while Estonian has acknowledged a debt to German (mainly Low German) and to the Slavic tongues, mostly Russian, but also to Belorussian, to Polish, to some extent, and to the Baltic languages — actually in the Baltic language group, by Latvian and Proto-Baltic much more than by Lithuanian. They are nevertheless both members of the Ural-Altaic super-family, and that close relationship between the two languages, distinct cousins, is noteworthy, as can be seen in the following pairs of words, taking the Finnish word first, and then following it with the Estonian word: *sana–sõna* ("word"); *pelto–põld* ("field"); *kutsua–kutsuma* ("call"); *mies–mees* ("man"); *oikea–õige* ("right, correct, straight"); *isa–isa* ("father"); *kaikki–kõik* ("all, everything").

There is notably a frequent occurrence in both languages of the double-vowel *–aa–*, as well as such clusters as *–ii–* or *y–* followed by any double consonant. (The letters *aa* and *u*, so often repeated, are to Estonian what the letter *j* is to Serbian — pullulating!) Finnish specifically lacks the Estonian letters *õ* and *ü*, and it lacks entirely the sound represented by Estonian *õ*. Finnish represents the sound of the Estonian *ü* by the letter *y*. Both the Estonian *ü* and the Finnish *y* have the sound of the German *ü*. The Estonian *õ* is not a nasalized vowel, by the way, but rather a mid-high, unrounded back or "guttural" vowel that specifically resembles the vowel of the English words "bird, burn, her, learn," pronounced a bit further back in the throat and without that identifiably specific "r" coloration that is usually given with the usual American pronunciation.

Carson McCullers in *The Mortgaged Heart* wrote, "I love the voices of Negroes — like brown rivers." Henry James said Scandinavian "danced." Australians seem to chew bark when talking. A bigot I know insists Chinese sounds like "a bunch of ducks trying to bite off each other's heads." Spoken Estonian actually seems to *bounce*, like many Scandinavian languages. There is a sky-glide to it, with many liquid *u* sounds showing what I believe has a strong labial and palatal touch to it, like Russian. I find Estonian has a clear, clean sound. Estonians tend to pronounce every letter when they speak, as Italians do in their language. There are no silent letters, except a widespread tendency to drop initial *h*s, but not at the cost of dropping, slurring, or weakening unstressed syllables. Nor can one find in the language those strenuous agglomerations of consonants that one hears in Czech, Slovak, and Serbo-Croatian Brno, Krk, Strbr, Hrdlička, Vltava, or Hrvatska, or even Latvian. Consider, for example, several real Latvian names, chosen at random — Uldis Stříbrný, Zdeněk Kārkliņŝ, Rozalija Ozoliņŝ! When pronounced, they actually sound like what an art critic from the *New York Times* said Marcel Duchamp's *Nude Descending a Staircase* resembled — "an explosion in a shingle factory." I can only picture being stopped in a car with four Estonians on board by an American policeman, among the meanest bastards on earth, and his taking down their names: Seppo Zappo, August Nikastama, Lepp Vaimulik, Korral Ehituskrunt — he would think he was staring into a goddamn clown car.

There is also in Estonian none of the Slavic profusion of sibilants like *s, z, sh, zh, ch, ts, dz*-type sounds. Nor can one detect any of that throatiness or those breathy sounds that one finds, say, in spoken Inuit or in Chinese or Greek. Nothing of the Mr. Scrabble sort, with its plethora of *zs, ks, gs*. I myself hear a lot of abrupt punch on stressed syllables in Estonian speech. Voices are always conundra, however. Do you remember in the classic tale of Edgar Allan Poe's *The Murders in the Rue Morgue* how in the chaos of the crime all the witnesses who had been listening heard two voices spoken behind the closed door but, in the end, got it all wrong, guessing that of the two voices they heard one was French and the other was "high-pitched," maybe Spanish? As it turns out, lo and behold, the sound they heard was not even a *human* voice!

The proximity of Estonian and Finnish words has its comical sides. When they speak of a wedding in Estonia — *pulmad* — it sounds like the Finnish word for a problem, *pulma* (pl. *pulmat*), causing no end of jokes. In an Estonian shop when one buys milk it is *piim*, but in Finland *piimä* is sour milk, so the careless pronunciation of an order by travelers in each other's countries can sometimes become a surprise. A simple vowel can make a major difference. There are slanting similarities. The Estonian word for town, *linn*, can be confused with the Finnish word for castle, *linna*. If an Estonian says she is cleaning her home — *koristada* — to Finns it sounds as if she is decorating it (*koristella*). Exit in Estonian is *väljapääs* — *välja* means out — but to a Finnish speaker it sounds — comically, and it invites puns — like the word *väljä* which means loose!

The first foreign literary or ethnographic notice of Estonia, incidentally, was made by the Roman historian, Tacitus, around 100 A.D. In his *Germania*, it was Tacitus who described the "Aestii," fishermen and amber gatherers on the eastern shores of the Baltic Sea. (Tacitus used "Aiščian" with two *i*s, other writers use "Aesti" with one *i*.) It is highly unlikely that Tacitus, about whose wider travels we know little, ever visited this land, as he also curiously described them as speaking a Celtic language, which scholars suspect for a number of reasons is a dubious possibility for that area. Some nationalistic 19th and early 20th century Latvian and Lithuanian philologists referred to the Baltic languages as "Aiščian" (pronounced *ighsh*-chee-an) languages as a nod to Tacitus.

Why the "east" in Estonia? Many say it is ethnic self-designation. Others believe that it derives from an early Germanic (Gothic or proto-Norse) term for "East" or "Eastern," meaning the people living to the east of Scandinavia. For whatever it is worth, the Estonian name for the Baltic Sea is *Läänemeri*, "Western Sea." (Not all seas on earth are equally salty, by the way: while the Red Sea and the Persian Gulf have water containing about forty parts of salt per thousand parts of water, the Baltic Sea has only two to seven parts of salt per thousand.) A few have even suggested that the name might actually be a shortened form of the Latin *Aestuarii*, "Estuary Dwellers." Medieval German, Swedish, and Danish chroniclers first began to use the various names *Esten*, *Ehsten*, *Estland* and *Ehstland*, but whether these were used in homage to Tacitus or were simply derivatives of ordinary Low German, Swedish, or Danish words for "Eastern" it is difficult to say. Early medieval Estonians, before their subjugation by Teutonic Knights, Danes, and Russians, were divided into a number of independent tribes or petty kingdoms who seem to have referred to themselves more often by their tribal designations than by any collective pan-Estonian ethnic name. This is still reflected in some of their neighbors' modern names for Estonians. Finns call them *Virolaiset* and Estonia itself as *Viro*, from the old northwest Estonian kingdom of Viru around Reval/Tallinn, also still reflected in the modern county of Virumaa ("Viru Land"). Latvians refer to Estonians as *Igauni*, a corruption of the old Southern Estonian kingdom of Ugandi. (The Romans, remember, always referred to all Hellenes as *Graeci*, after the comparatively insignificant ancient Greek colony of Graia or Graea.) Russians, by the way, have traditionally used a complete misnomer, referring to Estonians as *Chud* or *Chudi*, a corruption of *Teuti*, i.e., Teutons! For not very well-informed medieval Russians, everybody to the west of Estonia's Lake Peipsi were "Germans" or "Teutons." Strangely enough, Russians still refer to Lake Peipsi as *Chudskoye Ozero*, that is, Teutonic Lake. So much for the accuracy of names!

As I say, I knew I was going to write about the country but began to fear that like the questing Horacio Oliveira in Julio Cortázar's *Hopscotch* I would never get the full ball of yarn: "If he began to pull at the ball of yarn he would get a thread of wool, yards of wool, *lana*, lanadir, lunagnorisis, lanaturner, lannapurna, lanatomy, lannuity, lanativity, lanationality, lanature, *lana ad lanauseam* but never the ball of yarn.[8]

I daresay for most people, being neither from the Baltic area nor the former Soviet Union and not experts on Russian or Eastern European history or politics, Estonia as a place is largely the name of an unremarkably obscure country everybody has occasionally heard of in passing but few know anything at all about — it sounds like a typical name for a small fictional comic realm found, say, in a Marx Brothers movie or Peter Ustinov play or Alec Guinness film or a country one might like to allude to or use as a setting for a dark and intriguing spy-thriller or as the ancestral country for a character one might seek to portray as some sort of "ethnic" or immigrant. One of Arthur C. Clarke's technothrillers, *The Hammer of God,* a novel he wrote in 1993 involving a marathon race on the lunar surface, centers on the kidnapping of an Estonian physicist who has, of course, invented a super-bomb. (One memorable nugget in the book is a reference to a religious sect called Chrislam, originally founded by a female veteran of the Persian Gulf War, which believes it can convert a human being into a few terabytes of computer information!) Joseph Heller in *Good as Gold* casually mentions a character on New York City's Upper West Side going to Zabar's gourmet delicatessen to buy some Estonian bread. (Hey, why not? The country makes some of the best bread in the world.) These books all fall more or less under the formulaic heading of weak exotica. For such writers, the xenophobical name Estonia is a version of something like "Ruritania" or "Lower Slobbovia" or "Narnia" or the bankrupt "Freedonia" of *Duck Soup* or "Carpathia," the mythical country in the 1957 Marilyn Monroe film *The Prince and the Showgirl,* a kind of almost satirically distant, far-flung *ultima thule* comparable to the name "Megalomania" that the historical sociologist and cultural philosopher Ernest Gellner casually used in one of his books on nationalism as a generic term for post-World War I Eastern European national states (Estonia, Lithuania, Czechoslovakia, Hungary, etc.) and pre-World War I East-Central European dynastic empires (Romanov, Habsburg, Hohenzollern). Such mythic countries almost always prove in the end to be less than perfect societies, even dystopias, like the pluralistic society called "Kakania" which was invented by Robert Musil in his monumental novel, *The Man Without Qualities*, which mocked the highly stratified, multi-cultural garden of nationalities of Habsburg Vienna during the last thirty or so years of the Austro-Hungarian Empire. On the surface, the word is a coinage from the abbreviation KuK. (*kaiserlich* "imperial," *königlich* "royal"), but needless to say it carries the secondary scatological sense of "Shitland." recalling the word *caca* used in most European languages. Science fiction writer Poul Anderson in his 1974 novel, *Fire Time*, gives us the independent republic of Eleutheria. "Euphoria" is a Midwestern town in Edith Wharton's novel, *Hudson River Bracketed*, and in one of her stories she satirically names a small town "Halleluja." In Ben Katchor's ingenious *The Cardboard Valise* (2011) the capital city of his indescribably peculiar Tinsent Island is named Occupatia. Then think of the comic value that Evelyn Waugh got out of portraying such fictional worlds in his earlier novels, not only the right-wing Republic of Neutralia in his satirical spoof, *Scott-King's Modern Europe* (1947), which bears a striking resemblance to Tito's Yugoslavia where Waugh spent time as a captain in 1944 during World War II, but also the loony-bin backwater in *Black Mischief* (1932) in which buffoonish Basil Seal goes trundling off to the fictitious island of Azania off the eastern coast of Africa, spouting "Every year or so there's one place on the globe worth going to where things are happening."

On the other hand, who has to resort to satire when the Latvian name for Estonia is *Igaunija* and the Lithuanian name *Estijoje*? May not one assume that in terms of mouth-filling complexity Estonia is retaliating when it goes out of the way, almost impishly, to call France *Prantsusmaa* and New Zealand *Uus-Meremaa* and the Netherlands *Madalmaad* and the Cote d'Ivoire *Elevandiluurannik*?

The history of the tiny country of Estonia is a curious mélange of Finnish, Danish, Russian, Swedish, and German influences. There has been much confluence and influence in this particular area, especially since the early part of the 13th century. Foreign rule in Estonia roughly began in 1227, when that part of the world was conquered by the Germans and Danes in the "Northern Crusades" forcibly to Christianize the uplands of northern Europe but with probably less a sincere missionary impulse than the chance to grab as much land as they could. From 1228 to 1561, southern Estonia was ruled by the Livonian Confederation of Teutonic Knights (the "Livonian Brothers of the Sword"), a crusading religio-military order of German knights authorized by the Popes to conquer and convert "Livonia," as the eastern Baltic coast was then called, after the Livs or Livonians, a now extinct Finno-Ugric people related to the Estonians who were living in what is now Latvia. These Northern Crusades against the idol-worshipping pagans and primitives of what was then Estland has never commanded as much attention as has the better-known crusades in the Holy Land. It is not strange that the Knights of the Sword transferred their activities to the Baltic area, as the forcible conversion of these people to Roman Catholicism became a national German aim, but greed for land and predictable German bellicosity figures in. I have always associated the quaint name Livonia, incidentally, whenever I thought about it, with one of those quaint, imaginary, dwarfish European countries that were always being invaded (or defended) by plumed soldiers in one of those ditsy, ritzy operettas like *The Merry Widow* or *Die Fledermaus* or *H.M.S. Pinafore* or one starring Mountie Nelson Eddy with his adorable chinstrap and toothy Jeanette MacDonald with her fluttering eyelids singing right into his mouth! Or am I thinking of such magical realms as Sidonia? Harmonia? Begonia? Catatonia?

At the same time, Denmark took possession of northern Estonia. The Danes quickly took over the Estonian fishing village of Reval. As the main Danish stronghold, it became known by the Estonians as *Taaninlinna*, i.e., "Danishtown," the source of its modern name "Tallinn." Taaninlinna/Reval soon became a major Hanseatic seaport, still known to German merchants by its old Estonian name Reval. As in most Hanseatic towns, Reval's mercantile class was of mainly German origin. Northern Estonia remained a Danish possession until the mid-14th century.

The German name for Tartu, now Estonia's second largest city and a university town on the Emajõgi River in southern central Estonia, was *Dorpat* (from a low German word for "The Town"). The Russians called it *Yuryev* (Estonian spelling *Jurjev*, "St. George's Town.") It was the Russians who conquered the Tartu/Yuryev stronghold in 1030 A.D., long before the Teutonic Knights got control of most of the rest of southern Estonia. German presence has always been strong in Estonia. (I spoke German during most of the stay over there, whenever English was not understood.) The crusader-built castle set on the hill in the center of Tallinn — once a strong, visible center of German power — vies for architectural prominence with the elaborate Alexander Nevsky Cathedral there built in the 1880s. On the walls of the magnificent medieval Church of the Dome of St. Mary's (*Toomkirk*), a Gothic masterpiece nearby, one can still see, along with armorial epitaphs and tomb plates, a hundred German coats of arms and heraldic shields hung up all along both sides of the nave.

In 1343, the Estonians unsuccessfully tried to overthrow their German overlords in the *Jüriöö Mäss* ("St. George's Night Rebellion"), beginning on April 23, the eve of St. George's Feast Day. In 1346, the Danes sold their northern Estonian lands (including Reval) to the Teutonic Knights. Sweden in turn conquered much of northern Estonia in the mid-16th century. From 1561 to 1710, Sweden occupied Tallinn and its environs. In 1561, Poland took over southern Estonia from the Teutonic Knights but then ceded it to Sweden in 1629. Sigismund, son and heir of the king of Sweden offered to hand over to the Polish state his personal possession of Estonia, for which the Polish nobility showed no enthusiasm, since the Swedes remained in military occupation. It was the father of Gustavus Adolphis, King Charles IX of Sweden of the Vasa dynasty, who conquered Estonia, cutting off the Russians from the sea; he also proposed to conquer Livonia and Courland, and the Baltic fringe of Poland, as well, as to weaken his cousin as a claimant to the throne of Sweden. (Upon his father's death in 1611, the 17-year-old Gustav inherited the throne as well as an ongoing succession of occasionally belligerent dynastic disputes with his Polish cousin Sigismund III of Poland who, in the preliminary religious strife before the Thirty Years' War, was forced to let go of the throne of Sweden and give it to Gustav's father.

Sigismund III wanted to regain the throne of Sweden and tried to force Gustav Adolph to renounce the title.) In the early 18th century, Russia's Tsar Peter the Great wrested Estonia from Sweden for Tsarist Russia in the Great Northern War (1700-1721), introducing Russian serfdom at its most brutal to the Estonian peasantry.

So although Sweden, Denmark, Muscovy, and Poland fought for the spoils of the ailing Livonian order of Teutonic Knights from 1558 to 1582 in Latvia and Estonia, it was the signing of the Peace at Nystad in 1721 that left Peter the Great with Livonia, Estonia, Ingria, Kexholm, and part of Karelia. When Peter proclaimed himself the Emperor of Russia, that country in one stroke emerged as the dominant power in the Baltic, and power had shifted away fundamentally from divided Poland. Russia had managed to secure the lion's share of Sweden's former empire, annexing a string of territories in the Eastern Baltic.

It can honestly be said that poor Estonia has had more owners than a second-hand flea-market overcoat. Sarah and I used to have a sort of standing joke when things would be going wrong in Estonia. "What's the solution?" she used to ask, usually laughing, in some buggered-up situation or other. "To Estonia?" I would usually shrug and say, "Make it smaller and move it to the left."

In late-19th and early-20th century Russia, very similar ideas, ideals, and impulses inspired the heartfelt "Slavophile" ideology of many distinguished Russian intellectuals and, on a lower social and cultural level, Jew-baiting pogromist groups like the Union of Russian People (the "Black Hundreds"). The Black Hundreds' hoodlums enjoyed the covert behind-the-scenes official support of the Tsarist Secret Police, who also connived at the fabrication and early dissemination around 1905 of *The Protocols of the Elders of Zion*. The conflict between the "Slavophiles" and "Westernizers" among educated Russians is a main central theme of late-19th and early-20th century Russian intellectual and cultural history, closely paralleling the German conflict of "Idealist"/*Völkisch* versus liberal/Enlightenment outlooks. The dissident Soviet historian Alexander Yanov, among others, has pointed out the close parallelism of the Russian Slavophile/Westernizer polarity to the German "Teutonophile"/Westernizer opposition, and noted the frequent active "cultural exchanges" between German and Russian chauvinists and anti-Semites. Until late in the 19th century, by the way, there were hardly any Jews in Estonia, since it lay outside the Pale established for Jewish settlement in Russia. It is worthwhile to note that the proselytizing Betar movement, short for Berit Trumpelder, the activist Zionist youth movement which was founded in 1923 in Riga, Latvia, and which not only grew but gained a large following in Lithuania, never took hold in Estonia. But it is not an understatement to say that wherever it was that Jews resided, they were squeezed as much as squeezing.

It is well-known that, for all the Russian bullying, Estonians tended, still tend, to be more comparably amenable to the German mind, and although with the rise of the Nazis many Jews sought refuge from anti-Semitism in the seamless brotherhood imagined by Communism (as others did in the nationalist rebirth promised by Zionism) — a strong Judeo-Bolshevism may or may not have been a simultaneous scapegoating ploy, at least in the United States, against both Jews and the Communist party — but for decades poverty, paranoia, and tribal pride have combined to keep even Estonian Jews more in the German than the Russian camp. It may be noted here on this subject, by the way, that in the 1980s when Margaret Thatcher tossed a lot of the old Tories out of her Cabinet and put in a lot of parvenu Jews, elderly (and waspish) Harold MacMillan bitterly complained, "There are now more Old Estonians in the cabinet than Old Etonians..." — and this was taken to be coded anti-Semitism. One may therefore conclude that something of a sea-change has occurred.

I would like to point out that the resentful hatred of 18th century Anglo-French Enlightenment liberalism, tolerance, cosmopolitanism, and universalism infected not only the Germans, Austro-Germans, and Russians. It also infected the intelligentsia and educated classes of most of the peoples of Europe's Eastern-Central "Periphery." The virus also infected the Hungarians, Slovaks, Croats, Serbs, Romanians, Ukrainians, Poles, Finns, Latvians, Lithuanians, and Estonians. It became a spiritual cancer, a kind of ideological AIDS.

While East Europeans have long been split between well-recognized "Enlightment" and "Counter Enlightenment" mind-sets — a "clash of civilizations," to employ a phrase popularized by the American political scientist, Samuel P. Huntington, from his 1993 *Foreign Affairs* article of the same name — Estonians have always avoided the ration of fury that in the 19th century spawned a dark, illiberal, intolerant mood in people, the kind of chauvinist anti-modern, anti-urban, and anti-Semitic Völkisch drive that with its inborn penchant for ethnic scapegoating and militant racist tub-thumping prepared the way for the extremes of Nazism with its vehement contempt for the "weakness," "decadence," and "materialism" of Western European liberalism and humanism. Estonians, like other Balts, were and are of course ardent Russophobes and can manifest a certain and distinct xenophobia, but, as my friend, T. Peter Park observes, they did sidestep the murderous chauvinisms that were seen in other neighboring nationalities (Slovaks versus Czechs, Lithuanians versus Poles, Hungarians versus Romanians, Serbs against Croats).

Estonians never went in for pogroms. They have a widespread reputation for being phlegmatic, practical, slow, and level-headed in most areas of life, being more "Scandinavian" than "German" or Russian." They have never fostered anything close to the kind of pan-German zealotry or murderous and intolerant "counter-enlightenment" inter-war movements and tyrannies of Ferenc Szalasi's Hungarian "Arrow Cross" or the intolerance of Croatian fascist leader Ante Pavelić's Ustaše movement or the far right, ultra-nationalist, violently anti-Semitic excesses of Corneliu Zelea-Codreanu's Romanian "Iron Guard." The independent 1918-1940 Estonian Republic had a mildly authoritarian regime, the so-called "Silent Era," in the 1930s under President Konstantin Päts, but Päts was a much milder dictator than, say, either Hungary's Admiral Miklós Horthy or Romania's King Carol II of Romania who themselves were in turn overthrown by the even more ruthless Szalási and Zelea-Codreanu.

In the 1930s, an Estonian semi-Fascist movement, the *Vabadussôjalaste Liit* ("Independence War Veterans' League") or "Vaps," was formed, an organization somewhat comparable to Finland's anti-communist Lapua movement which began in 1929. But history has shown that the "Vaps" organization had nothing whatsoever of the viciousness of its Hungarian, Romanian, or Croatian counterparts and always aimed its demagogic animosity against the Estonian Republic's "divisive" party system rather than against, say, Jews or other ethnic minorities. Later, during the period of the Cold War, some younger-generation Baltic exile intellectuals and culturati formed their own pro-independence freedom groups, the

Baltic Appeal to the United Nations (BATUN, pronounced "ba-*toon*") to demand human rights and to restore national independence in mainstream Western liberal democratic terms. The newly restored post-Soviet Estonian Republic has been overwhelmingly "Western" and "Enlightenment" in its politics and intellectual life, much to the chagrin of many "Counter-Enlightenment-" oriented cranks, many of whom — to be quite frank — are angry, closed-minded, right-wing Estonian exiles.

It should be pointed out that the Soviet-German Treaty of Brest-Litovsk, signed on March 3, 1918, gave Estonia, Latvia, and Lithuania, among other nations, their independence — an often overlooked event. But the fact of the matter is it did not last. The ultimate German defeat in the First World War prevented that settlement from being definitive. The Civil War in Russia between the Reds and the Whites broke out in the summer of 1918. As early as 1932, the Litvinov Protocol was signed by Estonia, and in that same year the Soviet Union concluded a non-aggression treaty with Estonia, Latvia, and Lithuania. Although in 1933 the United States finally recognized the Soviet Union, by 1940 Estonia was incorporated into the USSR as a union republic fighting the Nazis.

To understand the dark hatred Estonians feel for Russians and the force of their merciless vice-grip, that is, until the Estonian Sovereignty Declaration was issued on November 16, 1988, look no further than the Hero of Alexandria's "law of reflection:" the angle at which a light ray is reflected from a mirror equals the angle at which its strikes the mirror. It is the land of sickle and hammer, of the ushanka hat, of the big bear, Misha, all teeth and claws, recapitulating for Estonians what poet EE. Cummings called the land of "un," "the world of was," 'the apotheosis of isn't," a "joyless experiment in force and fear," "a merciless and motley proletarian parade." He wrote, "O to be in finland/now that Russia's here."

Brown Shirts or Red Shirts?

The Molotov-Ribbentrop Pact of August 23, 1939 allowed for that brief, inexplicable, and forced marriage between the Nazis and the Reds, both spiritual grandchildren of the darker side of Romanticism, German Idealism, and plain "folkish" populism. This mutual non-aggression which meant little to Estonia ended the possibility of an independent country. In a secret protocol to this document, the Baltic states were left in the Soviet sphere of interest. One month later, Vyacheslav Molotov, the Russian Foreign Minister, pressed Estonia to accept a pact of mutual assistance which, in effect, meant the stationing of large numbers of Soviet troops on Estonian soil. Germany and Russia proceeded to divide up Eastern Europe. The Germans invaded Estonia in June 1941, forcing out the Soviets, and the Baltic States were now under the occupation of Nazi Germany with Riga the administrative seat. The Nazis were initially hailed as a liberating force, except by the Jews, of course. Compared to the more than 3 million Jews living in Poland during the Third Reich, there were far fewer Jews in the Baltics. But were they welcome? Hannah Arendt points out in *Eichmann in Jerusalem* that, relatively speaking, anti-Semitism was more cordially met (than in other places in Europe) "by those people in the East — the Ukrainians, the Estonians, the Latvians, the Lithuanians, and, to some extent, the Rumanians — whom the Nazis had decided to regard as 'subhuman' barbarian hordes." It is a gruesome assessment of Estonia and Estonians from any angle of regard. (It should be pointed out, however, that before 1917 the only university in the Russian Empire that admitted Jews was the University of Tartu in Estonia, and that this remained the case into the Soviet period. Jews believed that Bolshevism would liberate them and eliminate anti-Semitism, and so they embraced Lenin and later Stalin.) To the Nazi mind, of course, there were hardly any true Nordics outside of Germany. To them, Norwegians — except Quisling and his followers — had been corrupted by intermixture with Finns and Lapps and such. Alfred Rosenberg, Hitler's racist ideologist, although a Baltic German, was born and raised in Estonia. So was Hermann von Keyserling who was a philosopher and world-traveler with an interest in Eastern thought. (As was the short-story writer Werner Bergengruen.)

A word here about the Jews and the Nazi occupation. Estonia was the only country designated as *judenfrei* — free of Jews — at the Wannsee Conference in 1942, a terrible category in which to be placed, indeed, and one that continues to haunt the country in any discussion of its past.

For ages Jews were actually *banned* from living in St. Petersburg (then the Russian capital) and environs. "As an English visitor exclaimed at the time of Véra Evseevna's [Nabokov's] birth," according to Stacy Shiff in her book, *Vera*, "'I would rather be treated a swindler, a forger, or a vulgar assassin, than as a respectable Russian Jew!'" Estonian territory stood in the radius of this ring and so remained free of Jews until sometime in the 19th century when this law was changed. This is why strong Jewish communities formed mainly in Lithuania, Belarus, Ukraine, and Poland, later the desperately benighted region that Yale historian Timothy Snyder refers to as the "bloodlands," commonly called "borderlands,"[9] an entire area that experienced not only multiple occupation but mass killings on an unprecedented scale, not in acts of combat but by the deliberate mandate of extermination. Estonia's comparatively small prewar Jewish community, which numbered around 4,500, had been reduced to around 1,000 persons, thanks to the savagery of Soviet deportations, wholesale executions, and a general Red Army mobilization to drum them out. In comparison, there was a very large community of as many as 260,000 Jews in Lithuania, with 100,000 in Vilnius alone — 45% of that city's population, in fact, which is why the city was often referred to, not always with reverence, as the "Jerusalem of the North" — and as many as 420,000 in occupied Poland at the time. (Of Lithuanian Jews a full ninety-four percent desperately perished in the Holocaust, 225,000 according to official figures. Only about 15,000 escaped annihilation. Some 70,000 were shot at Panerai, a wooded hamlet about six miles outside the city where today a Soviet-era granite obelisk stands, dedicated to the "Victims of the Fascist Terror.")

Strange to find that the "Final Solution," was carried out, in part, in Estonia even before the shame of Wannsee, indeed even before Adolf Hitler decided to eliminate the rest of European Jewry.

There were no gas chambers in Estonia. Mass executions were carried out by police battalions and killing squads — local police battalions guarding the camps composed many of them, Estonians and Latvian Russians who were considered too much of a security threat to send to the front — who usually had to get drunk to shoot their victims. Anton Weiss-Wendt suggests in his book, *Murder Without Hatred* that Estonia's Jewish citizens by either their (a) lassitude or (b) ambition provoked their own murders. The Nazis and their Estonian collaborators, when they recruited them, went to great lengths to associate Jews with communism, although Jews frankly did comprise a disproportionate number of Estonian communists. There were plenty of native Estonian Communists who did collaborate with the Soviets (and the Nazis, for that matter). There is no question that, while many of them were conscripted to play ball with their occupiers, the majority of Jews in Estonia, just as in other European countries, became scapegoats for divisions within the Estonian nation itself; a way of placing the blame for the horrors of the Soviet occupation on a vulnerable, commonly disliked, and easily identified, if small, segment of the population.

As I say, Germans and Estonians, relatively speaking, have always felt more culturally aligned. They had seen the same western films, knew the same popular songs, and were culturally closer. In comparison, the Communist world under the Soviets which had flourished for 20 years seemed alien and dangerous. Who can explain it? Carrots prosper next to tomatoes. So do asparagus and beets. Cucumbers oddly do not. Celery dislikes parsnips but likes cabbage. Neither broad beans nor climbing peas grow well next to onions, garlic, or olives. Pumpkins dislike potatoes. Call it the "proximity equation." The heterosporous combination of cedars and European mountain ash kill the latter. This is one of the reasons why German rule was seen as comparatively milder by many Estonians, while the Soviets were seen as alien, brutal primitive boors out of the wastes; peasants and barbaric mesomorphs from a land of imprisoning and intolerable cold whose rude, leveling revolution had darkened Europe. Wherever you look, Estonia was circumscribed. There was Russia firmly rooted, the insufferable burdock with its prickly burrs and giant clubfoot-leaves throwing shade and holding the earth in a deathly grip. Estonia still suffers the fact that it is the only post-Communist Nordic country, a humiliation they feel and grudge they bear for the Russian population that is still in evidence all over the country.

A pejorative anti-Estonian neologism, *eSStonia*, appeared in the Russian media, on Runet, and at the street protests in the midst of the Bronze Soldier controversy in 2007. The term, a portmanteau of Estonia and SS, is of course intended to portray Estonia as a neo-Nazi state.

The Erna Raid annual international military exercise, held annually,

was again controversially held in Estonia on August 4, 2010. It commemorates a reconnaissance group that worked with German military
intelligence in World War II. Moscow believes that the exercise is an
attempt to glorify Estonia's collaboration with Nazi Germany. The Erna
unit was a Finnish Army formation of Estonian volunteers that spied
behind Red Army lines. The event has been held since 1994, with teams
from around the world taking part.[10] In that it has been met with disap-
proval, I am reminded of the satirical song Noël Coward did for the BBC
Forces Broadcast in July 1943 which goes in part:

> Don't let's be beastly to the Germans
> When our victory is ultimately won.
> It was just those nasty Nazis who
> persuaded them to fight
> And their Beethoven and Bach are really
> far worse than their bite.

> Let's be meek to them —
> And turn the other cheek to them
> And try to bring out their latent sense
> of fun
> Let's give them full air parity —
> And treat the rats with charity,
> But don't let's be beastly to the Hun.

Aurel Kolnai's *The War Against the West* (1938), an early critical study
of Nazi ideology by this Hungarian scholar, included slow, backward
Slavs, Balts, and Jews as the very antithesis of the "heroic" model of more
vital civilizations like Germany — his "west," oddly enough, was composed of capitalistic, liberal mind-sets — which held up higher ideals
and was prepared to fight for and defend them. It is my belief, however,
that Kolnai may have focused too narrowly on Germany and the Nazis.
My own observations and reading seem to show that throughout the
late-19th century and the first half of the 20th century many East-Central Europeans who hailed from the vast tract between the Rhine and
the Volga — along with Estonians, Latvians, Lithuanians, Hungarians,

Croats, Romanians, Ukrainians, etc. — equally loved to grumble about what they themselves saw as the luxury-festooned, over-advantaged, and materialistic countries like the United States, Canada, England, France, Belgium, and Scandinavia, where a lot of political and economic wire-pulling, effected on the quiet, was done by liberal bourgeois and cosmopolitan Jews. That whole European region has been dominated by the same polarity between "Westernizers" versus Counter-Enlightenment "Nativists" that so many historians had been noting in German and Russian cultures (e.g. 19ᵗʰ century Russia's "Slavophiles" and "Westernizers"). As I have pointed out, one can see that the whole East-Central European "Periphery," from the Baltics to the Balkans, was dominated by this "Nativists" versus "Westernizers" split. Dostoevsky in his day took up the topic endlessly.

Soon young Estonian men were being recruited, not into the Red Army, but rather into the Wehrmacht. Some 40,000 Estonians joined the German army to try to stop the Red Army. As a matter of fact, as many as 70,000 people also fled to Germany and Sweden. Everywhere was a nightmare of oppressors. Although the Germans were at first perceived by most Estonians as their liberators from the USSR and its repressive bull-headed regime, and while hopes were raised for the country's independence, it soon became quite clear that the Nazis were only another occupying power. They pillaged the country for the war effort and unleashed the Holocaust. During that occupation, Estonia was incorporated into the German province of *Ostland*. This led many Estonians who were unwilling to side with the Nazis to join the Finnish Army to fight against the Soviet Union. A brave Finnish Infantry regiment, the so-called *soomepoisid* ("Finnish Boys"), was quickly formed out of Estonian volunteers in Finland. Although many Estonians were recruited into the German armed forces — including the Waffen-SS — the majority did so only as late as 1944 when the threat of a new invasion of Estonia by the Red Army had become imminent, and it was clear that Germany could not win the war. It was always Scylla and Charybdis for Estonians, danger from the left, danger from the right.

There are films of the Estonian SS Legion — the crack military unit within the Combat Support Forces of the Waffen-SS Verfügungstruppe formed in 1942, consisting of Estonian soldiers — singing in chorus

Norway's "På Vikingtokt," the March of the 34th SS Netherlands Brigade, which evokes with chilling force the Nazi stormfront. Black metal on the hoof! Dawn of the heathens! Wagnerian Valkyries![11]

There were two distinct Soviet invasions of the country of Estonia: from 1940 to 1941 and from 1944 to 1991. Hope rose, faded, rose, faded. On July 21, 1940, the Estonian Duma, the Lettish Sejm, and the Lithuanian Sejm passed almost identical resolutions stating, naïvely, that they were each confident that admission into the Union of Soviet Socialist Republics would ensure their true sovereignty. In 1944 the Soviets proceeded to push out the Germans who fled in disarray into the disintegrating Reich. When the war ended, however, the Iron Curtain descended, and Estonia was locked inside. On March 18, 1919, Lenin, who had conceived of a Soviet Estonia from the very beginning, wrote, "We live not only in a state, but in *a system of states*, and the existence of the Soviet republic side-by-side the imperialist states for a prolonged period of time is unthinkable."[12] This is called "telegraphing." Stalin, the Mephisto, repeated those words with force until the very day he died. In 1945, with Stalinism back on course, agriculture was collectivized and industry nationalized, and another 60,000 were killed or deported. Over 20,000 Estonians were deported to the Gulags or to Siberia. The legendary *metsavenad* or "Forest Brethren" — intrepid resistance men who met in secret and took refuge in the woods — bravely fought Muscovite tyranny with guerrilla tactics. The Soviet assault on and domination of small Estonia was nothing less than outright *isnasilovanie* — "rape" — an outrageous ravaging invasion of a country mind, heart, and soul. The 20th century was not kind to Estonia. The Nazis visited, but the Soviets stayed. The Soviet NKVD (People's Commissariat for Internal Affairs) was later changed to the KGB, but under whatever name they went by they deviously infiltrated every sphere of the country. I have to say, however, that I always wondered why responsible Estonian leaders never took advantage of that endlessly prolonged, nothing-less-than rabid anti-Communist position of the United States throughout the long span of the post-war years to oppose as a nation the Soviets. Was not free Finland right next door? Did that not suggest a role — a right — of exit? Would a stalwart uprising not have had U.S. support? Was not the Estonian populace of one mind and able simultaneously to be roused? "The nose of a mob is its imagination," wrote Edgar Allan Poe. "By this, at any time, it can be quietly led."

So what happened?

More pointedly, what failed to happen?

Unhappiness is Indecent

Hannah Arendt in *On Revolution* found two old chestnuts — strictly canards, she felt — to be false on both counts, writing,

> Those who say 'better dead than red' actually think: The losses may not be as great as some anticipate, our civilization will survive; while those who say 'better red than dead' actually think: Slavery will not be so bad, man will not change his nature, freedom will not vanish from the earth forever. In other words, the bad faith of the discussants lies in that both dodge the preposterous alternative they themselves have proposed; they are not serious.

Forget Arendt's cynicism. The Estonian people, who actually had to face the fire of such desperate alternatives, and having to do so every single day, were certainly serious, not owlish groups of theory-pedants loudly gas-bagging for endless hours in comfortable Ivy League college seminars during the notorious, witch-hunting McCarthy era.

Why, however, did it take so long to get "involved"?

Estonians, arguably, were — are — shyly obedient. Dutiful. Highly serious. Earnest beyond words. The concepts all tend to merge. Or is such just-walking-along merely rote? I have heard accusations of servility. A diffidence may apply to them. I personally believe that Estonians are among the most courageous people in the world. May one suggest that as a nation, the people are too regulated, too orderly? The restlessness is certainly there, the pride, no question about the anger, but what about the concentrated discipline to *revolt?* It is not the case with many other countries in the world.. Professor Noam Chomsky in his *Latin America: from Colonization to Globalization,* for example, unequivocally states that

Nicaragua is "probably the least disciplined country in the world on the part of the population." He attributes this trait among Nicaraguans to "the lack of class consciousness of most of the population [that] is reflected in a natural dissidence, natural skepticism, unwillingness to obey," attributes, to my mind, quite un-Estonian-like. Estonians are a people who in their seriousness are manifestly *not* superficial. Chomsky indicates that a kind of insouciance, basic mistrust, makes for rebellion and revolution. "This is one of the reasons why you can have a phenomenon like the American peace movement, which would be difficult to achieve in other countries — spontaneous, unorganized, coming from all corners of the country."

After meeting with him in Tehran in 1943 President Franklin Roosevelt gave "Marshal" Stalin hegemony in Europe and it was only reinforced at Yalta in 1945 ("Take Poland, Uncle Joe"), when FDR was a dying and inattentive president. At Potsdam in 1945 Stalin refused to withdraw his troops from eastern and central Europe. In 1946 there were Communist movements — creating civil wars — in both Greece and Turkey. Why did not Estonia revolt, as well? Rage in the streets? Tear down the ramparts? President Truman and his Secretary of State Dean Acheson demanded that the USA draw a line. Truman gave as much as $400 million worth of aid to Greece and Turkey ("The Truman Doctrine") earmarked as military support, and under the Marshall Plan he provided food for humanity. There was no discernible rebellious action in — and so no aid or support for — Estonia. I do understand, of course, that at the time Estonia was part of the USSR and that no country in the East received or was even allowed to accept help, but should not the stirrings for such a possibility have begun on all sides? The so-called "Khrushchev Thaw," roughly from the years 1957 to 1964, amounted to virtually nothing. Were Estonians just gathered together, singing in a circle and doing nothing else? Why was so little done inside or outside? They were certainly circumspect; they were perhaps also too self-consciously civilized. Joseph Conrad for one — and it is a theme in many of his novels — was both skeptical of and dubious about revolutionary action as inevitably devolving into fanaticism, unreason, and bad faith. But when do the *malheureux* change into *enragés*? As the Jacobin Alexandre Rousselin declared, "Vengeance is the only source of liberty, the only goddess we ought to bring sacrifices to."

I have often reflected that cold-hearted Papa Stalin perverted the idea of Communism, when one may legitimately argue that as a pure political concept it is as true and as altruistic as any government. (I was, in my late teens, a novice in a Trappist monastery, a strong, giving, highly moral, productive, holy, society-in-small, where the only personal accessory a monk personally owned was his toothbrush, and that community, that commune, flourished with near perfection.) Betrayed, the revolution sank in horrors of inefficiency, disillusion, and despair. "The failure of [Communism] seems to be that although it set out ideologically to provide welfare for a people," noted the perceptive Jan Morris with a factually true if rather obviously Disneylandesque remark, "it utterly lacked the idea of giving its people happiness. It never took into account the human desire for happiness." What depressed me most about Estonia, in the end what became the most desolating, most beastly hobble of all, was that any evident human desire or real pull for happiness — I have no doubt it was there, but I rarely saw it — seemed missing. I am not certain that handing out pamphlets on "Cosmotarianism, the Religion of Happiness," invented by the flamboyant physical culturist Bernarr Macfadden, the push-up king, was any solution, either. Maybe there is something to defend in that over-simplistic, assbackwards existence-assertion, "I don't trust happiness. I never did. I never will," that the disaffected, alcoholic, hardscrabble, grizzled old country singer, tough Mac Sledge (Robert Duvall) confesses to his lovely new wife in the tearjerker movie, *Tender Mercies*.

It was quite the opposite for Frances Hodgson Burnett, author of *The Secret Garden*, one of these late Victorians who not only had a childlike confidence in the safety of childhood but also fearfully avoided unpleasant things and simply practiced a "doctrine of elimination on that which will not make me happy." Folks thought she was a Christian Scientist. She was not. "I am an artful dodger. I am a coward, a sneak," she admitted. She was a Pollyanna, in fact. Her life-long mantra was "See no evil and it won't exist." Unhappiness frightened this tubby lady so much that she actually refused to read newspapers ("I am sure to find my sense of horror aroused, and that makes me afraid"), avoiding at all costs the black horrors that rained down on the world. "Unhappiness is indecent, not respectable and futile," she wrote. "I believe our big creative powers of things intellectual are the powers that come from without. That is the real manifestation of the psychic." It seems to me that fearful and suffering people, *mutatis mutandis,* often take refuge in both extremes — those areas where the poet W.B. Yeats declared that no life exists — and that neither are healthy. The Russian Occupiers for decades found both types in Estonia, unduly pessimistic Sledges on the one hand, overly optimistic Burnettists on the other. It is almost a philosophical truism that no political progress could be made at either margin, on the far perimeters of either extreme.

It was in Estonia that the first large-scale non-communist political coalition, the People's Front, received recognition, in June 1988, and it was Estonia that proclaimed in November 17, 1988, the right to reject Soviet laws when they infringed on its own autonomy. On January 18, 1989, Estonian became the official language of the republic. The first public raising of the Estonian flag took place on February 24, 1989 over the Pikk Hermann Tower which is a corner of Toompea Castle, official residence of Estonia's president. It may be noted here that the Soviet Union retaliated. Fourteen Latvian independence fighters — martyrs — were later killed at the Vilnius television tower in 1991. That very September, however, the Soviet Union, forced to it, recognized Lithuania's independence, and that country was admitted to the United Nations. Soviet Prime Minister Mikhail Gorbachev drastically underestimated the power of nationalism in the Baltic area, as well as elsewhere, and at first tried to ignore or dismiss the struggling demands for recognition and independence. He tried in vain to check all nationalist courses of development, using persuasion, political maneuvering, even coercion, but now nothing worked.

Cicero was right. Freedom is participation in power, and without having a hand in your fate you are a slave. There is a bottom reached where a man suddenly discovers a paradoxical foundation. Aleksandr Solzhenitsyn wisely noted, "When you have robbed a man of everything, he is no longer in your power. He is free again."

It was in the late 1980s that the Soviet policies of *glasnost* and *perestroika* inspired the Lithuanian reform movement, *Sajudis.* The Estonians as a people were now spoiling for freedom. In 1989, to protest 50

years of Soviet rule in the Baltic countries, as many as two million Lithuanians, Latvians, and Estonians linked hands to form a human chain that
extended all the way from Vilnius to Riga to Tallinn, a distance of 400
miles. This extraordinary freedom-chain has been captured on film, and
to see it is to find a very moving testament to the solidarity of liberty-
minded people. (It may be of interest to note here, in passing, that Estonia is one of the countries, as of this writing in summer 2010, which has,
for weal or woe, committed soldiers to fight in the Coalition on the side
of the United States against al-Qaeda in Afghanistan.)

On August 20, 1991, dramatically, the country of Estonia formally
declared independence from the Soviet Union. It took place during an
attempt at a Soviet military coup in Moscow. The first country diplo-
matically to recognize independence for Estonia was tiny Iceland. It may
seem hard to believe, but the last Russian troops left Estonia — hate-
fully walked out — only as recently as August 31, 1994! Equally in-
credible is that before 1990 — *1990!* — Estonia's only direct link with
the world outside of the USSR was a single ferry steaming its feckless
little way from the port of Tallinn to that of Helsinki, Finland. Estonia has been an official member of the United Nations since September
17, 1991; of NATO since March 29, 2004; and of the European Union
since May 1, 2004. Much progress has been made, indeed, for a small,
poor, once-brutally-treated, post-Soviet but very brave state in demographic decline. Growth has been slow but steady and, as always, begins
in Tallinn. Some seven years after Estonia joined the European Union,
large-scale infrastructural and restorative work, including several rebuilt
museums, a waterfront promenade and a large arts venue, KultuuriKatel
(Culture Cauldron), are presently reshaping Tallinn's cultural identity,
as Charley Wilder points out in "41 Places To Go in 2011."[13] Much of
Northern Europe's arts community will converge on the city in 2011,
as it kicks off a yearlong schedule of European Union-sponsored events,
including the student-focused contemporary art triennial *Exsperimenta!*
and "Stories of the Seashore," a project that enlists writers, actors, artists
and musicians to reflect on the sea that has been so central to Estonia's
development. The transformation from Soviet satellite into one of the
European Union's potentially most vibrant young members reached another milestone on January 1, 2011 when Estonia officially became the

17th nation to adopt the currency of the Euro. So farewell francs, marks, pesetas, lire, guilders, drachmas, markkas, escudos, and now kroon! (Latvian lats and Lithuanian litas, regarding change to Euros, are pegged to the year 2012.) All three countries, Estonia, Latvia, and Lithuania now celebrate two Independence Days: the first marking their (short-lived) freedom from Soviet Russia in 1918; the second marking the collapsing Soviet Union in 1990-91.

A feverish period followed. What I call the "Gauguin Questions," the biggest ones to ask, were now being asked: "*D'où venons-nous? Que sommes-nous? Où allons-nous?*"[14] The fond hope was that now like all liberated people Estonians would come out into the sunlight at last and in celebration of freedom rejoice, experiencing in the joy of rebirth something of new life, recapitulating what André Malraux hopes for with Kassner and Anna in the final scene of his novel, *Man's Fate*:

> They were now going to speak, remember, exchange experiences…All this would become a part of everyday life, a stairway which they would descend side by side, into the street, under the sky eternally looking down upon the defeats or victories of men's wills.

It is a very strange thing about hope. In a queer way, hope simply pledges allegiance to another ideal, one out of necessity we simply deem — yearn to deem, pray to deem — better. "I have no money, no resources, no hopes. I am the happiest man alive," wrote Henry Miller in *Tropic of Cancer*. The dreams of hope one has are not always followed immediately by its disbursements even if some hope is achieved, and half the time its classifications are subjective, even fleeting, at times not even documentable. "Totalitarianism is not only Hell, but also the dream of paradise," wrote Milan Kundera in *Book on Laughter and Forgetting*. Mankind can yearn in a thousand ways, and it is only when we step back and take a look at those projected yearnings that we encounter mad paradoxes.

The Iron Hotel

Estonia can be a desolate country: its skies, the buildings, the cobblestone walkways of the Old Towns in the major cities, the color of the relentless stone. Wooden houses can appear like old hulks. The paint itself seems somber and uninspired. (I have heard the Soviets legislated that only three cheerless colors — green, ox-blood red, mustard yellow — could be used to paint them.) There is a drab chronic sameness here, defiant towers, an odd durability. The corrosive R. Crumb in the midst of Balkan bleakness — when he was 21 he visited the backward Soviet satellite of Bulgaria in 1964 on his honeymoon with his first wife, Dana — managed in a series of evocatively spare drawings to limn on paper the desperate kind of metallic grey in that country, the specific drabness, the hard grind of drizzling, unrelenting, casual rundownness. The artist Marc Chagall, who claimed that color came into his life only after he went to Paris in 1911 and began painting red and green rabbis, once said that he detested the color of Russia. He cryptically said, "Their color is like their shoes."

It rained a good deal. I was often soaked through in a rubbery way, looking like a draggled duck, and recall how Nathaniel West in *The Dream Life of Balso Snell* has Janey the hunchback imagine death to be "like putting on a wet [bathing] suit." There are about 160 to 190 rainy days a year in Estonia — say that out loud — and the snows, which can sweep through in an instant and can foster a need to huddle down, usually last from mid-December to late March. There is in the cheerlessness something also dolefully impressive. Dark. Iron. Solid.

I loved the Old Town of Tallinn with its old 14th- and 15th-century buildings and churches and castles with stout beech doors and crenellated towers and jumble of turrets, spires, and red tile roofs and vast walls constructed with small stone. Battlements, like the chill sky of Elsinore, 11th century Denmark. Bluish darkness. One hears the bells jussle in the high steeples that in their blackness look rubberized, and down the dark narrow streets below one can almost imagine old horse-drawn carts with oil-lit Blanchard lamps clumping along. The majestic Toompea Castle, built on the limestone hill in Tallinn in either the 10th or 11th century by residents of the ancient Estonian county of Rävala (Revalia), now houses the Estonian Parliament but originally served as a fortification. The military value of heights? Consider the Battle of Fredericksburg in the American Civil War and the strategic value of Mayre's Heights —13,000 Union dead compared to 5,300 Confederate. I think of Estonia as a place of survival. Stoicism. Endurance. The theme of all Chaplin movies. Soviets, Nazis, Soviets again, the collapse of the ruble, occupation, potato blight. Nothing could undermine the strength, resilience, and durability that the brave Estonian people have, that you feel when walking into that Town Hall Square and breathe its majesty. You can climb up one of the city's narrowest staircases in Oleviste Kirik (St. Olaf's Church) to get a high view of the city to survey below the cobble streets of this old Hanseatic trading town and, to sustain your medieval feeling go have a meal of elk, wild boar, juniper cheese, hot pottage, roasted capon, and honey beer.

I cannot fully recall or presume to say precisely when I first began to be disenchanted with Estonia — that specific moment of *crise*, that is, when, like Ludwig Bemelmans' Miss Clavel in the middle of the night, I pulled on the light and cried out, *"Something is not right!"* — but I think I can say I am not terribly wide of the mark when I point to the country's remorseless and unforgiving darkness, a darkness of the sort that can be felt, depth in a sense that involves or even calls into question the spatiality with things, a night-space of occlusive inky saturation almost destroying one's self when as you walk through it you are not so much in it as of it, a medium of thickness with a tangibly diffuse materiality that is not "held" at a distance, density like the ninth plague Moses sent against Pharaoh[15] — a darkness, lasting three days, so heavy that it was physically experienced. A seven-fold-colored rainbow, remember, needs some sun, even if at a low altitude angle. Hope may not always find a rainbow, I accept that, but can it thrive in such impassable, such impermeable darkness? The most spectacular rainbows occur when half of the sky is still dark with raining clouds and the observer is at a spot with clear sky in the direction of the sun. The result is a luminous rainbow that contrasts with the darkened background. I understand. I accept that. *But one needs some sun!*

After even a few months there, a simple look in the mirror showed me how beaten down and papery I had become. Ludwig Wittgenstein spent the winter of 1913 rusticating in the tiny village of Skjolden, Norway, however, and yet found it to be one of the most productive periods of his life, writing his *Logik* ("Notes on Logic"), which was the predecessor of his great work, the *Tractatus Logico-Philosophicus*. The relentless gray made every act seemed done under the cover of secrecy.

Akhenaten in his illustrious "Hymn to the Sun" — C.S. Lewis offers the possibility that the monotheism of this ancient poem from the 14th century B.C. may have given Moses himself his first concept of the idea of one God — suggests night *itself* is the enemy, a state beyond God's benevolence: "When thou [the Sun] settest the world is in darkness like the dead. Out come the lions: all serpents sting." Who would deny that Moses sending that devastating plague of terrible darkness to Pharaoh was an undisguised attack on Ra, the Egyptian sun god?

The apricity — the warmness of sun in winter — is zero. Its copperiness you could paint blue, in the late afternoon being almost wistfully metallic and sharp as flint. Possibly that critical moment of which I speak happened very slowly, a build-up of slow, accumulated *cauchemar*, when after weeks of purchasing this or that in the shim of shadowy shops and discovering that in not one transaction did any merchant or vendor or proprietor ever smile back — or even seem to care a whit that you gave him or her custom or courtesy — I suddenly thought: *bug, meet windshield!* Do you happen to remember the Heisenberg "uncertainty principle"? A particle's location limits what can be known about its speed at the same instant, and my position and momentum could not simultaneously be known to arbitrary precision![16] I was in a position, a bewildering place, in short, just exactly when and where I could not determine I could move. It put discernible constraints on me.

But was I an *electron*? A *particle*?

I can say I went from being sort of disappointed to fairly depressed. Disappointment I could take. I was disappointed that the word "chimney" was not in fact "chimbly" which, as a small boy, I judged the much better word. When I first learned that Y and W were vowels, feeling neither belonged in the list, I must say I was also disappointed. It was a source of grave disappointment to me to see the Boston Red Sox tank every year *until I reached the age of 65!* But depression?

The cold certainly did not help, either. All her life the novelist George Eliot (Mary Ann Evans) suffered from two negative sensations which I

did not share with her but could easily understand: an unusual suscepti-
bility to the cold which plagued her throughout her life, and the other,
crippling night terrors. She reported being happy enough during the day,
but at night "all her soul became a quivering fear." Dark, cold Estonia
would surely have put a crimp into this genius' output!

My dark epiphany, the unwelcome transcendental vastation I had in
the middle of the night, took place in our first backwater flat in Tallinn
at the Writers' Union, a unpersuasively dingy fleatrap, its construction
of faulty design disturbingly wrong in all its dimensions and in its drab
austerity and hollowness something along the lines of the dilapidated,
slightly run-down Hotel Earle ("A day or a lifetime" is the hotel's motto)
in Los Angeles in the movie *Barton Fink* where the hapless transients with
drawn brows I occasionally saw coming and going on the stairs sported
Barton Fink haircuts and even wore outmoded Barton Fink underwear,
and at any minute I thought I might find some wacko in a ratskin hat
come barging down one of those antique, subfuse corridors wielding a
double-barreled shotgun and howling, *"I'll show you the life of the mind!"*

"Ma naitan Sulle vaimu elu! (blam!) *Ma naitan Sulle vaimu elu!* (blam!)
Ma naitan Sulle vaimu elu!" (blam!)

I certainly did not want to leave the country on a dime — or in a huff.
(A day was too short, but a lifetime? Forget it!) Did not Augustus Hare
tell us, "Half the failures in life arise from pulling in one's horse as he is
leaping"? My disenchantment was merely that, nothing more, in no way
a repudiation of the country — simply a process of undergoing an experience that it was not a magical land. But it was tough. Our hands were
always dry and chafed. We slathered on unguents and lotions. A purple
and, if I may add, minatory tinge was always ribboning the lower sky
whenever we looked up. We slid and slipped on icy sidewalks and precarious walkways. We ate peculiar food, spent too much for too little, never
swam, and had to bring our own reading. (Before my final departure, I
dumped off several cartons of paperbacks in English at a Russian bookshop in Tartu, boxes that we had sent ahead of us, for I always travel like
the actress Eleonora Duse, a fanatical reader, who on her endless tours
was never unaccompanied by trunkloads of books — Dante, Schiller,
Shakespeare, Goethe, William James, Byron, and many of her favorite
authors, including the work of Gabriele d'Annunzio with whom she had

a tempestuous love affair for over twenty years.) We were repudiated by unsmiling natives who saw us as typical Americans, only yet another one or two more of those tall insufferable boasters who wore big shoes, overweight yam-in-the-mouths who mawkishly overpraised their kids, flag-wavers who absurdly placed their hands over their hearts at the sound of the national anthem, naïve dopes who in their smirking, googly-eyed, bowlegged fratboy G.W. Bush had a real dunce for a president. But it is to the darkness that I point — to the bleak, black, bludgeoning darkness, Dantean in its forbiddingness that, I swear, first drew blood. Punxsutawney Phil would have loved it there. So would Dracula and other notable heliophobes. Nights which never end or, turnabout in summer, never manage to grow dark, distinctly make it a place in its mad extremes — single it out with an accusing finger! — fit for repairing to bed with a pile of interminable epic novels like Samuel Richardson's *Clarissa* or Fielding's *Tom Jones* — or, hell, why not the longest, most brain-frying novel ever written, which is Jules Romains' *Les Hommes de bonne volonté,* a work that fills twenty-seven volumes. I bucked up, although I was never warm. I had heard Estonia got milder, that many are cold, but few are frozen.

Still, it is not good to be pampered, and I liked getting out of the real world, the formalities of workaday commerce, the polar regions of personal responsibility. Hard fare for a time is a fine alternative. I believed it. *Persicos odi apparatus* and all that. I have known monastic self-denial and thrived on it for a good while. Air-cushioned mattresses, it is now believed are the very worse to sleep on — actually *terrible* for the back. As to those high-tech running shoes? It is now thought among experts that no support is far better for the foot than all those gussied-up, cookie-constructed, rubberized boats which are now seen to be causing plantafasciitis. Animals are designed for a flat foot-strike. The best running shoes are the worst. Long live Zola Budd! I could still welcome the difficult and the dastardly. I was determined not simply to endure but to prevail.

But night at noon? That was not normal, that was not fair, that was not bearable. The Plutonian darkness got to me. It is so oppressive that it makes you begin to focus reasonlessly but compulsively on the means of illumination *itself:* candlelight, lamplight, streetlights, arc-light, the glow of shops, bonfires here and there, a salvific glow coming from the artificial light shining in the larger stores to the warming window-glow of distant farmsteads. It was on one of these days, blinking like a field mouse, that I recalled one of Ralph Waldo Emerson's apothegms: "The soul is no traveler; the wise man stays at home."[17]

It grows dark there in winter so brutally fast that anything like sunsets and horizons disappear. Around mid-fall, the sun starts coming up around 9 a.m., a weak metallic sun fighting shadows mixed with bluish black, and begins going down about 3 p.m. "There is always something missing about late afternoon on the East Coast," Joan Didion complained when she was living in New York. "Late afternoon on the West Coast ends with the sky doing all its brilliant stuff," she wrote. "Here [the East Coast] it just gets dark." I myself have always found California sunsets too elongated, peach-colored, overly-fruity, Renoiresque, and frankly over-angelic while in New England the sunsets are stark, pensive, stately and stern. The way it grew dark in Estonia threatened me, however. It is as old and portentous as the stark beginning of Genesis, Book I: "In the beginning God created the heavens and the earth. Now the earth was formless and empty, Darkness was over the surface of the deep."

I often had a sense of impending doom. A meaninglessness — isolation — seemed to grip me. It recalled for me Heidegger's assertion that he was neither theistic nor atheistic but adrift in a world from which God was absent. There were voices, however, if by voices one means signs. I never saw so many signs and flyers and posters in a given country. Truman Capote in his essay on New Orleans in *The Dogs Bark* remarked that that Louisiana city, like every Southern town, is predominantly a city of soft-drink signs: Coca-Cola, Dr. Nutt, Nehi, Grapeade, etc. I found Tallinn and Tartu fully plastered with posters, on walls, on store-fronts, in back alleys, stuck on walls, strung between buildings, across squares, and advertising just about every product, every play, every event from a rock concert to hair products to movies. It always seemed somewhat metaphorical to me that the pictorial symbol for all "exit" signs in Estonia is a stark running figure. Fleeing — flight — in Estonia is an exit strategy.

"The night cometh when no man shall work" was an apothegm that Rudyard Kipling had portentously inscribed over the mantelpiece in his strange boat-like mansion, "Naulakha," in Brattleboro, Vt. where he lived from 1892 to 1896. It was an unnecessary reminder during those dark days that came almost as a croak to me. My only prevailing question was, when did the night goeth?

I Spy

As we walked about the cobblestoned streets of Tallinn and its leaden outskirts in my black hat when I first arrived there, staying with Sarah at that Writer's Union apartment near the Old Town, I felt lugubrious. I began to picture, unwittingly, the paintings of the Danish artist Vilhelm Hammershoi. A reductive palette. Reduced images. Empty rooms. Haunting interiors. A person facing away. A solitary figure here and there, even the backs of women's necks. One could call it the poetry of silence there in that old, cold corner of the world. That grey tonal range, that hypnotic quietude, the dismal sense of non-disclosure, the melancholic introspection. I sensed a distinct secretiveness to the place. "Tallinn was known to be a centre for espionage, infiltrated by White Russian intriguers intent on blocking Stalin's access to the city," wrote Ian Thomson in an article in the *Times Literary Supplement*. "By controlling the Estonian capital, Stalin could protect the Soviet Union against assault from North-west Europe and command all Baltic territories."[18] I tried not to focus on the sad history I could nevertheless smell. "There is almost nothing bad that I couldn't say about humans and humankind," Elias Canetti wrote in *The Tongue Set Free*, and when I wandered through Tallinn and, squinting, tried to imagine — and through my imagination somehow managed to see — what the Soviet Union did to Estonia, I heard Canetti.

Or John Le Carré. I often felt in Estonia like Alec Leamas waiting near a crook by the Berlin Wall, in fact. The bleak urban landscape of Tallinn in the dead of winter shares many of Le Carré's own, a typically colorless, gaunt half-world of ruin, giant buildings of rising grey concrete still unfinished, a disintegrated environment flat, mournful, opprobrious, and incomplete, usually shrouded in slushy snow, rain, or fog which communicates a sense of moral and spiritual malaise, a scarred grey-white landscape like his Finland in *The Looking-Glass War* in which he describes figures and buildings "locked in the cold like bodies in an ice-floe." "Significant colour appears only once in all of Le Carré's Eastern European scenes," notes David Monaghan in *The Novels of John Le Carré*. "In the secret courtroom where Leamas is exposed as a double agent, red stands out in sharp contrast to the otherwise unremitting shades of black and grey."

Still, the central heart of Estonian cities is the Old Town around which has grown the outlying suburbs. The Old Town in Tallinn — *Taani linn* (Danish town) — is magnificently medieval. Surrounded by a huge, turreted medieval wall, and with a large cathedral that supports five gilded domes, Tallinn truly has a character all of its own. There is a weirdly fantastic, almost fairy-tale atmosphere about this venerable area due in large part to the enormously tall bell-tower of the Church of St. Olaf and to the tremendous width of the fat old-city wall. The more recent parts of this old city, the far-flung suburbs, the worn-out sections that one sees driving in from the airport, look like the depressing, down-at-the-heels inhospitable exurbs of Worcester, Mass. A third of all Estonians, some 400,000 people, live in Tallinn, the nation's only truly large city. You know you are in Europe but not quite where. I thought a good deal about Eugène Atget regarding the starkness of the deserted streets of Paris, almost always photographed like scenes of a crime, but there he also saw beggars, hand-organ players, fruit-sellers, horses, etc. — I tended to see, at least in my down days, only the empty streets, out-of-the-way corners, deadly wooden houses. There are the usual malls, of course, in the central city. (Malls in Estonia not only have small food shops but also feature supermarkets, almost always on the bottom floor.) Movies ("*Eesti keeles, ingliskeelsete subtiitlitega*") are big. Video shops are everywhere. I heard a crazed rock group playing in a crowded mall in Tallinn one afternoon that almost blasted out my ear-drums. Rock 'n' roll in various attenuated forms is popular there.

Music is a big Estonian thing. In tea shops, in restaurants, on street walls, one constantly comes across flyers, sheets, and hand-outs for concerts, pop shindigs, *muusikals*, and shows for rock groups. I seemed to hear the songs of Abba on loudspeakers wherever I went. I also heard groups like Genesis, the Bee Gees, no end of Beatles clones, a plethora of Mink DeVille and Ramones wannabees, a lot of European artists: Mirielle Mathieu, Jacques Brel, Charles Aznavour; but nothing for people

ready to really get down like James Brown — *owwww!* We are not talking
innovation, let's face it.[19] I not only heard The Doors at the University
of Virginia in 1967 but back in my day also managed to attend several
of the milestone concerts of Pink Floyd, for example, the amazing free
Hyde Park preview of *Atom Heart Mother* in 1970 (Syd in attendance),
even the launching of *Dark Side of the Moon* at Radio City Music hall in
1973, but why start there? — loving old rock-and-roll, 1950s stuff, black
groups, old doo wop, etc. I have to say has left me an exile, a willing refugee, for ages, a rueful cultural expatriate, by dint of it not being popular
anymore. I mean, I believe, not without logic, that real rock-and-roll had
already gone the way of the dodo by 1973, so you can imagine what kind
of bewildered misfit I was stranded in un-wiggy Tallinn with my head
exploding in 2009.

Don't misunderstand; there is much splendid music there. Arvo Pärt,
a genius if there ever was one, is internationally celebrated, as he should
be. Then there is Urmas Sisask. One would be remiss in failing to mention the powerful contemporary music of Erkki-Sven Tüür who from
1979 to 1984 headed up the rock group In Spe, a very popular group
in Estonia, and rose to write more serious, matchless compositions. He
wrote the music for *Wallenberg*, an opera in two acts in 2001 along with
choral, chamber music, orchestral work, and string quartets. I greatly
admire his *Requiem "In Memoriam Peeter Lilje"* for soprano, tenor, mixed
chorus and chamber orchestra (1994), his *Rändaja õhtulaul* ("The Wan-
derer's Evening Song") for mixed chorus a cappella (2001) and *Meditatio*
for mixed chorus and saxophone quartet (2003).

I mention the group Pink Floyd. I got to know the late, mysterious
Syd Barrett fleetingly just about the time that group was starting up.
There was a seedy old pub on Goodge St. in London called Finch's, a
dark, noisy place where I spent a lot of nights drinking when first I went
to England in the mid-Sixties. He was living with a few guys at 101
Cromwell Road in Kensington in 1966. I was off-handedly invited to kip
there several times, late nights when I had nowhere else to stay. I remember beautiful Susan Kingsford, his then girlfriend, I believe, who made
cups of tea for us. I was writing my first novel, *Three Wogs*. Syd played the
guitar all the time. This was before he became the hopeless drug casualty
of popular myth, for it is said he had a possibly acid-induced breakdown

one year later. When I knew him, the group was knocking at the gates of dawn, and he was the Pink Piper himself. Shine on, you crazy diamond!

Why do I mention Barrett and the Floyd here? They were not just four gerbils fobbing off a display of acoustic weirdness for musical art like so many Gothic loonies have since then. It was a period of shimmering fertility and creativity in the world of music, that's all.

Sometimes when the shadowy flats we shared in Tallinn and Tartu became too confining, on rare days when Sarah and I disagreeably began to grate on each other — "The couple's watches: never the same time," says Elias Canetti — I would throw on my coat and disappear, roaming to far ends of the city, looking no doubt like a demented, beaked corvid in my black watch hat and black all-purpose coat, not wanting to talk to or meet anyone, just processing information wherever I looked and no doubt embodying several features of high-functioning autism. Aloneness could be scarifying, but it never sent me to a shrink. "Be warned," comedian Conan O'Brien once told a graduating class of Stuyvesant High School, "Everyone has a weird roommate. If you don't have a weird roommate, that means *you're* the weird roommate." That would be me.

One comes across small, desperately lit discotheques all over Tallinn and Tartu and Põlva. They are usually ugly, soulless, out-of-date, neon *boites* located on the main thoroughfares, all making flashy but feeble attempts to mimic the hippitude of downtown Las Vegas (a place, pound for pound, much more decadent and far more sadly feeble, of course) which often advertised themselves by playing robotic music through speakers as loudly as possible, sometimes even live with that horrible kind of out-of-date European rock 'n' roll blasted out by caterwauling rock-groups — always four guys with bowl haircuts who look like Peer Gynt, singers with names like Urdu and Kiki and Livo (you pick the gender) howling hits that were popular in the USA sometime back around 1974! Glitzy gambling casinos, open all night, are fashionable in Estonia, highly visible money-traps with garish neon signs and heavy riveted wooden doors that always appeared to be locked. Estonian clubs, cafés, and combo bar-restaurants, often hidden, with side or back entrances only, have names like Garboo, Hollyvooood, Club Dietrich, Boogaloo, Coca-Cola, Plaza, Klub Konnect, *Rähn,* Galaxy, Nudeplay, Onyx, *Lepatriinu* ["Ladybird's"!], Scandal's, Sueycide, Omnivore, The Ratt and, of course, the ubiquitous Pussycat Doll. In the city of Tartu, one bar on a side-street off Town Square shows illustrated caricatures of Chaplin, Gable, Douglas Fairbanks and Mary Pickford. So hip! One rock group is called *Jäääär*. Others are *Lakkamatu, Tuberkuloised, Seos, Fanaatik, Trotslik*. Yet another was *Lõõtspillide*. Not to forget that great techno lezpop duo called *t.A.T.u* who came in third in the Eurovision Song Contest a few years ago, two passionate lavendricals who apparently sweatily kiss and paw and fondle each other while they are performing. People adore such stuff, which explains, at least for me, why democracy can never be a success. This may be the place to mention one unusual name for a cinema in Estonia, the "Bi-Ba-Bo" in Tallinn which, needless to say, has to be right up there with other "de-lite-ful" popular world theaters like the "Amusu" in Lincolntown, Ga; the "Jolly Talkies" in Muttom, India, the "Fo To Sho" in Ballinger, Texas; and the "Kosy Korner Kinema" in Bristol, England, except that those particular names, I believe, actually *mean* something!

Movie theaters are everywhere. The first feature film made in Estonian was Konstantin Märska's *Mineviku Vari* ("The Shadow of the Past") in 1924. It was Theodor Luts, however, a producer of both feature films and documentaries, whose *Noored kotkad* ("Young Eagles") in 1927 that is generally regarded as the cornerstone of Estonian cinema. The two other Baltic countries came to produce films relatively later. The first feature film in Latgalian, a dialect of East Latvia, was *Cilveca berns* ("The Child of Man") in 1991. Exclusive of the influences of Soviet cinema, which have been notable, certainly, one may cite *Onyte ir Jonelis,* a film from 1931, as being the first feature film of Lithuania.

Europe to Americans can seem odd, an interphalanxing structure of long-held peculiar habits, routines and manners.

This was *quaint* Old Europe, where there are things like kitchen yards, fairy tales are all about wolves, people write number 7s like arrows, no toilet flush is the same, people give little chocolates as gifts, couples shop for food carrying string bags, readers wet their index finger to turn a page, public statues show penises, apartments are cramped, ice-cream is sold as cornets, chair-backs are carved with gargoylish heads, and pop singers go by single names and sport huge dippy hair! Laced-dirndls appear in one form or another in endless national costumes, soap is hexagonal and brown, all toilet paper is stiff, novels come only in paperback, currency looks phony, people sport bicycle clips, and men love wearing Tyrolean hats with feathers in them. They waltz. They eat gelato. They go hiking and trumping about old forests with wooden staffs and whistle hearty songs. They find the films of Fernandel and Jacques Tati actually funny. They enjoy Euro-comic characters like Largo Winch and Diabolik and Asterix the Gaul which bewilder the few Americans who know about them. They know all the German lyrics, all the choruses, to the "Ode to Joy." They are rabid chess addicts and know all about Dan's Metric and Zugzwangs, Fianchetto and Pawn Chains. They wear berets and sit in outdoor cafés sipping espresso to discuss with high seriousness outré people like Mommsen and Von Treitschke and Saussure. They celebrate Europe Day (May 9) which no American has ever heard of and drink odd concoctions like pastis and mineral water, hang tapestries up on their walls, and actually eat Wienerbrod for breakfast. They still ride Vespas, thrill to accordion music, measure lengths in meters, drink midnight-black coffee in midget cups, love embroidered clothing, and in extreme fits of unappeasable anger actually shake their fists at the sky the way one sees it done in cartoons. They still recount by firelight stories of bridge trolls, erl-kings, and forest sprites. They quaff drinks like aquavit, potato schnapps, Trakehner blut, and Marjellchen. They like goofy puppet shows and cheese gone off and read authors we over here have never heard of like Vera Linhatova (Czech), Marek Bienczyk (Poland), Gudbergur Bergsson (Iceland), Selma Lagerlöf (Sweden), and Jens Peter Jacobsen (Denmark) whom the poet Rainer Maria Rilke in his day — hyperbolically? — rated among the greatest writers of all time! They call French fries *frites*, drink out of horns, stencil the outside of their houses, favor midget refrigerators and measure liquids in centiliters. They grow tulips along their walkways, carry chessboards about in their pockets, wear huge wristwatches that have compasses *which they actually use,* part their hair in the middle, and append their wallets to long chains! The men wear Speedos at the beach, silk shirts unbuttoned to the waist, and are as vain, autocratic, overconfident, greasy, exact, and flamboyantly temperamental as Robeto Orlandi (Rossano Brazzi) in *Rome Adventure* and Boris Lermontov (Anton Walbrook) in *The Red Shoes* — and even *look* like them! They hand out awards like the Palme d'Or and the Kossuth Prize and the

Giro d'Italia Medal that seem to be less internationally inconsequential than totally pointless. They love swoopy, loopy Scandinavian furniture — Alvar Alto and Eero Sarinen come to mind — with undecorated and scoldingly didactic lines but an organic soul! They buy packs of cigarettes from stalls and kiosks, love astrakhan hats, favor metal scraping mats, roll their *R*s like roller skates, and, as in just about every European city, their ambulances on emergency runs, instead of sirens, make the sound of alarming goose honks! They formally kiss each other on both sides of the cheek and hold cigarettes not like this but like *that!* They have *thin* Santa Clauses over there, and Christmas means marzipan, carp, reindeer games, and tree-hats with live candles! They listen to people like Charles Aznavour, Jacques Brel, Yves Montand, Edith Piaf, and even Leos Janacek and never manage to miss the delightful annual Eurovision Song Contest which launches such deathless song hits as "Diggi-Loo, Diggi-Ley" (Sweden, 1984), "Boom Boom Boomerang" (Austria, 1977), and "Sinu Sipilgapesa" (Estonia, 2008), and where at lugubrious parties with subterfugian casts right out of *Notorious* held in cryptlike high-ceilinged rooms, musty with the dust of ages and heavy fringed drapes swagged back with silken cords, you will never fail to meet at least one tall, preachy, rectitudinizing anti-Nazi bore ("Ve are all wictimized by evil!") who talks exactly like the unbearably earnest Paul Lukas playing Kurt Muller (a murderer himself!) in the World War II movie, *Watch on the Rhine*. I was floundering once again in the middle of whirling semantic moskoe-strom of progressive cultural Yurrup: *"Monsieur, où est le Burger-King, s'il vous plaît?" "Señor, yo quiero un otro Budweiser, por favor!" "Möchte ich für dies emit Visa oder mit Mastercard bezahlen, bitte?" "Igor! Davai mne dva peperoni-pitsy, pozhalusta, I dva klassikalichesky Kokakoly!" "Anata wa Heiniken-biiru ga arimasu ka?" "Ma tahaksin Tallinnas rentida Buickit või Toyotat kas Hertzilt või Aviselt, ja maksta Mastercardiga kui saan Tartusse!" "Dove sono I terminali qui d'Alitalia, di Lufthansa, d'Air France, e d'El-Al, per favore?"* I gotta tell ya, it was not long before I began seeing pinwheels and faces from Ronald Searle cartoons!

Who Dem?

Statues of all sorts can be seen everywhere in Tallinn and Tartu, usually busts of balding, bespectacled men that only a few have ever heard of outside of Estonia, such as, to but name a few, Carl Robert Jakobson or Jaan Koort or Johan Pitka or Jüri Uluots (the last legitimate prime minister of the Republic of Estonia) or the celebrated Field Marshall Barclay de Tolly or are set many of them up in niches. During Napoleon's Invasion of Russia in 1812 de Tolly assumed the supreme command of the 1st Army of the West, the largest of the Russian armies facing Napoleon. He proposed the now famous "scorched earth" strategy of drawing the enemy deep into one's own territory and retreated to the village of Tsaryovo-Zaimishche between Moscow and Smolensk. He is buried in Jögeveste, Estonia. The famous Estonian writer Oskar Luts, whose books can be found all over Estonia, merits a lot of attention, statue-wise. He worked in education. "It is easy to become famous in Estonia because it is so small," an Estonian professor told me, reminding me slantingly in terms of relativity of what the priggish G. K. Chesterton observed in *Sidelights* when he — foolishly, pompously — wrote of the genius Abraham Lincoln, "Nowhere else in the world could a man of exactly that type have been a *great* man; he would at best have been a good man, generally derided as an exceedingly dowdy sort of dunce or failure." (In Iceland, the most sparsely populated country in Europe with an average of three inhabitants per square kilometer — 60 percent of the people live in Reykjavik — it is said that everyone knows everyone else personally!) There are Bronze Soldier statues all around Tallinn.[20] I used to saunter along the banks of the Emajögi and often follow what I came to call the "Gnome Walk." This was a long meandering path, replete with very strange, tall and small, variably-shaped statues. A black statue of gnomish Hugo Hermann Furchtegatt, founder of a private school for boys, looked like the Mayor of the Munchkin City in *The Wizard of Oz*. Then there was an owlish monument to some begoggled (*kaitseprillid*) creature with the anagram-sounding name Auglap. I would never learn, despite research, exactly who this mysterious figure was or exactly what he — or it — did! Very impressive, then, is the overmuscularized statue of Kalevipoeg with sword in hand. Next, we encounter Oskar Luts, a peering, bird-faced fellow sandwiched between two rocks. Then came F.R. Kreutzwald who resembles J.D. Rockefeller. Scholar-types seemed to proliferate in Estonian statues. Schoolmen. Clerks. Writers of children's books. Estonians are Finno-Ugrics, and it is part of their nature, I am told, to contemplate the universe on a regular basis. Widely celebrated, it seemed, were people connected with folklore, and they are well-represented in busts and statues everywhere. Let me add here, parenthetically, that, as far as statues go, logic seems to play very little role in the United States as to who should be honored and why. There is no end of corruption in this matter. In the city of Boston, for example, with all sorts of politics involved, statues have been preposterously raised to a jailbird governor, a basketball coach (who was born in Brooklyn, N.Y.!), a baseball player, while the most dramatic bridge in the city, now its "location shot," was named for a contemporary Jewish lawyer who was born in Clifton, New Jersey![21] Passed over for that honor, if they were even considered at all, were such local notables as Edgar Allan Poe, Emily Dickinson, Ralph Waldo Emerson, Henry David Thoreau, James Abbott MacNeill Whistler, Childe Hassam, Samuel F.B. Morse, Oliver Wendell Holmes, John Singleton Copley, Alexander Graham Bell, John Singer Sargent, and Henry Wadsworth Longfellow, and Daniel Chester French who spent his happiest and most creative years in Massachusetts at his Chesterwood in the Berkshires.

My favorite statue in Estonia was that of the handsome, dashing poet Kristjan Jaak Peterson (1801-1822), standing dramatically in his long frock-coat with a book in one hand, a staff in the other — legend has it that he once walked from Tartu to Riga — on the windy top of haunting Toome Hill in the town of Tartu. A herald of Estonian national literature who died unthinkably young — four years younger than John Keats — at the age of 21, Peterson was the first student at the University of Tartu to flaunt his Estonian identity. His birthday is celebrated on Mother Tongue Day — March 14 — when one recalls his lines:

Cannot the tongue of this land
In the wind of incantation
Rising up to the heavens
Seek for eternity?

A fashion in Estonia on bronze busts and plaques found on walls throughout the cities is that for sculptural verisimilitude appendages *stick out* — noses, hands, chins. It is a good thing that Lord Byron is no longer around as, according to legend — in what mood your guess is as good as mine — he was notorious before leaving Brussels for entering the Royal Park and knocking off the noses with his cane!

I saw nowhere any statue of Louis I. Kahn, the world-renowned architect. (A portrait of him done by his illegitimate daughter, Alexandra Tyng, however does hang in the town hall of Kuressaare.) The strange, secretive, diminutive, scarred eccentric is widely thought of as being American, but he was in fact born of Jewish origin in Estonia, specifically Pärnu. He was brought on a steamer in 1906 to the United States where his parents changed their name to *Kahn* in Philadelphia. That his true name was actually Leiser-Itze Schmuilowsky (1901-1974) is only one of the many odd facts about the man who never married but juggled three separate women and three separate families, took every commission he could — the design of his much later celebrated Trenton Bath House (!) Kahn considered a watershed in his development as an architect — fought with pretty much everybody, and then upon returning from Bangladesh dropped dead in a Penn Station men's room in New York City where, because he had scratched out his home address in his passport, it took three days before the police and the world figured out the identity of the body that had lain in a New York morgue. After working in various capacities for several companies in Philadelphia, he founded his own atelier in 1935. While continuing his private practice, he served as a design critic and professor of architecture at Yale School of Architecture from 1947 to 1957. From 1957 until his death he was a professor of architecture at the School of Design at the University of Pennsylvania. Influenced by ancient ruins, Kahn's style tended to the monumental and monolithic; his heavy buildings don't hide their weight, their materials, or the way they are assembled.

No patriotic Estonian — perhaps a redundancy — is unaware of the Tõnismäe Monument debacle. The Tõnismäe Monument in one of Tallinn's central parks — the 6-foot bronze statue of a Soviet soldier, erected in 1947 — commemorates the "liberation" of Estonia from the savagery of Nazi rule on September 22, 1944. In actual fact, the five-day-old independent government of Otto Tief had been crushed by the Soviets who either shot or sent to Siberia most of his ministers. The Russian people living in Estonia who used to gather at this monument — maudlin nationalists, many of them from the region east of the city in the rural towns of Jõhvi and Kohtla-Järve with their heavy Russian populations, who refuse to see themselves as the unwanted (and, to many, malignant) people they are — cannot fathom why Estonians hated it so. Estonians for the most part have loathed this statue ever since the day it was erected more than half a century ago, and they have more than once tried to tear it down. On March 27, 2007 a violent riot broke out in the city when the Estonian authorities tried to remove the statue to the Defense Forces Cemetery outside of Tallinn, reminding me of what the Belgian playwright Maurice Maeterlinck once said: the dead would not exist if it were not for cemeteries. As many as 1,500 angry nationalists panfuriously demonstrated in a mêlée in which 44 were injured, 300 arrested, and one young man, a 20-year-old ethnic-Russian of Estonian citizenship, was actually stabbed to death. It wistfully recalls for me the "dove," a peace symbol, that Pablo Picasso drew for Louis Aragon as the Communist Party emblem — the artist later donated it the Soviet-backed World Peace Congress of 1949 — which has since become one of the most popular lithographed posters of Picasso's. John Richardson, Picasso's foremost biographer, recounts how the Spanish artist deviously confided to Aragon that he "kept these vicious birds in separate cages, otherwise they would peck each other to bits."[22] Like many, if not most, of the alien and, in many instances, unwelcome 300,000 Russians living in the republic (out of only 1.3 million Estonians) he no doubt felt injured and insulted, since the remains of many Russian soldiers are also supposedly buried nearby. Where the controversial statue once stood is — predictably — now an empty space. Memories, however, linger.

Who would ever deny symbol is statement?

At Home Abroad

Since the American dollar was fairly worthless in 2008 — I mean our money was essentially worth ratshit — for entertainment Sarah and I parsimoniously used to sit up at night drinking glasses of *Rahva Viin* (37.5% vol.), the cheapest vodka in Estonia at about 50 kroon a bottle — the kroon was worth about a dime in 2008 — and on her MacBook laptop download streaming videos of old movies — a slangism, at least in his mind, that Edmund Wilson actually went on record as fussily disliking as late as 1956 (see his *A Piece of My Mind: Reflections at Sixty*) and I mention this because he also states in the same book he could not "abide" radio, which we listened to constantly — usually arbitrarily selected and even found brand-new American movies on a Chinese website (*Tu dou*), which was probably illegal. The films we watched all seem to come in five segments of 20 minutes each: part I, part II, etc. We rationalized that the aggravation of watching movies so segmented mitigated the crime of piracy, and then what else was there to do? Fly-fishing in the Emajõgi? Go happy-wandering with scrip and staff to the outlying suburbs of Tartu which quickly gave way to such sweeps of emptiness it seemed as if the human race had vacated the world? Visit the Ant Kingdom in Akste, the largest colony of ants in Estonia, with over three billion "inhabitants," about 1,500 nests all communicating — as "the words go out in Formic" — with each other? Trek off to Raplamaa county to the village of Pahkla which is replete with old rocks and sit on the largest, the "King of Estonian Rocks," also known as the Pahkla Suurkivi? Take in the famous windmills of Saaremaa? Go to a dark, ear-splitting disco bar and watch *Fizz Superstar*, the *American Idol*-like contests so popular there? (A cute blonde from Elva, Estonia named Kerli who won the contest six or so years ago has become a celebrity and has since made an album called *Love Is Dead* which includes her hit "Walking On Air." ("I had my first big meeting with a record label guy," she told *Cosmopolitan* magazine. "I was this 15-year-old girl from the forest — I was nervous about whether I'd be able to eat correctly with a fork and knife.") Take a bus to sunny Riga? (It did cross my mind at one point to head down to Dvinsk, the Vitebsk Province of the Russian Empire, now Daugavpils in Latvia, to see where the depressing Abstract Expressionist suicide Mark Rothko was born before his family came to America in 1910, moving of all places to Portland, Oregon, but upon reconsideration I thought it might have a deleterious effect on my writing — I was still working on my novel — and that in despair I might meet that Russian-born manic-depressive's own ignominious end!)

We drank instant coffee. We dined at home and ate spaghetti a lot. We tried as best we could to regulate the heat, keeping it low. And as I say it was old-time radio and boosted movies for us. I look back and see us still, holed up in bed, winter chipmunks, on many a dark and cozy night drinking glasses of fire-hot vodka and getting zorched. Plastered. Dredge-fried to the hat. *Verfnyifkit*, as they say in Yiddish. Still, even though on occasion we woke up with faces like slept-on sheets we kept busy.

No, we set out, Sarah and I, sincerely determined to avoid what Harold Bloom legitimately called the "anxiety of influence" and the pernicious effect on our lives of the often moronic "triple screens" — television, cinema and Internet — but even though we had little money one can only read or paint for so long, especially in such a discalced country, before it is rubber-room time. Even the best of us crack. I remember back in 2005, after President Obama first arrived in the U.S. Senate, he was in the unfortunate situation of having to listen to a characteristically long, droning speech by the psychotic Vice-President Cheney he wrote down something on a piece of paper and handed it to one of his aides. On the paper, the young senator had scrawled in large letters, "Shoot. Me. Now."

Sarah and I were passionately behind then-Senator Obama and his race with the aggressive, pusillanimous pants-suit-wearing androgyne Hillary Clinton all through that winter of 2008, following him with — to swipe a phrase — the fierce urgency of now. Watching him standing at the lectern at the National Constitution Center in Philadelphia in March, flanked by four American flags on either side, and listening to that "A More Perfect Union" speech he gave that spoke to finally ending the long racial stalemate of white-black in the United States was truly profound, but we had been on-board for that born leader long before as throughout the campaign all of the other candidates, of both parties, in that seemingly endless two-year slog of merciless, malpractitioning primaries, seemed in comparison empty-souled manipulable hand-puppets.

We saw it on a computer. We watched no television in Estonia. I have always despised the goggle-box, anyway, a brainless mercantile shipping-container at best. "There is nothing on it worthwhile, and we're not going to watch it in this household. *I don't want it in your intellectual diet,*" said Philo T. Farnsworth, the man who *invented* the damned thing, the first electronic version of it, in any case, and who was the first to foresee its abuses and among the very first to regret it, immediately understanding how it was going to be badly misused. Television! The electronic marketing box! The thing is not buffoon-proof, is a major reason for obesity in America, makes major inroads into reading and intellectual growth, and, among other things, can make a moron — look at the dunces on cable "news"! — famous in a single day. I inevitably lowered my expectations and was soon only hoping that being in Estonia would allow me time to think, to dream, to write, and in general to detach myself from anxieties enough to examine them, making fastidious self-inventories, like J. Alfred Prufrock did and to take a worthwhile assessment of this strange country. Fatally immured like Radames and Aida I can frankly report we were not. But the concolorous darkness filled the overhead sky, and sealed in many a night we were. We were content; still, we needed entertainment. We were limited to films over the Internet, as I say, and tall glasses of 140-proof vodka. As an indulgence we at times brought back sweets for late-night snacks. *Kohuke* was a favorite, a curd snack — something similar to Latvian *biezpiena sieriņš* or Lithuanian *varškės* — that is made from milled and pressed curd with added raisins, jam or other fillings and sometimes glazed with chocolate or other sweet substance (glazed snacks often have no filling), such as vanilla-, kiwi- or woodland strawberry-flavored cream. Once in a while, on rare occasions, I would go out to splurge on a bottle of Bordeaux, "the best wine for conversation," according to the late, hyper-indulged Duchess of Windsor, who dismissed Burgundy as "deadly to the liver."

That's Entertainment?

As I say, our film-fare was not exactly of the Super-Duper-Special-Musical-Photoplay-in-Cineramic-Technicolor-on-Widescope-Triple-Screen variety. It would better be compared to sitting in wooden chairs in the back row of a dusky 1916 nickelodeon or perhaps squinting through a knothole in a fence to see puppet shows.

Among the films we watched, with endless "buffering," were: *Watch on the Rhine*; *The Go-Between*; *Amarcord*; an early Judy Garland called *Listen, Darling* (1938); *Dodsworth*; *Romance* (1930) where Greta Garbo was at her prettiest (no woman looked sexier wearing earrings); *The Lost Squadron* with weird bald Erich von Stroheim; *Last Year at Marienbad*; *The Sorrow and the Pity*; *The Big Sleep* with yet another one of those farcical Raymond Chandler plots ("Where's Eddy Mars? Who's Sean Regan? Why did Canino blackmail Little Jonesy? And exactly when did Carmen squeal?") — did people in 1946 really fall for that shit? — a couple of Woody Allen movies, which, to me at least, are always transparently autobiographical: a homely self-conscious Jewish kid from Brooklyn who never earned a college degree insistently trying to show, cannily by default, that he is an intellectual; *The Children's Hour* — the lying little brat, Mary, reminding me of a nasty niece of mine who when young was not only that monster's double in vileness but with her piggish up-turned nose and psychotic behavior, scarily, looked exactly like her; *Mr. Imperium* with fat, bloviating Ezio Pinza and an aging Lana Turner; *Gilda*; *Red River* — perhaps my favorite movie, although I cannot stand John Wayne — William Powell in *Fashions of 1934* (with a young Bette Davis in a beret who even looks pretty!); *The Gorgeous Hussy*; *Showboat*; *A Face in the Crowd* (1957) starring Andy Griffith as a vagabond soul who gives us far and away one of the greatest performances ever on film and was not mentioned for an Academy Award; Fred Astaire and Ginger Rogers in *Shall We Dance* (with officially no question mark in the title, thank you) — sunglasses in 1937 made people look like insects or sex-criminals! — where Fred and Ginger ingeniously tap-dance on roller skates! I marveled at the brilliant timing, the physical comedy, the great grinning wide-mouthed lunacies — as well as the signature yowl — of Joe

E. Brown, especially in his early films of the 20s and 30s, *Son of a Sailor*; *Fireman, Save My Child*; *Elmer the Great*; *Polo Joe*; *Sons O' Guns*. He seems always to be chawnking apples in his movies. He munches six of them all through *The Circus Clown*. We resorted to watching something like less than a quarter of a Marx Brothers movie — a cultural forgery still honors these purveyors of assless, second-grade humor when they were, every one of them, surely the unfunniest and least accomplished drips in film history — and I remember in desperation that we even watched some cipher of a movie with Jerry Lewis whose roaring lack of talent and shameless stupidity reinforced a remark I recall he once, I think revealingly, made to playwright Neil Simon, "I never read a book in my life." We tried to find the Andrei Tarkovsky film, *Stalker*, which was filmed in Tallinn but never managed to do so.

I was struck at the cold and soulless facility with which, literally across decades, so many movies glorified adultery and advocated it as a boon to delight and creative drama: *Brief Encounter* (1945), *Intermezzo* (1939), *From Here to Eternity* (1953), *By Love Possessed* (1961), *The Postman Always Rings Twice* (1946), *Autumn Leaves* (1956), *Tea and Sympathy* (1956), *Doctor Zhivago* (1965), *The Bridges of Madison County* (1995), *The English Patient* (1996), *Unfaithful* (2002), etc. — it is a theme in its casual sordidness that depressed me especially in the dire, light-amputated gloom of that secular country. What upside-down values! What a crippled practice to exalt! Seeing life through Hollywood eyes crazed with testosterone — or estrogen and progesterone — burn! We live in morally parlous times. It is hard to comprehend the vulgarity of 80-year-old, Gloria Vanderbilt who has been married four times in a high moment of what I can only call trashluxe proudly published a book in 2004, *It Seemed Important At the Time*, giving an account of all the famous lovers that she had in her lifetime in a last attempt, I gather, at self-aggrandizement by association. But precedents were surely set, examples made, by the adulterous marriages of Presidents Roosevelt, Kennedy, and Clinton, never mind Prince Charles, Lady Diana, and Camilla Parker Bowles. Søren Kierkegaard was right: "Society begins to die from the head downward."

When our eyes got bleary on late snowy nights we found music on the computer and listened to some of my favorite old tunes which, as a matchless treat for Sarah, I would often sweetly sing to her: Sam Cooke's "A Change Is Gonna Come," Ray Sharpe's "Linda Lu," The Coasters' "Searchin'" The Globetrotters' "Rainy Day Bells," The Short Cuts' "Don't Say He's Gone," The Skyliners' "Since I Don't Have You," The Fleetwoods' "Mr. Blue," Etta James' "I'd Rather Go Blind," Barbara Lynn's "You'll Lose A Good Thing," Buster Brown's "Fannie Mae," Joe Cocker's "Cry Me A River," The Elegants' "Little Star," Fats Domino's "My Girl Josephine," Lee Andrews and the Hearts' "Teardrops," The Penguins' "Ookey Ook," The Human Beinz', "Nobody But Me," Huey Piano Smith's "Don't You Just Know It," Dion & the Belmonts' "Where of When," The Magnificents' "Up on the Mountain," the Bee Gees' "I Started a Joke" — sorry, but I happen to like it — the Rolling Stones' "Under My Thumb," the Sir Douglas Quintet's "She's About A Mover," The Olympics' "Western Movies," etc.

I have to confess, I love old-time radio and am convinced that a good bit of impetus in my becoming a writer can be traced to my imagination being stirred there in the close dark of our bedroom when, as a boy, my brothers and I, watching the transfiguring dial-light above the mesh of our little clunker of a Philco radio, would listen in the dark to one dramatic show after another, programs like *Sergeant Preston of the Yukon*; *Beulah*; *Mr. Keen, Tracer of Lost Persons*; *Henry Aldrich*; *The Great Gildersleeve*; *The Jack Benny Show*; *I Love a Mystery*; *Name That Tune*; *Straight Arrow*, starring Howard Culver as Steve Adams/Straight Arrow ("Keen eyes fixed on a flying target," so the show began, "a gleaming arrow set against a rawhide string, a strong bow bent almost to the breaking point and then…[*thup* sound of an arrow hitting its target] Straaaaaaight Arrow!"), *Yours Truly, Johnny Dollar*; *Cavalcade of America*, brought to you by DuPont ("Better Things for Better Living Through Chemistry") and, among others, *The Shadow*. On many a night in Estonia or in the wee hours of the morning I would go through iTunes to the radio to find Talk/Spoken word (146 streams) and click on AM 1710 Antioch or The History Capsule or ACB Radio Treasure-Trove, and Sarah and I would be able to catch many of these original old shows, many of them new for Sarah, hailing from another generation, and no doubt another entertainment preference, I believed, but who soon became a passionate and devoted convert.

Night after night we cheerfully drank, squinting there in the dark like bulb-eyed lemurs, and once or twice even got toasted, waking up the next day on a dark, cold morning with the numbed, palsied tongue of dead vodka. Only once I can say did I get truly ossified. It began on a winter day and lasted into the night when I went grumpily walking far afield in the dark, out toward the direction of Tammelinn. I felt like one of the lurching drunks I saw down by the bus station saying "hello" and "goodbye" to the walls. I was as pale as a Canadian ghost. Sheet-white. I recall I started hearing music for the dreaded movie, *The Lost Weekend*, eerie theremin waves coming through the ether almost like the sound of mouse squeaks. Jeeves, the fictional butler in the Bertie Wooster novels, had an extraordinary concoction to deal with hangovers, but in all of the P.G. Wodehouse books, the recipe — the omissive quirk — was never revealed. I usually took a cup of strong gunpowder tea in consequence or went for a bracing walk by the river or the train station where, from a nearby stall (inside), in order to feel as much an inner gestalt of Spring as a cure for headache, I once bought and ate a handful of *les capucines* — nasturtiums. Nose twisters! Does that seem strange? This is the realm of the extraordinary, the unaccustomed.

For logic there, look everywhere, anywhere — it is not in great abundance, quite the opposite. I can vouch for this. I searched up and down, this way and that, over and under.

I left no Estonian unturned.

Anomalyville

Estonia, before all else, is anomalyville. It is not necessarily fully assbackwards but, to the orthodox Western mind, surely a country of distinct oddballism. They sell a beer there that is actually made out of fermented bread. Doors open outward. (I several times cracked my head trying to push one out. To abridge Elvis, I forgot to remember I was not in America.) In bookstores, the prices are always maddeningly penciled in at the back of books, never at the front. Toilet-paper rolls always sit loose on a straight open rod and so easily slide and tumble off. (In bathrooms there are IFÖ toilets, which one flushes by pop-pushing a top button: two buttons are provided, one a half-flush for economy.) Many people garden mother-naked in the summer, but then, ironically, will not deign to speak to you. Estonians are famously shy, or standoffish, yet many public statues showing men's "wedding tackle" — like the creepy Father and Son sculpture (same height, same unbuttoned mutton) on Küüni St. in Tartu done by Ülo Õuna (1944-1988) — and yet paradoxically a cold and stiff, frozen face is the national greeting. They adore children, but they rarely seem to touch them or fondle them or indulge them. I am reminded that when she started off peddling her kitchen-made oils, unguents, and face creams — excuse me, *crèmes* — door-to-door, Josephine Esther Mentzer from Corona, Queens, New York, the daughter of a Hungarian mother and a Czechoslovakian father who changed her name to the preposterous Estée Lauder familiarly, and needless to say vulgarly, always made it a point to *touch* her customers, as a sales ploy, in order to gain their confidence. (Elias Canetti begins his great book, *On the Nature of Crowds*, with a disquisition on the concept of being touched but relates it as a fear not as a reassurance.) Snowplows not only plow snow (from the front) but *sweep* it (from the back). They write number ones (1s) like *V*s so that in Estonia, weirdly, the number 11 resembles — seems to be — the number *77*. Canned beers, all of them, come with a thin, condom-like cap as a sanitary protection. While Estonia has over 1500 islands, the countries of Lithuania and Latvia have exactly *none*. Estonia has no vineyards, at least none that I saw. There are no serious mountains in Estonia, it is more or less entirely flat, and *Suur Munamägi* ("Egg Mountain") the highest hill in the country, is only 1043 feet — not much bigger than an egg. The country has no mountain peaks, no raging rivers, no spectacular fjords. You cannot get badly lost in Estonia. Drive anywhere for more than a few hours, and you'll go bang right into the sea or into Russia or into Latvia or into the filthy pig-run of some demented farmer in a pointed felt-hat who will look up and scream, "*Kes Sa kurat oled, Sa loll munn, ja mis sitta Sa kurat teed?*" ("Who the devil are you, you stupid prick, and what kind of shit are you trying to pull here?")[23] They worship light, sweep rugs instead of vacuum them, sing when they are unhappy, and drink wine hot. I never saw so many cultural deviations or departures from the normal or common order, form, or rule, at least the norms we all know. They sell milk in bags there (Kohupiin light brand), an innovation that is now very fashionable in Europe — a sign, it may be argued, that Estonia is ahead of the curve for once. They officially stop selling beer at 10 p.m. — for a time in Tallinn it was as early as 8 o'clock — but that same commodity can be purchased at any grocery store, gas station, or kiosk in the country. We all know that in Italy they have table wine, but did you know that in Estonia restaurants provide *laua vin* — table vodka? There are endless books on the subject of mushrooms in every bookshop, but it is next to impossible to find a copy of the Holy Qur'an anywhere — I tried — which only happens to be the largest-selling book on the planet. They have a market in Tallinn on Müürivahe Street expressly for selling knit-wear. In Estonia yogurt comes in an assortment of bizarre flavors chal-lenge the imagination. Forget vanilla and chocolate — how about rhu-barb-oat? Aloe-lemon? Lime-wheatgrass? Raspberry-pineapple? They are all in stock. (One afternoon Sarah actually, temeritously, bought a cone with tomato-basil ice-cream. *Tomato-basil ice-cream?*) You can buy scary processed meats there: in one package of sliced meats that I purchased, for example, the first listed ingredient was *water*. They eat pancakes not only for breakfast but at any or every meal, morning, noon, and night. Welcome to Estonia, land of bootleg absinthe and anatomically-accurate naked public statues, but also a realm of uneasy handshakes, atrabilious scowls, peevish glances, and xenophobic suspicion.

Certain Estonian words become splendidly comic to a speaker of Eng-lish. In Estonia, for example, a hog or pig farm is called a *seafarm*. A *mutt* is not a dog but a mole. The word *embama,* not at all funereal, is the noun for "embrace." A *praam* there is a ferry, a *kann* a pitcher or a mug, a *tool* is a chair, and, indeed, a *novell* is a short story. It is easy to remember your car-keys in that country because the word for "chain" is *kee*. Surely a joke resides in the fact that the word for "head" is *pea*. ("I feel dizzy" in Estonian is *Pea käib ringi*). Surely no country has a more vocative word for trick or practical joke than *vingerpuss*.

Most Estonian coins — the smallest ones, the 1, 2, 10, 20, and 50 *senti* are virtually worthless. What, maybe they can buy *närimiskummi* — chewing gum? A piece of Kalev or a Kamatahvel candy? A beet? The country is street-foodless, vineyardless — Sarah claims that she bought a sweet Estonian wine once, so I may be wrong — and too often freezing. I never laid eyes on a golf-course. It was said for years that the best jobs in the country were paid under the table: taxi driver, waiter, doorman, or bartender. There is even a joke that a father would rather his daughter marry a waiter than an engineer. Ground turkey meat costs more than ground beef. The Estonian word for appetizers is — I am not making this up — *eelroad*. Most Estonians eat their main meal, not at dinner, but at lunch. Veganism is completely unknown in Estonia, despite the fact that sour cream, cabbage in some form or other, and cucumbers appear virtually at every meal at any time at any place. Estonian spring rolls are 15 cm-length rolls of fried bread containing meat, cabbage, and carrots. You want anomalies? They eat blood pancakes, beer soup (*ollesupp*), berry froth, farina cream, meatloaf of peas, beet wine, and pig's feet in aspic. Start there!

It is an incontrovertible fact that Estonia has more accidents per capita than any country on earth. (Could one reason be rubber-neckers are watching folks garden naked as wheat straw?) People in Estonia walk very fast, old men and old women included who, even on dangerous ice, will go flashing past you like a shot off a shovel. Wearing a mask in Estonia can lead to an arrest. They love cash dishes. When paying for items in shops, the custom there is not to give money directly to a cashier but rather to place it on a small dish from which the cashier takes it, putting your change back in the same dish, whereupon you pick it up, like chess passes, and should you try to bypass this weird little dish they'll give you a face. Procedure is important among solemn and sober people. In Estonia one is always given a receipt, even for insignificant amounts. Although almost all of Estonia is wireless — people pay for everything on their mobile phones, including parking; they don't even bother bringing cash to the beach — the country is still almost fifty-percent forest, and wild boar on the island of Saarema are so common folk often shoot a boar a week just by standing at their front door to keep them out of their potato fields.

Wooden beer steins can still be seen there, and Tullik and X factory-produced brews have a whopping 10% alcohol count. The word for creation is *looming*. ("Why can't Estonians be more creative?" "Don't worry, it's looming.") The Estonian word for caviar is *kalamari*. Tallinn telephone numbers, which all begin with a 6, have no city codes. Punane Torn ("Red Tower"), the oldest building in Pärnu, one that has survived from the Knights of the Sword, is, of course, white. In a country where one cannot play outside comfortably for almost ten months, the biggest sport is basketball. Courts small and large can be found all over Estonia. Estonia's "Eiffel Tower" is curiously made of wood. The rickety 31-meter structure was built by Jaan Alliksoo in 2008 on Hiiumaa, Estonia's second largest island, to give tourists greater views of the island and the Baltic Sea. The question is: how long will it remain standing? Incidentally, one can actually go *surfing* in Hiiumaa, the second largest island in Estonia, separated from the mainland by a 22 km wide strait. Located in the eastern part of the Baltic Sea, the island of Hiiumaa and a number of small islets cover an area of more than 1,000 square kilometers.

Coats are always buttoned up all the way, even among teenagers. Doors swing inward, as I say, so one is constantly pushing when he should be pulling and vice-versa.[24] It is a country that not only boasts to being one of the largest makers of marzipan in the world but is also home to the rare game of ice cricket — cricket played on frozen lakes, with the country becoming an increasingly popular ice-cricket destination for touring teams from around the world. On the subject of ice, incidentally, they rarely if ever put ice cubes in your drink in Estonia, and, if you should ask for ice, it is you they find peculiar. In restaurants, they do not set out salt and pepper shakers at every table, by the way; there is often only one pair — by the cashier. The tune of the Estonian national anthem, "*Mu isamaa, mu õnn ja rõõm*," was composed by a Finn of German origin named Fredrik Pacius — and, an added irony, Finland often uses it as *its* national anthem!

When visiting people in Estonia it is customary to remove your shoes before entering their home, but I have often seen worshippers in church wearing hats. Tallinn's football team, with Estonia's toughest, meanest players, is mellifluously called "Flora." Estonia has — inexplicably — the highest number of meteorite craters per land area in the world. In the refrigerators of many hotels, you will find what is called a "good morning pickle." Do Estonians eat *pickles* for breakfast? Many indeed do. We usually ate a bowl of Rice Krispies. ("Snap! Crackle! Pop!" in Finnish is rendered "*Riks! Raks! Poks!*") I heard in one nightclub a band featured a lead singer who sang with a voice like Donald Duck accompanied by a tall tattooed violinist with wild, Klimt-like hair, shooting out like rays, who was followed by three girls playing purple violins while another in striped socks and an elf hat, seemingly zombified, watusied up and down in one place. Song titles were solicited from the stage. I heard requests for "I Vant to Holt You Hantz!" "It Doooze Net Metter!" — there is, inexplicably, something of a cult in Estonia for Depeche Mode — and, among others, Michael Jackson's "Beat It." I don't know why, the imp of the perverse, but I wanted to shout out, "Can you play Hoagy Carmichael's 'I'm a Cranky Old Yank in a Clanky Old Tank On the Street of Yokohama with My Honolulu Mama Doin' Those Beato Beato Flat On My Seato Hirohito Blues?'"There is so much that is topsy-turvy in Estonia, so much peculiarity, that it seems as if God, in a fit of inventive horse-play or whimsy, decided to create a trial or experimental country simply to test the concepts of oddness. What was the solution? All together: *Make it smaller and move it to the left!*

Modern valentine cards there show pictures of wooing men wearing outdated fedoras and women with hair-buns. Bad behavior, like orgies or mad drunken lunacy, is never formally "recollected" the following morning. Bathroom light-switches are located outside the room, and always maddeningly at waist level. They do not use shoe-scrapers, rather on the front stoops of many houses are shoe-brooms, parallel brushes, used to clean muddy footwear. The Estonian bagpipe, *torupill* also known as *kitsepill, lootspill,* or *kotepill,* was commonly made from the stomach of a grey seal, elk or, dog, and the story has it that the louder the animal howled while being killed made the instrument fashioned from his breadbasket play that much better. On the subject of greetings and good will, no one smiles in Estonian tourist bureaus where one of the goals, one had always thought, was to make foreigners seem welcome. The Estonian love of saunas is so pronounced they have built them even into buses.[25] It is an Estonian law — an official *dekreet* — that pedestrians wear small reflectors at night, which makes people who generally pin them to their coats or handbags look like blinking toys or clowns!

The country is upsidedownland and reverseville all at once. People there tend to sense direction not as a matter of front and back but as north, south, east, and west. It is their perverse habit, for example, to say not "in front of me" but "west of me" and so on. You would therefore be directed by a host to sit at the north, south, east, or west of the table, instead of to the "left or right." I began to wonder if this odd crotchet was exclusively a European thing. All things considered, I was often reminded for all the anomalies there of the old immigrant nonsense song from 1923 written by James Kendis and Lew Brown titled "When It's Night-time in Italy It's Wednesday Over Here," which goes in part:

> When it's night-time in Italy it's Wednesday over here
> When it's fish day in Germany you can't get shaved in Massachusetts
> How high is up I'd like to know
> How low is down and when will we have snow
> If you bump into Gallagher you'll find Shean is near
> When it's night-time in Italy it's Wednesday over here.
>
> When it's night-time in Italy it's Wednesday over here
> When it's washday in Picardy they're eating ice cream cones in Georgia
> Sixteen and four makes thirty one
> Take eight from fiver and your day's work is done
> There are people who hesitate but corn beef makes them cheer
> When it's night-time in Italy it's Wednesday over here.

There are virtually no antiques in the place. What, postcards? A wee bit of amber? Nazi memorabilia, armbands, flags? An 1898 mustache-trimmer? Oil lamps? Puttees? Old issues of Крокодил? A steel Finnish helmet? Sport badges? An Adolf Hitler stamp-block of four? A few lithographs? Certainly these, but nothing of real value. I can say that I did come across some beautiful lace shawls from Haapsalu, triangular ones, true works of art. I saw some splendid old clocks, as well. And rustic furniture. An old lady bookseller in a small room in the outdoor market in Tartu, where one saw small stalls filled with purple potatoes, shiny clothes, and ugly shoes, sold mainly old books, some pornographic magazines, mainly postcards. *Tullid*. Postcards of plain flowers were all cheap. Also postcards with Christmas themes. Valentine postcards. It is the old, colored Russian postcards or historic postcards that cost the most. Stiffness at formal dances keeps older partners unsmiling and moving by rote, often pairing up simply by being proximate. Another anomaly is that when it is your birthday in Estonia, it is the birthday boy or girl, man or woman, who is obliged to buy food and drink *for all the others*. Lavishness, in short, goes the other way, and it is you who must do the honors. Whenever birthday parties are held in offices and various workplaces, they tend to be elaborate and rigid, involving line-ups, bowing, handshakes, and awkward and officious speeches. They sell hot-dogs and hamburgers in their gas stations, like Statoil, meatwiches served with sloppy sauces, one of the more common ones a sickly-sweet pink sauce. Are the hot dogs greasy? I used to buy mine from a wordless and po-faced old lady, who looked like a chinless oyster cook on a hand cart, and the deathless examples handed me were rumpled pale blue horrors, but the hamburgers weren't bad. She seemed to feel that my (*my*, mind you) good manners were missing. The grumpetta as she fumbled about in a steaming tin box for meat distinctly put me in mind of *Cymbeline's* vivisectionist queen and her nasty games with the poison:

> Which first, perchance, she'll prove on cats and dogs
> Then afterwards up higher.

Post-offices in the country queerly sell shampoo, dish detergent, and sanitary pads. On ancient buildings, twenty-feet high up on walls can be seen *doors*. Doors that opened out to exactly nothing — thin air. There are more billboards in Tartu for the single McDonald's fast-food outlet there than there are McDonald's restaurants in any average American city. (France, by the way, has more than 1,000 McDonald's food emporia.) "We believe that the Germans copied our hamburger, the Russians copied our piroshki and the Finns stole our sauna and went international with it," said American-Estonian Ell Tabur in a *New York Times* article[26], on the making of blood sausage. Of interest is that the McDonald's outlets are probably the single best places to go in any Estonian city, not merely for the usual now world-wide identimeals (very salty there) but to be assured of finding a person — he or she will almost certainly be relatively young — with whom to speak or chat in English. Young people there take pride in their ability to do so. Another anomaly, an outstanding one — a truly classic example of European curiosa — is love-related.

Mooning young couples will traditionally snap a padlock on a tree limb or a bridge strut or a grating and then dramatically throw away the key, thus sealing their feelings with a visible bond forever. Eternal love. Married couples, unlike in the USA, wear their wedding rings on their *right* hands in Estonia. It is a country where they have midget strawberries and hats the size of wheelbarrows. Estonians do not wrap gifts of flowers in furled cones with top-blooms but rather in opaque sheets, *completely covered and stapled*, so that no one can see them, usually with the explanation that they will be a surprise, but I suspect a better reason is that the donor simply does not want others to know his business. As Henry Wotton enigmatically tells Oscar Wilde's Dorian Gray, "The true mystery of the world is the visible, not the invisible."

I can think of other anomalies. License plates which never vary on vehicles are all — always — composed of six figures: three numerals and three letters, an unalterable alphanumeric fixture. I saw no American cars, certainly none of our seventeen-feet-long jobs. Not one. Only Opels, Saabs, Hyundais, VWs, Olympics, compact cars with mouth-organ faces, several with their unattractive tin bums elevated *à la française*. (I thought, searching the streets and roads of Estonia, that I might come across some old American classic clunk-failures and automotive disasters like the 1949 Kurtis/Muntz; the 1936 DeSoto; the 1951 Henry J — an econocar with no glovebox, armrests, sunvisors, or trunklids (access was through the fold-down seat) — the carp-mouthed, bug-eyed 1958 Packard; the 1983 AMC/Renault Alliance; or the 1970-78 Gremlin, the first American subcompact, but I have to say I saw nothing of the sort, not a Frazer, a Crosley, a Nash, or Checker, or any other shaky or shrunken cars from the past.)

Seeking similarities in Estonia, but finding only differences — mainly the occasion of delight for me, I promise — did however make me think quite seriously that at times I had actually wandered onto the pages of a Zippy the Pinhead fable.

There is no limit to the incongruities, oddities, or unpredictable anti-cultural alarums in Estonia. *Kalevipoeg*, the Estonian national epic, is a manufactured compilation of oddball sources and probably the least-read central work of literature on earth. The mainstay Estonian beer, a premium lager named Saku, has what seems to be a Japanese name. The other main brand — A. LeCoq — sounds French. Estonians go cane-pole fishing and ice-fishing and electric-shock-wire-fishing. *Electric-shock fishing?* How do they go about this, I wondered, drag rolls of electric wire down to the ponds from some sort of distant plug? The University of Tartu was founded by Gustavus Adolphus II (*Fundator Universitatis Dorpatensis*) — who was (drum roll) a Swede. Were you aware that Estonia still holds the European record for the most bird species seen in one day? 191 different birds. Chaffinches, willow warblers, pipits, you name it. Storks, even. One sees storks everywhere. You may be interested to know that Estonia still has wolves — real wolf packs popularly hunted. It remains one of its stark medieval touches. I am also convinced — just another anomaly — that Estonians have a predilection for rail-less stairways, interminable flights of stairs that go forever up, up, up in a winding, circular way, for I had several definitive David Balfour experiences in that country!

While winter in Estonia is coal-bin dark, if you want to go blind from glare, visit the "Baltic Glint," a long stretch of raised limestone banks, about 1,200 kilometers from Sweden to Lake Ladoga in Russia. You can see the Ontika cliffs which rise 50 meters above the coast. It is from this coast that ships go forth to the seven seas, laden with butter and eggs with flax and bacon and potatoes, the major exports and importing raw cotton, iron, steel, and all-important fertilizers. The Baltic Glint is spoken of like electricity. What, to provide shine, like snowlight, to read a newspaper by in the grip of a January noon?

Singing — bold and proud lusty song — symbolizes protest for many if not most Estonians. The earliest mention of Estonian singing dates as far back as Saxo Grammaticus' *Gesta Danorum* (c. 1179), in which he speaks of Estonian warriors who sang at night while waiting for battle. Older folksongs are also referred to as *regilaulud*, songs in the poetic meter, *regivärss*, a tradition shared by all Baltic-Finnic peoples. The love of singing is a national boast in Latvia and Lithuania, as well. Runic singing was widespread among Estonians until the 18th century, when it started to be replaced by rhythmic folksongs. For fifty years, the act of singing protest songs was for Estonians their sole psychic defense against the occupying Soviets.[27] It does not matter what kind. They sing madrigals, novelty songs, flag songs, pop songs, hiking and knapsack songs, campfire sing-a-longs, choral performances done by huge groups and massive gatherings, wedding songs, and *zupfgeigenhansel* songs of the old German folklore sort. *Laulupidu* (singing) was essentially the voice of revolution. It is a singular source of hope, but in its sweet ineffectiveness wistfully reminds me somehow of sheep in distress. A sheep's solitary defense, a depressingly ineffectual one, is stamping its leg. God in his egalitarian mercy and counterbalancing forethought gave snakes venom and fangs, bears claws, lions teeth, even bees nasty stingers, but what for defense or protection did he endow sheep with? Nothing. They can only scream, defecate or stamp their feet.

"The quickest way to win a war is to lose it," George Orwell wrote, and I wonder if that was not the paradoxical Estonian gambit. In any case, they temporized. Did it work? A mass demonstration — an "*Eestimaa Laul*" — took place when the dark Russian troops departed Estonia on August 31, 1994. Can you fathom the angry patriots John Hancock or Samuel Adams, Dr. Joseph Warren or Capt. John Parker all *singing* to rid themselves of those seven-foot British Grenadiers? Yet power can be unpredictable. It has been said that a mouse can fell an elephant. One of the greatest enemies of the shark is the Moses Sole (*Pardachirus marmoratus*) a highly poisonous fish — weirdly toothless, small, and about as flabby as a wet jellyroll — which contains a milky toxin that is capable of paralyzing any large creature foolish enough to swallow it![28]

Still, singing has a force like nothing else. It is for the nostalgic and idealistic, the sustenance of an irrepressible people with dreams and root-stirring vision. The Latvian poet Imants Zeidonis (b. 1933) has written, "My child, put your spoon back into your bowl when a song is being sung. / Don't look at that man eating, do not learn from him./ He has eaten all his songs. He cannot tell the difference between songs and lettuce." I recall a funny old *MAD* magazine in the 1960s listing national stereotypes of the "one-two-three-formula" kind. ("One Italian is a pizza. Two Italians is a barber shop. Three Italians is a Senate investigation. Four Italians is an opera," etc.) What did I compose for Estonia?

One Estonian is a secret society.
Two Estonians is a beauty parlor.
Three Estonians is an anti-Soviet demonstration.
Four Estonians is a song festival.

But back to the anomalies. I never once saw a person eat a steak in Estonia. Only Swiss steak, once, in a restaurant. It is there. I am assured it is. Simply, I have never seen one. They do not bother with steak. But I am just beginning. I have read that the sunniest month in Estonia is *March*. I heard that fishermen in places used pan-pipes to attract fish. At the post offices in the larger cities in Estonia no one ever queues up, as one does in every other country I have ever visited, people walking inside officially take a ticket as in a delicatessen. One ticket for the stamp line, another for the package line, etc. Customers, strangers all in one big official room — standing alone at separate points and places — wait, holding their tickets. A buzzer with your number/window goes off to let you know when your turn comes. By number, by rote, by rule, by law, by procedure. There are three kinds of mailing boxes for sale: big, medium, small. A thick book chained on the post office wall explains exactly how to address a letter. I once whiled away a whole afternoon in the main Tartu post office on a dark, wet, freezing day writing out a whole list of questions I hoped to ask some willing soul one day over a hot cup of fermented goat-piss. It was either that or take a walk and get my head wet again or go to the movies where I would understand none of the words for films were not dubbed and it was lighter inside than out and there were no Raisinets or Milk Duds or Jujyfruits, having a "a large box of" which the inventive if vulgar film director John Waters exclusively defined as his "idea of perfect happiness."[29]

The country is so old-fashioned. At a tiny cinema, you buy a ticket and the lady at the window asks you — zig-zagging the cursor of her computer — where you want to be seated, as if the place was Dallas Cowboys Stadium with 80,000 seats. I mention this, because at the *Tartu Athena Keskus*, where we went for movies several times, had only about 150 seats. An usher with a flashlight — shades of the old Roxy — was in attendance. There were rich classical murals of Greece on all the walls. One saw red plush seats, soft carpets, and high chandeliers. This was 1940s Hollywood, shades of the Trocadero, Carole Landis, red-carpet premieres, klieg-lights scanning the sky. A seat cost 50 kroon — about $5.00. Quaintness is so Estonian. At Christmas time, parents put a toy dwarf into their children's slipper, as a friend. The owner of the slipper is then in a position to negotiate directly with this dwarf to order whatever surprise he or she wants. An out-of-date aura maintains. Weddings there seem to be, at least in part, a public event. I once saw out in the countryside on a bus ride from Tartu to Tallinn a bride and groom, with a handful of guests, right out in the middle of nowhere waving to every passing automobile. Sarah saw pretty much the same thing in Kadrioru Park when a wedding party drove up in a Mercedes and the couple got out, waving and jumping about with antic gestures. I recall once taking a walk in Tartu and seeing in the window of a pizza parlor a poster of the once-celebrated, now forgotten McGuire Sisters, with Phyllis in the center, all holding up bottles of Coca-Cola and toasting any fans of theirs who are still alive. I saw decades-out-of-date ads for Snow Crop orange juice, Squirt soft drinks, and Lustre-Crème Shampoo. A large sign for Van Houten's Cocoa recalled for me the lines in Vladimir Mayakovsky's madly brilliant rant, "A Cloud in Trousers: A Tetraptych"

> Very good,
> When the cry
> 'Drink Van Houten's Cocoa'
> hurled in the very teeth of the scaffold

which is in reference to a condemned Russian prisoner who just before his execution — in exchange for a lump sum of money to be paid to his widow — grotesquely agreed to shout, "Drink Van Houten's Cocoa!"[30] A lot of the toilets and bathrooms in houses, flats, and hotels in Estonia are antiquated, many just about functioning. Gym showers are like water fountains in the United States. In order to keep the flow of water going, one has to keep fretfully jabbing an "on" knob every ten seconds. As Chinua Achebe once perceptively wrote, "Show me a people's plumbing, and I can control their art."

There are no flea markets in Estonia, at least in winter, none that I saw. I found only one flea market in Tartu, a feeble one, with stalls that sell mainly cabbages, potatoes, bags of garlic — Khabar, Yugoslavian porcelain, Ferganskij (turbaned), Siberian, Carpathian purple, and mainly Estonian red, a hard-neck variety — polyester pants and faux-leather gloves, ugly coats and grotesque black market shoes. ("Kood cloath-est," cheeped a Russian oldster, rubbing the nap of a used overcoat, but then why mock the poor dear, since "clothes" is a word that no one — English-speakers included — pronounces correctly.) They are not popular, not like, say, the *Gariunai* on the western fringe of Vilnius where one can buy things shops don't sell. Estonians don't have a lot to sell. I saw no garage sales. (Tag sales or yard sales are an American thing.) I did notice a few shops where they sell postcards and faux-Nazi memorabilia mostly, some Czarist money, a few paintings. The Nazis marketed — and indeed hid — many looted Russian antiques in Estonia. Boxcarloads of paintings. Vases and rugs. Wooden crates of leather-bound books and manuscripts. Cameos. Sculpture. Almost all with museum inventory numbers and tags. In the city of Võru, a repository was found filled with furniture stolen from the Catherine Palace in Russia. Who can say, perhaps the fabled Amber Room, that rare chamber that was actually stolen, pirated away, from that very same palace by the exploiting Nazis during World War II, a complete box-set of priceless amber panels backed with gold leaf and mirrors, is lying in Estonia somewhere. After all, it had been brought as far as Königsberg which is not much more than a rock-throw from Estonia. Six tons of amber, the complete, elegant 18th-century chamber decoration of amber panels — still missing — often called the "Eighth Wonder of the World!"

Antiques

You see a lot of amber sold in Estonia. Amber comes in 250 colors — green, pale, yellow, even black to brown to golden. A "white" amber actually exists. It contains one-million gas bubbles per cubic millimeter. (A genuine test of amber is if it sinks in salt water, polished amber is a dud.) I found a beautiful amber pendant in a small shop in Tartu for Sarah for her birthday, on March 26. There was not a large selection of jewelry. I had looked at various stones, never diamonds though. I once read a remark by the DeBeers chairman, Nicky Oppenheimer, which I never forgot and even wrote down: "Diamonds are worthless, except for the deep psychological need they fill." What a scam! (The word "jewel," revealingly, goes back to the Latin word *jocus* which meant a plaything, a trinket, which then became a joke!) As to greed in the diamond industry, in addition to diamond engagement rings, it was the guileful DeBeers Co. who also came up with the ratty idea of "surprise proposals." It turns out that the company learned that when women got involved in the selection process, they actually chose rings that were cheaper! By encouraging surprise proposals, DeBeers shifted the purchasing power to men, the less cautious and more obliged spenders. What kind of diabolical churls run the international diamond industry with all these subfusc maneuvers and pea-and-thimble tricks? Such underhanded schemes remain several of the prevailing reasons I have never been taken in by any of the tendentious and self-serving political statements of Israel — the country, with its web of worldwide connections, that has monopolized the diamond business — or the brutalizing, unfairly stacked Jewish Agenda in the Middle East against the beleaguered Palestinians, whose lands have receded, inch by inch, ever since the Partition in 1948. (Israel typically put the clamp on foreign journalists hoping to record any of their movements when they brutally invaded Gaza in January 2009 but then of course permitted all of them to cover first-hand and in-depth Hamas' rocket response in Israel.) Israel's ban on foreign journalists, only a handful of countries that do this, has been levied repeatedly, skewing all reports. Make this charge, level any such criticism, and what is the result? An uproar of objurgation that one is a flaming anti-Semite, no small joke since the Palestinians, like all Arabic people, Biblically considered to be the descendants of Shem, son of Noah, are — ancient and modern — true Semites.

We bewail the Soviet Union occupying Estonia. But today China occupies Tibet. Russia occupies Chechnya. North Cyprus is occupied by Turkey. There are various parts of Azerbaijan occupied by Armenia. Western Sahara is occupied by the unrecognized sovereignty of Morocco. Spain and Argentina even claim that Britain occupies, respectively, Gibraltar and the Falklands. What about Ethiopia in Eritrea, the USA in Iraq — who is leaving and when? Israel to this very day with impunity — and indeed with America's *nihil obstat* — occupies the West Bank, the Gaza Strip, much of the Golan Heights and, until 1982, the Sinai Peninsula. Israel has also annexed East Jerusalem by some ginned-up bullshit called the "Jerusalem Law," a wily and unscrupulous contrivance of the present-day fascist Knesset where at least one-third of the members are identifiably anti-democratic. When President Obama in May 2011 insisted they go back to the 1967 boundaries, Israeli yowled, "Unfair to us!" It is always one-sided. They give nothing away. Take as look at the original 1948 boundaries between Israel and Palestine and compare them today.

The wall that Israel nefariously began constructing on June 16, 2002 against the Palestinians — a blatantly illegal act — consists of a series of 25-foot high concrete barriers, trenches, barbed wire and electrified fencing with numerous watch towers, electronic sensors, thermal imaging and video cameras, unmanned aerial vehicles, sniper towers, and roads for patrol vehicles. The Berlin wall was 96 miles long with an average height of 12 feet. The Israeli wall, still under construction, is expected to reach at least 403 miles in length with heights of 25 feet. It has been roundly condemned by both the World Court which calls it "a gross violation of international law and basic human rights," as well as by the UN General Assembly which has demanded "that Israel stop and reverse the construction of the wall in the Occupied Palestinian Territory, including in and around East Jerusalem, which is in departure of the Armistice Line of 1949 and is in contradiction to relevant provisions of international law. (A/ES-10/L.15; A/RES/ES-10/13 of 21 October 2003.) Nevertheless, Israel continues to build it, maintaining that this racist eyesore, a monstrosity, is a temporary structure physically used to separate the West Bank from Israel and thus to prevent suicide attacks on Israeli citizens. The wall's location, however — in some places reaching up to as much as 8 miles inside Palestinian territory — and projected length, currently almost 500 miles despite a border with Israel of less than 125 miles, suggests it is quite emphatically an additional effort to confiscate Palestinian land, facilitate further colony expansion, and unilaterally redraw geopolitical borders, all the while encouraging an exodus of Palestinians by denying them the ability to earn a living from their very own land, have access to their schools and work places, be able to reach essential health care, or come into any contact with water resources.

So the Israelis continue freelancing lies and with their hair on fire for more and more land ratlining the wall further and further into the rocky farms and stunted olive groves of poor Palestinian farmers, daring them with their American-paid-for Merkava Mark IV tanks with 120mm main guns to make a single squawk.

There is indeed documentable evidence that Israel seeks to deprive the Palestinians of water. Mekorot, Israel's national water authority, has drilled 42 deep wells in the West Bank mainly to supply Israeli cities, according to a 2009 World Bank report, by indifferently exploiting any and all Palestinian needs for water. Israel uses four times as much water per capita as Palestinians, much of it for agriculture…enough water to fill their swimming pools, water their lawns, and irrigate miles of fields and greenhouses," writes *National Geographic* reporter Don Belt[31] "In contrast, West Bank Palestinians, under Israeli military rule, have been largely prevented from digging deep wells of their own, limiting their water access to shallow wells, natural springs, and rainfall that evaporates quickly in dry desert air. When these sources run dry…[they] have no choice but to purchase water from Israel for about a dollar a cubic yard — in effect buying back the water that's been taken out from under them by Mekorot's pumps, which also lower the water table and affect Palestinian springs and wells." One need not revert to old bullying Soviet aggression to see what subjugation and oppression looks like today. This is the face of Occupation with its ugly lineaments in evidence and its profile undisguised. Israeli wells go 2000 feet deep. Palestinians have to buy their own rainwater.

In the meantime, while as many as 400 Palestinian villages and 25,000 Palestinian houses and buildings have been bulldozed and utterly demolished from 1967 to the present day! Jewish-only settlements and "outposts" are daily, hourly, being swiftly built on confiscated Palestinian land by grabby, conniving, and dishonest hustlers, opportunists, and rat-thieves. Talk about a brutal occupation! It is nothing less than a policy of force, a semi-fascist ideology — ironically, a demand for expansionist *Lebensraum* — a regime of blatant and shameless apartheid. The Palestinians are "unpeople," as Noam Chomsky points out in *Failed States*, the owners of their land originally but nothing now but a million disenfranchised souls largely cut off from contact with the outside world by land or sea, policed like concentration camp inmates, which they are, with few means of sustenance, lacking even water to drink, victims — in the uncompromising words of Maskit Bendel, the intrepid director of projects in the Occupied Territories for Physicians for Human Rights-Israel and a woman who was not only born and raised in Jerusalem but currently lives in Tel Aviv — "living in the largest and most overcrowded prison in the world."[32] Let the Israeli historian Benny Morris tell it, who in his searing book, *Righteous Victims*, writes,

> Israelis like to believe, and tell the world, that they were running an "enlightened" or "benign" occupation, qualitatively different from other military occupations the world had seen. The truth was radically different. Like all occupations, Israel's was and is founded on brute force, repression and fear, collaboration and treachery, beatings and torture chambers, along with daily intimidation, humiliation and manipulation. True, the relative lack of resistance and civil disobedience over the years has enabled the Israelis to maintain a façade of normalcy and implement their rule with a relatively small force, consisting of a handful of IDF battalions, a few dozen police officers (rank-and-file policemen were recruited from among the Palestinians), and a hundred or so General Security Service (GSS) case officers and investigators.[33]

The expansionist plans of the Israeli government with its unapologetic greed for territory and hypersucrotic thanks to the United States for turning a blind eye to these crimes while the so-called "settlers" — shtarkers, land-grabbers, and thugs — are annexing land by the minute and building houses on every available space as fast as they can. ("There is a settler in every Israeli," charges the brave Israeli journalist Amira Hass, daughter of two Holocaust survivors, who was born in Jerusalem.) Having that negative trait of what historian Thomas Carlyle in his *History of Friedrich of Prussia* called "an abundance of vulpine,"[34] they heed nothing and are vengefully immune to pleas or fair play. They boast that God gave this land to them. As any good Talmudist can tell you, however, the word *Hebrew* means, "One Who Crossed From Beyond One Region to Another," for it is well-known that these tribes were aliens themselves and originally haled from the faraway Chaldees. Abraham, born in Ur and patriarch of three religions, was not a Jew. A case can even be made that the worship of Yahweh originated with an ancient pre-Israelite people from the Levant, specifically in Midian. An Egyptian inscription connects the wandering *Shasu* (Egyptian: "those who move on foot") — a nomadic group who lived south of Palestine during the Egyptian Empire on the eve of the Bronze Age collapse[35] — with the non-Israeli name *yhw*, antedating the oldest occurrence of the name of the Hebrew tetragrammaton, YHWH, found on the Mesha Stele (or Moabite Stone) of 840 B.C. by over five hundred years.

Fair play, however, is not an Israeli trait. I am reminded of what activist Israel Singer once said of the late egotistical Nazi-hunter, Simon Wiesenthal: "He only listens when he's talking." Amos Schocken, the brave publisher of *Haaretz*, the liberal Israeli newspaper, who has repeatedly gone to the wall for justice in the matter of his country's unconscionable land-grabbing savagery has compared the Arabs living in these occupied places, once their very own, to "a helpless imprisoned population," intrepid reporter Dov Alfon to "inmates living a life sentence."[36] I once yearned to believe that the Israeli "left" was fiercely open, undogmatic, heroic, and ethical, "*les justes,*" in Camus terms, but even that is a nest of rats. So deep is Zionist hypocrisy, that the activist Tikva Honig-Parnass, who both fought in the Israeli Army at the beginning of what the Palestinians called the *Nakba*, or catastrophe, and as a soldier even participated in military operations that expelled 750,000 Palestinians, points out in her shocking book, *False Prophets for Peace* — scandalously *uncovers* — the indefensible fact that many activists and intellectuals of the Zionist Left are not only not helping the Palestinians but are actually complicit in actually *fostering* the criminal treatment of the Palestinians while secretly spoiling for a Jewish-only state. The devilish act of repeatedly echoing the words of the old Zionist narrative that they desire a state for their victims in the occupied territories is the very definition of moral paralysis. The bitter irony is that the persecution of and racist scorn for the Palestinians today by Israel recapitulates what the Germans did to the Jews during World War II, the exact opposite of the principle for which the saintly pastor Dietrich Bonhoeffer was martyred. Where exactly is the level of outrage by the American people while all of this is going on? It is virtually non-existent. Another, stronger pen than mine would be required to do justice to the full story here, but I can state that since the October War in 1973, Washington, not merely shielding and coddling Israel while merely pretending the Palestinians are an equal party — Jewish pressure on Congress is incessant, its power in the media truly bottomless — has provided Israel with a level of support dwarfing anything like any amounts provided to any other state. In fact, Israel has been the largest annual recipient of direct U.S. economic and military assistance since 1976 and the largest total recipient since World War II. The U.S. which yearly provides Israel with *$8.2 million per day* in military aid in turn gives the Palestinians exactly nothing. Total direct U.S. aid to Israel amounts to well over $140 billion in 2003 dollars. *Israel receives about $3 billion in direct foreign assistance each year, which is roughly one-fifth of America's entire foreign aid budget.* In per capita terms, the United States gives each Israeli a direct subsidy worth about $500 per year. This largesse is especially striking, and indeed grotesque, when one realizes that Israel is now a wealthy industrial state with a per-capita income roughly equal to that of South Korea or Spain.[37]

As to wealth and/or per capita income, I was among the low rollers in Estonia, and content to be, but more than content or satisfied. I enjoyed poking in old shops and did find a small wooden nesting-doll to buy of Marilyn Monroe (one inside another inside another) with her name predictably misspelled "*Merilyn*" and the painted portrait of her in a Hollywood white fur looking more like a chubby, slightly older Simone Signoret. Actor David Niven once observed that Marilyn Monroe was "not beautiful unless her mouth was slightly open." My little matryosha-doll of her met that requirement, closed, I mean, not open. Pianos of the Estonia Klaverivabrik Tallinn are, reputedly, among the most valued ones in the world known for their pure sound. I wanted to find one, especially to hear one played, but I never managed to do so.

One antique that I saw and loved was a kind of round-topped hooded all-purpose chest that one sees all through Estonia and even in many country houses. It is the national antique and is traditionally called a *kirst*. That word came to be used for "coffin" or "casket," although for a time there was a more polite or elegant word for coffin — *puusärk*, literally "wooden shirt." I am told that the word *puusärk* never really caught on in Estonian popular usage, and *kirst* began to be used more and more for "coffin," and so it is almost never used any more for "chest." A *kirst* is sturdy, capacious, and medieval-looking. I looked everywhere to buy one but, alas, in vain. No one in Estonia of the many who have them apparently wants to part with one. These chests are national treasures and are usually passed down in families. They are not owned by wealthy people in particular, I've seen them everywhere, in bookstores, in old shops, even in bars. (There is no noble class in Estonia, as such. No aristocrats that I could make out.)

But was the country itself an antique?

Erick Erickson once offered the idea that "a nation's identity is derived from the ways in which history has, as it were, counterpointed certain opposite potentialities; the ways in which it lifts this counterpoint to a unique style of civilization, or lets it disintegrate into mere contradiction." Was the point-counterpoint of the Estonian character the German/Russian polarities, although similar in totalitarian horror, that it had to face and, facing, had to resolve — and if so what did all the contradictions, never mind the pain, lead to? Are they the weaker for it or stronger? Were they stimulated by it all or simply subdued? More importantly, is the nation now a vital and progressive body, growing by the day, or a white elephant?

What About Negroes in Estonia?

There are none.

Xenophobia

There are no Asians I saw, either. What, maybe two or three — tourists. My wife who is half-Korean and beautiful found this as passingly strange as I did. "*Jaapan!*" muttered a group of rowdy boys, bigots obviously in need of "cultural diversity training," as they muscled past us in the street, rough-housers who, I swear, if Mrs. Montessori herself spent a day with them arranging their building blocks, could not have *spelled* the words China, Japan, or Korea. I saw no *hiinlane* (Chinese) or *korealane* or any *muhameedlane* in kerchiefs, for that matter. Xenophobia is rife. I have heard the same about Latvia. (White guys with Asian tattoos on their biceps or running up their arms — an oddity that has by now become fairly universal — may be the one exception.) A provincial churl or *juntti* in Finland will spit out the pejorative word "*neekeri*" for any type he dislikes, Jews, blacks, strangers, you name it. Many natives in Estonia seem to consider anything different as odd, by simple definition. It reminded me of the quaint if peculiarly conceptual phrase some people from Maine have for strangers. "They're 'from away,'" you will hear them say. People who seemingly have no *from* greatly intrigue an Estonian — and no doubt a native of Belfast, Maine — and can become the occasion of an extended sour glance. Surely St. John's invective-fueled declaration at the end of Revelations 22:15, "*Outside* are the dogs and sorcerers and the sexually immoral and murderers and idolaters, and everyone who loves and practices falsehood" [my italics], became the template for millennia on the policy of suspicious non-inclusivity and the worthlessness of strangers. An entire Samaritan *village* rejects Jesus in Luke 9:51 Still, a hermeneutical point not to be ignored is the fact that it is neither a priest nor a Levite who takes the time to stop and help the poor hapless Jew who, going down from Jerusalem to Jericho, was beaten by robbers and left naked, but specifically an "outsider," indeed a Samaritan — a supposed "enemy" of those people. When I say there are no black people there, I mean it. There are no black people in Estonia: *none*. I mean, not a single Negro face. Anywhere. Was I looking for one? Not particularly. What slowly dawns on one after awhile, however, is that something is distinctly missing. It was only upon that realization that I began to look for one. In the popular nationalistic film, *The Singing Revolution*, a two-and-a-half hour documentary of the country, focusing especially on its battles with and interminable domestic misery from Germany and the Soviet Union, not a single black human being appears in mobs of tens of thousands. I looked. In wide-screen mob scenes, not a black face. No Negroes. Not one hiding in the back. I wrote a poem about it:

A Tanzanian in Tartu

Jews from Pskov were welcome

even in the Tsarist days, but a cold frost

greeted Wilfred Bgoya from Dodoma
when in Tartu he muttered "Jambo"

to a man in a reindeer-hat
who did not so much scowl as drop his jaw

when again he blinked to see
a smiling black head as perfectly odd

in that snowy Estonian city as seeing
the devil! Mr. Kauplema almost shit!

"*Tumm! Trumm! Trummeldama!*" he boomed
and made a quick applaud

to snatch the attention of three runty
passersby, one a truculent harridan

carrying a cane — people gathered —
and all now began regarding Mr. Sambo.

"*Praak!* said Mrs. Uha, cane high.
"Scrap!" "*Lõõtspill,*" screeched another,

miming an accordion. Wilfred, bug-eyed,
in the meantime with true delight

in the icy darkness of the Old Town Square
at noon, grinning at Mrs. Bgoya,

reached down to present two pigtailed
Bgoya girls twining through his legs

to show them they liked music, *too,*

drums and horns and big accordions,

but not before two dwarf men cachinnating
awfulness the way a beggar begs

began bouncing up and down,
one making extra lips while the other gave

as if to brush his face. Horn-hat hissed.
"*Valgeks värvima!*" "Paint it white!"

The society of Estonia could have been a country club in Durban in 1950, except that there one had colored waiters. It is not that you cannot find *rassism* or *rassists* in the country, for, as I say, you can. There is simply small occasion for exercising such a thing. They have the names for it. A name alone looms large as an indication.

My Name is Rumplestiltskin

I love Estonian names. To my mind, many of them seem to be the names of elves, dwarves, trolls, country bumpkins, giants of fable, big dumb drum-bellied glad medieval foresters, Wagnerian mountain people, oafs in big hats, funny pie-men out of storybook lore going to the fair. They also all have a slightly futuroidal sound. Start off with men's first names — Anti, Eero, Leek, Elmo, Livo, Ain, Hardo, Ott, Väino, Ivi, Mall, Yuso, Argo, Tarmo, Gerli, Anders, Veikko, Henno, Pearu, Tõnis, August — it means "from a hole" — and Õnnelamb. Amazing! Women are given names like Olga, Lilly, Eva, Õilme, Marika, Indrek, Leen, Epp, Aap, Triin, Iris, and Elo. Saara is of course our Sarah. Laine, literally "wave, ripple" is a fairly popular pretty Estonian name that may have originally been suggested by English Elaine. I think maybe the funniest woman's name there is Lagle, the Estonian word for Canada goose! (In the first few years of Estonian independence, there was an Estonian woman politician named Lagle Parek.) How about full names like Peep Pukks, Tiit Priiks, Ants Oras, Otto Mutso, Karl Sööt? Charles Dickens would positively have loved to read any roaring roster of names in an Estonian telephone book! Nikolai Reek (1890-1942) was an Estonian general. Cyrillus Kreek (1889-1962) was a well-known composer. As was Eero Liives. The music of Rudolf Tobias (1873-1918), the first Estonian professional musician to write instrumental works is monumental, grandiose, and in a way massive, not qualities normally associated with Estonia, but I have been stunned by the majesty of his 1909 oratorio, *"Joonase lähetamine"* ("Jonah Sets Out on His Mission") and his 1900 *"Eks teie tea"* ("Know Ye Not"), a setting for 1 Corinthians 6, "Know you not that your body is the temple of the Holy Ghost." Anto Pathique (born in 1966) is a writer. Marie Under (1883-1980) is a poet. Say those names out loud. Eero Liives! Anto Pathique! Marie Under! They sound like revolutionary slogans! Heraldic mottos! The rebellious cries of embattled students! (It is my firm conviction that every Estonian name is an anagram.) Other memorable Estonian names I stumbled across were Rein Rannap, Tuuli Oidekivi, Tõnis Hurri, Tiit Tomika, Hani Honka — the printer Joannes Gutenberg's name was originally Gensfleisch, meaning gooseflesh, so he adopted his name from the quarter of Mainz where his family lived — Iris Lomp, and Karl Parts. I even came across, giving me something of a cheap thrill, one Alexander Taru, surely my Baltic doppelgänger. By the way, do you know how to say, "Barack: his own land" in Estonian? *Barack Omamaa!*

We Americans have our own nominal oddities, do we not? One can often identify a person's region in the United States by nothing more than his quirky name. Names are addresses, to a degree. I mean, only in the American South would you discover people with names like Horton Foote, Narvel Felts, Earlene Peawiggle, Jimmie Lee Thigpen, and Babytater. You would never hear names like that in New England. There people have names like H. S. Peabody, George Dodd Wythe, Flemister Drayton, Chauncy Ballwyn, Meldrum Wheelwright, and A. S. Mars. Black girls in the East, given monikers by their mamas to make them feel special and original, have names like Chevelle, Ureene, DeDonda, Twylite, Desharius, Aisha, Moonetta, and Shenacqua. Ours is always an ongoing ethnic potpourri, as well, in the way that old World War II movies showed unshaven grunts of all shapes and sizes with a spectrum of names like Dombrowski, Needleman, Kobold, Flaherty, and DeMasi. I wonder what an Estonian reader of P.G. Wodehouse's books would think when he came across such fascinating nicknames as Oofie, Catsmeat, Bingo, Stilton, Tuppy Glossop, Gussie Fink Nottle, Cyril "Barmy" Fotheringay-Phipps, and Major Plank?

A pedantic sod named Nosewheel, an objectionable Fulbright whom I will soon have the occasion to complain about more fully, argumentatively insisted that the names Jäppinen and Yannick were Estonian names. I explained that the former was distinctly Finnish and that the latter was in fact an Israeli name and that if it were a legitimate Estonian name it would be Jannik, which resembled Jaanike, "Dear Little Johnny," the endearing diminutive of Jaan, "John." Nosewheel, who loudly insisted that he knew everything about the cultural pulse of the country but whose arguments I could already determine even in the thankfully brief interval of meeting him were always crooked as a snath, smugly explained that he was "an historian." And so? I hung fire. Nosewheel abruptly turned on his heel and walked away. Oh dear, I thought. I saw this man can not afford to be wrong. The clown Lance in *The Two Gentlemen of Verona* declares, "I think Crab, my dog, be the sourest-natured dog that lives." I gotta say right off, Shakespeare's Lance never met Nosewheel.

Names are also stories, are they not? A name is a character that goes in a certain direction. I once told an acquaintance of mine with the surname Della Chiesa that his name indicated that an ancestor of his might very likely have been a foundling. He became unpredictably upset with the implications of bastardy, but I was right, of course. It is a well known fact that certain given church-related names like D'Angelo, Engel, Ange, Iglesias, DeBenedictus or Benedetto, Kyrka, Kirche, and De Donne suggest that unwanted babies given such names might have been found at a church door and been taken in by the church authorities. Even Vondeling (foundling), Verlaeten (abandoned), and Bijstand (welfare) "Children of misery" they were called. They were frequently named by the person who found them or by the hospital staff where they are taken.

Foundlings (also, paradoxically, lostlings!) had to be christened and given a surname by the church authorities or whoever adopted it. Some were named after the spot in which they were found (e.g., Church, Porch, Churchstile, Bridge, etc.) Some were named after a saint's day, the name of the church, or even the name of the street in which the baby was found. There is an apt passage in Gabriel Chevallier's *Clochemerle* (1936), a novel about the comical goings-on in a small provincial French town and one of my favorite books, in which the author points out in passing that many French names going back to the 11th century had their origins in some physical or moral peculiarity of the individual, very like among the Plains Indians in North America, and, more frequently still, were suggested by his trade. Chevallier mentions that:

> the baker's name was Farinard, the tailor's Futaine, the butcher's Frissure, the pork-butcher's Lardon, the wheelwright's Bafère, the Carpenter's Billebois, and the cooper's Boitavin. These names are evidence of the strength of tradition at Clochemerle, and show that the different trades have been handed down from father to son in the same families for several centuries.

One Italian surname commonly given to such a child was Esposito, literally meaning "exposed" (from the Latin *expositus*, past participle of *exponere*, "to place outside"). Among other connotative Italian names given to foundlings were Orfanelli ("little orphans"), Povarelli ("little poor people"), Trovato/Trovatelli ("found/little foundling"), Demandoti ("I ask you"), and Dittami ("dictate to me/speak to me"), the last being the given and perhaps spontaneously made-up surname of my maternal grandfather, the man for whom I was named, a luckless boy who was born on June 17, 1880 — the child of a notable senator[38] who rejected him — and raised in an orphanage in the town of Cento in the province of Ferrara, Italy. What was he doing in the town of Fiume (now Rijeka) in 1899? No one knows. How long had he been in the Italian Army? That is not recorded. His early life remains a complete mystery. At the age of 20, he sailed alone across the ocean to New York City where after many wayward days and as many unsheltered nights before he took up the trade of tailor, he often slept, as he told my mother, in the "Hotel Peppino," that is, outside on the grass in Washington Square Park under the statue, unveiled in 1888, of the Italian revolutionary Guiseppe Garibaldi, "Peppino" being that hero's nickname and indeed that of all boys named Guiseppe. Equivalents in Estonia would be something like *Preeili Mahajäetud* ("Miss Abandoned") or *Preili Inglikink* ("Miss Angel-Gift") or *Treppide Lapsuke* ("Little Child of the Stairs"). I allude to the phenomenon because traveling I came across — and made a point of collecting — Estonian surnames such as *Kirik* ("church") and *Õnnis* ("Blessed") and *Õndsus* ("blessed") and *Proua Vaenelaps* ("Mrs. Orphan"). I even encountered complementary bookends of a sort, a *Härra Sohipoeg* ("Mr. Bastard") and a *Härra Ingel* ("Mr. Angel")!

An Estonian name is always a mouthful. I remember the people of Qwghlm — also a language — who can be found not only in Neal Stephenson's galactically vast novel, *Cryptonomicon,* but also in other outsized slabs of postmodern fiction of his so-called Baroque Cycle, an invented word the author himself has gone on record as stating was actually unpronounceable. "I never say it out loud," he helpfully pointed out in an interview. "It's like one of those languages used in southern Africa that have sounds people can't make unless they've grown up in that culture." Coincidentally, the realm of Qwghlm is also a northern European country with people, as Stephenson once put it, "who suffer from a lot of frostbite." *Teretulemast Estisse!*

You Fish On Your Side, I'll Fish On Mine

A sign of the ultimate tribalism of Estonia — and the region in general — is that very few Estonians *know* the languages of Latvia or Lithuania, although the countries are all part of that stackbox world, nor do most Latvians or Lithuanians know each others' languages. Proximity, contiguity, means nothing. It reminds me very much of England and environs. Birmingham, for example, is near Wales geographically, but culturally it is light years away; they could be on different planets. Consider Cornwall, Scotland, and Wales — they might as well be separated by vast oceans. A mad disconnect prevails. I once had the occasion of speaking to an Estonian college student at a sports gym, a guy about 22, who confided to me that he had never been to Latvia — Riga, by the way, is a mere three hours away from Tartu — and that the only Latvian word he knew was the word for ice-cream, "*Rujiena*," which it turns out is not only a *brand name* but is a name taken from the Latvian town where it is produced and where it remains that town's largest industry. It turns out that most Estonians take Rujiena ice-cream home with them wrapped in newspapers! (A Finnish ice-cream whose name I positively love is *Pingviini!*) Curiously, in my stay there I also never once come across a single Estonian person who spoke either the Latvian or the Lithuanian languages. (Did you get that, dear reader? *Not a single Estonian person who spoke either the Latvian or the Lithuanian languages!* It is truly a mind-blowing fact.) I suppose that the simplest explanation is that all three of these difficult languages are completely — *stupendously* — dissimilar. It is different rain on a different umbrella! Added to that, speakers of "small" or "minor" languages, even immediately neighboring ones, rarely bother to learn other "small" or "minor" languages, which is to say they would not go out of their way to learn such languages, say, as Tsiili, Rootsi, Island, Hiina, Taani, or Madalmaad. (That would be to you, respectively, Chile, Sweden, Iceland, China, Denmark, or the Netherlands! That is just a mere glimpse of how difficult — how uniquely isolating — the language can be.) People understandably lean to learning with the locally dominant "major" cultures and nationalities. The normal urge is to try to join the local "majority" rather than another "minority", just as, presumably, any group of ambitious, upwardly-mobile Vietnamese shrimp fishermen in Louisiana, for example, would try to imitate — and become — WASPs rather than to follow blacks. Analogously, Estonians have clearly long felt it unnecessary to learn the Latvian language as long as they could get along perfectly fine with Latvians using Russian or German — and now, more increasingly, English. And as far as the future of languages go, especially regarding the relative obscurity and notable lack of success of such artificial "international languages" as Esperanto, Volapük, and Interlingua, learning English, French, or German is certainly more practical to an ambitious Basque or Wend than learning Estonian. Students in Estonia would choose to learn English, Russian, and German, not a language in some demanding and operose minor chord. (The comic, googly-eyed Latvian buffoon played by Martin Koslek in the Hitchcock movie, *Foreign Correspondent*, spouting what sounds like arrant nonsense, summarizes, I'm afraid, most people's view of the mystery of that country and the Baltic tongue in general.) Other than Hungarian and Finnish, the Estonian language has no widely spoken relatives. The U.S. State Department ranks it as one of the world's most difficult languages.[39] Many Russians refuse to learn the language, of course, but a good many who do, having gone that far, still have small empathy with Estonians or the country. "Russian children," an émigré Estonian businessman named Jüri Estam wrote in *City Paper*, "are being raised in Estonia in the spirit of denial." During my visit, I heard several lamenting people express the fear that the Estonian language will eventually disappear, not only because of its relative difficulty to learn and the sparsity of use throughout the globe — it has competition, for there are as many as 6,900 languages spoken in the world today! — but also due to the very low birth rate and dwindling native population. Gaelic is more or less a museum language. Welsh is spoken by comparatively few. But then Yiddish, frankly, is no longer a living language either.

Through 2010 but continuing from time past, Estonia has long been mounting a determined campaign to elevate the status of its native language and to try to marginalize Russian, the tongue of its former colonizer, and this seems to be the reason — according to Merlyn Mannov in the *New York Times* (June 8, 2010) — why public schools like Pae Gymnasium, one of the best schools in Tallinn, where children have been taught in the Russian language for many, many years, "have turned into linguistic battlegrounds." Mannov notes,

> The National Language Inspectorate is in charge of ensuring the Russian schools teachers' knowledge of Estonian language, but according to the *N.Y. Times* the local Russians are not pleased with inspectors' work: 'The agency has only 18 inspectors, it is such a provocative symbol of the country's language regulations that even Amnesty International has criticized its tactics as heavy-handed.' In December 2008 every third teacher of Pae Gymnasium failed the language exam. One of them was 57-year-old biology and geography teacher Olga Muravjova who has to learn a devilishly difficult language at her age. Even the teachers who passed the exam said that it was difficult. English teacher Natalja Širokova said that it was very stressful because of the fear of making a mistake. Ilmar Tomusk, director general of the National Language Inspectorate, told to the *N.Y. Times* that the greatest challenge in Estonia's language policy is the Russian schools

teachers' level of Estonian language, because it is lower than what is demanded from students.

There is a primitive cast to Estonian speech, an aural jabberwocky (if only to foreigners) that suggests a primitive tongue. One must not forget that Lord Monboddo (1714-1799) who eccentrically believed that "orang-utans" (as all anthropoid apes were called in his day) were primitive men, essentially human except for lacking language — a view satirized by the novelist Thomas Love Peacock in *Melincourt* (1817) with the speechless but otherwise civilized and well-bred African ape Sir Oran Haut-ton *who even gets elected to parliament* for the rotten borough of Onevote — was one of the very first linguists to observe that so-called "primitive" languages were paradoxically often long-winded and polysyllabic, the direct opposite of the traditional reductive and comic stereotype of them speaking in a language consisting of short monosyllabic grunts loosely strung together in the cinemagraphic "Me Tarzan, you Jane" fashion: "You ugh big hunter, me hit you head, you die!" (Of course, young Monboddo — his Christian name was James Burnett — also believed that all human beings were born with tails which dutiful midwives universally cut off!) Early men, in Monboddo's sober view, developed language as a survival tool, and I often thought of that whenever I found myself, United Nations-wise, in the midst of a hectic tornado of explosive Estonian conversation.

I am very much interested in speech patterns, a tremendous source in writing of comedy and characterization. No one has the same speech patterns, so if you can catch and then capture the speech patterns of a person — his or her lilt, sounds, dialect, quirks of delivery even speech defects, repeated words and phrases, tone included, etc. — you have gone a long way in describing that person. Charles Dickens pulled many such rabbits out of his commodious fictional hat.

Although one notes a degree of extreme grammatical and syntactic simplicity in East or Southeast Asian languages like Chinese, Thai, and Vietnamese, no one would equate their language with caveman grunts. Surprisingly, there is a rich polysynthetic complexity in such languages as modern Eskimo, Nootka, Kwakiutl, Shawnee, or, say, Lakota, Yana, or Mohawk. Linguists emphasize that so-called "primitive" or "tribal languages" like those of Native Americans, sub-Saharan Africans, Melanesians, and Australian Aborigines are structurally complex enough to discuss quite adequately all of the complexities and subtleties of contemporary physics, mathematics, and philosophy if need be; they are merely in need of developing or borrowing the necessary terminology from English, German, Chinese, or Japanese. Estonian translates "computer" by *arvuti*, literally "figuring-thing" or "counting-thing," from a root *arv-* ("count, figure, think,") also found in *arv* ("number,") *arvama* ("to think, to guess, to suppose, etc.") plus an ending *–ti* meaning "tool, instrument." Actually, regarding polysyllabic long-windedness, Estonian, which in terms of circumlocution I am told is surpassed by its Finno-Ugric cousins, Finnish and Hungarian, can also show, paradoxically, a certain brevity where in certain observable cases the phrase in English can get comparatively complicated. One can say, for example, "*Minna-kse sööma*," ("They're going to eat" or "People are going to dinner") or "*Ollakse rôômsad*" for "They are happy" or "Everyone is happy." It is the same with Finnish. The wordy English sentence "You will be able to have some of my apples" in Finnish goes simply, "*Saat emenoitani*." That same phrase in Estonian is the also brief, "*Saad môned minu ôuntest*." "Please undress" is the tidy "*riisuuntukaa.*" ("*Vôta riided ära!*" or "*Riietu lahti!*" ["Dress (yourself) free!"] in Estonian.) On the other hand, "I love you" in Finnish is the somewhat cheek-filling "*Söisin mieluummin salmiakkia*." (In Estonian, the phrase is, "*Ma armastan sind*" or "*Sind armastan!*" with *ma* or *mina* ["I"] being understood.)

I would not hope to deny that we in the United States have our own periphrasts and endlessly gum-beating tub-thumpers who somehow never seemed to shut up: W.C. Fields, Huey Long, Hubert Humphrey, Alexander Haig, Joe Biden, the late William F. Buckley — the wordy conservative host of TV's Firing Line and editor of the *National Review* who, to signal his own objections to a chiliastic or utopian confusion of religious and political hopes, while happily using several words and phrases he loved, coined and popularized the slogan "Do not immanentize the eschaton!" which even became a political bumper-sticker.

For its oddities, uniqueness, and rarity in the world Estonian would make for excellent codes. Just as WBVKXJQZ are, in order, the relatively least used letters in the English language, Estonian lends to the same outré quirkiness. As a pre-teen, having a nerd-like fetish for good-natured secrecy, I loved the cryptic and used to study codes — transposition codes, substitution codes, rail-fence codes, position codes, you name it. Invisible inks thrilled me, as well. I caught the bug from early radio detective/mystery programs. Decoding was a big subject circa World War II. Lemon juice was a standard for invisible writing, but I tried onion juice, vinegar, even a teaspoon with *honey* in a glass of water worked, and, yes, Coca-Cola which contains sugar and works very much like sugar solutions. (If color shows up in writing, always dilute it with water.) Writing with *milk* I also successfully employed — milk is not a chemical compound but a mixture of many organic chemicals — and when the paper with the message was heated the writing appeared as a warm brown color. The process is so simple that is almost amazing to see a message written in milk gradually appear as the paper is warmed! ("One way to communicate [in Robben Island Prison in South Africa] was to write messages with milk," writes Nelson Mandela in *Long Walk to Freedom* (as prisoner #466/64) explaining how he and his fellow prisoners devised ways in their communication for writing without being seen or deciphered. "The milk would dry almost immediately, and the paper would look blank." Whiteness reverting to the whiteness of a transparency, *not* to be seen! Unfortunately, Mandela adds, their success was, alas, short lived. "For the disinfectant we were given to clean our cells when sprayed on the dried milk, made the writing reappear.") At 10 years old, I can boast, I knew the Masonic cipher, had fabricated old hand-made rods for the amazing Spartan scytale, and was an amateur expert in bigrams, digrams, and piegrams. It led to a later interest in dead languages, *Carian*, for example, a language of a people who seem to have moved from Crete to Asia Minor long ago. Then there is *Oscian*, a bit like Latin and a tad like Greek. Very few people could decipher a document in these languages, or, say, even in *Geez, Vedic*, or *Coptic*. Anyway, there were many times during my stay over there that I would ponder the delights of writing a short whimsical novel using the Estonian language as code! The country is the perfect setting, especially in their dark winters, in the old cities, the grim back alleys, for grim stories of sedition, suspicion, sabotage, and spying.

At a critical linguistic impasse, I noticed, Estonians will often quickly try out German on you — or is it that I looked like I was from Munich? — but younger people will offer an English word or two to test the waters. Once alone in a hall at the university, I was buttonholed by a fat red-headed goop eating large gum-drops from a bag, potentially a wheelbarrow full of crazy, I thought. I had seen him looking at me suspiciously with his boss eye, sizing me up as a stranger. He profusely shook my hand — his hands were warm, like exuded liverwurst — but when he asked me to print out my name, he said in halting German, the mutual language we had inadvertently settled on, on, that he hated the French. What misstep had I made? Interrupted him? (Estonians are not fond of conversational overlap and think ill of someone who interrupts them while they are speaking.) I noticed that a lazy eyelid he had began to quiver. Garrulous, parasitical, weird, I thought. We were standing, I remember, in the midst of a beautiful because rare sky-light that morning coming from an overhead window which I hyperbolically commended to him as being an Estonian delight. He suddenly looked, rodentlike, like someone who stored praise within his cheeks. Was he a professor? "But what is wrong with the French?" I asked, somewhat nettled. "They invented the suit, the tie, and the handkerchief! And the sewing-machine! The coffee-pot! Forks and knives! How about aspirin?" I repeated in English, "They gave us aspirin! Teflon-utensils. Voltaire!" I paused. "Anyway, I am an American." Upon hearing that — and put into English — his face went tighter than the mouth of a drawstring bag. Immediately he fled. Older people there tend to be more self-conscious than younger people about speaking the few words of halting English they know, often shyly glancing away after temeritously trying out a phrase or two with a gulp that they well know means taking a risk, and one always heard something garbled like, "*Sthreet shnow! Mebbe you gets runned over by cabsitac!*" or "*Dat tog go to Vilnius not not!*" or "*Dis zoop is feet for kink!*" or "*Der pengvinne go 'prrrp, prrrp.' Unnerstand, meester man and dis vife of you?*" It always sounded to me like some sort of blundering variation — cack-handed and buffoonish — of the illiterate Lindbergh kidnapping note, quote: "Dear Sir! Have 50.000$ redy 25.000$ in 20$ bills 15.000 in 10$ bills and 10.000$ in 5$ bills. After 2-4 days we will inform you were to deliver the Mony. We warn you for making anyding public or for notify the Police the child is in gut care. Indication for all letters are singnature and 3 holes." As I say, for young people the act of learning

English in school buys you the USA, the British Isles, Canada, Australia, New Zealand, South Africa, and many other places, as well. Over 85% of the people in Jamaica, Malta, Guam, and the Bahamas speak English. *India* has the highest number of English speakers in the world! Cross the border merely one *mile* into Latvia with all of your hard-won Estonian and no one — *no one* — will understand you! There, or any other place on earth. *Across the entire earth! No one!* Same with a Latvian studying Estonian, or a Lithuanian studying Latvian!

The Law of Diminishing Returns

It is worthy to note that Russian is widely spoken as a secondary language by thirty-to-seventy-year-old ethnic Estonians, simply because that was the unofficial language of occupied Estonia from 1944 to 1991 — almost half a century of the Russian bear hibernating in your own dwelling! Russian was taught as a compulsory second language during the Soviet era. First and second generations of industrial immigrants from various parts of the former Soviet Union (mainly Russia) do not speak Estonian. You hear Finnish being spoken a good deal in Estonia and some Swedish. Historically, large parts of Estonia's north-western coast and islands have been populated by indigenous ethnically *Rannarootslased* (Coastal Swedes).

The majority of Estonia's Swedish population of 3,800 fled to Sweden or were deported in 1944, escaping the advancing Red Army. Many Russians stayed.

It is hard to believe that while 873 million people in the world speak Mandarin Chinese and 366 million speak Hindi, less than one-and-a-third million speak Estonian. But nothing fails to surprise me. I am surprised that France is the world's most popular tourist destination, that salt is the only stone we eat, that the town of Nazareth is never once mentioned in the Old Testament, that Red Sox slugger Ted Williams batted left and threw right, that ant colonies are always female, that the intrepid mariner Joshua Slocum who sailed around the world could not swim, that the overweight pussyfoot FBI director J. Edgar Hoover, who began his working life as an obsequious paper-pusher in the Justice Dept., was not a policeman, not a military man, and never carried a gun in his whole life.

I believe it is an ungainsayable truism that the majority of east Europeans hate to speak Russian. As I said earlier, when not finding the occasion to speak English, German was my language of choice, sometimes French. I hasten indeed sprint to add that although I tried as hard as possible to speak the language, my smattering of book Estonian conveyed too little meaning and was routinely treated as a foreign tongue. So resigned to the idea that mystery grows with knowledge, as Flannery O'Connor wisely points out, I coped as best I could to make myself understood in a land where much of a much was between-worlds and lost messages. As I said earlier, German was my language of choice there, sometimes French. Estonia, like Poland which is often called the "Christ of Nations," was, like its neighbor, also crucified between two thieves, Russia and Germany. Whithersoever they seemed to go — politically, geographically — the hand of fate was against them. Poland, however, which was hit even worse by World War II, lost 40% of its wealth, 60% of its schools, 50% of its public transport, 20% of its population. (Britain lost 2.5% of its population, Russia 11.2%). No, a true Estonian is a guaranteed Russophobe.

Vichyssoise! Rhubarb!

Estonia is one of the smallest countries in the world to have its very own language. (The smallest European country, population-wise, with its own language is Iceland, with a population of around 250,000 compared to Estonia's 1,300,000 or so. Andorra in the Pyrenees Mountains uses Catalan as its semi-official language.) No other country in the world so small has such a strange language, I am certain, a language that sounds like one spoken in the land of Blefuscu! *Esiteks* — first of all — the language is hard as hell to learn. I have tried it, I know, and I have studied

— and, like St. Augustine, wept over the irregular verbs of — classical Greek, which I happen to be able both to read and write only from doggéd application. Regarding complexity in Estonian, are you looking for cognates? Assimilative roots? Etymologies? Cognates? Greek does not help. Neither does Latin, the language of exorcism. Frankly, Estonian as a language is maddeningly inaccessible. I mean, in a country where a washing-machine is confoundingly called a *pesupesemismasin* and the simple word "proclamation" is *väljakuulutamine* and the uncomplicated sentence "I like chocolates" becomes the incredibly difficult, astonishingly periphrastic, jaw-breaking *mulle meeldivad šokolaadikompvekid*, what possible chance does a non-Estonian speaker have? I remembered learning for a junior-high school project on world-wide words the name of one tropical fish in Hawaii is *humuhumunukunukuāpua'a*. The longest word in the Icelandic language is *Haestarjettarmalaflutunesmanskifstofustulkonutidyralykill* which means "a latch-key belonging to a girl working in the office of a barrister." So I wondered what the longest Estonian word might be. My friend, T. Peter came up with the serpentine gem, *tuletõrjekompaniitervishoiukindlustuskassalaekur,* which means "Treasurer of the Firefighters' Company Health Insurance Fund." Scandinavian, German, the Baltic languages, and Inuit or Eskimo-Aleut: in these languages one can find some doozies! I have always loved the bold *saucissenkartoffelbiersauerkrautkranzwurst,* a Cologne sausage that Mark Twain always insisted was his favorite dish!

I wonder what that interminable, eight-page long single sentence in Donald Barthelme's story, "Sentence," in *City Life* would look like translated into Estonian! A plunge into a depthless Chuck E. Cheese ball pit to crawl through a thousand colorful plastic balls?

Pronunciation of Estonian words matters hugely. But is it different in any other country? I am reminded of the comic dilemma of an American in Denmark inquiring of a native where the home of H.C. Anderson is located. He will get nowhere unless he asks for the home of "*Ho Tsay* Anderson.*"* Some near-homonymous Estonian word pairs are almost identical in pronunciation except for a normal or "hard" (or, as I tend to think of it, dark, dull, dry) versus a "soft," palatal, or *y*-colored pronubiation of the final consonant. Compare, for example, several Estonian words pronounced with a hard final consonant, *kas* ("if, whether;") *tall* ("lamb, kid, baby sheep or goat;") *palk* ("wages, salary") with their homonymous counterparts pronounced with a "soft" (or, say, bright, shiny, wet) final consonant — an almost flirtatious softness that recalls for me that of the French *gn*, the Italian *gn, gli*, and the Spanish *ñ* — *kass* ("cat,") *tall* ("stall, stable, compartment,") *palk* ("log, beam.").

Another important Estonian phonetic difference between near-homonyms is between a weak or normal versus strong *stress*: e.g., the weakly stressed *kastis* ("in a box;") *linna* ("of the city or town;") and *saada* ("send!") as opposed to, say, the strongly stressed *kastis* ("he dipped or sprinkled;") *linna* ("into the city or town;") and *saada* ("to get or receive"). T. Peter Park, agrees with me that there is a tonal difference involved compared to that of many Oriental languages. Take the word *dong* in Vietnamese, for example. Pronounced alto it means "thunderstorm." Soprano it means "to close, shut." Bass — "winter." Mezzo-soprano indicates "East or orient." Several other tonal variations of this same word can mean "freeze," "numerous," or "to measure." A weak stress on a word has a level tone, whereas a strong stress has a falling or falling-then-rising tone. In this respect, Estonian echoes not only Chinese, Japanese, Thai, Burmese and Vietnamese, but also Swedish, Norwegian, Lithuanian, Serbo-Croatian, Classical Greek, and Proto-Indo-European! Could Plato and Kreutzwald, Homer and Tammsaare, Confucius and Lydia Koidula have easily picked up the proper intonations of each other's respective native languages?! It is the English and Americans with a language highly inflected who have to make do with a crude blunderbuss stress-only accent! Estonians for some reason do not like to stress the point, but Estonian is a tonal language.

It is tone — the pitch in language — that makes Chinese, the most widely spoken tonal language, so difficult to learn for English speakers — and, remember, it has 56,000 characters. Dong, a Tai-Kadai language spoken by about 1.5 million people, has as many as nine contour tones. There are six tones in Cantonese — high and level, high and rising, middle and level, low and rising, low and falling, low and level. Maddeningly, linguistic tones, unlike musical tones, are not set at specific, absolute pitches like *do* or *re* or C flat but instead are completely relative. Take the word *ma*. Depending on tone it can mean "mother," "hemp," "horse," "to curse," and even many more meanings when it is combined with other words.

For example, *ma* in the first tone can mean "to wipe" but when combined with the word *lang* means the word "dragonfly." In a Chinese dictionary there are 24 different characters alone with the pronunciation "ma."

Any amble through an Estonian city reveals no end of signs that are fully impenetrable. I often thought of that one brief crazy chapter in Blaise Cendrars' profane novel, *Moravagine* (1926): "The Only Word in the Martian Language" in which he claims that word is "written phonetically: *Kay-ray-kuh-kuh-ko-kex*," adding "It means whatever you want it to mean."[40] I have tried to learn the language several times, times without number, merely sitting down or just walking along, but as soon as I began conjugating the simplest verbs and trying to memorize them I found they fell out of my head as dead as smelts. Do you happen to recall what high-school drama teachers, when directing a play that called for a crowd — Shakespeare's *Julius Caesar* comes to mind — commonly told their actors to repeat on stage in order to mimic a mumbling crowd? First, divide the gathered group on the stage and then have one side keep repeating the word "vichyssoise" while the other side in turn simultaneously begins repeating the word "rhubarb." The combined sound makes for a most memorable mutterance. Estonian, alas, sounded like that to me. I felt like poor Agassiz striving to decipher the impressions of dead fossil-fish on the ancient stone slabs of the Jardin des Plantes. What, for example, would you make of:

> *Kokkusaamiseks On Põhjust!*
> *10-15 märts Tartus TTU 90, juubel*

or, in the post office: "*Käsud Sees*" or "*Meil Pakutavaid Teenuseid*" or "*Müüa Krunt*" or "*Ratta viskamine*"[41]?

Five Sides To a Square

Walking along I used to ask myself, pondering the roots of words as I have in many a country during many such a walk, and wonder, *why* would a carrot be called a *porgand*? A pineapple an *ananaas*? A book a *raamat*? A cross a *rist*? A priest a *papp*? Wait, a priest being called a *papp*, I quickly saw, must have been born of *papp* as in papist and papistical and popery. (There are only 3,500 Catholics in the whole of Estonia, by the way.) In typically confusing Estonian fashion, *papp* is also the word for cardboard! Wolf is logically *hunt*, but greyhound is weirdly *hurt*. Necktie is *lips,* musical instrument is *pill*, gentle is *hell*, and bench is *pink*. Words that were not risible were intriguing but in fact they were both. *Joon* means both "line" and "I drink." There is a popular slightly ribald Estonian pun, "*Mis Sa sealt pudeliga tood? Kust?*," which can mean both "What are you bringing in a bottle? From where?" and "piss," as *kust* is both the locative demonstrative "whence? from where?" and the accusative case of *kusi* "piss." *Too* means both "that, that one" and "bring!" In the sense of "bring," I suspect it may well be a very distant Nostratic etymological cousin, with a reversal in meaning, of the Indo-European root for "give" found in Latin — *do, dare* — and French — *donner*. Estonian *toon* can mean both "tone" and "I bring." While *munn* is the most common Estonian word for "penis, prick," it has close rivals in the Estonian street slangwords *tūra* — and in *titt!* (Inconveniently for travelers, in Swedish the word *munn* means mouth.) But the rest? It became a source of middling depression to me, the legacy of Babel and all that. But I mean, are not words, spoken sounds, written representation, the only means that we have to sort things out? "All that has been said and known in the world is in language, in words," reflects the overly-cognitive if brilliant Miriam Henderson, the eccentric protagonist of Dorothy Richardson's epic *Pilgrimage*, "all the dogmas of religion are words," when she then adds, "the meaning of words change with people's thoughts," whereupon she desolately (and erroneously?) concludes,

> Then no one knows anything for certain. Everything depends on the way a thing is put, and that is a question of some particular civilization…language is the only way of expressing anything, and it dims everything. So the Bible is not true it is a culture.

If her conclusion was not mine, the lament was.

Speaking of anomalies, as we were, that monosyllable *papp*, I later discovered, which comes from the Russian word *pop* — while *papp*, cardboard, is a derivative of *paber* ("paper") — is used only to refer to Eastern Orthodox prelates and never in reference to Roman Catholic priests who in Estonia are always called *preester* (plural *preestrid*), occasionally *paater* (plural *paatrid*). Still no logic ever held as far as studying the language went, as far as I'm concerned, which reminds me of a joke. An Estonian, a Dane, and a Swede get together for a dinner. Immediately, the Dane, typically fun-loving, pops open a beer and calls out, "Drink up!" The Swede, cautious, serious, not unaware of the enormous taxes on alcohol in his country levied to discourage such wild frivolities as drinking, replies, "Hold on, not so fast! I haven't had time to examine the contents on the label yet." The Estonian bewilderedly peers at the label, slowly looks up and inquires, "*Kas keegi saaks palun seletada, mis keel on siin kirjutatud?*" ("Could someone please explain what language is written here?")

The Estonian language is a non-Indo-European language, in the Finno-Ugric chain. The Finno-Ugric languages all share:

1. An absence of gender (the same pronoun for both he and she)
2. The absence of definite-indefinite articles (*a* or *the* in English)
3. A plethora of long words, due to language structure
4. Many grammatical cases
5. The use of postpositions rather than prepositions
6. No syntactic equivalent to the verb "to have"

There is no gender in Estonian. So he = she! There is no future tense. No articles are used. So articles and pronouns are completely missing; therefore, it is *mets* meaning forest, not *a* forest. I saw all of it as five sides to a square! Inexplicably, for example, one would say not "under the piano" in Estonian but "*klaveri all*" which means "the piano under." Prepositions are rare. There is no real specific masculine suffix in Estonian, while the suffixes *–tar, –anna, –inna* can be used to indicate the feminine. (*Vürstinna* is "duchess;" *krahvinna*, "countess;" *jumalanna*, "goddess;" *kuninganna*, "queen;" etc.) Certain words can mean either "he" or "she." The only cases vaguely resembling gender are word-formations. *Tantsijator* is necessarily a female dancer, *lauljanna* a female singer, but you cannot tell if *tantsija* or *laulja* is a male or female performer. When speaking Estonian, any conscientious Indo-European speaker is freed from the burden of using politically-correct pronouns. It is a linguistic phenomenon.

The Estonian language was drastically reformed in the early 20th century by the Estonian philologist and language reformer, Johannes Aavik (1880-1973), who actually invented new grammatical forms and coined dozens or scores of new words from English, German, and Russian prototypes. Finnophile, he also happily borrowed from that language. Many of his word-coinages have entered the everyday Estonian language, though few of his grammatical innovations have become popular. Thus, Aavik too in effect created an artificial Estonian language which nobody actually speaks in real life. As T. Peter Park has observed, "Modern Israeli Hebrew, too, is in effect a constructed language — which Zionist enthusiasts have actually gotten people to speak in real life!"

It is observed in an article in search of the world's hardest language, "Tongue Twisters," in *The Economist* (December 19, 2009), that "some European languages are far harder than are, say, Latin or Greek. Latin's six cases cower in comparison with Estonian's 14, which include inessive, elative, adessive, abessive, and the system is riddled with irregularities and exceptions." So which is the hardest of all languages? "On balance *The Economist* opts for Tuyuca, a language of the eastern Amazon, explaining succinctly that it has:

> a sound system with simple consonants and a few nasal vowels, so is not as hard to speak as Ubykh or !Xóõ. Like Turkish, it is heavily agglutinating, so that one word, *hóabãsiriga* means, 'I do not know how to write.' Like Kwaio, it has two words for 'we', inclusive and exclusive. The noun classes (genders) in Tuyuca's language family (including close relatives) have been estimated at between 50 and 140. Some are rare, such as 'bark that does not cling closely to a tree', which can be extended to things such as baggy trousers or wet plywood that has begun to peel apart.
>
> Most fascinating is a feature that would make any journalist tremble. Tuyuca requires verb-endings on statements to show how the speaker knows something. *Diga ape-wi* means that 'the boy played soccer (I know because I saw him)', while *diga ape-hiyi* means 'the boy played soccer (I assume)'. English can provide such information, but for Tuyuca that is an obligatory ending on the verb. Evidential

languages force speakers to think hard about how they learned what they say they know.

Parallel complexities exist in Estonian.

Amazingly enough, beyond that, there is no verb "to have" in the Estonian language — which is in a sense like having one hand! (The other hand is, of course, the verb "to be.") For a language to possess no verb "to have,"[42] does it not force speakers of the language into all kinds of bizarre and even comic circumlocutions and ridiculous preterimposterous alternatives? Instead of the verb "to have," Estonian is forced into inventive co-constructions with "to be" — that is, *mul on* ("I have"), *Sul on* ("You have"), *tal on* ("he has"), *mul oli* ("I had"), *Sul oli* ("you had"), *tal oli* ("he had"), literally "with me is," "with you is," "with him is," "with me was," "with you was," "with him was." In other words, *minul on raamat* (I have a book) is, literally, a series of short cave-man-like grunts saying, "book with — or on — me." Literally translated word for word, *koertal on sabad* means something like "with the dogs, [there] are tails" or "with dogs are tails," from *koertel* "with, at, or on dogs." (The word *sabad* means tails; *on* means is or are.) Therefore we have: *koer on pruun* ("the dog is brown"), *koeral on saba* ("the dog has a tail"), *koerad on metsikud* ("the dogs are wild or fierce"), *tal oli raamat* ("he or she had a book"), *nendel olid raamatud* ("they had books"), *lehmad olid paksud* ("the cows were fat"), *lehmadel olid sarved* ("the cows had horns"). Russian and the other Slavic languages use a somewhat analogous method; thus, Russian has no actual verb for "have" but uses a preposition *u* ("at, with [the possessor]") — e.g., *u vas kniga* for "you have a book," literally "with you (there is) a book." And as for our "have" as a perfective auxiliary verb, Estonian likewise uses the verb for "to be" — e.g., *ta on jooksnud* ("he or she has run"), *nad on lugenud* ("they have read"), *ta oli tulnud* ("he or she had come"), *na olid tulnud* ("they had come"). It sounds like Cloud Cuckoo Land. It may be of interest to mention here that in the 1920s Aavik, out of a national linguistic need to have it, actually *tried* to introduce into Estonian a neologism for the verb "to have" and came up with *evima* — *ma evin* ("I have"), *sa evid* ("you have"), *ta evib* ("he has"), etc. — but it never really caught on. Some Estonians also use *omama* ("to own") for "to have," as in, say, *Ma oman Sinu kirja* ("I have your letter"), literally "I own your letter," but such odd linguistic jogs and swerves are generally considered quite clumsy and substandard Estonian, a transparent imitation of English, Swedish, or German usage.

As Estonian has no definite or indefinite articles, no words corresponding to the English "the, a, an;" the word "book," say, *raamat,* can mean either "book," "the book," or "a book." Among younger-generation Estonians growing up in the United States, Canada, Germany, or Sweden, a tendency exists that is still frowned on by purists to render "the" by the word *see* ("this") or *need* (plural, "these") and "a, an" by *üks* ("one") — exactly as in the Romance languages (French, Italian, Spanish, etc.) and German, where the definite and indefinite articles are historically derived from the Latin or Old High German demonstratives ("this, that, these, those") and the numeral "one." Although condemned by linguistic purists, such words have long been used in Estonian poetry and song for the sake of meter.

Estonian also lacks Finnish possessive suffixes like *–ni* ("my"), *–me* ("our"), *–si* ("your"), etc., which is another example of the grammatical simplicity (or strangeness) of the language. In Estonian, as anyone can plainly see, the letters K, V, P and L clearly predominate. Yet in the peculiar alphabet of theirs, at least to us, there is no letter X, Z, Y, C, Q, or W! F you will find but almost always used in names and words of foreign origin. The letters Z, Ž, and Š appear in loan words only. So, one asks, how in all get-out do they write all those knotty Czech and Polish names? One answer would be that to make up for these absent letters, they conveniently provide us with nine vowels (a, ä, e, i, o, ö, õ, u, and ü), many of them lovely little sea-going characters like Ö and Á and Ú with tildes and umlauts like little sailor hats on them. But then to add insult to injury, many words have four vowels in a row in them and at least one umlaut, if not a billion of them — *jäääär, tooov, kuuuurija, araablan.*

In contrast, there are only 12 letters in the Hawaiian alphabet, five vowels (a,e,i,o,u) and seven consonants (h,k,l,m,n,p,w). It was adapted from the English alphabet in the early 19th century by American missionaries to print a Hawaiian Bible due to words with different meanings being spelled alike, the use of the glottal stop became necessary. As early as 1823, missionaries there made limited use of the apostrophe to represent the glottal stop, but they did not make it a letter of the alphabet.

Vowels appear in Estonian like currants in a fruitcake. Consider the tongue-twister *Õunapuu õitseaeg on Jüriöö ülestõusust jõululaupäevani* which means, "Blossom-time of an apple-tree is from the Jüriöö uprising until the Christmas Eve" or *Asjaajaja ja jaamaülem* which means "procurator and stationmaster," a phrase actually used by the police in Estonia, to be repeated, as a sobriety test. The word for "workaholic" is *tööööbik.* "Horrors of the night" is *hauaööõudused.* "Those living underground" is *maaalused. Kahetsusväärne* means "deplorable."

It is all of it a rather phantasmagoric experience. I am reminded of one episode in the TV sitcom, *Married … With Children.* "Why are you watching Spanish television?" teenage Bud Bundy bewilderedly inquires of his pretty but not overly-bright sister, Kelly, when he sees her sitting and staring blankly at the television set. She mindlessly replies, "Spanish? I thought that they were just English words I didn't know." In a way that describes my blundering experiences with the Estonian language. I began to believe it was all words in a language I had diligently applied myself to study but could never quite learn — English words I didn't know! I began to take a sad but self-replenishing refuge in a Jean Cocteau remark: "Since these mysteries are beyond us, let us pretend to have devised them."

The language is a vowel dump, an explosive alphagram-drill full of repeated letter-combinations with multiple bingos! It is positively *made* for Scrabble, splendid for word games. Back in 1990 an Estonian fellow named Mati Soomre playfully concocted a delightful Estonian neologism which consists of only vowels — *ööõoieoaeoaiaõuuiuauõu.* It means "a yard so named in honor of an idea of having fear of a garden where one can grow shoots of beans for their blooms which blossom only at night"! Suffixes alone are a field for fun. So he made up an Estonian one-stem word, *segu* (mix or blend) with fifteen syllables — *segunematustumisliustatavusenigi,* which means "even to the potentiality of achieving immiscibility." Ponder how utterly impossible it is, for example, for a non-Estonian person — even a Norwegian or a Swede — to pronounce common Estonian words with such eye-crossing strings of vowels and diphthongs as *õueäärne* ("yardside") or *ajaleheväljalõige* ("newspaper clipping") or *iseteenindussöökla* ("cafeteria"). One particular abstruse phrase popularly cited for the humiliating hems and haws required by non-natives to pronounce it, *Jüriöö ülestõus* — it refers to St. George's Night, a rebellious episode in Estonian history, comparable, say, to the Magna Carta or the Boston Tea Party, when in 1343-1345 the indigenous Estonian-speaking population of Northern and Western Estonia rose up against rulers of foreign (mainly German) origin — is phonetically daunting although it is only two words.

Would you like to try out a few lovely Estonian tongue-twisters? Try *Habemeajaja majarajaja ja jaamaülem!* ("Barber, house-builder, station-master"). Or *Eminemi esimene esinemine* ("Eminem's first performance"). *Kummikutes kummitus kummitas!* ("A ghost with rubber boots haunted a chest of drawers").

The explosive buckshot of vowels is of course not limited to Estonian alone. Norwegian and Danish are riddled with *As*. So are Hawaiian and Samoan, Mandinka and Maori. And how about Wolof? I swear, I could not tell half the time if a speaker in Tallinn or Tartu was not a Senegalese speaking Wolof in which the word "stamp" is *tubaab*, "honeymoon" — *céetal*, "war" — *waaw*, and "drunkard" — *daajukat!* In Wolof one says *Aala bi mungee lakka* for "The bush is burning." Will you insist I am crazy for confusing a West African tongue with Estonian? Wrong! Believe me, you had to be there. You should know that even in small English dictionaries one can find perfectly legitimate words like aam, aaru, and aioli, among others — they're simply never used. An orange was once a "norange," and many years ago one did not sneeze but rather *fnesed!*

About multiple vowels, there is a lovely quatrain in "Nostratic," the hypothetical prehistoric precursor of the Indo-European, Uralic (Finno-Ugric-Samoyed-Yukaghir), Altaic, and Afroasiatic (Hamito-Semitic) language families, found after his death among the scholarly papers of the pioneering Russian linguist Vladislav ("Slava") Illič-Svityč (1934-1966), a poem inscribed on his tombstone. It represents a language that the linguist believed to have been spoken between 20,000 and 12,000 years ago, probably somewhere in the Middle East. It goes,

K'elHä wet'ei 'ak'un kähla
k'a ai palha-k'a na wetä
a da 'a-ka 'eya 'älä
ya-k'o pele t'uba wete[43]

How about another confounding twist to the Estonian language, something it heavily shares with Chinese — one word can mean several things. For example, *tee* means (1) a road (2) tea, and (3) do! (an imperative form). *Sool* means both "salt" and "intestine." There is also *koor* which can mean "tree bark," "cream," but also "chorus, choir." *Täht* means both "star" and "letter of the alphabet." Then we have *tuli*, "fire" and "he came," and *tule* "of fire" and imperative "come!" There is *või* "butter," "or," and the negative form of "may, be allowed, be permitted." Similarly *võid* means both "butter" (accusative case) and "you may." *Saada* with a normally long *aa* means "send!" but with an extra-long *aa* means "to get, to receive." Likewise, *kastis* with a regular *s* in the middle means "in a box" but with an extra-long medial *s* means "he dipped" or "he sprinkled." There are also near-homonyms like *sa* short form of *mina* the pronoun "I" and *maa* "land, earth, country" — and *sa* short form of *sina* "you" (singular) and *saa* "get." Again, *reis* can mean both "thigh, pants leg" and "trip, journey," while *viin* means both "booze, liquor" and "I bring" or "I carry." One might also point to *kuid* "but" and "months" (accusative case) — or *kas* (with plain *s*) "if, whether, interrogative particle" and *kass* (with palatalized *s*) "cat."

Other examples include: *jää* "ice" but also imperative "stay!"; *saar* "island" but also "ash tree"; *tint* "ink" but also "smelt" (small fish); *joon* "line, stripe" but also "I drink;" *mees* "man" but also "in honey"; *meel* "mind, sense, frame of mind" but also "in or with honey"; *kuul* "bullet, cannonball" but also "on the Moon, in a month"; *kuule* imperative "hear!" but also "bullets, cannonballs" (accusative case) and "to the Moon"; *kaos* "chaos" but also "he disappeared"; *laod* "stocks, stores, deposits" but also "you load, you heap or pile up"; *sead* "pigs" but also "you arrange"; *mao* "of a snake" but also "of the stomach"; *maod* "snakes" but also "stomachs"; *soo* "swamp, marsh" but also "of sex or gender"; *sood* "swamps, marshes" but also "sexes, genders"; *nael* "nail" but also "pound sterling"; *puud* "trees" but also "*pood*, old Russian unit of weight (equal to 36 pounds)"; *need* "these, those" but also "curse, malediction, damnation"; *luud* "broom" but also "bones"; *teod* "acts, deeds, actions" but also "snails, slugs"; *tassi* "of a cup" but also imperative "carry, drag, lug, haul!"; *tahe* "dry, dried" but also "will, volition, desire"; *rohi* "grass" but also "drug, medicine" (latter sense perhaps originally meaning "herb," hence "medicinal herb"); *pead* "heads" but also "you must"; *nisa* "teat, nipple" but also an ending in place names meaning "cape, point, headland" as in "Lindanisa" (perhaps derived from Swedish *-näs* of the same meaning, originally signifying "nose").

The language also thrives on confoundedly gooning-up the names of just about every country with an extra, slightly elate, almost comically superfluous letter: *Iraak, Itaalia, Jaapan, Aafrika, Etioopia* and haphazardly running words together, as Germans do with their rebus-esque language, when half the time one cannot discern the controlling word. I would repeatedly see the word *Samidatheater* in Tartu and ponder, is that a cinema or a *samidath* eater, an eater of samidaths?

But when you think about it, is the dupled, drawn-out *Iraak* so bad? I have been hearing no end of hopeless ignoramuses in the United States now for eight years, from cretins in the streets and all over the airwaves, radio and television, mispronouncing Iraq as *Eye-rack!* The same half-wits and bigots who say *Eye-talian* and *Eye-ran* — many of them actual paid, professional broadcasters!

Ithy Oonts and Long-Haired Plomets

It is a tongue cloven with difficulty. One intuits there is a system not so much by listening as by hoping to catch in the rhythm any audible entrance or by watching the involved speaker's face, hoping that the voice shaping the sentence is eager to be understood. When an Estonian is speaking, the sentences seem to obey no rhythmic system the ear can apprehend, as one hears what poet Wallace Stevens comically called in another context "hoobla-hoo:"

> Pure coruscations, that lie beyond
> The imagination, intact
> And unattained…
>
> We enjoy the ithy oonts and long-haired

Plomets, as the Herr Gott
Enjoys his comets.[44]

We do, we quite enjoy the oonts and the long-haired plomets. There is also a balletic lilt to Estonian. I have often thought that when the language is spoken it sounds lovely, like a babbling brook. Still, we feel that impossible language can mime the world we know only by a kind of coincidence, with us searching, as it were, a stain on wallpaper for what resembles a human face. For in Estonia the thing is different. It is in that place one comprehends how arbitrary language is. One studies the verbs, learns vocabulary, listens hard, but then when you look up,

...still the grossest iridescence of ocean
Howls hoo and rises and howls hoo and falls.
Life's nonsense pierces us with strange relation.[45]

A violent order is disorder. It is true. A great disorder can always be *found* in order. Also true. These two things are one. They are hard words. I once tried to study — negotiate the morphologies of — Albanian with a view to reading the great novelist Ismail Kadare in the original, novels of his like *Agamemnon's Daughter*, *The File on H*, *Chronicle in Stone*, or *The Palace of Dreams*. It became next to impossible. Albanian in a way seems to resemble Estonian. Albanian is an Indo-European language, however, and thus of course not related to Estonian. It is the sole member of its own separate branch of Indo-European and not really closely related either to Greek or to the Slavic or Romance languages. It is often held to be descended from ancient Illyrian, an Indo-European language of the ancient eastern Balkans of which not very much is really known.

I can assert without fear of contradiction that it is a real help in Estonia to be able to speak French, German, or English. One language in the Baltics seems never enough. That truism is actually one of their proverbs. "*Ühest keelest ei piisa kunagi.*"[46]

Rock star Patti Smith might be someone who would love the Estonian language. Coincidentally enough, Sarah happened to meet — bump into — the punk singer in Basel, Switzerland in the Spring of 2008 at the Annual Art Fair. But I mention her here because I recall once reading about the anger she felt the first time she received a letter addressing her as "Dear Ms. Smith" when the outspoken punkstress exploded, saying, "A word like Ms. is total bullshit. Vowels are the most illuminated letters in our alphabet. Vowels are the colors and souls of poetry and speech. And these assholes take the only fucking vowel out of the word Miss. It sounds frigid." In a sense, the Estonian language with its soft, open, and repeated vowels, unique gender peculiarities, and oddments of illogic is what the critic Hélène Cixous might include as part of *écriture féminine*. In her essay, "The Laugh of the Medusa," she points out that women's language "does not contain, it carries; it does not hold back, it makes possible" and she goes on to define *écriture féminine* as poetic, nonrealist, antilogic, and rich.

"One speaks in one's own language, one writes in a foreign language," gnomically wrote Jean-Paul Sartre in *The Words*. There are quite a number of "click" languages in the world — it is called Khosan — especially notable among the Nama in Namibia and the Sandwe in Tanzania. When speaking, the Beami people in Papua, New Guinea *whoosh* and click. I remember reading that, when driving an elephant in India in a *pilkhanna* or grouping of them, the command for "sit down" is "*beht*," "*oot*" for "get up," and to get an elephant to make a pathway the mahout gently sings, "*Dalai, dab. Dalai, dalai, dab,* and at each "dab" the beast makes a renewed effort to clear the path. Klingon, the artificial language which made its debut in 1984 in *Star Trek III*, is actually studied, there is a Klingon Institute, and a Klingon translation of the Bible is presently underway. The Klingon Language Institute oversees it all. Let me add that there is also available in Klingon a full translation of *Hamlet* — *The Tragedy of Khamlet, Son of the Emperor of Qo'nos*. Can you recognize the opening of this soliloquy, reader?

> *taH pagh taHbe'. DaH mu'tlheghvam vIqelnIS.*
> *Quv'a', yabDaq San vaQ cha, pu' je SIQDI'?*
> *Pagh, Seng bIQ'a'Hey SuvmeH nuHmey SuqDI',*
> *'ej, Suvmo', rInmoHDI'? Hegh. Qong—Qong neH—*
> *'ej QongDI', tIq 'oy', wa'SanID Daw"e' je*
> *Cho'nISbogh porghDaj rInmoHlaH net Har.*
> *yIn mevbogh mIwvam'e' wIruchqangbej.*[47]

So there are no surprises in the area of language. But as far as Estonian goes, whether speaking or writing, we are all at sea, at least in my mind. We are all galley-slaves, we are all tattooed.

With verbs, there is no future tense in Estonian. (*Estonians do not believe in the future!*) In each of the tenses, the ending of a verb depends on the person and the number. Very awkwardly, each verb has two infinitives, and one has to know when to use which. Even funnier, both infinitives can be declined! Infinitives sound like Dutch surnames! To swim is *ujuma*. To smell is *haistma*. To sew is *õmblema*. To stab is *pussitama*. What is *lurtsema*? I knew a person with that name. The word for chair is *tool*. School is *kool*. Tomorrow is *home*. The word for friend in a land of big drinkers is *sober*. Train is *rong*, which does not seem right! By the way, there are a number of Estonian dialects, broadly divided into a Northwestern or "Tallinn" in contrast to a Southeastern or "Tartu" group. The most divergent is probably the Petseri dialect, spoken in the extreme Estonian Southeast, is practically a separate language. The Saaremaa dialect, which one hears spoken on that large offshore island, is also rather distinctive as an extreme version of Northwestern Estonian. There are a few vocabulary differences, but dialects and sub-dialects there differ mainly in pronunciation and phonology. It may seem strange that even in a small country like Estonia one encounters dialects, but as many as seven dialects of Aramaic were spoken in the vicinity of Judaea in Jesus' time. (Does that surprise you? As many as five distinct dialects have been discriminated in Mark Twain's novel, *Huckleberry Finn*, indices of five different classes!) Aramaic, not Hebrew, is the main language of the Talmud, remember — and it is older than Hebrew! The official literary language in that country is — not surprisingly — based on the Tallinn dialect. Tallinn is the capital, and what they say there, goes. Have you ever noticed that the worst language-snobs on the planet — choose any country on earth — are always those arch, always pushy, self-appointed aristarchs who happen to inhabit the capital city of a country, even though in myriad ways many of them may speak like provincials, partly because 70% of any capital's population blew in from the boondocks? I mean, people in New York City ludicrously say *toime* for "time" and *hart doorg* for "hot dog" and *hah* for the word "her," right? It is really a joke. But the precious inhabitants of Madrid, Rome, Berlin, New York, Tel

Aviv? Impossible snobs!

The Estonian third person plural *nad* or *nemad*, "they," is sexually neuter exactly like the English "they" and the German *sie*, in contrast to, say, the French *ils* and *elles*. When his parents would quarrel, my friend T. Peter Park told me, his mother would mock his father's original childhood Kodavere district accent (a sort of Estonian version of Georgia or Arkansas "cracker or broad Yorkshire," one might say), by using the local Kodavere rustic third-person plural *neie*, "they," for standard Estonian *nad, nemad*. "That was sort of my mother's Estonian way of accusing my father of saying 'dem' or 'dese' or 'dose,'" he explained. "When my mother imitated the Kodavere *neie on* ("they are") for standard Estonian *nad on*, she was implying that my father was a rube and had grown up saying 'Dem dere folks is' or 'dey am.'" But as to language, we Americans from Maine to Georgia, from Mississippi to Idaho have our own loony dialects — in Massachusetts we still say *hoss* instead of "horse," *cah* instead of "car," *Indier* instead of "India" — to say nothing of our quirks and crotchets. Americans, horridly, now say "absolutely" instead of the word "yes." There is ridiculously something of space-age terminology involved, I don't know. We substitute "basically" for "kind of" or "I think," repeatedly misuse the word "hopefully" as a sentence adverb, and conventionally offer the truly idiotic tautology "It is what it is" as a pronouncement of the deepest gravity. Virtually no one knows what *per se* means although it is used in conversation with reckless abandon. I hear *folage* and *foilage* for "foliage." Wolfie "graduated college." The list is endless. Television and movies spread the bad habits, and broadcasters are some of the worst offenders. Teenagers who rarely read books anymore talk too fast in robotic rhythms — as a way of impatiently looking, what, intelligent? cool? — and maniacally rely on the word "like" with jittering constancy. We no longer face problems — people shrink from the word which has the connotation of desperate hand-wringing — but rather "challenges," so ringing is that crusader-like euphemism. The verb "grow," a soulless think-tank word — Bill Clinton loved to use it — that has its origins in bland Rand Corporation-"speak," now applies to everything from vegetables to stock portfolios to the economy. I have no idea what the dorky word "pro-active" implies to most people, but it is hellaciously overused. We use "fellowship" as a verb. The dunderheaded present-day overreliance on the word "closure" is almost scandalous. Every last moron calling a talk show repeats like a mindless parrot the conned phrase, "Thank you for taking my call." Then there is all that Twitterspeak — LOL, OMG, BFF, etc. The NPR/Cambridge, Mass. academic crowd in the unlikeliest way constantly relies on the pretentious verbal sound-effect "sort of," a catch-phrase/palliative wantonly inserted just about everywhere in a sentence, which they feel somehow endows speech with a faux-posh Oxford University-like stutter or hesitancy. The one verbal crotchet that really sends me up a wall as far as spoken English in America goes has become nothing less than a national epidemic — the universal abuse of the word "well." Have you ever noticed how compulsively, how inanely, how obsessively, how brainlessly almost all Americans begin *every* answer to *every* question by, saying, "*Well*"? "Well, I guess I —" or "Well, what you should know is —" It is ALWAYS the first word said, a responsorial starting-gun. Why this almost demented excess is not the cause of an immediate lexicographical investigation is truly beyond me. It is a mad verbal tic, actually a discourse marker, an enclitic of sorts, a weak rhetorical crutch so frequently repeated by so many dopes and deludinoids without thinking that as a lamentable conformity it is depressingly almost as if every chuckle-headed American has to say the word — is actually *forced* to say it — in order to make any reply.

I heard *vabandust* ("pardon?") and *ma ei saa aru* ('I don't understand") repeated enough in Estonia — mainly from my own tentative and uncertain lips — to endow both phrases with the ringing and bothersome equivalence of what in spoken English irks me with the cursed word "well." (Let me add that I also badly overused the phrase *Andke andekas* — "sorry". Travelers tend to say "sorry" a good deal, even when someone else is at fault, ever notice?) Would that I had the gift, the time, to be able to read more widely in the tongue, particularly in the area of fiction.

Words, Words, Words

The great Estonian novel has yet to be written. Some people in the know may disagree and insist it is August Gailit's *Toomas Nipernaadi* or Anton Hansen Tammsaare's masterful *Tõde ja õigus* ("Truth and Justice") or Lennart Meri's *Hõbevalge* ("Silverwhite"). I am not qualified to say, being unable to read them well in the original. Until 1900 very little secular prose was written in the Estonian language. One must mention the social-critical novels of Eduard Vilde (1865–1933), a man who led an adventurous life in Germany and Denmark, and who, although he turned Estonian prose toward a realistic direction, also wrote about the Maltsvetian movement and the mythical "White Ship," a metaphorical phrase in Estonia for expectation, a theme in the national culture that we will come to look at shortly. Along with Vilde came a rise in both the novel and in poetry. Among some of the more notable contemporary writers are Tõnu Õnnepalu, Peeter Sauter, Mats Traat, Viivi Luik, Ene Mihkelson — a woman novelist — whose fiction deals, among other things, with the doom-dark days of Soviet occupation, and Jaan Kaplinski, who is probably the best known Estonian poet and intellectual. As I write, the plays and short stories of one Andrus Kivirähk with his absurd, irreverent, and deadpan humor have become very popular. The book that made Kivirähk's name is his satirical novel of 1995, *Ivan Orava mälestused ehk minevik kui helesinised mäed* ("The Memoirs of Ivan Orav, or The Past As Azure Mountains"), a spoof, a hilarious travesty of 20th century Estonian history that pokes fun of national myths. There are very serious thinkers and intellectuals presently writing in Estonia. Philip Roth once quipped that in the West anything goes and nothing matters, while in the East nothing goes and everything matters. I believe that he meant, among other things, that good books — not agitprop or popular trash — do not sell. Who can explain who reads what and why? There is a strange if predictable arc in Estonian tastes. In Estonia, silly, fatuous gossip magazines like *Kroonika* far outsell — by light years — serious, insightful cultural journals like *Vikerkar* ("Rainbow') or *Looming* ("Creation"). But when was not ours *mundus indiscriminatus*? Most people prefer to read Stephen King, Victoria Holt, and Danielle Steel than Anthony Trollope, Thomas Hardy, or James Joyce. Imbeciles, fatheads, and clods want to read more about Hannah Montana than Simone Weil, are fascinated more with Britney Spears than Ingeborg Bachmann. I blame Original Sin. Agatha Christie is the second most translated author in the world (after Walt Disney books) and the pen-pushing hack Nora Roberts is thirtieth, one slot after Karl Marx! Stendhal and Defoe, Villon and Borrow had all scraped and grubbed for money. Melville could not earn a living either. He stopped writing altogether to take a crapulous and demeaning job at the New York Customs House. Poor Stephen Crane, who wistfully divulged it in his letters, could not turn a dollar with his stories. Fyodor Dostoevsky told his publisher in 1849, "I struggle with my small creditors like Laocoön with the serpent." *The Desire and Pursuit of the Whole*, like almost all of Baron Corvo's books, was written by a man who was nearly starving. Knut Hamsun was almost always badly impoverished. Thomas DeQuincey's career was spent tethered by debt to the periodical press. Adversity plagued many. Consider the works that were written in jail. Sir Thomas More's *A Dialogue of Comfort Against Tribulation* was composed in jail. So were Oscar Wilde's *De Profundis*, Dietrich Bonhoeffer's *Letters and Papers from Prison,* Aleksandr Solzhenitsyn's *One Day in the Life of Ivan Denisovich,* and many of Ezra Pound's *Cantos,* along with several of St. Paul's letters. Boethius wrote *The Consolation of Philosophy* while detained before he was executed without a trial. John Bunyan wrote *Grace Abounding to the Chief of Sinners: Or Brief Faithful Relation Exceeding Mercy God Christ his Poor Servant John* during one of his incarcerations. Cervantes began writing *Don Quixote* while in debtor's prison. And Jean Genet's *A Thief's Journal* was written in jail, on bumph. Who that had the occasion to read it can fail to remember how a mortified Henry David Thoreau was dismally driven to buy back 706 unsold copies of the first edition of all but a thousand printed copies of his book *A Week on the Concord and Merrimack Rivers* after pile upon pile of them had lain conspicuously, sonorously, unsold on the publisher's shelves in Boston and Cambridge for four years? It is wistfully touching to see the gallant if self-conscious notation in the pages of Henry's homely diary:

I have now a library of nearly 900 volumes, over 700 of which I wrote myself. Is it not well that the author should behold the fruits of his labor? Nevertheless, in spite of this result, sitting beside the inert mass of my works, I take up my pen to-night to record what thought or experience I may have had with as much satisfaction as ever. Indeed, believe that this result is more inspiriting and better for me than if a thousand had bought my wares. It affects my privacy less and leaves me freer.

As far as royalties went, *A Week on the Concord and Merrimack Rivers,* the book, people tend to forget, that he wrote during his stay at Walden Pond, earned Thoreau the lordly sum of $96.67.[48] So much for his "experiment in living." Although he valiantly tried to put together a lecture tour throughout the Midwest and Canada, much of the trip had to be cancelled owing to lack of interest. He spent but ten days traveling. ("I fear that I have not got much to say about Canada, not having seen much; what I got by going to Canada was a cold.")[49] Following a misbegotten attempt to break into the publishing world in New York City, he wrote to his mother, "My bait will not tempt the rats; they are too well fed."

The best Estonian fiction and poetry, to no one's surprise, least of all mine, sells practically not at all in that country, the same pattern of course that we find among some of the very best writers in the United States. Check out any best-seller list from the *New York Times* from forty, fifty, or sixty years ago — nothing but eighth-rate books. Less than mediocre work. A waste of trees. It may sound off-puttingly elitist but the common people, I'm afraid, are wanting in taste.[50] Consider the hack-writers now selling widely in the United States, and it makes a person want to weep. (Elbert Hubbard's dippy *A Message to Garcia* [1899] and Jacqueline Susann's prurient *Valley of the Dolls* [1966] remain, respectively, the ninth and tenth best-selling books *of all time* — check it out for yourself.) How different it was ages ago, when the written word was held to a higher standard. You say *Hamlet* was not popular in Shakespeare's day? Wrong — it was a best-seller, published in quarto five times, if not more often, during the playwright's short life. Sadly, it is a rare individual in the United States nowadays who makes a special conscious effort singlemindedly to go out to a bookstore to buy, with hard-earned money, a new work of good fiction.

On literary misappropriation and the vice of conditioned values? All my life I have considered the Gettysburg Address to be, although a pithy and heartfelt speech, vastly over-rated — and I who revere Abraham Lincoln take not a jot of worth away from the man[51] —a classic example, less of ancestor worship, than the penchant for a kind of inherited, unassailable, knee-jerk respect for the traditional as well as a bourgeois fear of breaking ikons. It is a splendid and succinct speech but also a formal rhetoric, conned from the ages with both received phrases and hoary notions that are like old, well-thumbed coins, smooth to the touch.[52] Ralph Waldo Emerson's lengthy "Address to the Temperance Society," given in the small town of Harvard, Mass. on July 4, 1843 — there is not a single contemporary account of the event — is an infinitely deeper, far greater address, and until 2010[53] *the lecture had never been published!* I would go so far as to say that President Obama's "A More Perfect Union" speech given in Philadelphia on March 18, 2008, an impassioned and inspired oration renouncing the extreme of black nationalism without giving up black pride, is as great an address as any American statesman has ever made.

It was an Estonian, a fellow prisoner in the gulag named Arnold Susi, who disabused the novelist Aleksandr Solzhenitsyn of any belief in Marxism, but Solzhenitsyn also hated snobbish Russian intellectuals, "the well-read ones," he snidely referred to them. Russians in the mass — particularly peasants — he alone seemed to care for, and he was as hidebound as Mohandas Gandhi was in hating machinery, industry, and scientific agriculture. Vision, weirdly, often looks backward instead of forward. As the holy mystic Simone Weil once wrote in *Illusions*, "Necessity is essentially a stranger to the imaginary." I have to say however that a Russian poet giving a public reading in Russia, even back in the days of the Soviet Union, could fill an entire stadium. I remember evenings in both Moscow and Leningrad hearing poets read to thundering applause.

But back to the *baffling* Estonian language and the difficulties that it presents. Take, for instance, the words of St. Paul to Timothy, "No longer drink any water, but take a little wine for your stomach's sake and your frequent infirmities."[54] The Greek Testament equivalent for the first ten words of this exhortatory sentence would be, roughly, "*Me hydropotei pleon, de metacheirizon oligon oinon.*" The words *me* and *de* must necessarily be learned without any association, but all the other words can be remembered with ease, because they have derivatives in common speech. One finds *hydor* in hydrogen, *potein* in potation, and even the compound word *hydropots* is, like the word water-babies, applied to tee-totalers in England. You have *meta* in metaphysics, *cheir* in chiromancy. *Oligon* we find in oligarchy, government by the few. *Oinon* is the same word that we find in Latin *vinum*, the German *wein* in our own wine. In this sentence no artificial memory need be involved, merely a proper regard to the philological relations between the known English and the unknown Greek, which is a far better aid to your memory than all the artificial mnemonics in the world.

But in Estonian, the sentence, "Drink no more water, but take a little wine," etc. becomes in translation the jaw-breaking mouthful *Ära joo enam ainult vett, vaid võta pisut veini oma kõhu pärast ja oma sagedate haiguste pärast* where with haws and huffs and no end of gnathic adjustments one has no more recourse to an Indo-European cognate than to the *appellation* St. Paul had in mind to imbibe!

Translating "wine" by *viina* is not too felicitous, as *viin* actually means "booze, liquor, vodka, spirits" while *vein* — I have made previous comment on the chilling overtones of this Draculine coincidence — is the more normal Estonian word for "wine" from grapes. "*Viin* and *vein* are words of respectively Russian and German origin, trailing culture-historical aromas respectively of vodka and Riesling or Liebfraumilch," T. Peter Park tells me, he whose translation of the Pauline exhortation stands above. He went on helpfully to explain, "It is pretty much a toss-up whether you use the verb *võta* ('take') or *tarvita* ('use'), as both, I feel, are acceptable. Also, it is a toss-up whether you use *sageda põdemise* for 'of frequent illnesses' — *haigus* for 'illness, sickness, disease' is a bit more idiomatic and colloquial, the words my parents would invariably have used, while *põdemine* ('being sickly, convalescent') is a bit more literary, what Americans would call a 'five-dollar word.' The postposition *pärast* translates variously as 'because of, on account of, for the sake of.' Instead of *pisut* ('a little') you can just as well use *natuke*, of exactly the same meaning. My parents and I used *natuke* a bit more often ourselves. My hunch is that *pisut* is ultimately derived from German *bisschen* (cf. Yiddish *bissl*). The prohibitory particle *ära* ('don't, do not') has the original primitive meaning of 'off, away.'" But whatever etymological notes or niceties are provided, the Estonian language is still enormously difficult, to say the least.

It seems almost unfair in that neck of the planet that while Estonian is so nut-hard-tough, Swedish, Norwegian, and Danish with some slight exaggeration are all pretty much one language. As the American linguist John McWhorter in *The Power of Babel* writes, "What is today 'Norwegian' was just 'the way they speak Danish in Norway' until Norway broke with Denmark in 1814 and gradually began explicitly working out a standard form of what was an array of nonstandard local dialects." People speaking these "languages" can be all fairly conversant.

The majority of words in conversational English are stressed on their first syllable, as in the words "social," "language," "challenge," "monkey," "jungle," or "differ." (Southerners in the United States with their contrary pronunciation actually follow this convention with pronunciations like: *um*brella, *ci*garette, *in*surance, etc.) Estonian words and names of native Estonian or Finno-Ugric origin are usually stressed on the first syllable. However, words and names of foreign or international origin are usually stressed on the same syllable as in their language of origin (whether Latin, Greek, French, German, English, Russian, or "generalized Western European") — hence, words like korpora*tsioon*, organisa*tsioon*, dimen*sioon*, retsen*sioon*, masturba*tsioon*, a*bort*, distsi*pliin*, ping*viin*, poli*tsei*, po*lii*tika, demo*kraa*tia, orga*nism*, krititsism, sotsia*lism*, kommu*nism*, kapita*lism*, fa*shism*, karika*tuur*, tempera*tuur*, ling*vist*ika, astro*noo*mia, bio*loo*gia, psühho*loo*gia, filo*soo*fia, and the whole class of the Estonian –*eer*ima verbs which are derived from German –*ieren*, e.g., telefo*neer*ima, kritit*seer*ima, mastur*beer*ima. The same is true of names like Ma*riia*, Lo*viis*a, Julia*an*a, Kris*tii*na — though Aleksander and Konstantin are usually stressed on the first syllable. Finnish, however, has a mercilessly invariable initial stress which has always sounded a bit "funny" to me — e.g., *ka*pitalism, *so*tsialism, *kom*munism, *tem*peratuur, *kor*poratsioon, *his*toria, *fi*losoofia, *bio*loogia, etc.

There are literally *no* Estonian words taken over into English. Should anyone be surprised? A Cold War-era *Look* or *Life* magazine article from the 1950s, bizarrely enough, explained the Soviet Communist term *kulak* ("rich peasant") as derived from the Estonian word for "fist," whereas of course it is the Russian word for "fist," originally a Russian slang term for

124

"tight-fisted money-lender." (I love this subject. Did you know that, for years, the Russian word for typewriter was simply "*Underwood*"?) There are scads of modern Estonian words of general international origin, like *närv* ("nerve"). Two common Estonian words, *roim* ("crime") and *siiras* ("sincere") were specifically coined by the early 20th century Estonian language-reformer, Johannes Aavik, from English "crime" and "sincere," based specifically on their English pronunciations. He also coined a noun *sóu* ("show") — as in stage show, radio show — from the English word. (I looked but could not manage to find it in Paul Saagpakk's extremely comprehensive dictionary, the *sine qua non* of Estonian reference books, not that I can use more than six percent of it.) Contemporary Estonian habitually uses *printer* for "computer printer" (rather than a possible *trükkija*), and *printima* "to print on a computer printer" (rather than *trükkima*, "to print on a printing press"). Incidentally, although Aarvik himself did not create them, there are two rival contemporary Estonian words for "computer," *raal* (of inexplicable origin) and *arvuti*, from the native Estonian stem of *arv* "number," *arvama* "to figure, guess, calculate, suppose," and *arvestama* "to calculate, compute," plus the modern suffix *–ti* "tool, instrument, body organ"). Of these two forms, *arvuti*, with its derivation from a familiar Estonian stem, is by far the more popular, *raal* of unknown origin being only rarely used.

I found no examples of the kind of linguistic stage comedy one hears, for example, in Israel where the rear axle of a car has comically trans-mogrified into "beckexle" while the front axle is therefore logically called "front beckexle," which sounds like the Molly Goldberg or Milt Gross version of American. Estonians call American-style hamburgers *ham-burgerid* — I have to say that several times I heard Americans over there with a kind of dogged insistence trying to masticate this particular word: "I wanna haaamboorger, Ed!" — reserving the word *hakklihakotletid* or, more familiarly, *kotlet,* for their Estonian-style chopped beef and pork hamburger patties. *Dzhentleman* has become fairly common as a pho-netic spelling of English "gentleman." So, too, is *dzhäss* for "jazz." (I write out these awkward words with some reticence but don't feel too bad: Huckleberry Finn could not spell Pennsylvania. Why should he have been able to do so, you ask? What people forget is that Huck, not only a celebrity at the beginning of that novel but also rich and famous — that's what drags his exploitative, opportunistic Pap back to see him — was *schooled* to some degree by both Miss Watson and the Widow Douglas.) Endlessly I tried speaking Estonian. I have no respect for people who in their travels flatly refuse to try out a new language. I am afraid that in most of my attempts to communicate with Estonians in their language, I sounded sadly like Spencer Tracy speaking "Portuguese-American" [sic] in *Captains Courageous* ("Wad do you gomplain for? I make wid da moosic and sing a dis zong!") which was worse than bogus, more like a bloody calumny against Portugal, and after the laughter dies down and the comic ebbs surely has to be one of the stupidest, most indefensible acting and directing mistakes in the history of Hollywood cinema, that is, if it was not outvulgarized by the talentless Cher desperately trying to sound like a real Italian in the awful film, *Prizzi's Honor.* Spelling Estonian words is alone like negotiating a thicket of thorns. No, young Huck could not spell Pennsylvania, but I was not much better.

I once bothered to compile a small list of more common English words taken over pretty much bodily into Estonian: *beebi* ("baby"); *spiiker* ("speaker [of the house]"); *dzhemm* ("jam"); *treening* ("training"); *seef* ("safe"); *ragbi* ("rugby"); *leedi* ("lady"); *kiibord* ("keyboard"); *dzhamper* ("jumper [jacket]"). But, as I say, no words that have entered the English language in the manner of *smorgasbord, ombudsman, piano, forte, concerto, sauerkraut, kindergarten*, etc., have ever been taken over into English from Estonian. You could better hunt for them from Tulu or Malayalam, Tlingit or Eyak, Haida or Gilyak, Wolof or Pushtu!

Some Reflections on Feet-Folk

I can say I was somewhat surprised on my flight east after passing through customs in Stockholm to find the small plane filled with so many different-looking, exotic people (all heading to Tallinn on a snowy *February* afternoon!) and recalled reading how astonished was the writer M.M. Kaye, author of *The Far Pavilions,* when at Nairobi airport she once heard the announcement — she would later cite this as the inspiration for her novel, *Trade Wind* — "Will passengers for Mombasa, Tanga, Pemba, Zanzaibar, and Dar Es Salaam be kind enough to take their seats?" I remember looking down from the plane to the Baltic Sea and reflecting how Tonio Kröger in Thomas Mann's novel loved it as much as he did his violin, his books, and the old walnut tree in his father's garden. When not craning my neck to look at the shining glint of that expanse, I found diversion in a small book I had bought, *Hilarious Estonia* (Eesti Instituut), certainly one of the unfunniest books I have ever read. It stated that there are still places in Estonia where humans have never penetrated, which seemed unlikely, but who knew? The Bible is also a planet where entire spots are never visited. I mean, I have always thought that there are places in Scripture where no one ever goes, ignored books like Zephaniah and Nahum and Haggai and Nehemiah. Who ever reads *those* books? I have always been amused at what people find fun and began to ponder various examples of hilarity instanced in *Hilarious Estonia*. Riding ice-floes is a sport in Estonia, it asserted. So is wife-carrying, wife-throwing — *ratta viskamine* — and wheel-throwing. In the competition of wife-carrying, the traditional "Estonian Carry," a hitch that my book blithely insisted is known throughout the world, is — not surprisingly — different than any of the others. Why would it be the same in Estonia!? Whereas in many if not most such events in other countries, dutiful wives are either slung over one of the shoulders of the husband or alternately carried in both of his lifted arms like a bride over a threshold, in Estonia the wife is hung backwards like a just-slain deer, her face staring at her husband's butt, her twammy on the back of his neck, her legs jutting out like a desperate pair of raised, wagging windshield wipers! It is embarrassing image to contemplate, even if vaguely aerodynamic! Generally, the popular prize for winning this hearty contest wherever it is held is to win one's wife's weight in beer, another elegant moment for all the poor muddy-bottomed wives who must simply love having their avoirdupouis divulged in public — by megaphone — to a howling crowd! I have read that the greatest wife-carrier in the world is the muscular blond Estonian, Margo Uusorg. There is a limerick lurking there somewhere.[55]

Estonians, you see, love games. Or what passes for games. Song contests are very big there. People in national costume stand in rows and sing songs that they have been practicing and polishing for centuries. A man with a nose long as a ring-measure sitting next to me — he sported a fulsome mustache and with a mirthful squint had something of the leer of band-leader Xavier Cugat — put a question to me, "*Käivitub motor, ina avab usu?*" — or something like that. We landed. I entered Tallinn on February 19, 2008 and immediately noticed on the car-ride in that white brick Soviet buildings were popular there. Was it the dismal specter of the World War that I, who had not been back to Europe for decades, found in the flat depressing pale creams, apricots, and dark pinks of those Baroque buildings? Nazi art, Soviet apartment buildings, Dictator architecture. "The logical result of Fascism is the introduction of aesthetics into political life," wrote Walter Benjamin in his essay, "The Work of Art in the Age of Mechanical Reproduction." There is a gloomy post-war air, I believe, in the very way that the republics of eastern Europe insistently try so hard to glorify all progress from the year 1945, a sort of obsessional pertinacity that almost pleads — nothing like the mood that was emphatically present in the devitalized, berubbled East Berlin that I witnessed in 1965 crossing both ways — at night, past dogs, by Vopos! — through "Checkpoint Charlie" which the East Germans officially called *Grenzübergangsstelle Friedrichstrasse*. I looked at Tallinn. The brick was grey and not as white as the heavy cotton-balls of snow filling the air. I began to feel a seasonal affective disorder and seemed to hear in my mind coronachs and threnodies and lamentations like the "Adagietto" of Gustave Mahler's Fifth Symphony accompanying me everywhere I went, a fitting backdrop from the composer of a Christless "Resurrection." (*"Der Mensch liegt in grösster Noth! Der Mensch liegt in grösster Pein!"*)[56] I knew immediately why everyone went out of their way to tell me, "Make sure you come in summer. Estonia in winter is a prison."

At the same time, generally speaking, the air in Estonia is fresh and clean. To walk through old Tallinn or any of its parks like Hiiu, Varuvärava Mäe, Kadrioru, or Toompark — the trees glazed schneeball and majolica and porcelain — is to discover an ice kingdom. It is a fresh, uncluttered, little country, its spaces seemingly endless, its vistas wide. The land can breathe. Sarah insightfully observed, "The cultivated land seems just one step away from turning wild again. But one feels safe in the countryside." I worried about that, for Sarah was a landscape painter who worked mainly outside, and her beauty is of movie-star quality —

an all-too obvious target for lecherous passing motorists. Regarding her extraordinary good looks, I would often hearken to a passage in a little-known Conrad Aiken story, "By My Troth, Nerissa!" where he writes, "My dear Sara: why is it that you are made of flesh — indeed, if God, as it is reported, created you in His image, did He not dispense for once with the common straw and clay and dip His hands into the clear brightness of the ether?" But Sarah also has a circle of grace around her. She told me, "When I paint outdoors, no one bothers me, cars and truck drivers don't wave and honk their horns, shouting stuff like 'Way to go!' In a rare case in the countryside, local people might come up to see what I am doing, but they are usually very polite and don't stay long. One woman in fact who approached me with great enthusiasm from a distance like a long lost sister, as soon as she saw my foreign face" — as I have mentioned, my wife, Sarah, is Amerasian — "immediately turned and walked quickly away as if I were a ghost. It was comical." Sarah who drove around a good deal there added, "In terms of cars, some just drive too fast by me, young people with green-leaf stickers on their cars, which I first thought meant had some connection with Canada, until it was later explained to me that they were reserved for new drivers to warn others on the road to beware of them." Sarah and I of course were "feet-folks," as Bram Stoker in *Dracula* several times refers to tourists. We tried to fit in and ignore it when they were rude, but it was like quitting a bad cigarette habit. "It gets easier each time," or so goes the comic pronouncement on that subject, but by algebra it proved to be *harder* each time.

My worst thought of Estonians was that they were prayerless footlings in extreme maleficence diligently not noting other people's needs, but I was quite determined there that whoever it was who despised what he did not understand was not going to be me.

I tried to outface such things, taking up their own notion of *ootame, vaatame* ("wait and see"). Estonia is a nation that has survived, within living memory, two World Wars, a war of independence, six occupations, three regimes of terror, repeated economic depressions, and if I in my person happened to bother them as only yet another example of a drip-faced foot-folk beefwittedly trenching onto their national soil and it bothered them, so be it. I can honestly say and want to go on record as feeling that in spite of the fact that, although I often found them to be often cauterizingly unsentimental and offensively bad-mannered, many times I personally felt sorrow for marginalized Estonians. Poverty cannot hide. Knut Hamsun wrote about it insightfully and so did Sigrid Undset. I would never come across luckless hoboes or hopeless indigents sleeping outside along the cold, dark, muddy banks of the ice-strewn but still flowing Emajõgi in the dead of winter or, huddled by watch-fires blazing in a barrel, sitting under huge oak trees on the crooked limbs of which, even in the extreme of winter, still waggled a few parcels of desiccated leaves — I was reminded of the ancient belief that the wisdom of Zeus was whispered by the oak leaves — and fail to recall that short but highly memorable passage from *On the Road* when after he was summarily kicked out of a railroad station in Harrisburg, Pennsylvania by the station master Jack Kerouac reflected:

> Isn't it true that you start your life a sweet child believing in everything under your father's roof? Then comes the day of the Laodiceans, when you know you are wretched and miserable and poor and blind and naked, and with the visage of a gruesome grieving ghost you go shuddering through nightmare life.

Places sharply — and subjectively — shape memories. Jack Kerouac fixed on Harrisburg as a city forever to hate. ("Cursed city!") On the other hand, he drew a universal truth about Iowa simply by having passed a bevy of lovely high school coeds in that state one arbitrary afternoon. ("The prettiest girls in the world live in Des Moines.") He loved the way everyone — anyone — out west liltingly pronounced the name, "L.A." but of that centerless, smog-filled, rat-trap of a city he also wrote, "I never felt sadder in my life. LA is the loneliest and most brutal of American cities; New York gets god-awful cold in the winter but there's a feeling of wacky comradeship somewhere in some streets. LA is a jungle."

It is an almost incontestable fact that in any tribal, rustic, or non-industrial world, the people are invariably open or closet animists who love nature. Estonia is one such place — bonfires, for example, they adore. They set them up on virtually any occasion, on St. John's Day, on Christmas, on wedding nights, on birthdays, on the anniversary of Russian evacuation. I have nothing against nature, understand. Who would deny, however, that people who pointedly take refuge in nature as a life style, solipsists like Henry Thoreau, John Muir, and that ilk, just like those intransigent and autocratic women who find sanctuary among apes, are invariably not very good with people? But I mean, hey, what is wrong with a holiday night when one can get drunk and decide to howl? Run through the woods naked? Do cartwheels in the shrubbery? Indulge in aestival mudbaths? Roll around in the cloverthatch? Engage with threesomes in a sauna? Munch mushrooms and channel the ghost of Tharapita? Invoke forest-spirits with sticks? Chase lynx or wild boar or wolves? (There are many of all three roaming around in the republic.) I am reminded of some lines from "Potato Thief" by the Finnish poet Pentti Saarikoski (1937-1983):

The year was long and dark
The forest was pushing through the museums.
It is a chthonic country.

I would offer that in their capacious attention to nature many Estonians may have over time located what others may call faith, may have substituted such worship for what others in their orthodoxy choose to deem religion. Other thinkers may associate or credit God with all natural bounty. The paradox is that, while acknowledging the idea that God creating Nature brings both God and nature into relation, it also separates them. The Creator and the created must be two, not one. Therefore, the doctrine of creation in a real sense either empties Nature of divinity or, as with curmudgeonly, indeed angry poet Robert Frost who often blamed God for Nature's cruelties, indicts God for its extreme savageries.

As the churches have all transmogrified into small crepuscular galleries, there is only silence and the smell of old brick as you enter one and sit in a pew. Forests are treated like churches there. It is not at all glib to find sardonic twists and turns in Estonia. I remember a man once coming up to me on a street in Tallinn, a fat man with an *en brosse* hairstyle — "a pig with a pasty face squealing for cookies, kinned by poor pretense with a noble house," as John Crowe Ransom put it, I think in his poem, "Dead Boy" — and suggested I was a foreigner by dint of my hat!

Scrap Irony

Estonian irony is widely known. Impishness is prized. Wryness. Sly exchanges. It goes without saying that one has to know an Estonian before one hears anything like the midnight of a chuckle. There is a cast of resignation to them; it could even be self-deprecation. I never got fully close enough to know. I suspect that they do not expect people either to approve or appreciate them. This yields you the breezy benefit of not having to appreciate them in return, which is a blessing. "Who fears laughing will die of farting" is a favorite Estonian proverb. So they do laugh — at least the author of that proverb did. You just don't see laughter happen very often. What there is in the Estonian soul — once you get a glimpse of it — is an antic, self-gratifying, jokiness, ludic pep, a slightly peculiar but mischievious playfulness, a distinct gene for simple fun — of the practical-joker sort. They love to clown, to cod, to play the dozens with a stranger. This is their kind of humor. Thimblerigging humor. Taking the mickey out of you while winking to a friend. It is the syndrome of the "prickly pear" (L. *Opuntia*): a sweet nature beneath a forbidding exterior. It is a humor that conveys doubt, friendship, cynicism, scoffing, pasquinade, understanding, playfulness, and the antic all at once. There is a distinct innocence to it. Their attitude of gentle mockery, that arch reminder or hint that its author considers almost nothing serious, absolute, or credible, convinces me that underneath those long, drawn faces and grave, peevish personalities that so often recalled for me what the French referring to a hardcover book call a *couverture rigide* can be found — dare I say it? — a warmth. The hunch in this corner is that deep down Estonians are actually sweet. You have to hang around some to see it, to *discern* it, but it is there. I have to say that in my experience, impolitic as it may be to say so, for just plain sourness and a kind of black disgruntledness no one comes close to matching the American Irish, many kind and harmless, of course, but in the main, for envy, spite, contempt and injustice-collecting, among the coldest, meanest, bitterest, darkest-hearted, grudge-holding, passive-aggressive bastards on the planet, their heads, as Mercutio tells Benvolio in *Romeo and Juliet*, to borrow an apt phrase, "as full of quarrels as an egg is full of meat." The star of television's popular

132

All in the Family, Carroll O'Connor was asked in an interview about Irish culture and, whenever returning to his old neighborhood, how proud his friends and neighbors must be of his success. He said, "Oh, you know, the Irish would much prefer that you come back a failure." James Joyce in *Ulysses* referred to Ireland the "sow that eats its own farrow."

I feel that I should add, by way of fairness, that Aleksandr Solzhenitsyn, who from his somewhat mystical perspective saw less of a spiritual crisis in Europe than in the United States, at least back in 1978, declared in his famous speech at the Harvard Commencement in that year (I was in attendance) that he "could not recommend today's West as a model" for his countrymen. Eastern Europe, he felt, was far ahead of the West. "The complex and deadly pressures bearing upon our lives," he said, "have developed characters that are stranger and more profound and interesting than those developed by the prosperous, ordered life of the West." The spirit of rationalism, infecting both communism and capitalism, had left both the U.S. and Russia spiritually bankrupt.

Bawdiness figures in much of Estonian humor, what perhaps unkindly might be called "poor people" wit, which is a phrase of Ned Rorem's who in his book *Pure Contraption* states, "Humor is tone based on irony, a Janus head. Children, being literal-minded, have no humor." Does he mean that they will laugh at everything? *Anything?* It is probably true. When I was a little boy, crayon drawings that we scribbled off on cheap paper on rainy days of turds falling out of a cat or a dog's bum ("Holy smoke, don't let *Mom* see that!") could send us into hysterical gales of laughter. Where American jokes tend to concentrate on sex, Europeans — Estonians, especially — fix on scatology, cuckolds, simpletons gulled. Slow-witted piemen. Stupid husbands. Wily, mobile wives. There is a wonderful earthiness beneath it all. I have often thought that the one Estonian proverb, "Do not choose your wife on the way to church," sums up best, from several aspects, their cheeky humor and wry irreverence and practical outlook.

A truism is that the jokelore of every nation is always directed at any closely neighboring country. It is competitor discord, the automatic grudge from propinquity. Focus, typically, always deals with their canniness, sexual oddities, cowardice, drinking problems and, of course, their stupidity. Worldwide universal targets include stingy Jews, sexual Negroes, and thieving Gypsies. Estonians themselves mock dumb Chukchis (Russians), workaholic or ambitious Mulks — inhabitants of Viljandi country, a southern area said to be the cultural area of Estonia — and the rustic *talunik* or *talumee*, poor farmers. Freud once observed that there is no such thing as a joke, implying they are all true.

As I say, drinking or drunken Estonians figure in many jokes. Alcoholism is on the rise there. According to the Estonian Institute of Economic Research, Estonia in 2008 had the second highest alcohol consumption in Europe, France having the highest. (The institute found that the average Estonian drank 11.9 liters of alcohol that year.) It has been blamed for a rise in dissolute youth, lack of production, driving accidents, the wholesale plunging of the country's birth-rate and notion of national extinction, and general acedia.

The national slag coming from Russians on poor Estonians is that they are slow. You hear anti-Russian slurs coming from Estonians in the words *vanka* (from the name Ivan) and *tibla* (a slang corruption of Vitebsk.) *Saks* for German (from Saxons, Saxony) is used as a slightly sarcastic or mildly contemptuous term for any rich man or a "big shot." There is a good-natured nickname for Finns, *mehud*, literally "cranberry juicers," alluding to the Finnish fondness for that drink — a berry to a Finn is what paprika is to a Hungarian — but it is not as rude, contemptuous, or malicious as the words *itsked* (singular *itske*) from *Yidsky* or *Yitzhak* which is used for Jews. Nicknames feed the kind of jokes used to mock or lampoon the most proximate neighbors. You hear "Juhan Juurikas" (Johnny Root) used to cod Estonians — John Root or Johnny Tuber — the way that monikers like "Hans Wurst" and "Marmeladinger" and "Piefke" have long served for Germans. I've heard generic tags like "Reinis Bērziņš" applied to Latvians, "Vilkas Kazlauskas" to Lithuanians, "Päivi Heikkinen" to Finns.

I inquired about jokes. Jokes about a country, its people, are always revealing and, in my opinion, invariably true. Totalitarian countries tend to produce a lot of jokes. It is a form of *samizdat* or a chance to mock softly with impunity. There are many anti-Soviet jokes in which Russians are portrayed as a race of dirty, lazy, shiftless, irresponsible, drunken, dim-witted bums and thieves, Saturday night barroom brawlers, wife-beaters, rapists, and dunderheads. (It may be pointed out here — doubters may consult the UN Demographic Yearbook — that Estonia is officially *the* most accident-prone country in the world! Weirdly, Latvia comes in second.) Endless jokes of course are told about Estonian rustics, provincials, and boobs, jokes of the broad Chaucerian sort, what scholars of that English poet in fact call "estate" comedy — jokes about types. Finns tell thousands of gay jokes about Swedes. Swedes mock Finns for being country bumpkins Norwegians telling Finnish jokes invariably give the protagonist the very common Finnish name, Pekka, which means "penis'" in Norwegian. A negative stereotype of a Finnish guy is an alcoholic with an old-fashioned mustache, a bad fashion sense, and an abusive wife, who lives in the woods, hunts bears, listens to black metal, and whacks himself with birch switches in the sauna. Even Estonians find Finns withdrawn and solipsistic. Q: How can you tell the difference between a Finnish introvert and a Finnish extrovert? A: When he is talking to you, a Finnish introvert looks at his feet. A Finnish extrovert looks at yours. Latvians and Lithuanians are widely regarded by Estonians as lazier and more emotional than themselves. Latvians are commonly lampooned for adding milk to everything, indulging in sexual activities, for being too "soft on Communism" and maybe a bit too pro-Russian — or not quite anti-Russian enough. Lithuanians are considered an undisciplined, over-emotional and backward lot. There are a variety of Russian cabbage-jokes, often fart-related, that disparage Estonians. (*Boche*, of course, was an offensive slur in both World Wars I and II for German soldiers.)

Estonians, like Finns in Scandinavian jokes, are depicted as being stubborn, taciturn, dolt-headed, morose and perpetually tardy. The Estonian accent, with its sing-song lilt and lack of gender in grammar, is mocked, as is their common use of long vowels and consonants both in speech and orthography which leads to their not only satirized stereotype as being slow in speech, thinking and action but also lends itself to unwarranted but easily lampooned portrayals of blinkered approaches and comic inefficiency. More than anything, Russians mock Estonian slowness. Laziness. Aimlessness. The syndrome of lethargy they call *Oblomovshchina*, from the bed-ridden protagonist of the Goncharov novel. Estonians are seen as snail-paced. Over-deliberate. Dullards, with no tractive effort. A Russian joke has it that they do not teach physics in Estonian schools because any study on the subject of speed will confuse Estonians. (In

Italy, a slang word for slow-witted types is *"Polenta!"* — stodgy and un-stirrable.) "What is the favorite sport in Estonia?" a leering Russian asked me, his tongue resting on his lower lip as, grinning, he waited, ready to launch the punch line. "Sheep-racing!" he clucked. "Your idea for a bridge across the river is a good idea," says a smart Russian to an Estonian who becomes the brunt of his comic zap. "Your great-grandchildren will get around to building it." "I told some Estonian workers that they were slow," complained a Russian. "What did they reply?" "Nothing, but they beat me up the following day."

The jokes are of course in the main all rather vicious calumnies, sim-ply due the old saw, the greater the truth the greater the libel. "Did you hear about the Estonian tea-kettle? It will boil in a week." "They shit and flush a week later" goes another joke. The Latin slogan on the attractive Angel Bridge in Tartu bears the somewhat comic inscription: *Otium ref-icit vires* — "Strength is restored by resting."

One multi-barbed joke goes: two Estonians are sitting by a campfire. "Christmas is nice," says one of them. A half hour later, the other one replies, "Yes, Christmas is nice, but a woman is better." Another half hour later, the first man replies, "Yes, a woman is better, but Christmas comes more often." The book *Famous Estonian Comedians* will be found in the same section of the library as *Notable Irish Teetotalers, The Eskimo Book of Etiquette, A History of African Jockeys, Jewish Sports Legends, Ethiopian Tips on World Dominance,* and *Lawyers' Codes of Ethics.*

American hustle is surely no better than Estonian deliberateness, let me hasten to add. I have often thought that, to select one figure, Captain Kangaroo, star of the longest-running children's television program of its day, with his almost studied passivity would be my choice for a counter-balancing corrective, trying to set an example perhaps for children in the Sixties, Seventies, even Eighties. He was *the* definitive non-frantic man. No furious movements to create intensity. No nervous or anxiety-driven activity. (OK, there *was* Mr. Moose and Bunny Rabbit and the ping-pong balls!) No hysteria, no violence, no wigging out, simply measured speech, old persona, gentle mien. A dark unidentifiable uniform with large pockets. Carefully knotted tie. Tubby. He was a bumbler who, like the hapless Robert Benchley, another butt of innocent jokes, was always bested by gadgets. His passivity was purposeful and his soft-paced *modus operandi*, I suggest, a redress or remedy to American haste.

There are a lot of "Leida Peips" jokes in Estonia. A humble Estonian milkmaid, Leida — who incidentally was a real person — had some thirty years ago energetically devised certain techniques for super-efficient milking and monitoring cow nutrition. Rearing and training young heifers was her particular specialty. In the 1980s, after the Soviet Union awarded her prizes for milk yields, with Leonid Brezhnev personally giving her a medal, she attracted unwanted attention, was pitilessly mocked, and became a national figure of fun.[57] One typical wheeze about Leida Peips — a blue joke, needless to say — goes as follows:

> Sculptor: "*Leida juurde tuleb kunstnik ja utleg: Teeme büsti.*"
> Leida: "*Ei ole aega.*"
> Sculptor: "*Teeme büsti ruttu ära, see ei võta palju aega.*"
> Leida: "*Ewaeg ei ole püsti teimud, teeme ikka pikali.*"

Since there are no voiced plosives in Estonian, at least in word-initial position (not in the middle or at the end of words), the sound "*büsti*" can mean the genitive case of "*büst*," as well as "stand up" or "upright." Approaching Leida, the Sculptor earnestly says, "Let's make a bust [of you]" — a suggestion understood by her as "Let's do it." Leida replies, "I have no time." He responds, "We'll do the bust [do it standing up] quickly. It won't take long." So Leida candidly tells the Sculptor, "I've never done it standing up. Let's do it lying down instead."

I had the chance to speak with a Russian in a bookstore in Tallinn who with a lightness and an accompanying wink he hoped would be interpreted as charitable mockery, summing up Estonians, referred to the "Land of Fools" in Nikolai Tolstoy's fable of 1936, *The Golden Key, or The Adventures of Buratino* — Buratino, a wooden puppet, is famously the son of Pinocchio[58] — which is a legendary locale in literature and folklore where the foolish get scammed. Estonians are seen as embodying such types: rubes, naïfs, boobies, dolts, airheads, dingbats, and simpletons — we frequently come across the type in the stories of Gogol: Cherevik the cuckold; the barber Yakovlevich who is hen-pecked by his shrewish wife; Manilov in *Dead Souls,* the dreamy misguided manager — who on the one hand are half-wittedly fixated on the past, slavishly bound to their former miseries, and on the other dunces given to planning futures that never seem to appear. Old Varavka, chewing his beard and sipping seltzer with cognac, says the very same thing about Russia in Maxim Gorky's *Bystander,* when he cynically mutters, "Russia is inhabited by two tribes: the people of one tribe are able to think and speak only about the past; the people of the other, only about the future, and, inevitably, the very distant future. The present and tomorrow interests almost nobody."

Let us close this interlude of jokes with:

"Top 10 Reasons You Know You Are From Estonia:"

1. Sour cream tastes good on everything.
2. There can never be too much sarcasm.
3. You are disappointed that Jan Kross never won the Nobel Prize.
4. When someone asks you, "Where is Estonia?" your immediate reply is that it is located in Northern Europe, close to Finland.
5. You believe that any beverage below 31% is non-alcoholic.
6. Words like *ülemnõukogu* (the Supreme Soviet), *keskkõrvapõletik* (inflammation of the middle ear), and *põhjapolaarjoon* (Arctic Circle) sound perfectly pronounceable to you.
7. You bring crampons and oxygen to climb Egg Mountain (318 meters).
8. When in the emergency of running out of lightbulbs, you employ a potato.
9. You attend a song festival at least once a month either as a performer or as a spectator.
10. You and your wife have decided to have only four children because you read in the newspaper that one out of every five babies born in the world today is Russian.

Watchman, What of the Night?

I love to read the "agony columns" in newspapers (Sherlock Holmes, incidentally, also did the same), and before going anywhere I always turn first to the deliciously informative "Dangers and Annoyances" section of the *Lonely Planet Travel Guides* to learn what is sociologically diagnostic about a people. In that section, you will detect more than a small undercurrent of bawdiness in Estonia. Organized sex-tours are popular there, and the country has become a magnet for partying Swedes, Finns, Brits, and others who go there in search of cheap alcohol and sex. (In Fodor's priapic 664-page *The Men's Guide to Europe*, however, a features series published in the 1950s, the country of Estonia — I checked — is not mentioned even once.) Sex shops can be found in the larger cities. I heard that Estonia had the usual problem with young people and drugs, with one of the more popular items among the fast crowd there being Rohypnol — called "roofies" — which were usually connected to sexual assault in bars. Same-sex marriages are still banned in Estonia. But I do not see that would ever bother them. "Estonians are a nocturnal people and like to stay out all night," wrote a young Graham Greene in one of his Foreign Office circular dispatches on April 27, 1937. He certainly would have been one to know, for the novelist was an inveterate frequenter of brothels after his first visit to Estonia in 1934 when he visited "for no reason," he wrote in his memoir, *Ways of Escape*, "except to escape to somewhere new." As a matter of fact, it was one Baroness Budberg, a Baltic exile living in London and a mistress of the writer, H.G. Wells, who had recommended to young Greene a special brothel famed for its antiquity and discretion and which he sought out when he was staying at the Golden Lion Hotel on Harju St. in Tallinn, coincidentally the same street on which the Writer's Union Apartment was located where Sarah was staying when I first landed in that country, a grim little walk-up behind a crumbling courtyard just off the Old Town, a catafalque with a double door, big locks, and a passel of big weird keys. Estonians who generally enjoy off-color jokes do not seem to have any hang-ups at all about sex. Would this penchant be filed under "Scandinavian practices"? (Tina Brown in her book, *The Diana Chronicles*, mentions how Princess Diana, both when a young girl at Althorp House and then later when a princess at Buckingham Palace, often went below-stairs to have prurient chats with the help, a laxity, certainly disapproved of by the Queen. "Scandinavian practices" it was known as, after mildly depraved European royal families.) It seems that any latitudinarian act in the world is considered a "Scandinavian practice"!

Tallinn is the location of much seedy, organized crime in the late

Swedish writer Stieg Larsson's popular second novel, *The Girl Who Played with Fire*, published posthumously in Swedish in 2006 and in English in January 2009, which shows us an underworld of teenage prostitutes, sex-slaves, and abused prostitutes. Finnish-Estonian novelist Sofi Oksanen's noir fairy tale, *Purge* (2010), documenting the crime and cruelty of human trafficking in the former USSR, has an escaped Russian sex-slave collapse in front of a dilapidated house in Estonia. The recent sweeping phenomenon in Europe of a genre for which the Germans gave the name *Schwedenkrimi* — Swedish crime writing — fits nicely with the sort of intrigue that seems to resonate in the dark streets of urban Estonia. The direct terrorism threat to Estonia from any of the many fronts there are continues to be low; there are neither national nor international terrorist groups and, according to information from the Security Police, there are no supporters of such groups either, but one heard racist mumblings against Muslims and the shameless kind of bigotry that nowadays shamelessly passes in common parlance in the United States with complete impunity.

By the way, Estonia is — would have been — classic Graham Greene country. Although he had a strange fixation on the Catholic Church (and often slept with a crucifix under his pillow), he loved not only brothels, drugs, and spies, but seediness of the sort one comes across in this louche country where maleficence can be found in many corners, especially by any visitor with a vivid imagination. (He personally disliked Americans, however.) George Orwell complained of Greene, "He appears to share the idea which has been floating around ever since Baudelaire, that there is something rather *distingué* in being damned. Hell is a sort of high class nightclub, entry to which is reserved for Catholics."

There is a notable gay profile in the country. Estonia has traditionally always been one of the most relatively gay-friendly or at least tolerant of the former Soviet republics. (Sweden became the first country in the world to remove homosexuality as an illness and is considered to be one of the most gay-friendly in Europe.) During the Soviet period, Estonia became something of a Mecca for gay Muslims from Kazakhstan, Uzbekistan, Turkmenia, Tadzhikistan, and other Soviet Central Asian republics. Gays have found far more acceptance, or less harassment, bullying, and hate crime, in Tallinn and Tartu than in Alma-Ata, Frunze, Dushanbe,

Ashkhabad, Bokhara, or even Moscow or Leningrad. (W.H. Auden, who wrote a travel book in prose and verse in 1937 with Louis MacNeice, *Letters from Iceland*, often made the comment that in that country he found almost no homosexuality.) Adolf Hitler, remember, introduced a severe homosexuality law. Inversion only ceased to be a crime in Germany as late as 1969 when the severe Nazi "Article 151A" was dropped. When I was a student at the University of Virginia back in the late Sixties I remember that miscegenation was literally listed as a crime until 1967.

I am reminded of how the great traveler Bayard Taylor who, by the way, not only visited Iceland but also wrote on Swedish life, language, and literature — his long narrative poem, *Lars* and his *Northern Travel: Summer and Winter Pictures* are worth reading — was vilified for his 1870 novel, *Joseph and His Friend: A Story of Pennsylvania*, which has been called America's first gay novel.[59] The last and most unconventional of Taylor's four novels, it recounts the intimate, if disparate, relationship between two men, 20-year-old Joseph Asten and older Philip Held. ("I guess your thought, Philip," Joseph then said. "But the things easiest to do are sometimes the most impossible.") A hundred and fifty years may pass, but clearly the obloquy does not cease.

One small verse that Taylor penned in his poem, "The Metempsychosis of the Pine" aptly applies:

Another life the life of Day o'erwhelms;
    The Past from Present consciousness takes hue,
And we remember vast and cloudy realms
    Our feet have wandered through.

A Gay Pride march, held in mid-August in Tallinn, has become an annual event. It began in 2004. Tallinn was the first Baltic country, in fact, to hold such an event. However, violence marred 2006's Tallinn Pride march when 15 people were injured when they were pelted with stones, eggs, and excrement by weapon-wielding skinheads. Although homosexuality was legalized in the country in 1992, there is a radical hate fringe, mainly skinheads, that are still resolved to cause trouble. The Dutch Ambassador to Estonia, Hans Glaubitz, in 2006 scandalously (because publicly) asked to be reassigned to another country after his male partner claimed to have suffered repeated racist and homophobic abuse on the streets by the odd *vertikaalidioot dendrodebiilik* (loony jackass) or *intellektioponent fekaalovaal* (stupid shitwheel) passing by.

Glaubitz requested to be posted to Montreal Dutch Embassy following the insults to his partner, a black Cuban dancer. "It is not very nice to be regularly abused by drunk skinheads as a 'nigger' and to be continuously gawped at as if you had just stepped out of a UFO," he unappeasably declared. The turmoil of sexual ambiguity is bad enough — "My type doesn't know who I am," confessed Tennessee Williams, according to legend — but to be the cynosure of all eyes on the street and be screamed at? By the way, while 32 million people in the world presently have AIDS (one million in the USA), Estonia has the highest HIV and AIDS infection-rate in the European Union. (Is that why Finland is now criminalizing all sex purchases and services there?) Two of the more prominent gay clubs in Tallinn are Club 69, the first gay sauna ("40 lockers") in Estonia as well as the only one in the Baltics; and Club Angel, a member club ("Students and soldiers are welcome free of charge"). Another one I used to pass outside on Tartu called Mari — it means "berry" — allowed me to reflect on a possible ad slogan for them: "Eat, Drink, and be Mary." One day a student at the gym I sporadically attended in Tartu slyly questioned me brimming with amusement when I once mentioned the Russian bear. I discerned a distinct twinkle in his eye. Apparently, a "bear" in LGBT slang is a heavy-set, hairy invert who loves wearing flannel clothes and drinking beer. He himself was slight and had the delicate pointed face of a medieval page-boy, and I recall him winking and saying to me cryptically, "I say shop in your own closet."

I notice above I include Muslims with the marginals. Muslims in Estonia — in 2002, the most recent census, there were as few as 1,387 — are mainly Sunni Tatars and Shia Azeri whose ancestors immigrated to Estonia after the passing of old Livonia and Estonia into the Russian Empire in 1721 and who (the overwhelming majority) immigrated during the Soviet period (1940–1991). From 1860, the Tatar community started showing activity, their centre located in the city of Narva. A Muslim congregation (*Narva Muhamedi Kogudus*) was registered there under the independent Republic of Estonia in 1928 and a second one (*Tallinna Muhamedi Usuühing*) in Tallinn in 1939. A house built for funds received as donations was converted into a mosque in Narva. In 1940, the Soviet authorities typically banned the assembly of both congregations, and during the fire bombings of World War II in 1944 the buildings of the congregations were destroyed. There is no mosque in Tallinn, where an apartment has been adapted by them for prayer purposes. May not one suggest they would be good neighbors in spite of the vicious and hectoring racism against Islam not only found everywhere nowadays but that is, as I say, widely and popularly *accepted* — in many places literally encouraged — especially in the United States? Estonia could very well learn from a Muslim community. It was General Lew Wallace who, after spending twenty years in Constantinople, declared that while Christian drunkards were daily to be seen in the city streets, he never once saw a drunken Muslim. You will never find an ASPCA in Muslim countries — they do not need them — except in such cities there overrun by Christians. Alfred W. Martin in *Seven Great Bibles* insightfully notes, "I have observed in Turkish countries, the four corners of the slabs that cover graves are grooved to catch the rainfall, so that the birds may drink and sing over the places where their human brethren sleep." It is a testament to humanity. How can Americans *today* treat Arabs the way that Nazi treated Jews?

No world cities more than Tallinn or Tartu with their winter-jail of staggering darkness, the Bard's "solid darkness stain'd," could better evoke or more readily summon the lines from John Rechy's gay *City of Night*: "And ghostfaces, ghostwords, ghostrooms haunt me: Cities joined together by that emotional emptiness, blending with dark-city into a vastly stretching plain, into the city of the night of the soul…that world which I've loved and hated, that submerged gray world…"

The Russian Footprint

Today almost 27% of Estonia's inhabitants are Russian. Nearly all Estonians nowadays speak Russian. Russians born in Estonia before 1992 have to pass a language test and memorize the answers to questions about

Estonia's new constitution. In a very real sense, Russians deserve much of the contumely of Estonians. They were the Unjust Judges. The Soviet occupation, the KGB, the NKVD — choose your favorite — was unforgivingly endless, and Kremlin rule was brutal, picayune, unfair, cruel, officious, demanding, ignorant, belittling, smug, terrifying, and murderous. The Soviets occupied the best buildings, shipped out for themselves the very best local produce, raped the women, framed regulations, passed arbitrary laws and legislation, smashed the national statues and, worst of all, tried to break the spirit of the small nation they invaded. They uglified the country where they began to spread and in several cities, like Narva, are still resented for choking out the native populace like overreaching coreopsis in a perennial garden killing other plants. It is hard to believe but the Soviets in Estonia cracked down not only on the wearing of wedding rings but also the cultivation of tomatoes and roses, all elements of the bourgeois past. They sought to outlaw Christmas trees, as well, and, when they failed, compromised by officially calling them "New Year's Trees," a denominational vice that has lately reached America where craven pusillanimists, under political pressure from minority religions, have yielded to the bland "Happy Holidays!" over "Merry Christmas!" and "Fright Festival" for "Hallowe'en" with its Christian origins. (Ours is a country of freedom of religion, not freedom *from* religion!) The Russians also imported a Scandinavian Yuletide custom of exalting goats and deer plaited from straw, which they called "New Year's Goats." (In the USA, Estonian refugee intellectuals and cultural activists regarded as too "soft" on the Soviets, not quite hard-line enough, were nicknamed "New Year's Goats.") Many Russians in Estonia today seem to feel not the slightest compunction for the past savagery of their bullying, ass-kicking occupation. When one looks at the buildings they raised and left behind, or razed and did not leave behind, one may very well ask with Milan Kundera: is revolt against Communism aesthetic or ethical in character? It is a question well asked. What repelled the character Sabrina in the novel, *The Unbearable Lightness of Being*, "was not nearly so much the ugliness of the Communist world (ruined castles transferred into cow sheds) as the mask of beauty it tried to wear — in other words, Communist kitsch." Appearance here was being fobbed off as reality. Kundera believes kitsch to be the absolute *denial* of ugliness, excluding everything from its purview which is essentially unacceptable in human existence. "Shit is a more onerous theological problem than is evil," Kundera bitterly wrote. "Since God gave man freedom, we can, if need be, accept the idea that He is not responsible for man's crimes." The idiotic Soviet tautology, "Long live life," as you can imagine, is a joke to every thinking Estonian.

Incidentally, Kundera who extols the recognition of a new, postwar Europe, "born of an enormous defeat unparalleled in its history," as he says, has also expressed in 2010 the somewhat disconsolate belief that as it became liberated it was also somewhat smothered, even oppressed, by the domination of the United States and Russia.

Russians and Estonians. Owls and crows. The deep hatred for each other is elemental. To the crow, the owl — whose range coincides with theirs across all continents — is its chief terror and nightmare. The enemy, well-identified, is always nearby. Crows who are survivors and sleep in groups at night scream less to elicit anger than to summon help as they try to drive predators away by force of numbers, swarming — "mobbing," it is called — any invader with utter contempt. "Crow remembers Owl's transgressions all the day of its life," notes Charles Fergus in *The Wingless Crow*. I composed a limerick on Russian/Estonian relations:

There was a man from Estonia
Who thought Russians couldn't be phonier
As a taunt at each pass
He pulled out of his ass
A flaming red-leaf begonia.

We attended a small dinner party in Tallinn toward the end of my stay. It went poorly. I got into a heated exchange with a pompous Jew from Vilnius who claimed to be "like za art cridic Bernard Berenson, of the 'Jewish aristocracy.'" I had to laugh, being a Bostonian myself and knowing full well that Berenson with his salty intolerance and puffed-up credentials had been nothing but a self-mythologizing, opportunistic, bullshit-slinging, jumped-up little Litvak who had entirely reinvented himself in America and got his start in life as a so-called "connoisseur" and "art historian" by hustling pictures like a common pimp for the eccentric, trusting, and sporadically gullible millionaire, Isabella Stewart Gardner. Mr. Maggid — this dinner-party poltroon — was no more a distinguished European aristocrat than that vulgar little speedball, sweaty Sammy Glick in Budd Schulberg's *What Makes Sammy Run*. Born in the shtetl of Butrimonys now in the Alytus district in remote Lithuania, Bernhard Valvrojenski — the family later fabricated the name Berenson — was not only a peasant whose immigrant father was a peddler of junk and jumble who went door to door in the slums of Boston's grubby North End hawking his wares but, as a penniless student at Harvard, owed his presence there to wealthy Bostonians impressed by his gift for languages. Berenson's was an entirely *derivative* life. He came into the world with two hands already flexed to grab and taloned to grip. As literary critic Alfred Kazin, himself a Jew, once wrote, "Being a Jewish aristocrat does not diminish one's foreignness but transfers it to another plane — like the American Negro who went South with a turban on his head and was welcomed everywhere as a foreign potentate." So I knew that the loud, shoe-cracking, self-important European dwarf with the ascot opposite me at the party was a phony himself.

What caused the contretemps with Maggid was that he claimed that Ashkenazi Jews, descendants all of eighth-century converts, the Khazars, immigrated to Europe from the Caucasus, and then proceeded to insist that his argument refuted anti-Semitism by showing that European Jews were not even related to those Jews whom anti-Semites blame for killing Christ. I had heard the theory before. It had been proposed by Arthur Koestler in his book *The Thirteenth Tribe* (1976), an idea which I pointed out to Maggid was popular not only with the Arabs, since it implied that all of the many European Jews settling in Israel were returning to the wrong homeland, but it also delighted the neo-Nazis, since it suggested that Diaspora Jews constituted a pseudo-nation constructed on a racial myth, and that Jews should either immigrate to Israel or assimilate — and where had that got them with the Soviets? I have already alluded to that kind of sanctimonious ornithologist who knows only one bird. Maggid was this fellow in the flesh, except that in the case with my colleague he was neither tall nor imposing nor dramatic. He was pushy and wore a tangerine ascot and his right hand was paralyzed into a claw. "Ze Nahahzis vere fah, fah vooooooorse zhan ze Sawietzs," declared Maggid as if by fiat and theatrically raised and knocked back his drink with a periodic flourish as if that were the end of it. His gassy exhalation, as he breathed on me, wheeze, waft, whisper, made his words more offensive. "Rabbis all have bad breath," comedian Mel Brooks once complained. "There was no surviving rabbi's breath. God knows what they ate…their breath would wither your face."[60] Well, Maggid's was just as bad. I looked at his fox-red hair and clipped vanity. Did this man's wacky Eurocentric elitism extend as far as rewriting history and making himself a Khazar prince? He wore glasses, kept ducking up and down, and resembled one of those squeezable rubber toys one sees that are fashioned with a hideous softness called phthalates. "Total horseshit," I said. "Do you honestly think that, simply because you're Jewish, Lenin was somehow kinder than Hitler? The Soviets enslaved this country for half a *century*. Occupied it by iron rule! You believe that was an extended vacation?" I was a panegyrist for neither dictator, I can promise you, but a non-sequitur couched in a last unforgiving afterthought of his wounded me. "John Demjanjuk — I-van zet Tewwible — vas an American. A guard at Sobibor. So you defend harbowing that goon, alzo?" "Demjanjuk was a Ukrainian Russian who initially fought on the Soviet side but agreed to work for the German SS after being captured in 1941," I replied. "After several years in a displaced persons camp in Germany, he later settled in Ohio and worked in an auto factory, according to all court findings." It got all heated, I have to admit, as my weirdly presumptuous little counterpart began theatrically reciting the racial aspects of war, discounting the pain suffered by every single race except his own. I have always believed that the same qualities that go into charming people also go into deceiving them.

It was later that Demjanjuk, a 91-year-old man supine on a gurney, was wheeled out of court and sent to jail. Revenge as justice. The Law of Talion, one of the most bankrupt and perverse concepts ever conceived, is to me part of the reason why Jewish karma is so heavily-laden with noxious fumes, and why any religion that makes a practice of forgiveness is the only one to which to cling. Doubtless, the teenager Jesus saw too much of this and became Christ the tiger, overturning the Mosaic laws and preaching love, where once there had been vengeance. Israel can never be a whole or integrated country for this reason. I notice that the absence of vengeance in Vietnam has contributed to its prosperity.

Novelist William Goldman once said, "I have always understood the Nazis because I am of that sort by nature." As I saw it, Maggid was one of those sharp-elbowed and aggressive herberts one cannot avoid in life who out of perverse malignity immediately assumes an extra-level knowledge of things, an intolerable presumption of "knowingness" that is born more of ego than anything else. It was not conspiracy theory he was dishing out, merely the idea that any obvious thing, by dint of being obvious, cannot be the truth, rather only what is behind it, the chapter-and-verse of which could be smugly divulged only by someone who knows what is really going on. It is the left-behinds' panicky refuge against a dizzily changing modern world. *Dietrology,* a term extrapolated by one Alisdair Spark meaning the study of what is behind something — *dietro* (Italian) means behind — generously applied here, no question about it.

Queerly, Maggid was later to give me a cinematic epiphany. I realized upon reflection (by the algebra of having met him) that it was the savagely cruel, surreptitiously subversive zipperhead Mel and not at all the loudmouthed country bumpkin, an Arkansas hobo, "Lonesome" Rhodes in the movie, *A Face in the Crowd* — I have already alluded to this movie as being a masterpiece, one we watched six or seven times on cold Estonian nights on illegal free-streaming video — that is the truly evil one of the many negative characters in that movie. Pay attention next time you watch it to see how silent, calculating, and envious the basically scorned character Mel Miller works ("All mild men are vicious," "He's dangerous," "I think I'll just be a pal and hope he chokes on a Vitajex pill") and how subtly vicious is his continued connivance to detract, to subvert, to kill.

I would also be reminded of Maggid when, after years of deceit and subterfuge, it was finally disclosed in November 2009 that those secret hideout prisons that had been staked out abroad by the Bush administration — CIA torture centers for Muslim terrorists — were located, characteristically from my point of view, in creepy dark, Soviet-haunted Vilnius, Lithuania, to which access, even after the disclosure, was still not given. The buildings were once a riding academy. This scandalous breach of all ethics, never mind human decency, was kept well-hidden from public knowledge for years.[61] No reporter ever investigated. But the obsequious American press not only allowed an illegitimately elected president to get away with it, in their craven way they tacitly allowed that same president to wage an illegal and barbaric war on an innocent country; I wish I had access to power to whistle-blow it all. I was not only without access to power. I was stuck instead in remote Estonia and ignorant of my own government's vile machinations. As a thug says in an old Jack Benny movie, *The Horn Blows at Midnight*, "If only I had of knew."

Former Vice-President Dick Cheney has never backed off from his deranged advocacy of "enhanced interrogation techniques," or EIT, declaring on Fox Network in August 31, 2009 that, regarding the rendition of human beings — it might have been 1209 and he was an official inquisitor — he was actually "proud of" torturing such prisoners as Khalid Sheikh Mohammed, the alleged organizer of the 9/11 attacks — or as al-Qaeda called those flying assaults, the "Holy Tuesday" planes operation — who was waterboarded 183 times. Cheney went so far as to state, in one particularly chilling remark, that he fully supported those torturers who went *beyond* their instructions and engaged in interrogation methods that even the Bush White House had refused to pronounce legal. "It was good policy," this human ferret proclaimed. "It was properly carried out. It worked very, very well." He sounded in this almost *exactly* like the notorious Soviet Chief of Secret Police and Security under Josef Stalin, Lavrentiy P. Beria — the two even *look* alike — who with his weasely cunning and almost diabolical contempt for humanity was responsible for the deaths of countless of thousands of Russians but in the end got what he deserved when he was brought to trial in 1953 and summarily shot. When the diabolical Beria was alive and in charge of operations, every room in the Soviet bloc was potentially "Room 101," the torture chamber mentioned in George Orwell's novel, *Nineteen Eighty-Four* in the Ministry of Love in which the Party attempts to subject a person to his or her own nightmare, fear, or phobia.[62]

Many arguments have been advanced for torture. Forget that it is barbaric, that it is counter-productive, and that our own soldiers when caught will in turn be abused in the same fashion — it is immoral and illegal. On what grounds is it defended — its effectiveness? All criminal activity is undertaken to advance the interests of the perpetrator. Stealing results in riches, plagiarism in advancement, and fraud in success. That such savage treatment can be discussed in an open forum shows how truly bankrupt we have become in this country.

There is an entire roll-call of anti-human savagery. Secretary of defense Donald Rumsfeld literally micromanaged ("Make sure this happens!") the use of torture at Guantanamo and Abu Ghraib, leading to a landmark lawsuit by the ACLU in May 2005. Condoleezza Rice, President Bush's Secretary of State and personal lapdog, an obsequious marionette and astonishing incompetent, on April 23, 2009 personally approved a CIA request to use "waterboarding" and other harsh interrogation techniques. Jose Rodriguez Jr., the leader of counterterrorism for the C.I.A. from 2002-2005 when Khalid Shaikh Mohammed and other al Qaeda leaders were captured, was directly responsible for driving the CIA clandestine activity. (It was Rodriguez, who also ordered the destruction of interrogation videos.) Then flabby John Yoo, the former Bush Justice Department lawyer/lapdog and author of the infamous "torture memos," twisted the Constitution and the Geneva Conventions into an unrecognizable mess to excuse all torture. William Haynes, Paul Wolfowitz, George Tenant — they were all dirty, all complicit, all beating the drum for the most medieval cruelty, all in direct violation of the Nuremberg Code of Ethics.

I beheld with despair an almost gleeful defense of torture from the fascist harridans, drumbeating Ann Coulter and dopey Laura Ingraham, as well as from the likes of the rubber-lipped Bill O'Reilly, the living antonym to Edward R. Murrow and a sectarian cheapjack on the Fox News Network, "whose knowledge of history," according to MSNBC's Keith Olbermann, "seems have to been drawn in equal parts from comic books and the German apologists after the Second World War."

Lawyer Alan M. Dershowitz is smugly in full agreement with the diabolical Cheney regarding torture. This hustlingly ambitious, jumped-up gnat-catcher and argumentative logic-chopper who races to enter every hole like a rat up a drainpipe has cynically gone on record as saying that *in extremis* torture should be used[63] — used for "mass terrorism," Arabs, needless to say, apparently not convicted traitors like the Israeli spy, Jonathan Pollard, the American Navy employee/intelligence analyst who was convicted and received a life sentence in 1987 for spying for Israel, stealing classified documents, and also selling information to Pakistan on multiple occasions, not out of any altruism but strictly for money —

cash — and diamond and sapphire rings. A terrorist whose treason endangered U.S. combat forces, according to Caspar Weinberger, Secretary of Defense in the Reagan administration, Pollard finds a continuing ally and friend not only in Dershowitz who to this very day continues to defend and support him but also in someone as high-ranking as the Prime Minister of Israel, Benjamin Netanyahu, who has repeatedly voiced particularly strong support for Pollard, even visiting the traitor in prison in 2002. Israel granted Pollard citizenship in 1995, while publicly denying for thirteen years — lying outright — that the man was an Israeli spy. "I think that if we ever confronted an actual case of imminent mass terrorism that could be prevented by the infliction of torture, we" — *we!* — "would use torture (even lethal torture) and the public would favor its use," asserts Dershowitz. The frenetically mulish making the savage legal sounds even more grotesque. What sort of villainous and delinquent age do we live in? "Judges should have to issue a 'torture warrant' in each case," Dershowitz went on to say with hairs-splitting distinction on November 8, 2001 in a commentary for the *Los Angeles Times*. "Thus we would not be winking an eye of quiet approval at torture while publicly condemning it."

It was in the small town of Uttoxeter that old Dr. Samuel Johnson, age 70, stood bareheaded in the pouring rain for an hour, exposing himself in the marketplace to the sneers of passersby at a time of high business, as penance for a sin of disobedience that he committed earlier on that spot against his father, the *only one*, he explained, that he had ever committed against him. His father, confined by illness, had begged him to take his place to sell books at a stall, which young Sam had refused to do. This was back in 1779. What a different sensibility exists today.

We regress, we devolve, we go downward.

Before I left the country, I visited with Sarah the Soviet-bloc flat she was going to rent for her last few months there, as the apartment that we were renting in Tartu was too expensive. She was back in the Mooste area. The flat was set in a complex of ugly rectangular block apartments — *art brut* is too lovely a phrase — built out of part of what was a large factory that produced vodka. The buildings set up to house collective farm-workers during the Soviet period had become an eye-sore, crumbling concrete, the mindless proliferation of similar units, dark deserted hallways of stained concrete, block stairways with metal railings, and not a lift or an elevator. It was a Gradgrindian delight that had all of the reduced, unadorned utilitarianism of those rebarbative public buildings of Coketown described in Charles Dickens' *Hard Times*. The place was located in a "village" artificially created from a large private estate. There was no town square, no church, and no stores except for a very small shop selling beer, chips, preserved pork, cookies, candy, hard liquor, some stationery, and various hygiene items, and it was there that Sarah bought the small wursts, spaghetti with Felix spaghetti sauce, sweet mustard squeezed from a tube, and *Saku Tume* (dark porter) that she lived on. A shabby post office was run by one woman with a receding hairline and a crinkly grin who looked like the actor Martin Balsam who himself looked like a common meat-cutter. She was absolutely the slowest human being on the planet; after licking the stamps for you would take seventeen years to stick it on the envelope.

We had been drily told that the flat to be rented was attractive, an assurance I consigned, with experience, to "The check is in the mail" and "There will be peace in our time" and "My knowledge of nymphets is purely scholarly," *Lolita*-author Vladimir Nabokov's solemn affirmation to the public after writing that novel. The flat Sarah chose to take was fitted out with hysterical wallpaper showing a different pattern for each room: loud purple with gold, heliotrope with green, pink circles with yellow. There was a fake parquet floor insanely glossed under a cheap chandelier. The doors were very cheap — punky wood — the sort of which cigar boxes are made, and not one door to any of the rooms closed properly. It was especially disheartening to see that Sarah would have no refrigerator to keep food, no stove to cook on and only a small hot-water pot to make coffee or heat soup. A single electric burner stood lonely on a counter in the minuscule kitchen. The bathtub was gaily stained around the rim in rusted Rothko-orange. For food in summer, she had to purchase a small hotel-room-sized refrigerator. Of the three or so months that she lived in that flat, there was no hot water for the span of one entire month, the explanation when she complained about it to the landlord being that it was (a) the "summer regime" and (b) a water main was being fixed. The toilet was bizarre to the point that directly in the center of the bowl there rose an actual ledge or landing (!) so that, until a weak stream of water carried off whatever was there into a very dark narrow hole, it uniquely remained.

Sarah with her bright vision was daunted by neither inconvenience nor irritation. She who received her B.F.A. from University of Pennsylvania, her C.F.A. from the Pennsylvania Academy of the Fine Arts, and her M.F.A from Indiana University, educated, not merely trained, was also never satisfied to follow strict academic rules but trusted her own contrivances, setting up her tall easel in the unlikeliest places in Estonia — balancing on a slippery angle in a courtyard; perched at a high oriel window of a dark well of a staircase; plunked down in the midst of a marshy meadow — always turned out brilliant painting after painting. She would travel to survey what she needed to see and always sensed what, in seeing, she chose to select of what to record. She often worked to music on headphones, sometimes in deathly silence. She banked on her confidence no matter what she took on and traveled widely, from Põlvama to Lake Peipsi to Rõuge to Tartu to Muhu Island, to Riga and to Basle to the upper reaches of Finland and even by bus to and from St. Petersburg, where the wind blows from four directions, according to Gogol, but where, in spite of that, Sarah executed several good paintings. When the mood was right, we used to line up all of her paintings against the wall in our flat and on certain nights — seated, listening to music, sipping ice-cold vodka — choose among her treasures what we best liked of her canvases: *Pair of Oak Trees in Evening, Road to Viisil with Airplane Trail, Manor House, Mooste, Suurjärv Lake, Rouge, Window View of Sunset at Tamse, Muhu Island*, and, among my favorites, *Courtyard in Tallinn, Estonia* and *St. Nicholas Church Tallinn*. I often thought of the lovely lines from a Stephen Spender poem whenever watching this beautiful woman deftly ply her brush:

Again, again, I see this form repeated:

The bare shadow of a rock outlined
Against the sky; declining gently to
An elbow; then the scooped descent
From the elbow to the wrist of a hand that rests
On the plain.
    Again, again,

That arm outstretched from the high shoulder
And leaning on the land.
   As though the torsoed
Gods, with heads and lower limbs broken off,
Plunged in the sky, or buried under earth,
Had yet left arms extended here as pointers
Between the sun and plain:
   had made this landscape
Human, like Greek steles, where the dying
Are changed to stone on a gesture of curved air,
Lingering in their infinite departure.[64]

Sarah managed to catch the many moods of the many places through which and to which she traveled, city and country, capturing on canvas various landscape, passages, Finnish and Swedish moments, even the spectral Russian touches here and there. Needless to say, it is essential to the Estonian psyche to repeat, and not without the distinct sound of something like self-convincing force in it, that this was not Russia. State-regulated aspects of Estonia — like hospitals and health care — are still as yet unreformed. As had been pointed out, Estonia was briefly, almost too fleetingly to remark upon, an *independent* republic between the two World Wars. It is a fact people tend to forget. Hope is aligned to reachable goals. The memory for a market economy to Finland has also been a great boon to the Estonian dream of freedom. During the Soviet occupation, Estonians could watch Finnish television, when no other Soviet territory could do so. So much still remains to grow taller.

Comparisons between Estonia and Finland, within hailing distance across the narrowest water, are inevitable. Again, Estonia suffers in the match. Of the Top Ten TV-Owning Countries, Finland — according to the *World Telecommunication Development Report*, 2002 — is impressively the 8th. (Qatar is first, USA second.) Estonia can say that it does come in 8th in the Top Ten Radio-Owning countries. Finland, second only to the United States, I believe, in the number of inventions, can also boast as having the 10th fastest rail journey in the world, Salo to Karjaa, as well as being officially (ESI ranking) the *most* environmentally friendly country in the entire world. (Weirdly, Finland has the highest crime-rate in the world.) Neighboring Norway, Denmark, and Sweden are, surprisingly, at least to me, the 2nd, 5th, and 10th richest countries in the world. I have to state that as of the year 2010 Estonia in this department ranks a relatively lowly 106, sandwiched between Paraguay and Honduras.

We Matter, We Count, We Belong

It is a point of pride for Estonians, however, that they are now EU members. Sweden and Finland heavily invest in Estonia. Estonia's GDP growth is currently running at 10% per year, putting it up with the burgeoning ranks of China and India, without having any of those country's festering ills. The standard of living grows. But it needs to grow. Lennart Meri, Estonia's first independent, reform-minded president, who died in 2006 — he once referred to politicians who got rich while in office as "scum on the surface of the state cauldron" — once held an apologetic press conference within a public toilet when he learned that a Japanese diplomat had complained about Estonia's then-appalling (though typically Soviet) public restrooms. Much tension without a doubt could be alleviated by depoliticizing the world that we all live in, let's face it. I have come to believe that for the most part politics is virtually *all* theater. When former president Bill Clinton was asked personally by Kim Jong Il to come cap in hand to North Korea in August 2009 to ask for, almost to kowtow to get, the release of the two American women, Euna Lee and Laura Ling, who had been captured the previous March and who had been harshly sentenced to 12 years of hard labor as spies, I saw it as the performance it was, pure drama, the kind of public cadillacking the toady Clinton, a lifelong dyed-in-the-wool applause-freak, could never pass up. Images make up the drama of confrontation, positive or negative, at every turn.

Czech-English Cambridge University philosopher, anthropologist, and historian Ernest Gellner (1925-1995) found a tentative hope for a certain muting or softening of nationalist passion in affluent late-industrial societies, a suggestion that he offered as half speculation, half wish-fulfillment, and saw as perhaps endowed with a small dose of factual support, as well. In his *Nations and Nationalism* (1983) and in *Encounters with Nationalism* (1994), Gellner suggested that the objective conditions of modern industrialism and technology might create a world-wide cultural and linguistic standardization that would reduce the semantic differences between languages and with luck also lead to an eventual toning-down of nationalistic hostilities and brutal ongoing rivalries that never end.

As I say, Gellner suggested in *Encounters with Nationalism* that late industrialism "leads to a diminution of the intensity of ethnic sentiments and hostilities," and that "generalized affluence diminishes intensity of hatreds, and gives everybody that much more to lose in case of violent conflict." In other words, grossly to oversimplify and somewhat vulgar-ize Gellner's own rather subtle, guarded, and tentative speculations, if there initially had been more of an all-pervasive "McWorld" culture of widespread Americanized hedonistic consumerist materialism in Leba-non, Bosnia, Kosovo, Rwanda and East Timor, people in those places on all sides might have been less interested in both risking their comforts and pleasures and interrupting their careers and amusements with jihāds and ethnic cleansings. In Gellner's admittedly hopeful scenario, not only would generalized affluence make wealthy consumers increasingly reluc-tant to sacrifice their comforts and standard of living in ethnic wars and bitter conflicts and open hostilities, but the increasing standardization and homogenization of worldwide industrial consumer society would render national cultures pretty much alike, as well. It is an argument.

Worldwide industrial consumer society if Gellner was right, would eventually erode many of the "serious" cultural differences — e.g., Medi-terranean and "Third World" attitudes about the proper role and behav-ior of women and girls, or the sacred duty of all right-thinking children of the Fatherland to be everlastingly on watch against our age-old evil, dastardly, brutal, satanic Russian, German, Greek, Turkish, Hungarian, Romanian, Serb, Croat, Arab, Israeli, Muslim or Christian enemies. As Rutgers University political science professor Benjamin R. Barber put it in *Jihad vs. McWorld* (1995), the two contending world-wide cultural and social trends in our day are "McWorld versus Jihād," international corporate capitalism mesmerizing and homogenizing people everywhere with fast music, fast computers, fast food, MTV, Macintosh and Mc-Donald's, pressing all the world's nations into one commercially homogeneous world-wide theme-park, versus a resurgence of fanatical, blood-thirsty ethnic, tribal, and religious militancies — both of which forces Barber sees as inimical to democracy and to civic values. As I have noted, however, Gellner hoped that "McWorld" would eventually win out over "Jihād," or at least dampen its fervor in advanced industrial countries, and that "McWorld" might not be too hostile to North American and Northwestern-European style democratic and civic values.

I myself also see a third cultural force arising, in competition with both "Jihād" and "McWorld," that neither Gellner nor Barber pay much attention to but I myself personally find generally fascinating and even possibly hopeful: the tendency of "McDonaldization" to create its own antithesis in a compensatory aesthetic and pop-cultural — but largely non-political — revival of ethnic and cultural "local color" to relieve the deadly stifling monotony and boredom of a "nothing but McDonald's everywhere you go, all the world's airports look exactly the same" homogenization by the cultivation of local cuisines, costumes, dances, folk-songs, architectural styles, etc. A world-wide industrial consumer-culture might well erode many of the "serious," "profound," and "sacred" cultural traits that grim, humorless nationalist and religious fanatics of our planet's hundred blooming "Jihāds" cherish: the insistence that women wear the veil in public or at least dress in mourning for five years after their husbands have died, narrow-minded restrictions on the personal freedoms and career choices of girls as opposed to boys; the Muslim fundamentalist stoning of adulterers to death and chopping off of thieves' hands; the Hindu caste system; the excesses of Israeli torture, wholesale thieving of Arab land, and insolent, illegal building; the sadistic persecution and oppression of homosexuals and lesbians in so many countries; angry and humorless litanies of the everlasting hostility; perfidy, and untrustworthiness of our nation's age-old national enemies (Russians, Germans, Serbs, Croats, Greeks, Turks, Arabs, Indians, Pakistanis, Vietnamese, Cambodians, Chinese, Japanese, whomever). Such emotional, cultural, and political garbage the world indeed would be far better off without, as far as I am concerned. At the same time, though, there does seem to be a resurgence of what might be called the "light," "fun," or "decorative" side of ethnic and national cultures — Estonians for whom, unpredictably, it may seem, "play" is an important cultural *topos* tend strongly to such celebrations — foods, festivals, dances, songs, costumes, etc., all cultivated largely in a light-hearted disregard of the political demagogues and warlords, of political thugs, *trumbeniks*, fat dictators, and religious fanatics, of the booming-voiced lachrymose nationalist and super-patriotic orators. (Native Estonian folk costumes are almost archetypally European, with women wearing colorful stockings, festive ornamented aprons, glass and stone beads, and tall headgear almost like mitres!) This "light," "fun" compulsion with its earnest cultivation of traditional intricacies and subtleties of food, song, and dance, may well be cultivated by the most "cosmopolitan" and "Americanized" members of various national and ethnic cultures, the ones most indifferent or even actively hostile to their own group's "Jihād" zealots.

I have personally observed that this dynamic seems in fact to operate within East European refugee and émigré diasporas in North America. Many of the most "hard-shell" Cold War-era émigré politicians, ideologues, and journalists, I have noticed over the years, have a drab, mousy, dowdy cultural style, an aura of seedy old-fashioned 1930s' or 1940s' suits and of wives in 1950s' hairdos, while the diligent cultivators of Estonian, Lithuanian, Latvian, Ukrainian, etc. cultural and "fun" ethnicity, such as the people actively involved in the annual New York springtime *Eesti Kultuuripäevad* —"Estonian Culture Days" — festivals, are serenely non-political or sometimes even openly at ideological odds with the "hard-shell" ethnic politicians. In Eastern Europe itself, my impression has been that there is indeed a sharp cultural life-style gulf between the "political" and "cultural" nationalists, with neither side exactly too enamored of the other. The cultural enthusiasts, as I see it, have usually been far less interested than the professional political patriots of their respective countries in madly demanding the expulsion of all Arabs from Israel, all Hungarians from Romania, all Muslims from India, all Tamils from Sri Lanka, all Bosnians from Serbia, all Roma (Gypsies) from the Czech Republic, all Poles from Lithuania, all Russians from Estonia or Latvia. The "culturals" have been far less insistent than the "politicals" on the innate incurable eternal genetic untrustworthiness and perfidiousness of all members of one's traditional enemy or "other" nation. In return, the "politicals" often regard the "culturals" as less than perfectly patriotic or national. They are stuck in the middle of old dead mud.

Younger Than the USA

Still, Estonia, by one queer definition, is a *young* country, which is a paradox I, in pointing out, ask you to consider. When Hugh Kenner in his book, *A Homemade World* explains how the poetry of T.S. Eliot in the 1920s "reads like a compendium of a decade's symbols" and that "no other twentieth-century decade has yielded in that way to being summed up in images" — and he also finds in passing the fictions of Hemingway and Fitzgerald in being as equally rich as equally powerful — he was pointing to the experience of the kind of vital modernity that gave the United States a dimension of *experience*. It should be remembered that Gertrude Stein, their stubborn expatriate friend in Paris, never ceased to go on affirming that the unalloyed preoccupation of her writing was with America — note — "*the oldest country in the world*," as she said, "*because it has been living in the twentieth century longer than any other country*" [my italics] — by which she meant since the Civil War. Beyond that, we do in fact have the oldest Constitution of any country on earth. The United States. In a very real sense, it is less a country than it is a world. As the poet Samuel Taylor Coleridge once cogently put it: "A nation of a hundred millions of freemen, stretching from the Atlantic to the Pacific, living under the laws of Alfred and speaking the language of Shakespeare and Milton, is an august conception." There is in the vast and reinvigorated dream of America, its bold refusal of obstacles, its energy, its accommodating temperament, its virtuosity of accomplishment, its incessant even if often blundering optimism and openness so often embodied in the energetic heroines of Henry James — what George Bemberg was getting at in his book, *The American Abel and His Brother Cain* — a hard, bullish affirmation. It is this mythic sense of a toadless Eden that communicates at least the notions of a modern narrative. We have bullheadedly refused to trace the old paths, even if the new ones can lead to recklessness. I look at the young people of Estonia, "Generation E," as the young adults of Europe are generally referred to these days and for whom the whole continent of Europe is now said to be home, with their mobile phones — and the GSM system "makes it possible to send a 'txt msg' to any user on any network in any GSM country," according to John Reid in *The United States of Europe* — and notice that English is overridingly the main language. The language of Eurovision songs. The language of Anti-American rallies. The language of text-messaging. The language of business. The language of flirting. The language of airports. The language of the Internet. The language of Facebook.

I have alluded above to Shakespeare. In his plays, he never once mentions Estonia. He mentions Africa, the Netherlands, Tripoli, even Mexico. He certainly mentions Denmark. He refers to Arabia, Ephesus (Turkey), Belgia, the "Bermoothes" (Bermuda) in *The Tempest*, and he makes reference even to a land that the Anthropophagi inhabit, probably "India Orientalis," maybe southern Africa. He sets part of *Othello* in Cyprus. In *The Comedy of Errors* he even mentions America[65]. Still, as we all know, his geography was wonky. He notoriously gave Bohemia a coastline in *The Winter's Tale*. (The country, needless to say, is landlocked.) He mistakenly refers to Verona and Milan as seaports in *The Two Gentlemen of Verona*; in *All's Well That Ends Well* he suggests that a journey from Paris to Northern Spain would pass through Italy; and in *Timon of Athens* he believes that there are such substantial tides in the Mediterranean Sea that they take place once instead of twice a day. Not once, by the way, either in *The Merchant of Venice* or in *Othello* are the canals of Venice mentioned. So much for the travelogue. It is up to you whether these are gaffes. But could he not have had the well-traveled Prince Hamlet at least once — on some college or court errand or other — dodge up to Esthonia?

I would like to add, being a Cape Codder, that Shakespeare even alludes to my wee peninsula, at least indirectly. In one of the Bard's last plays, *Henry VIII*, the Porter — perhaps bawdily — inquires, "Have we some strange Indian with the great tool come to court, the women so besiege us?" It is very likely that this figure was inspired by Epenau, a Wampanoag Indian from the Cape who was captured and brought to England as a curiosity in 1611. (Shakespeare was a vibrant 47 in that year.) Epenau found his way home three years later, tricking his captors into bringing him back to Cape Cod with false claims of gold ore. So the punch-list is quite long of named territories in Shakespeare.

Still, he never mentions Estonia.

Robots Look Straight Ahead

There is a terrible inflexibility in the Estonian personality, which I found to be too often suspicious, removed, buttoned-up, and mum. It involves a kind of horrible *proceduralism*. A native once assured me that in that country once something is written down on paper, a rule, a law, say, or a policy, it then becomes gospel, come hell or high water. I saw repeated there in the kind of doltish functionary mind a need to be in command in the same way Ernest Hemingway said he liked to hunt because he liked to kill. One morning, Sarah and I set out to take a bus from Tartu to Riga, about a three-hour trip. We had our bus tickets in hand, having purchased them the day before. What we had not reckoned on was the Daylight Savings Time (April 1). We found to our dismay that we had missed the bus, but since the tickets were expensive — $50 each — we inquired of a bus driver if we could use the same ones the next day. He shrugged. We approached a husky lady in the ticket office and pleaded our case, while a lot of impotent, po-faced Estonians standing by merely ogled us.

The verdict was: *Nothing doing!*

We sat down on a bench, trying to deliberate. Not quite certain what to do but determined not to make a scene — looking to be civil — we let some time pass, stacking pencils, so to speak. A smug oaf sitting next to us was disgustingly wolfing a big sandwich and gulping a drink. As he ate, he moved his elbows as if he were shoving his way through a crowd. To my mind, outside of picnic circumstances, there is nothing that can quite match for crudeness, for appalling lack of manners, the utter and undisguised piggery, of a vulgarian nonchalantly eating in public in a big way, the near-equivalent to me of toilet matters. The smacking sounds of satisfaction, the finger-sucking, the burps, the graceless ham-handed *cluelessness* of the thing is beyond description. (Damned close is any Neanderthal in a closed public space loudly gasbagging on a cell-phone.)

I decided to see the manager.

I tapped on the inner-office door. A scowling, hornet-eyed woman got stroppy and window-washed a finger at me: no go. I asked her again, but she defiantly looked past me with eyes of flint and refused to listen to us. I expected as much. Robots look straight ahead. Anyone who has ventured near any El Al check-in desk will know this drill all too well: cretinous Israeli suspicion, vulgar questions, rude attitude, pushy demeanor, angry confrontation, and uncivil delays are commonplace procedures with them, where grilling you involves sniffing your hair, spitting fury, and even pushing and prodding you with rifles. I seriously began wishing that they had made Estonia smaller and literally moved it to the left, I mean *for good*, right into the goddamed Baltic Sea! The Ecolines Company, this bus company, would do nothing to help us, no matter how much we explained or importuned them. The Fines of Ecolines!

Sarah wondered whether we should call the head honcho of the busline itself. Doubtful, I tried helpfully reminding her of what that mastermind President George W. Bush once sagaciously advised, "If we don't succeed, we run the risk of failure!" But we telephoned the bus company. They also refused to help us. Again I tried to explain what had happened. It was all to no avail. No calls to the bus official at headquarters in Riga, no explanation, no pleas mattered a jot. The ruthless bus official, a rude, ignorant, semi-literate, low-echelon, cold-hearted, paper-shuffling, dunderheaded, incompetent Latvian functionary, cretinously hung up the telephone on us, twice. What was the *passe-partout* here? Kindness? Anger? A stern voice? An attempt at flattery? The short and simple answer was exactly *nothing*. Delay. Arseholery. The letter of the law held. Procedure prevailed. *We have never seen this before! This is irregular! Ecolines procedure must be followed, do you not understand?*

There is no equivalent word for "sophisticated" in the Estonian language, by the way. But there is a phrase, "stick a finger through your throat!" *Pista sõrm läbi kurgu!* On that day I was ready to be out of that country like spit through a trumpet.

A dogged need to be in control is, to my mind, one of the worst aspects of stubbornness, and stubbornness is the worst aspect of stupidity. It is my belief that intractability in a stiff-necked person is almost always about fighting fear — the fear in a literal, simple-minded person of losing self-control. Speaking of the maddeningly procedural, that kind of moronically blind, irreversible, doctrinal, fist-faced close-mindedness that is by definition closed to discussion, never mind solutions, I have been told that for a person getting caught fishing without a license in Estonia fines can be assessed for hundreds of dollars. It is said no amount of logic, even in the throes of despair, can dissuade officials from levying that fine. Think of it. Dunned for dropping a line in four miserable feet of water. *Procedure!* I realize that to say that something *actually happened* is the defense of the bad novelist, but this was what transpired on April Fool's Day in Dumboville except that the authorities were not fooling.

And having to make all those telephone calls? It was like a pinball maze, a bagatelle in an insane playfield, all mad circuits, flippers, knobs, bumpers, and bells. Talk about confusion. Forget calling Riga — that was like trying to reach Thomas Pynchon. Estonia was bad enough in itself. Tallinn numbers all begin with the number six and have seven digits, but numbers in small towns like Vändra or Rapia or Mustvee have only five digits, and yet Tallinn, unlike other Estonian cities, has no city code; so to call Tallinn from outside on the digital system, you have to dial Estonia's country code (372) and then the number. In most instances thereafter, we resorted to using Skype and looking for *wee-fee* everywhere. Blissfully, it lowered the confrontational quotient.

Rule-bending, I suspect, is generally not a European thing, however. They seem to be brassbound dogmatic, inflexible, almost fractiously narrow-minded. Christ constantly bent — broke — rules for a higher good, irking the Pharisees. When Jesus said, "The Sabbath was made for man, not man for the Sabbath" (Mark 2:27), His point was that the Sabbath was made to serve people, instead of people being created to serve the Sabbath. Hollow rites seem always dead, blind obedience sad. On the other hand, maybe America's vice is that we are lax about rules, stupidly indifferent, wanting in rigor, slipshod. Criminals often walk on serious charges. The country is hopelessly drug-crazed. All Congressmen are brazenly bought off by lobbyists. Wall Street bankers who cause financial disasters are given multi-million-dollar bonuses. Just look at professional sports — in NBA basketball players to a one all "travel;" second basemen in Major League baseball rarely touch second on a double — or so-called "neighborhood" — play and get away with it; in football holding, with impunity, is commonplace, and half the dunces are jacked-up on steroids. Speaking of fraudulence, sport in the United States openly supports an entire population of semiliterate talk-show hosts, mal-educated broadcasters, pompous and moralizing unathletic lackeys, critics who think they are creators — sportswriters can actually go into the Hall of Fame! — an entire subculture of ungrammatical boeotians and self-promoters and hangers-on.

The extreme is always the forerunner of grief.

And Something Phrenological

Do my descriptions of Estonians seem unfair? St. Augustine says that human beings are actually disguised by their bodies, and that only God can look through "the lattice of our flesh" to see what we are really like. So that lets me out in terms of authority. But why not try.

Scowling is malice, hate homely, the sweetness of generosity a kind of beauty in most countries. But I saw faces, figures, bodies in Estonia that somehow often had no specific parallel in the United States or elsewhere. What do Estonians look like? In Estonia, faces in general are often round, turnip-nosed, bulbous. You see snout-faced, pouched-face, sharp-faced. Brown hair is often oddly potato-colored and limp like the Chaucer's Pardoner's. Cheese faces, dumpling faces, a good many troglodytic. (I often called Sarah *Minu Klimpikene!* "My Dumpling!") I must add I also saw in that country some of the handsomest young men I have ever seen, anywhere in the world. It is my conjecture that the sort of isolated, sequestered history of Estonia seems to allow for — to validate — the possibility of a physiognomic truism of Emerson's who wrote, "Every man finds room in his face for all his ancestors. Every face is an Atrium." Countries have predominant blood types. In China, over 99% of the population has Rh+ blood, for example. Almost all Estonians have Type B blood — can this signify in looks, even personality? In Japan, the concept of blood type as personality type is so popular that the Japanese will ask "What is your blood type?" about as often as many Americans inquire "What is your sign?" Some will insist that such an argument is scientific racism. Many men in Estonia also seem to be bony and awkward-looking, however. Take a look at a picture of the Danish author Hans Christian Andersen — many men look like that: raw, high cheekbones, fairly close-set eyes, almost Asian in instances. A lot of them in the rural world look like the Fabulous Furry Freak Brothers, scary and hairy. I pictured that vile Ecolines bus official with whom I spoke on the phone to be a hairy manner-bereft wearing a rubber necktie and hideous polyester pants. Estonians are a tallish people, although when I once heard a woman point and scream, *"Lilliput!"* I turned and actually saw a midget. Adolescent boys tend to be loud, with pudding-bowl haircuts. So many of them look different from the ordinary young people one sees elsewhere. They seemed to *loom.* I sensed an unpredictability in them, a feral restlessness. When Sigmund Freud looked up and suddenly saw Salvador Dali in London in 1938, the 82-year-old psychoanalyst whispered to others in the room, "That boy looks like a fanatic." I often felt that way, to a degree, as I looked around. As I say, however, many of them without effort have movie-star looks. Students and young men walk with a good deal of earnestness, long intense strides with a fixed straight-ahead focus, and have a sort of vulpine look with eyes close together. To me many of them more or less facially resembled the late great chessmaster Bobby Fischer, along with wearing dark clothes and backpacks strapped to both shoulders the way nerds always used to wear them — and be mocked for — at MIT. I would walk along with my phrase-book, checking out words of the physique: *Nina* — "nose," *kõrv* — "ear," *hammas* — "tooth," *suu* — "mouth," etc.

"I know inside you are seething like a volcano with lava about to pour out of you, but, trust me, nothing is happening to your face," the frustrated director Vincent Minnelli told "Method" actor George Peppard trying to play the part of the illegitimate son, Rafe, when, filming the movie, *Home from the Hill* (1960), he looked and saw nothing but an empty, soulless puss. Very often I felt the same way walking past the endless parade of inexpressive faces in the gritty cities of stony Estonia.

Please know my observations have to do with neither bias nor bigotry. I hasten to add, furthermore, that no claim is being made in what I say or what I saw that I was standing, in stage slang, "fireplace center." Racial assumptions one abhors. There has surely been no shortage of ethnic bigotry down through history. Henry Cabot Lodge called the Irish "scum." Rudyard Kipling called Germans "dogs." Edna St. Vincent Millay who was also Irish and grew up in lower-middle-class Maine while living in near poverty at times, with her mother carting her and her sisters from room to room, flat to flat and often sponging off various relatives, wrote later in life, after conveniently having married a multi-millionaire, "The only people I really hate are servants. They are not really human beings at all. They have no conscience, no heart, no sense of responsibility, no memory of kind treatment or past favors. Even their sins are not human sins, but the sins of spiders and magpies, of monkeys, serpents, and pigs." Painter and sculptor Frederick Remington wrote to a friend, "I've got some Winchesters, and when the massacring begins, which you speak of, I can get my share of them and, what's more, I will. Jews — injuns — Chinamen — Italians — Huns, the rubbish of the earth I hate." Here is Mr. J.W. Steele, the great authority on the American Indian:

> Brave only in superior numbers or in ambush, honest only in being a consummate hypocrite, merry only at the sight of suffering inflicted by his own hand, friendly only through cunning and hospitable never, and above all sublimely mendacious and a liar always, the Indian as he really is to those who, unfortunately, know him, seems poor material out of which to manufacture a hero or frame a romance. Mollified by semi-annual gifts and pacified by periodical talks about the Great Father and blarney about brothers, he has only the one redeeming fact upon his record, that he has never been tamed and never been a servant. Neither has the hyena.

Henry James wrote that Jews "smelled badly." Karl Marx always referred to his rival, Lassalle, as a "nigger Jew." Opera diva Kirsten Flagstad called musical conductor Erich Leinsdorf "a damned Jew." At the end of World War II, toughboy General George Patton singled out the "Jewish type of D.P. (displaced person)" as "a sub-human species without any of the cultural or social refinements of our time." He opposed the war crimes trials calling them "not cricket" and "Semitic." He constantly dismissed Jews as "vengeful" people trying to implement Communism, and blamed

Nuremberg on the "Semitic influence of the press." "I have never looked at a group who seem to be more lacking in intelligence and spirit," he wrote. "Practically all of them had the flat brownish grey eye common among the Hawaiians which, to my mind, indicates very low intelligence."

Oscar Wilde's dislike of Switzerland extended to its inhabitants. The country, he declared, had produced nothing but theologians and waiters. The Swiss were ugly, shapeless, colorless, like cavemen: "their cattle have more expression." Harry Lime (played by Orson Welles) in *The Third Man* was no kinder, stating, "In Italy for 30 years under the Borgias they had warfare, terror, murder, and bloodshed, but they produced Michelangelo, Leonardo da Vinci, and the Renaissance. In Switzerland they had brotherly love — they had 500 years of democracy and peace, and what did that produce? The cuckoo clock…" Anti-Scandinavian prejudice can be thrown in, as well. A stanza from "Beach at Evening" goes:

In Lapland are dirty people,
flat-headed, big-mouthed and small;
they squat over fires, fry fish, and
squeak and scream.[66]

I was looking for nothing like perfectibility in Estonia and cite the above examples of intolerance and cretinous bigotry solely to condemn them. Still, I found Estonians to be mainly of a distinct type. I detected in many people there a concave, vaguely worn-out appearance. People glumly hidden deep in rubbery winter coats, puffy as soufflés, do not radiate the temperaments of either Malibu or Al'Azīzīyah. It is not the land of angel fish, piña coladas, mango sunsets, or perfervid heat. I saw muffled despair too often. I would assert there are three types of faces: muffins, crullers, and donuts. You see kids with absurd hair shaped — *sculpted* — like absinthe spoons or rooster combs or garden rakes, characters right out of a Fritz Lang movie. The scientific-racist quack Carleton S. Coon, the virtual dean of faux-anthropology, in his rather cranky, racialist report, *The Races of Europe*, a bastion of soft-knowledge, observes that Estonians or Nordics are "generally thick-set and stocky, brunet to fairish…rugged-boned, prominent nosed." To Prof. Coon the "East Baltics" (e.g., Prussians, too) were generally "medium snub-nosed, broad-headed, and heavy, part Mongoloid." Americans whom I saw walking among the crowds there all seemed to be taller and to have bigger heads and ears and louder voices and longer shoes and more brightly-colored clothes.

Speaking of physiology, it was on a long winter perambulation one day going west along the snowy banks of the Emajõgi that I struck up a conversation, mostly in German, some in Russian, with an itinerant Russian with a hawk-nose in a very sharply outlined face — not a Russian-type at all — whose oddly flattened skull, which seemed to have prevented him from growing vertically allowed him to grow in width, I will ever associate with a song that he offered as a parting gift for me to take home as he energetically shook and re-shook my hand:

> My legs sing 'Whither am I going?'
> My head sings 'Wherefore am I talking?'
> But my flesh sings 'Why am I living?'

Greyhoundesque Beauties

Estonian women, who in large numbers are quite foxy and beautiful, all *adore* tight jeans in combination with long boots with high heels. I would love to be in the cobbler business in Estonia, not only to meet beauties, but for the lovely income, as the city streets there are invariably cobblestoned where a shoe can be wrecked in a single long walk, ground down like battered shells. Why must women waste their sole leather? Is it to gain the strength of striding? (Noisy footwear, I quite realized there, sends a distinct power to the wearer!) Middle-aged women, tubby and short, look like creamers, wear big hats, and most dye their hair henna. Young Estonian women, pale, ferox-faced, aloe-eyed, dark and light hair, to a degree resemble the tennis-star Martina Navratilova. Many of them for glam went with smoky black-cat eyeliner and gunmetal grey eye-makeup that I do not recall seeing since the days of Audrey Hepburn and Sophia Loren. They are many of them thin, lithe, tough, girly, statuesque, purposeful, elongated, they *walk* purposefully and tall — no faint water-colorish girls with pastel dresses here — and many wear sleek expensive footwear, like commandeering Reynold Heydick black boots with locks on them. "A representation of Hell — a stylish shoe," as one of G. I. Gurdjieff's subjective sayings goes. He also said, "Unhappiness on earth is from the wiseacring of women." I must say I did hear a lot of insults from snippy women there. Which of us has not allowed for the hauteur of beauty, however? Disdain increases one's illustriousness. Pouting, sulking is sexy. The women of Estonia are sensuous and sharp, like Japanese drawings. *Maintain that mask,* I remember thinking. *Do not tell me who you are. I want to worship you.* The Estonian population is 54% female, 46% male. Women dominate. Women control. Women rule.

Greyhoundesque is a word that actually describes Estonian women: sleek, pointed faces, shapely. Peter the Great married an Estonian woman. So did Rupert Murdoch. They are lovely, if occasionally sardonic and scarily self-contained. I noticed that when, handing you back your change in shops, they often coldly look past you. I would like to add that I do not know why the idea of such perfect beauty being found in Estonia should seem such a challenge to probability; there are times and places when and where nature's whim, in defiance of circumstance, rank, education, location, etc., produces a masterpiece. Is it not true that the first place to look for something is the last place you would expect to find it? I rather thought that was among the central themes of *Cinderella*, and no one, certainly not children, ever question the whys and wherefores of the pulchritude of that lovely third sister — daughter of another mother in the main version, by the way — who was a girl of unparalleled goodness and sweet tempered, as well. Aschenputtel, La Cenicienta, *Cendrillon ou La petite Pantouflede Verre,* Cenerentola, Askungen — Tuhkatriinu in Estonia, from *tuhk–, tuha–,* "ashes." (I am reminded here of a small bar in Tartu in which I would occasionally stop in for a drink, where five or six mustachioed *gnocchi,* men dark as Tophet who never stopped staring at me — I grow more resentful than intimidated at uniformity — I secretly began referring to as the Flying Tuhatoos, the Estonian word for "ash-tray" being *tuhatoos.*) No, the beauty of Estonian female is for the most part angel music.

Why since the inception of the Miss World Pageant in 1951 has not a single winner of the pageant ever haled from Estonia? It is nothing less than a scandal. Both India and Venezuela have won four, Sweden three, and even tiny Jamaica has won twice.

The women there are efficiently brisk with a sense of strength in them, a no-nonsense attitude, a feminist suasion. (The Estonian language has no titular handle for marital-status-neutral female corresponding to our "Ms." by the way, if you do not want to specify "Mrs." or "Miss." There, "Mrs." is *Proua*, abbreviated "Pr.", "Miss" is *Preili*, abbreviated "Prl.") Many young Estonian women eagerly dye their hair crow-black. Eurogoths with little creepy streaks of color in it — magenta is big — love raven-black hair which is worn at times with an all-the-way-around-your-head helmet look. They also sport lots of steampunk jewelry and jelly bracelets and decorate their eyes with metallic and shimmery, piratical-looking eyeliner and emo eyeshadow, a kind of Boho Chic in high evidence in Tallinn. There is a bar in Tallinn dedicated totally to Depeche Mode, the English electronic music band for which, by the way, the entire country holds a morbid and unfathomable fixation. I wonder if on stage they have wild, leather-vest-clad, kick-ass stand-ins with tats, playing guitars with their teeth, nightly howling "In Chains," "Pimpf," "Zenstation," "Barrel of a Gun," and "Fly on the Windscreen." As I say, women tend to have pulled faces, and pouts; are possumesque; chinless often with long necks. I see the Modigliani morph distinctly iterated. The cold air, the brisk winter nights, only seem to give the women an extra glow. Anger up the blood. Brighten the complexions. Put something of rose or blush into alabastrine smoothness. I found that Estonian women for the most part are in much better physical shape than their American counterparts. You rarely see in the streets glaring examples of *pesanteur* — heaviness. Is it diet? Pride? Vanity? Some young women are so glowingly blond they look irradiated.

We forgive beauty anything, do we not? The women Monsieur Verdoux kills are, scrutably, all ugly.

There is enough fascination with beauty and fashion with Estonian women — earrings, bracelets, hairstyles, kicky shoes, etc. — that I could not help but think of how with his rolling invectives that baffling Old Testament figure Isaiah would have thundered against them, he who believed that all the "nose jewels," "crisping pins," "wimples," and "tinkling ornaments about their feet" and "round tires like the moon" that the Hebrew Women — *Heebrea Naiste* in Estonian — sported were used to hunt souls. "Thus saith the Lord God: behold, I am against your pillows wherewith ye hunt souls!" Was it because I found all those charms coupled with their shrugging secularism?

Curiously, the *seriousness* of Estonian women adds to their sexiness, in the same way paleness of cheek does. (Curiously enough, the word for "cheek" in Estonian is *pale!*) Greta Garbo always seemed prettier when she was *not* smiling, which I gather was most of the time. She was clearly more attractive in *Ninotchka* as the severe, unsmiling Bolshie commissar wearing that plain white short-sleeve shirt and Soviet neckerchief than, later in the film, when "stylishly" wearing that steeple-like cone hat or that foolish, strapless, gilt-edged gown which she uncharacteristically dons trying to please that fop and dullard, Leon. Although one costume Garbo wore in *Mata Hari* took eight Guadlajaran needlewomen nine weeks to complete,[67] nothing could match for splendor the elegantly simple robe and collar she wears at the end of *Queen Christina*, standing as a silent figurehead at the bow of that caravel bound for Spain with the wind blowing through her hair. After she laughs out loud for the first time in that workingman's café in *Ninotchka* — a face-splitting yamph that incidentally does nothing for her looks, at least for me — Comrade Lena Yakushova Ivanoff transmogrifies into any other woman in love, face it — a mere filly. Her hair style even changes, going from that shinily chaste handsome pageboy to a dopey example of preciously worked hair. Love has made her womanly, perhaps, but submission has made her weak. The square-shouldered beauty that she previously embodied is compromised. Forget "Garbo Laughs!," that cheap slogan for the movie that tried to sell it to 1939 audiences. Aside from the fact that a Swede as to good looks is not two jumps away from an Estonian, it is the pale, efficient, dry *sobriety* of Garbo that, even if exaggerated, gave Ninotchka originality and panache. (Peculiar though you may think it, I feel the same way about the glowering Presbyterian martinet Katharine Hepburn plays as Rosie and the sour, recalcitrant, ill-shaven Humphrey Bogart playing set-in-his-ways Charlie Allnutt in *The African Queen*: both sets of lovers are far and away more fascinating as combatants before they fall in love.) In *Notorious*, the beautiful Ingrid Bergman actually looks much

Old Town, Tallinn, Christmas 2008

Kaido Ole with Sarah, two painters

Giant pig at the *Torg* (market), Tartu

Old Gate and McDonald's, a cultural anomaly, Tallinn

Rooftop view of Tallinn, looking toward Finland

Main buildings, University of Tartu

Icy Emajõgi River in January, Tartu

Town Hall, Raekoja Plats, from Toomemägi, Tartu

Three-dimensional wall statue, Tallinn

A lodging in Tartu

Old house in Tartu

Old stone oat-barn in Mooste

Wooden animal sculptures on the island of Hiiumaa

Sarah in Springtime, near Lake Peipsi

The author in early Spring on the Emajõgi

Tallinn Rooftops (oil on panel, 10" x 9")

St. Nicholas Church, Tallinn (oil on panel, 18" x 15")

Courtyard in Tartu (oil on canvas, 11" x 8")

better, far sexier, in the etiolation of illness when she is being slowly poisoned and wasting away than when she is dressed up with that almost campy devil-horn of hair she wears at the Sebastian's party trying to slip suave Cary Grant the key to the basement wine cellar. Remember how in his poem "Adam's Curse" W.B. Yeats told us that beauty must not reveal the labor necessary to achieve it? Informality is in a sense an aspect of flirtation, a laxity that becomes available. The Ninotchka who smiles is a needy Ninotchka. A smile in a photograph does more than date you; it waves away precaution. In its breeziness it confesses too facile a freedom. It is a moral act to flagellate a walnut tree.

I could not help but notice that many Estonian women in the street, in shops, walking about, wear sleek furs, quite elegantly — mink coats, beautiful ones — and, although I was once of the opinion that no one could look better in a mink coat than Katharine Hepburn in *Woman of the Year,* at her peak in 1942 — at the beginning of that splendid kitchen scene in which, trying to prove wifely efficiency, however ineptly, she proves she cannot even handle an egg and buggers up the waffles, coffee and toast — I was wrong.[68] An Estonian woman in furs is fireful! There are beauty salons (*ilusalong*) everywhere in the cities, on just about every street, it seems, and beauty products seem to sell big. It is understandable perhaps in a country where there are economic difficulties: you master what you can, or as Janet Flanner wrote in 1937, "In Europe, when bread becomes costly, beauty becomes cheap." This trend is commonly known as the "lipstick index." The thinking is that, rather than spend money on a new outfit, women will instead buy new make-up to refresh their appearance. Paradoxically, then, lipstick sales famously go up during a recession, so there was that, too, for the economic turn-down of 2008 reached everywhere. I believe it all fit in with my idea of Ninotchka the Communist, in any case. "Sexiness," as the writer Ned Rorem once noted, "comes from the financially underprivileged. The rich do not need to be sexy." The women in Estonia, at least from my experience there, are not at all like those classic pie-faced, high-smiling, waving — and I daresay brainless — American Beauty Roses who always seem to be from the South that walk the runways in bathing suits and manage to win all of the beauty contests in the United States. Estonian women who are both light-skinned and dark seem to have a fascination for pale-blue eyeshadow, what one might call graveyard lipstick, and space-age jewelry. I would smile, recalling a line from the John Payne translation of the *Arabian Nights*: "How many a leveling among them, eye-painted with languor, abode?" A cool remoteness somehow adhibits to most of them. In one way they reminded me of perfectly decorated houses in which nobody actually lived. One Estonia-boosting tract that I came across quite cheerfully, if boastfully, explains: "The concentration of beautiful and interesting women in Estonia is apparently among the highest in the world." No foxier women wearing blue jeans can be found on earth. Young women generally give off a clerk-at-the-post-office efficiency and make quick replies which are not necessarily answers — or even very helpful. It is about no nonsense. They also seem to love boots. Berets. Jewelry. Make-up. Hair-dye. Dove-tailed nails. (As to the boots, I have been told that most of the women wearing them are mostly Russians, not Estonians, who thrill at vamping men!) There is a high gonzo quotient to fashion, a kind of avant-garde roguery that is patently ridiculous, I think. It is not leather that women wear, but "pleather," a faux-material. I noticed that pleather jackets, in black, in brown, even in purple, are popular, and whenever I saw them I thought of comedian Paul Lynde's crinkly-nosed response on *Hollywood Squares* to the question, "Why do motorcyclists wear leather?" — "Because chiffon wrinkles!" (Lynde also insisted that what the Scarecrow "really wanted" in *The Wizard of Oz*, was "for the Tin Man to notice him.") Looking cool is looking hot. "Tallinn boasted what I can say were — without fear of hyperbole — the most jaw-droppingly beautiful women I have seen in my life," wrote Tom Bissell in his article, "Rolling Estonia," in *The New Republic Online* in 2007. I heartily agree. In the words of the poet Austin Dobson:

Beauties that Fragonard drew;
Talon-rouge, falbala, queue.[69]

Poutiness. The word was made for Estonian women. Sullen otherwhereness, with side-long glances. Could that contribute to the fact that in terms of divorce-rate Estonia is as high as 7th in the world? There is a fatal beauty to the female face in Estonia, giving credibility to Prof. Harold Bloom's assertion that all angels are fallen angels.

You see lots of dress shops, milliner's shops, modistes. In Estonia you do not find the kind of specialty shops one finds, say, in Manhattan, precious places that sell delicate items like monkfish or dragon fruit or those signature shampoos and artisanal pastas. I noticed in old Tallinn many quaint — cute! — department stores here and there, emporia like the endearing Matuschek & Co. in the film, *The Shop Around the Corner*, which, remember, is set in Budapest — look for the strange words *"Pengo"* (dollars) and *"Filler"* (cents) on the cash-register of the shop — although I daresay it could be any shop in any city on earth; I am certain, as well, that many of the shop-clerks in those small Estonian shops probably had the same kind of wonderfully evocative old-world names that are used in the film such as Ilona, Flora, Hugo, Ferenc Vardas, Mr. Pirovitch, Klara Novak and Alfred Kralik. That thick snowfall falling on all the busy shoppers on Christmas Eve, as Mr. Hugo Matuschek peers in his own store-front windows, is pure Estonia — and notice that, among the special delicacies Mr. Matuschek offers to the new stockboy, Rudy, for the Christmas dinner to which he invites him at the end of the movie is cucumber salad with sour cream, an Estonian *ne plus ultra!* More than once Sarah and I took coffee or tea and pastries in lovely little tea-shops on the side-streets in Tallinn and Tartu with those old 1920s' ice-cream chairs with backs of looped or whorled metal design and old marble-topped tables and wide creaky wooden floors and silver Russian tea-holders-with-glasses just like those that one sees in the Café Nizza in that great Ernst Lubitsch film, where fetching Margaret Sullavan — the star-crossed actress (she would later commit suicide) that of all Hollywood actresses the incandescent Louise Brooks most admired — sits primly waiting for the stranger she is certain she is in love with, a rose semaphorically stuck in the pages of her copy of *Anna Karenina* for easy identification. Why, the shop is even located on Balta Street!

Estonia is a quaint country. Traditions are maintained. The old ways are preferred. Habits remain, mostly. At Christmas which has virtually no Christian elements to the holiday decorations, you will not see a manger scene anywhere, as is also the case in Sweden, Denmark, Norway, and other notoriously non-church going countries — the Norwegian word for Christmas, *jul* is a pre-Christian Viking drinking festival; both countries, basically devoid of religion, celebrate a "festival of light."[70] People in the dark and dead-of-winter badly in need of a spirit-boost crave light, the return of the sun, longer days.[71] On New Year's Eve many traditionally-bound Estonians will see to it that they will sit down to dinner around a brightly candlelit hay-covered table topped with a cloth and serve twelve chosen dishes, one for each month of the coming year. I have to admit I love the challenge of trying to picture in my mind a Breugelesque banquet just to ponder something of happy foolishness — *narrus* — in Estonia. It is a quiet place, for the most part, a perfect place to sit down in a café with a hot cup of Löfbergs Lila with a few lovely raspberry friands or a piece of moist *munavalgekook*, Estonian egg-white cake. Did you know that late Russian novelist Aleksandr Solzhenitsyn traveled specifically to Estonia in order to complete his book, *The Gulag Archipelago*, hiding in friends' homes? He lived both in Tartu and in a countryhouse in Vasula, near Tartu, after the KGB had confiscated his materials in Moscow in 1965.[72] William Wordsworth, after all, did declare that the sublime was to be found in the solitary.

It is also a relatively safe country to travel in. As I said, I always enjoy looking at the "Dangers and Annoyances" section of modern travel manuals, for nothing quite discloses the quirks of a people more than its special threats and antagonisms. I remember reading that at Oxford, W.H. Auden always slept with revolver under his pillow, but I wasn't that paranoid. Of Latvia one reads, "It definitely pays to be streetwise here." In the several books I consulted, Estonia rates no admonitions at all, unlike its Baltic cousins. It is rated the sixteenth least-corrupt country in Europe, far ahead of any former Soviet state and better than the founding EU member, Italy. There is hedonistic nightlife in Estonia — I am told young Englishmen love to come to Tallinn for pre-marital "stag parties" — and one sees in the cities a plethora of "Casino" gambling huts. Prostitution, by the way, is legal in Latvia — any woman alone sitting in a foyer can be propositioned — but not in Estonia. I simply did not want to find myself on some backstreet in the middle of the night to get a metal shampoo — or worse — by some aggrieved Estonian nationalist with a long memory mistaking me, wearing the wrong hat, for some kind of crass Soviet lout! Coincidentally, the Estonian word for memory as a concept is *mälu*, and *mälestus* for the personal faculty of memory, but it seems somehow fitting in a country with such painful memories — could

the word share a distant inheritance from Uralic or Indo-European? —
that in both words we find the prefix for evil.

Men in Sun Helmets (Not)

Hats are a big item here.

In Estonian, hat is *kübar*, and cap is *müts*. I see the typical Estonian
kübar as an Alpinish all-feature, and the typical *müts* as a wool pull-on,
a golf cap, bicyclist's cap, or sailing cap. They also love duck-billed field
marshal caps and even those Jersey "buckets" favored by the Japanese.
Hailing back to the long-ago days of *The Student Prince*, most of the
college students in Estonia wear — and quite proudly — a smart sort of
sea-captain's cap to identify their college affiliation. Very Victor Herber-
tish and/or operettaesque, in my opinion. These caps are short-brimmed
and feature muted colors, and the ones I saw worn often seemed to be
striped at the crown adorned with the Estonian flag colors: blue, black,
and white. These multi-colored caps signify various student fraternities
and sororities — the blue, black, and white cap represents the biggest
one, *Eesti Üliopilas Selts*, "Estonian Student Society." An old Estonian
proverb goes, one no doubt seeking redress for the many strange versions
in this sartorial grouping, "Make fun of the man, not of his hat."

One sees all sorts of headgear and shitty chapeau, including (at least in
tourist shops) Viking hats with *horns!* Nazi gauleiter caps. Woolen M43
Nazi field caps (*Einheitsmutze*). Norwegian Olympic-style pullovers on
guys. Train-conductor caps, Old-World leather Russian jobs with flaps
like the kind that buggering redneck wore in the movie *Deliverance*.
Watch caps. Hooded ones. Crownless ones. Brimless happy hooligans.
American Legionnaire "cunt caps," as novelist James Ellroy so elegantly
puts it in *Hollywood Nocturnes*. Elfin hats. Biker helmets. Unblocked va-
rieties. Odd cockahoops. Floppy medieval hats like tea-cozies, the kind
you see in the paintings of Pieter Bruegel the Elder. Chinese Communist
leather hats with three flaps, one in front, and one on each side. Burglar-
ious-looking Balaclavas and Peruvian chullos and top-flopping barretinas

— popular mid-winter items. Fedoras. Berets. Sable ushankas. Forester's hats. Cartwheel hats like the kind the crazy poet Marianne Moore always wore (when she was not wearing a tricorn!), which I saw fetchingly being worn by a model one morning in Tallinn. Sort of hoop hats. Who would have loved it here? Bing Crosby, who would wear anything on his head. George Bernard Shaw collected hats. So does Lady Gaga and Aretha Franklin. As did Hedda Hopper and Frank Sinatra, or were his all baseball caps, saving of course the so-called "Fedora Lounge" he made famous by way of preference (size 7 1/8), those narrow-brim, wide-ribbon, high-crown Cavanaghs of the late 50s and 60s, worn with attitude? I once saw a heavy, hirsute man coming to the gym I used to frequent wearing on his head what I can only describe as the unbecoming top of a basket. Many wearing such hats had pronounced R. Crumb faces, the gnarled, outlandish kind one often sees in his explosive illustrations. We know a man by his hat, in a sense. "The importance of its hat to a form becomes/More definite," writes Wallace Stevens in "The Pastor Caballero," a character about whom we know very little more although what he is wearing seems enough to know him by:

The Flare

In the sweeping brim becomes the origin
Of a human evocation, so disclosed
That, nameless, it creates an affectionate name,
Derived from adjectives of deepest mine.
The actual form bears outwardly this grace,
An image of the mind, in inward mate,

Tall and unfretted, a figure meant to bear
Its poisoned laurels in this poisoned wood,
High in the height that is our total height.

The formidable helmet is nothing now.
These two go well together, the sinuous brim
And the green flauntings of the hours of peace.

The hat indeed enfolds the head in a vital ambiance. It may very well be a reflection of classes — the differences rather than the similarities — of people seen walking down the street sporting various headgear, each indicating differences in expectation and privilege, of wealth and opportunity; it is not tension or aggression or muted nuttiness, but often a sort of a symbol of guarded indifference. Panache is snobbery. People, at least to me, choose to coexist rather than create communities.

It is not a national habit to look happy there.

Faces are stony as plates.

Rõõmutu.

Cheerless.

Hornets with Squints

A gulag temperament is conveyed in winter especially, when you are as unlikely to see a smile as find a unicorn. (I always had to fight off a depressing image of Estonian life under the Soviet boot-heel whenever someone acclaimed to me, as happened several times, "*Jätku leiba!*" — "May your bread last!") Soviet glumness was mocked in virtually every anti-Communist movie in Hollywood from *Walk East on Beacon* to *The Spy Who Came in From the Cold* to grim books like *The Cardinal Mindszenty Story* and Herbert Philbrick's *I Was A Communist for the FBI* to Al Capp's comic-strip *Li'l Abner* which satirized secret agents and Soviet suppression along with mocking remote places like "Lower Slobbovia" where kulaks, sucking-stone poor, walked around in ratty clothes with blue icicles hanging off their noses. The syndrome of suspicion, surliness, and secretiveness of spies, agents, and double-agents has still not ended and probably never will. The film sketch conceived by Graham Greene shortly after the war, "Nobody to Blame" and which concerns a British sales representative in Estonia ("Latesthia") for Singer Sewing machines, who turns out to be an SIS spy — a film which was never made, as it poked fun at the Secret Service — was the film that contained the bare bones of what was to become *Our Man in Tallinn*, which as I have already pointed out became, in 1958, *Our Man in Havana*. ("Alas, the book did me little good with the new rulers of Havana," Greene ruefully confessed later. "In poking fun at the British Secret Service, I had minimized the terror of Batista's rule.") Again, Ian Thomson is revealing on this topic:

> In 1988, anticipating my first visit to Tallinn, I had written to Greene asking why he moved *Our Man in Havana* from Estonia in the 1930s to Cuba in the 1950s. Greene explained that a Secret Service comedy about a Hoover salesman who gets sucked up into espionage would be more credible in pre-Castro Havana, with its louche nightclubs, than in Soviet-occupied Tallinn. He concluded: 'I already knew Cuba and my sympathies were with the Fidelistas in the mountains… One could hardly sympathise with the main character if he was to be involved in the Hitler war.[73]

And my point? Comedy and Estonia do not mix either! Remember, Alec Guinness is quite an elfin delight as Wormold.

They were not given to trust, were almost *invigorated* by the lack of it. Herrlee Glessner Creel, the American sinologist and an authority on Confucius, succinctly concluded of his saintly subject, "He trusted the human race." The man who has been duped and exploited, however, soon comes to recognize in an abstemious and defeated way what he can no longer approve in anything, for what has been taken away from him, even if it is eventually returned in a distorted way, might indeed never again be his. Paranoia is the Estonian's counter-disease to Soviet oppression. The echo of the Kremlin's brute force remains a humiliation for Estonians. There also lingers as well the curious if perhaps distastefully paradoxical argument that many Estonians may have never lived so intensely, so concentratedly, as when commiserating under the burden of occupation. Did not André Malraux in *L'Espoir* describe the almost sexual arousal of men in battle? It is perhaps part of the national agony now that many Estonians may inevitably feel that sense of lift. While Nietzsche, who specialized in disagreeable remarks, observed that suffering may deepen a man but didn't make him better, he did not say that it failed to heighten or give him focus. "Anxiety may give one an aspect of brightness, purely because it sharpens all the faculties," asserted A.N. Whitehead. "It makes all one's impressions more intense." That one cannot escape history is arguably the most desolating idea of all truisms. In the final analysis, one may legitimately ask do Estonians merely suffer, or do they explore their pain? Approaches signify. On his birthday, Jonathan Swift always read the book of Job, and before going to sleep Rainer Maria Rilke sought consolation by reading Baudelaire's *Petits poèmes en prose*, especially the one which runs *"Enfin! La tyrannie de la face humaine a disparu, et je ne souffrirai plus que moi-même."*[74]

Feeling injustice is one thing; but being captured as a nation with a dormant grievance from the past that can make you interiorize all pain is quite another. History is not a zero-sum game in which a lesson of equal value springs forth from every tragedy. The Roman poet Lucretius in *De Rerum Natura,* arguing that death destroys personality, in lines composed more than a century after the Second Punic War when Hannibal evacuated Italy, addressed the horrors of that invasion which held such terror for men that the mere memory of it ("…just as body takes monstrous/diseases and the dreadful pain/so mind its bitter cares, the grief, the fear…") made oblivion for them seem preferable to personal immortality. One questions, should the present-day Estonian take hope and find solace or grow depressed by Mary Tyrone's somewhat enigmatic pronouncement in *Long Day's Journey into Night*, "The past is the present, isn't it? It's the future, too"?

There is also the matter of the salvific act of disclosing, divulging, connecting, even confessing. Osman, the energetic protagonist of Orhan Pamuk's novel *The New Life*, in a notable passage "What is Love?"[75] pleads not only for the value of personal exploration — to "plunge oneself in the thick of the commotion called Life" — but also stresses the deep importance of communicating, whether a passion, a problem, or a pain. Osman echoes Pamuk's own recent political outspokenness in Turkey over the Armenian Genocide of 1915-1917. "You see, I was not able to say anything new. But still, I did manage to say something! I no longer care if it's new or not. Contrary to what some pretentious fools think, it's better to say a couple of words rather than remain silent."

Silence is safe, and, far too often, talking — loose-lipped or "flannel-mouthed" chat — led to the salt mines in Siberia, or worse. It struck me that the habit of not exercising free speech in Estonia is an aspect of the climatological darkness there, a backdrop of inward displacement, as it were. Nobody knows better than they the cost of uncalculated utterance during the totalitarian regimes they suffered through. But the policy of keeping mum seems never to have left them. Free speech, however, is an empty formality and rarely made use of at the best of times, or so felt Mark Twain who, as he so often did, put his finger on a cynical truism. "There are not fewer than five thousand murders to one (unpopular) free utterance," he wrote in his essay, "The Privilege of the Grave":

> There is justification for this reluctance to utter unpopular opinions: the cost of utterance is too heavy; it can ruin a man in his business, it can lose him his friends, it can subject him to public insult and abuse, it can ostracize his unoffending family, and make his house a despised and unvisited solitude....we suppress an unpopular opinion because we cannot afford the bitter cost of putting it forth. None of us likes to be hated, none of us likes to be shunned.

Let us get to the point. None of us frankly likes to be dead, either, a likely outcome during the Soviet occupation for not merely idle or subversive talk. *Just talk!* Mark Twain satirically offered that free speech is the privilege of the dead alone, the monopoly of the dead. Better be hypocritical and mum. And safe.

Do you happen to know the Ogden Nash poem, "A Plea for Less Malice Toward None"? It begins,

> Love is a word that is constantly heard,
> Hate is a word that's not.
> Love, I am told, is more precious than gold,
> Love, I have read, is hot.
> But hate is the verb that to me is superb,
> Any kiddie in school can love like a fool
> And love is a drug on the mart,
> But hating, my boy, is an art.

There are no big hugs or kisses in Estonia, no thundering huzzahs, no exuberant greetings or goodbyes, no tears shed on a comforting shoulder, no patting of hands. No easy familiarity. No physical demonstrations of affection. Think "Still Life With Crows." Most cultures shake hands upon greeting. In Japan they bow. Thais honor each other with a wai. A Kikuyo will commonly hold his right forearm with the left hand as he shakes the hand of another, while the Masai just touch palms. In Venezuela when two friends meet or two people are introduced one will place his right hand on the other's left shoulder, and vice versa. I noticed in Estonia a sort of stutter-nod, a hasty, jerky, slightly nervous but scrimp unobliging duck-down with the head curtseying into a nestling neck accompanied almost always with a haunted look in the eyes. I remember a baleful reference in the movie, *A Thousand Clowns*, to "the wide stare that people put in their eyes to show their mind's asleep." So it seemed at times in the emotional desert of Estonia. Why? Was it from worry? Frustration? A desperate sense of inadequacy? Lack of attention? Stress? Anxiety? I am convinced as an amateur gardener that roses, easily the fussiest of all flowers on earth for demanding to be watered and needing to be fed in order to bloom, show jealousy to each other if they have to fight for room in the sun. I know for a fact that too many squash plants placed too close together in a space will not blossom. "Humor is a cloudy wonderland," we hear in that same movie, "from a blue, blue sky." Alone I would follow my nose through the cities on many days, trying to keep out of the way of my wife, who was painting but who in social situations was often more enthusiastic or outgoing than I, and frankly I began to think in my travels I created gloom in those flat, textureless personalities that forever seemed to be saying: take your bag of groceries and keep moving for we have no time to chat and we will not be bought off by smiles. A country so coldly and incapaciously unable to tell its heart to foreigners must surely recognize its flaw, its rough-hewn awfulness. If happiness could be put in sail-language, utter joy would be "Main-sky sail top sail!" Sails in Estonia, figuratively speaking, are furled. I honestly have to admit that at bottom whether that unshakeable surliness was born of shyness, stubbornness, I never fully concluded. Dante uses the verb "to smile" only once in the *Inferno*.[76] "The most natural explanation," writes Etienne Gilson in *Dante the Philosopher*, "is that if the word is encountered only once…it is because Hell is a place where opportunities to smile are somewhat rare." Laughter is the peculiar attribute of man, thinkers point out. Gilson insists, however, that Hell was not created by God to harbor the peculiar attribute of man. Whatever its infernal name, Limbo, Sheol,

Hades, or the Dark Reaches of Pluto, I could conjure up not a *riso,* a *sorriso,* in all of Estonia that could light up the smallest glowworm's crotch.

I have to say we found ourselves laughing a good deal there, over experiences both good and bad, fortuitous and frustrating. Sarah's laughter is not unlike that described by Proust when comparing that of the Comtesse Greffuhle's to the carillon at Bruges. What else can you do in the dead of dark winter, carless, with a very weak dollar and a platter of cold pork? Worry can give a small thing a big shadow, and, aside from the wobbly political primaries in the USA, we had banished anxiety.

Glowering in Estonia seems to provide in old and young alike a kind of social protection. Smiles are rare. A given smile there reveals you as a stranger. I promise you, I am not being insensitive, merely dislike churls. I yet have nightmares about Gilbert Osmond and can still tear-up when reading again of sweet Cathy Morland being coldly and brutally sent home in the middle of the night by General Tilney from *Northanger Abbey.* Estonians actually consider people who smile a bunch of *gladhanders,* clouted buffoons of a sort, indiscreet, yam-in-the-mouth, overfraternizing yahoos. Italians are always smiling. It is the same in Thailand. In Japan, before the Meiji era began, any person who failed to smile in the presence of a social superior could legally be killed then and there by the superior in question. This may explain why travelers find the Japanese a smiling race. Not so in Estonia. In Estonia, not a soul returning your change, giving you a direction, booking a room, selling you a book, wrapping up a package, pouring you a coffee, or thanking you returns a smile. As a visitor, do not expect it. Take it off the table. It is too expensive. It gives too much away. It demands too much commitment. "We must prefer real Hell to an imaginary paradise" is the way that the eccentric but holy mystic Simone Weil expressed a certain kind of low, stepped-down attitude, a scabrous over-sober presentation, grimness of face. I am extrapolating Weil to explain Estonians. (She was spiritual; they are material.) Paradise, like smiles, is fake, people there seem to be saying. "A test of what is real is that it is hard and rough," wrote Weil in *Illusions.* "Joys are found in it, not pleasure. What is pleasant belongs to dreams. We must try to live without imagining. To love the appearance in its nakedness without interpretation. What we love then is truly God." Weil was trying to find a way to learn to accept — even love — suffering.

To what I suspect is most Estonians, mostly older ones, suffering seems to be a reductive fact. Suffering is to an Estonian what wetness is to Walla Walla. I often got the impression that they were in mourning for the First World War. I saw many books and postcards on that endless savagery. I also saw that much depression ensued from World War II and years of depression that followed. Suffering is real, actuality without interpretation, the upshot of real life — secular, iron-clad, unavoidable — which can be harsh and difficult. What rules is real and what is real is rough. Estonians, like Norwegians, frankly think it is abnormal to go around idiotically smiling. It is a simpleton's look. It indicates oafishness to them, tomfoolery, dottiness, irresponsibility. Possibly an aspect of madness, idiocy. Any analysis of whatever social deictics regarding this state draws heavily on data unavailable to me, I promise you, but a long memory for wanton cruelty, empty promises, abraded hope, and deathless bullying cannot be discounted. Coldness — rudeness, if you will — is the *methode* there. It is accepted and acceptable, not holding doors, cutting in front, the refusal not only to stoop to pick up for you something you have dropped but to recognize that something has fallen. That beatitude is missing. You are but an obstacle, a hindrance, one they choose briskly to circumnavigate. It is a grotesque habit among inconsiderate Estonians, just as it is among insensitive, intolerant, self-centered, selfish, tactless, thoughtless, and uncharitable Americans to pay not the slightest heed to anyone standing behind them trying to pass, people whom they block, hinder, and inconvenience with lumpish indifference. We too often do not look to accommodate others nowadays. It has always bothered me, self-important buffoons who fatassedly block a supermarket aisle, motor in the left lane of a highway as if they own it, hog a doorway while they blithely chat. It might be one of the glaring vices of democracy, the belief that every space is yours and, dammit, no one's going to occupy it but you. I recall more than once hearing a Southern lady down in Charlottesville, Va. declare, not without a poetic turn, "She hated him with the tenacity of a hornet with a squint." It seemed to apply in Estonia in all sorts of ways.

There always seemed to be meanness behind the coldness. All of it became indissolubly connected to my life there. It was not for nothing that I began to refer to the country — stiff, hard, dark, and cold — in any notes I kept or postcards I sent as the "Iron Jail."

In instances of crucial, flagrant rudeness in Estonia Sarah and I, needless to say with irony, would often break into that old Judy Garland song, "Lose That Long Face,"

If as, and when you've got a long face

Rearrange it

Don't be contented with the wrong face

There's a way to change it

Does the day look painful?

Is the future glum?

Does the sky look rainful?

Hey there! Say there:

Are you in a vacuum?

All that stuff and nonsense

You can overcome...

and one night even went so far as to compile in order to watch a film-list we called "Theme Night for Old Estonia; or, Sour, Disagreeable, and Unlikeable Film Protagonists" which included, among other entries: Billy Bigelow (Gordon Macrae) in *Carousel*; Ethan Edwards (John Wayne) in *The Searchers*; Sol Nazerman in *The Pawnbroker*; Waldo Lydecker (Clifton Webb) in *Laura*; Mr. MacAfee (Paul Lynde) in *Rye Bye Birdie*; Harry (Gregory Peck) in *The Snows of Kilimanjaro*.

A reporter is supposed to be disinterested in the same way, I would say, that a spectator in front of a female nude in Western painting is presumed to be a man, a stranger, let us say, with his clothes still on. "The principle protagonist is never painted," John Berger observes of this fellow not only standing before the nude painting but who is, so to speak, actually implicated in it. I was trying to be honestly objective in my observations. But I was "in" the painting — principle protagonist. Frankly, seeing Estonia — disrobing her — was my focus.

It may be normal there, but being from the greatest nation in the country, as the yo-yo Spiro Agnew used to refer to the United States, I found it wholly depressing and never got used to it. It is an annoyance and not normal and blackens the day. I found I had to brace myself to buy a beer or ask a question. Maybe the country should import Thais. Thailand, the politeness capital of the world, is their opposite number. I can with all seriousness say that in my next life I hope to live in that country surrounded by kind faces and salaaming people. Brusqueness in Estonia is a kind of autism — a sort of mind-blindness. "What, you *expect* me to be kind to you, friendly, civil?" everyone seems to ask as he or she stands there in your sunshine. Confide in you? *Get personal?* You must be joking. (But even this implies conversation, communication, a personal narrative.) The obtuseness provides them with some angry payback. There were many times in that country when, as the result of such behavior, I mentally joined with the insane German novelist Robert Walser who declared from his mental institution in 1933, "I am not here to write, but to be mad."

The Whole Squalid Crew

I mention the States. The American Fulbrights to Estonia — a small group of seven, all men except for Sarah — were typically odd fish, but intelligent. Nerds. Naturopaths. A guy in computer science. One in social work. Another a textbook miser. Someone in philosophy. People whistling Mozart. Sarah was the only painter. I inadvertently bumped into the lot of them when several times they got together and I accompanied Sarah. A couple of hefty sapphonics from the previous Fulbright year who had stayed on, both Brillo-headed like the fat little heroine of Ernie Bushmiller's comic-strip, *Nancy*, were coping in an icy apartment in Tallinn. They wore serviceable shoes and net hats. Esther Oyster and Alice Klamm, or so I named them, whenever they appeared were tight and always showed up together whatever the occasion like some befuddled Scientology auditee with her dark-purposed "handler" in tow, with each scrambling the other's brain. I used to see the two canoodling in a remote corner of a nearby pastry-shop in the Town Square eating dessert dishes of *kissel* and drinking Madeira, an out-of-fashion wine that I thought perfectly suited them. Several older American students who drifted about and whom I could not manage to avoid — graduate students or something — disconsolately reminded me, as if I needed further proof, how a shadow always attends a shape. There was gormless right-wing economics major, Carl "Lymph" Knode, of whom I can report nothing save that he always wore a submarine tie-clip. That, and a Mickey Mouse watch. I thought it was a fitting prop for poor, vague Carl, at least regarding the analogy to the most famous cartoon character in the whole world, who, or so I was going to point out, is without any remarkable or even identifiable traits at all, probably the blandest of all imaginative creations, at least personality wise, but it turns out that the *original* little guy, the one with the pie-cut eyes and manic bounciness, was quite the ass-kicker[77] before he was sanitized and embalmed as the Disney logo, so apologies to Mickey and — why not? — to my man Carl. A loser named Marvin Muttley Mewshaw, a semi-ungulate with a headful of skunk-white hair and an indistinct affiliation, traveled about the country looking for things like green amber and red resinite and blue carbuncles — we all called him "Quackwatch" — all the while jotting down notes, clichés spatchcocked onto stale commonplaces, that he later mercilessly insisted upon reading to everyone as lectures in the *kohvik* that were so culturally acrid and hilariously uninsightful and just plain bad that they put everyone to sleep, except me and Sarah — we attended regularly strictly for the well-frosted cupcakes they served afterwards — who, scrunched up in the back row, nudging each other at every goony gaffe and wrongheaded remark of his, were often brought to risible tears. I was reminded of the quip someone once made regarding the campaign addresses of old Senator Henry Cabot Lodge — a dismal speaker, from all accounts — about the necessity of getting to the hall early to be sure to get a seat in the back row. A banana-nosed person named Sairey Golomb with orange bagpipe curls and oedematous ankles went endlessly rabbitting on with rapturous anger and pushy notice-me volume about the bad food of the country and kept repeating "*Nedugehdach! Nedugehdach!*"[78] It was not only her sour conniptions but castrating intemperance and bad vibes that reminded me of the freakazoidal mother in Melville's *Pierre*, that jealous, creepily frigid, pride-choked, rivet-eyed, fire-spitting, thin-lipped queen bitch who in the midst of one of her uncontainable and record-breaking shit-fits spitefully hurls a fork through a portrait of herself. I must say, however, that at times I myself felt thrown in with the odd, harebrained lot of that very same novel with all of its victims, riddlers, self-absorbed exiles, lonely souls, odd sex-elves, drama queens, and ambiguators with all of their crotchets, rivalries, and mad preoccupations. The irony was that this hard-faced, indeterminate-aged glowerball was there out of some kind of high-minded program regarding the plight of Baltic women — she was "funded," of course — which simply led me back to George Orwell's incontrovertible truism, "A humanitarian is always a hypocrite." The Butterheads, academics of some sort, had elongated academic heads, wore open-work sandals, and big efficient watches, were thin and tall and painfully earnest, and on any given day could always be found huddling in the far corners of restaurants and out-of-the-way cafés together eating big wet bunny salads and looking weirdly folklorish.

A lot of the students were aggrieved that the allotted stipend was so dismally small: as little as $16,000 devalued American dollars to cover travel, housing, food, incidental expenses, with a tiny addition earmarked for spouses that wanted to come. The Fulbright contingent for 2007-2008 were officially obligated to fly both ways in American planes, so no cheaper flights or fares were allowed. Lodging in Estonia — even for sub-mediocre flats and benighted apartments — was outrageously costly. Expenses were even higher for artists, painters, who, on top of all the luggage they had to carry (winter clothes, boots, etc.), were also saddled with an easel, tubes of paint, brushes, and unwieldy canvases to lug around, major bulkitude, to say nothing of having to cart them hither and yon by bus for any art-shows or exhibitions that were held and that all Fulbright officials of course encouraged. Sarah who had committed to three such exhibitions there, one in Mooste, one in Põlva — for which she won first prize — and a major one at the University of Tallinn, twice had to take thirty or more canvases three hours by bus both ways from Mooste to Tallinn! No pleading to the Fulbright Committee for parity ever got her a penny more. As far as they were concerned, if she wanted more money, fine, she could go carve penny-whistles and hawk them in the thoroughfares. She received not a jot of understanding. In the end, she had to spend much of her own money to survive. How different it was for me back in my day. In 1969 all of the Fulbrights sailed over together on the *S.S. United States* and were left alone abroad, and I not only remember having money to spare while living in a six-pounds-a-week flat on Pont St. in Knightsbridge across from Harrods but enjoying meals like steak-and-kidney pie, roast beef and Yorkshire pudding, and lobster *biryani* on large platters for about 13 shillings a pop!

The Estonian group, along with many former grantees, mainly guys and couples, who stayed on but made their presence known, were mostly in their late twenties or early thirties, friendly, confident, some bossy with the kind of self-importance associated with college sophomores. As Estonia was an "outpost," many of the students seemed self-conscious for that. Their chief frustration, along with a devalued dollar, was the remorseless darkness and the cold in that country. The prevailing and never abating sour face and the unfriendliness of the natives was not exactly a boost, either. Some students walked around in incandescent holiday sweaters trying to sell their zeal. Others tried to spend as much time as possible traveling — illegal during the grant period — in nearby countries like Finland, Denmark and Germany. Still others manfully dug-in in order to explore themselves, applying their wits and their resources to the task at hand, writing, studying, researching, getting to know the natives. One small guy, Gribble, in a perfect but seemingly workable self-deceptive bird blind, told me he simply pretended that he was living in northern Maine, surely a novel option on a foreign grant. One of the other Fulbrights bought a dog, defending his crazy impulse to purchase that little mutt with absolutely the worst cliché of all among dog-owners — and always with a screech — "She is a *born* comedian!" I met another guy named Ron Currants who was a foodie, an instinctotherapist who lived on raw vegetables, and when speaking always seemed to be addressing himself to an unseen audience, largely because no one was ever listening to him. "They serve eggs separately in plastic bags here, notice! Are you with me, people? One egg is 71 percent of a daily recommended cholesterol level, but we" — he had befriended another Fulbright named Queel and they were tight — "we decided we'll eat nuts. Why not, folks? Vitamin E, protein, fiber, and they don't crack being carried home!" Currants was bullet-headed with a low-slung jaw like a piranha and snapped out words whenever he spoke. Queel thrilled to his pronunciamenti, unlike an attractive young Norwegian woman taking a course there whom, with mad American zeal, he was always trying to convert to his health

views and whom I once heard when walking away from him exasperatedly whisper, *"Graatass!"* — a word I later looked up and which meant
"gnome." Currants and Queel, Queel and Currants. Their views echoed.
"They don't use pesticides here, but, tell me, does 'no pesticides' mean
'added nutrients'? Not on your tin-type, fans! I can tell that I am going
to swell up this year from MSG. It exists in fish, meat, why even in some
carrots and mushrooms, folks. Are you with me?"

One of the worst was an impossibly domineering shitter-wit named
Belk who was thin, pasty-faced, and had a face like a Thurber seal, chinless and fork-eyed. We used to call him Mr. C.D.E. Floptz, playing on
the sequential letters of the Snellen eye-chart, because he blinked a lot.
Sarah experienced a chemical loathing for him at first sight. He was par-
simonious in the extreme and walked around large-and-in-charge, reimbursing himself for his own inferiority by peevishly doing things like
cornering his wife in order to dole out her shopping stipend — he once
sent her out to the grocery store for *a single* organic tomato to bring back
for a dinner of six — and miserishly limiting his kids' food-intake to *half*
an egg, *half* a slice of toast, and *half* a tomato and toward the end, to
the scandal of the community, contriving to get two Estonian workers
to spend four days helping him move huge heavy furniture to a another
flat and then refusing to pay them with the outlandish claim that giving
them money would "offend them." I have always said our vices are our
virtues, but this was truly unique. This ingenious skinflint not only saved
money by stiffing those guileless workers, fleecing them outright, but
then, a consummate pietist, demanded that he be seen as a man of *virtue*
by doing so!

When one morning I complained that I needed some daylight and
something like a recognizable meal to jumpstart me after a dark week,
one of the sapphonics stridently declared, addressing me with closed eyes,
"Adrienne Rich — the poet? — believes that it is the lesbian alone in
women that makes them creative, that," she speechifyingly quoted, "'the
dutiful daughters of the fathers in us is only a hack.'" Her partner, grave
Alice to laughing Allegra, whom I had heard more than once was suffering from *ballonnement* or *gêne abdominale* — the word for constipation
in Estonian is *kôhukinnisus* — and whose big sweaters, I noticed, always
gave off the fatty smell of charred wool — dittoed her in such a fish-eyed

way, stating crisply, "She also didn't think men were necessary for pro-creation," I became convinced without further word of the argument of our origins being aqueous. Let me say ours was not always a gay time, if I may impertinently appropriate the word, a fine old English one with roots deep in the language, but alas now rendered unusable.

Taking in the lot of them, they reminded me of the comic crew in Lewis Carroll's long poem, "The Hunting of the Snark" — including the Barrister, Banker, Beaver, Butcher, and the doomed Baker — who all headed off on their perilous boat-trip in uncharted seas in search of a sinister but wholly unimaginable creature, including the *darkness* —

> They hunted til darkness came on, but they found
> Not a button, or feather, or mark,
> By which they could tell that they stood on the ground
> Where the Baker had met with the Snark.

— eventually to vanish into thin air.

One of the Fulbright grantees was a short actor with side-burns, Johnny Jump Up we called him because he was always "upstage center" looking for attention. Is acting the vainest or the dumbest profession on earth? I can never quite decide, so great are the arguments for both. I once came across an article revealing how desperately all of his life NBC's Brian Williams wanted to be a news-anchor. What else was that but a confession of vanity? Motives indict. (How different from the unassum-ing George Orwell, no glory seeker, who wrote about London during the Blitz in a garret under the searchlights, typing through air raids and the sounds of sirens, after long hours drilling with the Home Guard!) Why else do people become *actors* if not out of conceit, self-love, and narcissism? As Marlon Brando, said, "An actor is a guy who, if you ain't talking about him, ain't listening." During interviews, the movie star Paul Newman with a perfectly straight face and all of the gravitas of a funeral director always soberly referred to his "instrument," by which he meant his acting talent, as if he himself — in the flesh — were a Guerneri vio-lin. Actors surely have to be the biggest pains-in-the-ass on the face of the earth. The coddling! The pandering! The blasphemous amounts of money they receive and do not deserve! The publicity! The narcissism!

The endless dopey awards! All those prissy, self-regarding characters ga-
lumphing up to the podium on Oscar night to fill the air with all that
insincere and craven cant. "Best actor." "Best short subject, live action."
"Best original score, not a musical." "Best hand gestures in a B-film!"
"Best cheekbones." "Best well-fed ego in a Disney farce." It turned out
that Johnny Jump Up had received his Fulbright to study stage techniques in Estonia, something he could have done just as well with a small
repertory in Dennis, Mass. or Hoboken, New Jersey and with probably
much more success, given the thorny language problem. I was always giv-
en serious pause whenever I was in his company about the advisability of
government funding for the arts. In the end, I was told that the irrepressible Johnny Jump Up eventually hooked up with a Jewish girl from New
Hampshire named Putzel who played the oboe and wore bubble hats and
whom I mainly remember for arbitrarily disquisiting during the pause of
my once holding a door for her on the value in cold weather of unguents
and creams ("Skinfood is nutrition, mister"). I later heard that the two of
them had gone native and having joined a commune somewhere in the
Pakri Isles were inhabiting a hand-made reed hut — *pilliroog-onn* — and
living on black beans and rice, studying Reiki, and preaching that oxygen
was a sacrament.

Another Fulbright I came to pity as I got to know him, that is before
he just disappeared and decamped to Denmark, or so they said. I will
call him Waystacks. I happened to get into a chance conversation with
him while both of us were watching a local pointy-headed mountebank
entertain a handful of people by playing a tin-whistle in Raadi Park, rare
in Estonia in that it was a street act. The busker might very well have
been a lunatic. Waystacks who looked about thirty-five or so was sporting
a St. Louis Cardinals cap. I had seen him before on the streets of Tartu
once or twice, wearing a shabby coat, staring blankly through shop windows with tormented, underslept eyes. He wore thick eyeglasses and was
a small, vague-so-as-to-be-indescribable endomorph who had a lateral
lisp or slush-at-the-corners, saying, for example, "militia" for Melissa and
"Schanter Claus" for Santa Claus. We exchanged a few words. He had
a sensitive face and a kind of forest-animal shyness. We got along well
so we ambled over to the quaint Püssirohukelder (Gunpowder Cellar),
where we had a few beers and some munchables, he a meat pie and I a

platter of potato skins. The old cavernous place, brick-domed and medieval, reminded me of Auerbach's Cellar where Goethe spent some of his student days drinking mugs of ale. There were checkered tablecloths, but there are also checkered tablecloths at the 21 Club on 21 West 52nd St. in New York City where you can find $1000 wines. I saw when he took off his jacket that he had the kind of fallen-in chest that Donald Barthelme in *Snow White* describes as being characteristic of guys coming from the far west. He had an eye-tic. He was a fidgety, neurotic button-twister. I was glad to see him eating. He was very thin, with a sallow, somewhat fulvous complexion, enough to make me worry that because he had little money he was subsisting on nothing but decorative soaps, shoe leather, and spoon-bites of margarine. He spoke freely, and, although a seemingly educated fellow, he infelicitously shared with the notoriously slow and virtually illiterate President G.W. Bush's the indefensibly bad habit — a cretinous reader's — of repeatedly saying "I have *ā* headache" instead of "I have a headache" or "Let us take *ā* walk" instead of "Let us take a walk," a kindergartenesque cacogloss, at least to me, that is almost as bad as that cringe-making Ozarkian misconfiguration in one's personal handwriting — it is called "camel case" or "intercapping" — of writing small letters next to large in the same word, as in such popular significations as iPod, eBay, iTunes, etc. which few would argue is a distinct sign of illiteracy. (At least Waystacks did not, like our then reigning jingle-brained president, repeatedly say *nukular* for nuclear.) Waystacks, who had the nervous habit of polishing his glasses on the fat end of his tie, like John Le Carré's blinking detective Smiley, confessed that he was depressed over a situation in his family which, out of pain, he shared with me. He had two fat scheming sisters who with their vile husbands had coldly fleeced their doddering and aged mother of almost all her money — stealing it to give to their own children, buying them houses — managing as well to wangle out of her two houses that had been jointly owned by the family, a family as dysfunctional as could possibly be. He confessed with a maladive smile and not without a little embarrassment that out of stress and depression he had begun to wet the bed — in Estonia. "I thought I might go down to have a look at those bats" — *batsch* — "or whatever they are in Piusa," he said. I looked at him. Was I hearing things? "Bats?" Now *I* was getting depressed. "*Kaks ōlut*," I called to a waiter, ordering two more

beers. "Did you say bats?" "Yeah" replied Waystacks. "Bats. In Setumaa."
He shrugged. "I've already been to Rammu. But there are supposedly
these sand coves down in Piusa where I've heard they mine glassy-sand,
or used to — white and red." *Piooscha. Schand covsch. Glashy-schand.*
He raised his glass once more. "Yeah, I've heard that they have a lot of
bats down there. What else is there to do here?" Again he flipped off his
glasses and began shining them on his tie as he stared at me. We departed
that night, and I never saw him again. He disappeared in the end like a
lost Minoan. Maybe he went back home. But where and to whom and
why? I confess that I often thought of him when watching the lights at
Christmas flickering on and off on that iron bridge-crossing in Tartu, one
blinking bright, one blinking dark.

One of Sarah's new acquaintances there was a tall, hefty, semi-lumber-
jackish guy from California who was stationed in Tallinn. He had a head
the shape of a can, like the actor James Garner's. His flat was in a remote,
far end of the city, and it was a mess. He hated the place, not just his flat,
but Estonia. "I can't stand the goddamn whipped-cream here — do they
foam it?" "I go into a bookstore, right? All paperbacks! Priced on the back
— and expensive!" "You guys try one of the tomatoes here? *Stone*, man!"
He was tired and moth-eaten and homesick and had lost his camera and
couldn't meet a chick and wanted reading matter, *anything at all*, written
in English, "none of this gobbledygook, dude," and he fussily added, "I
prefer sci-fi." But by then I had honestly had quite enough. "Ursula K. Le
Guin insists the correct shortcut is *sf.*," I said coldly smiling. This did not
endear me to him. Frankly, I knew I was being petty and small-minded.
But I couldn't help notice that Dudelington was also a bit sweet on Sarah
which is what annoyed me more than his pretzel-shaped attempts to explain his less than infectious complaints about expatriate life. While he
growled at me, he spoke to my wife as if he thought he was handsome,
the way cool Troy Donohue spoke to Connie Stevens in *Palm Spring
Weekend* and to Sandra Dee in *A Summer Place* with that soft, hot fudge
of a voice and curl-over-the-forehead charm. What was this, a stoplight
party?

I could sympathize with his grim view of much of portentous Tallinn,
its bedizened and gloomy suburbs and outskirts, especially, slum-sad and
darker than the inside of a cow, recalling as he complained that beautiful

Helen in the *Odyssey* disdainfully even refuses to say the name Troy (*Ilion*, in Greek), referring to it merely as that *kakoilion* city, "dreadful." No, I could not in all good conscience duplicate for Tallinn Ezekiel's paean/ lament for Tyre (27:1-36), "the most glorious description of a city in all literature," according to Guy Davenport. But as I listened to this guy from California, I thought they deserved each other.

Our friend, in any case, had won a Fulbright grant to finish his Ph.D. in art, in spite of the fact that back when I was given a grant one already had to have his or her doctorate in order to apply. We shared a cup of coffee and cakes with him in a quaint tea-shop one sleety, pewter-dark afternoon in February, and I recall little but a storm of complaints. He was planning to attend an art show in Tartu — it was "You guys know a good tailor here?" and "You guys ever tried any of their cockamamie pizza with all that *oliivióli* shit on it?" and "You guys planning like me to cut out early and put Estonia in the rear-views?" and "You guys happen to have an extra room where you're at?" and "Any of you guys able to spare a twenty, American, 'cause I'm, like, hurtin'?" and, you guessed it, Sarah, a devout, unimpeachably charitable, overly generous, God-fearing Christian, but one of whose glaring, reductive, and I personally find un-bearable character flaws is the, to me, bourgeois and low-brow belief that it is a sign of corruption to have an exclusive friendship in marriage, one that his or her spouse for any of any number of reasons cannot or will not share, an inevitable and in honorable people always innocent condition of life since couples just do not necessarily like the same people, in a fit of truly misguided magnanimity invited this muttjack — Captain Bring-down, as we used to say back in the Sixties — to stay overnight at our apartment located virtually next door to the University of Tartu when he came down to the second city. My paying for the coffee and pastries failed to stem his crankiness.

"I half-expected to see some sunlight, but —" I said, looking up at a grey pewter sky, but he interrupted.

"What do you mean half-expect?" he grizzled. "How do you *half-*expect anything?"

A vocal stickler? I could scarcely believe it.

"It's just a turn of phrase."

He stood crotchety. "Tell me, how do you *turn* a phrase?" he angrily inquired, his chin jutting out. An angry pause held. "Look, before I come I've got to go clean the goddam mess in my flat which was left a pigpen by the guy who lived there before me and could get me the boot."

"Could?"

"What?

Snapped this observer, "Could? Of course it *could!* Just as it could tickle your arse with a feather!" His mouth hung open like a hippo with a hoopoe. "*Might*, you half-wit, *might!*"

And I walked away, taking Sarah with me.

I must say I hated myself. Grammar snobbery, the vice to which we both resorted, is always the recourse of a scoundrel. I am sure that Sarah wanted to go up in a balloon.

Fate, however, kept on happening, as Anita Loos so aptly put it. Late one snowy night back in Tartu our telephone rang, and it was — my name for him — Benny Profane. Tin Can Head. He had come down by bus and was hungry. ("I had a Big Mac in Tallinn and one of those, what, coffees, I mean do they *foam* the goddam cream?") I reminded Sarah it was her go, so she dressed, went out, and thoughtfully met him at the bus station, they stopped for a beer, and when afterwards they came blundering noisily into the flat late, all cold coats, fat gloves, and monstrous backpack, she gave him the best bed in a nook right next to the refrigerator, sink, food pantry. Like a post-party fraternity boy, Benny slept deeply — snoring like a grampus — until way past noontime the next day, never stirring unless to roll over with loud slams, when we not only had to tip-toe gingerly around that outsized body of his, prone like a dead pharaoh, but miss our porridge breakfast, as well. My hospitality bar is fairly high, but he was clearing it in street shoes. Starved, I left for the gym at 7:30 in the morning, and when I returned two hours later Benny was still horizontal, zonked, as content as an angel half-full of pie. I should have gone to www.wasteoftime.com on my laptop to complete that lost and pointless day. At the same time, I could not help but compare this sloth, this West Coast faineant, to all of the resourceful puffing, calorie-expending aerobicists at the gym and, in doing so, reflect on why no one has yet come up with a way to harness the incalculable amount of physical expenditure in all the gyms in all the world, now going nowhere, as an energy source. Has this been looked into by anyone?

A few American-Estonians, non-Fulbrights, who lived there year round made appearances among the visiting grantees. One of the more memorable was a large, cheery big-breasted half-Swiss miss with rubicund cheeks and gumball-sized faux pearls whom I called "Miss Lucerne Switzerland" as she was constantly comparing the themeless puddings of the Estonian seasonal festivals to the more delightful feasts of Fasnacht and Guggenmusigen back in Alpenville. A pal of hers, always in duck boots, Sententia — my name for her, anyway — had wandered in like a moonbat from the Kahlil Gibran Universe of Soft Knowledge and went around spouting fortunecookieana, optimistically to cheer herself up more than anyone else, in my opinion, with such upbeat gems like, "Plant roses, not thistles" and "Better to ask the way than simply go" and "The most important person you will ever be is the one that you are right now." What made it unintentionally comic — and why I found something ordinarily awful less annoying — was that she had an endearing comic lisp. I would have given a 5000 kroon to hear her say (after a priceless Bea Lillie sketch from 1937, entitled "Dinner Napkins): "One dothen Double Damathk Dimity Napkinth, pleath!"

Another woman, Katarina, who had inquired if I'd give a reading from one of my novels but because I never got around to it, spitefully began to peck at me at every opportunity. "Why would you want to *do* that?" she squawked when she once asked what book I was holding and I told I was reading Guiseppe Ricciotti's *Life of St. Paul*. "Are you serious?" I replied, "or are you ignorant?" It turned out she was both. She was married to a American plumber whom she also browbeat, and although she spoke good English she did so — especially when angry or provoked — on a voice frequency range somewhere between a virtually subsonic .01 kHz and 10 kHz which is roughly that of a squirrel's, pinched and hectoring. I believe her family was from Idavirumaa in the north-west and although I have since forgotten the crux of her long complicated story I do remember that it all led to the fact that she hated her mother and harbored a lot of grudges against her. We visited them one Sunday afternoon in their prettified but less than commodious apartment. Her husband Koit, who was the absolute soul of kindness and generosity opened up for us a new bottle of Vana Tallinn, a heady liqueur, somewhat brandyesque, that I tasted for the first time. It is never cloying, has a wonderful, warming, almondy, high alcoholic fizz to it, and goes well with coffee, in Coca-Cola, and on ice-cream and crêpes. I had heard that, mixed with sparkling Russian wine, it was called a "Hammer and Sickle" and was so named because, according to local legend, it hit the drinker on the head and cuts off his legs. We took it straight. At one point when Koit began to explain how effective his Estonian fire-stove/chimney — a funneled *laevakorsten* — was in winter, his wife belittlingly scorned its effectiveness, which offended him. Later that very night, reading *The Diaries of Dawn Powell* — the two boxes of paperbacks that we had thoughtfully sent ahead as an anodyne against the endless forbidding winter we had to jettison in the end — I re-read one particular entry with a scrutinizing eye:

> I saw the movie *Gaslight* the other night again. Every time I see it I think what is so ghoulish about this — it's the history of every marriage. Men and women have been quietly murdering each other for centuries with tender lack of understanding and believe me, lack of understanding can be more affectionate than understanding. The only way to get along in marriage is to surrender at once, don't have the bedtime Ovaltine he hands you laboratory tested, don't resist, just say Yes dear, of course I'm nuts but let's just keep it light while we're playing.

Katarina in a rather thrusting way, purported to be an intellectual and once lent me a book about Djuna Barnes which she felt after a week I had kept too long, refusing to accept my apologetic note, tucked into one of the pages, that I had had a hard time finding their flat in trying to do so. She later told Sarah, in a manner somewhat sniffingly perturbed, that my choice of the word "hard" carried some gender luggage with it. I later composed a sonnet, one of many I wrote on a slatted bench down by the dung-brown river, and called it "No Woman Hated By Her Mother Is Sane," which I emailed to Katarina the Crank in thanks. She hated the poem, it turned out, which I append here to see if you agree.

No woman hated by her mother's sane
Who ingesting all the bile she's got
Vomits up the hate and scorn and pain
On those who have become her lot.
A savagery the duplicating daughter

Like the mother viciously repeats,
As if by doing so she madly *sought* her
Choice to echo all that bitch's bleats.
A daughter apes her mother to a T,
Can never mask by guile her real face.
Neither wants the option to be free.
It is toward the final villainy a race.
No monster of a daughter as a scold
Is not taken from her mother's mold.

The most idealistic Fulbright, a naïve, good-hearted, toothy, Peace Corps-type with a hale-and-hearty Tom Tuttle handshake (see the movie *Volunteers*) — his name was Doodle — was gung-ho on Estonia. "Did you know that the word *Emajõgi* means 'Mother of Rivers?'" he asked me breathlessly, his face beaming, as if had just discovered radium. In the Fulbright program he was affiliated with the University of Tartu and was teaching classes there. He became a happy convert. He proudly began wearing a college beanie. In his flat with his family, he kept an over-sized Estonian flag — the *sinimustvalge* (literally "blue-black-white")[79] — tacked high onto the wall behind his desk in front of which stood a shelf filled with volumes of Estonian histories, dictionaries, and novels. His mother was a Southerner, but his father was of Estonian extraction which gave Doodle the impetus to take the country very seriously, so much so that he became a fervent convert to nationalism and when talking about its history he would positively mist up. No complaint about the country held water. Estonia was heaven for him. He spoke of the place with an almost religious zeal. Behind the superficialities of Doodle's being moved a larger distress, as with all hasty pursuivants or anyone so readily given over to a new identity. "Ain't it a wonder here? I know, I know, believe me, it's confusing at first," he would spark. "I keep walking by the sign *Hambaarst* and get hungry for a Big Mac, except that the word means 'dentist!'" "Let's see," he said, taking out a bottle of vodka. "The word for 'faculty' is, um, *õigusteaduskond* and the word *õigusteadlane* is 'law-yer.'" He banged a tray of ice-cubes. "Drive you nuts, huh? The word *spioon* is for 'spy'. *Spioon!* You gotta love that! *Spiiiioooooooooon!*" "The word *tige* means 'angry,' but the word *tigu* means 'snail!'" He swallowed laughter. "Go figure!" They were a sweet, generous, and uncomplicated couple, true believers, and had invited us over several times for cake, beer, and strawberries. One night Doodle reverently took down to show me a special copy of the *Kalevipoeg* that he had purchased, with gilt pages, one that looked like a very expensive edition. I will never forget the slow reverence with which he slowly, deftly, turned each of its big stiff pages, hovering behind me.

"Ice-cubes, one or two?"

"Three."

"Sarah? I believe you said ginger ale, right? One *ingveri-sooda* coming up!" Making drinks, Doodle gleefully bounced several ice cubes into her glass and handed it to her. "*Jää-kuubikkud*," he squealed with delight. "Ice cubes! Drive you nuts, huh?" He pointed to Sarah. "Could Kooby give her an ice cube? *Ya! Kooby could!*" Doodle, who was in his element, positively beamed and iterated, "Honest! I never want to leave this place."

I didn't want to say anything cruel.

We toasted them. "Here's to you both."

"*Elagu Eesti*," he proclaimed, raising his glass.

I remember when Doodle got up to get me the copy of *Kalevipoeg* how thoughtfully he gave it to me, reverentially with a bow and both hands settling it onto my lap as if he were a monk placing a psalter on the altar. Was I supposed to start reading it right there? I asked him about the rack of horns hanging on one of his walls. "They're reindeer horns," enthused Doodle, helpfully waggling fingers by his ears as a visual aid to our recognition. "*Põhjapõdra sarved!*" He sat down next to me and began dutifully to explain that it was common in Estonia, an old tradition, to give bones and horns of white reindeer as sacrificial gifts. "Cross the foot-bridge — the *purre* — and you'll find a shop selling them down by that old movie theater, straight ahead about a mile." He walked his fingers through the air. "Near the small food market? By the wooden church?" He asked, blinking. "Where they show old *tummfilm* on Friday nights?"

"We shopped over there once, I believe."

"For black pudding? Me, too. *Verivorst!* I love it!" He happily rubbed his tummy. "Ever try the *tanguvorst*?" Whenever he spoke about the country his face grew innocent and loopy and stupid with love.

"White pudding, right?"

Doodle nodded in assent, but he was on a roll, as he offered us a small dish of radishes. "Don't get me started I love 'em all. Egg pudding. Bread pudding. Swedish baked-apple puddings. Estonian flans, custards, mousses, curds." I knew the Japanese ate radishes for breakfast, so do the Pennsylvania Dutch, but in this country it surprised me. "Want to try on my *müts*?" He quickly reached into a closet, fumbling from a back shelf a college cap which he rakishly donned. It gave his jollity a desperate touch. "Or how about my university beanie?"

I forbore, with difficulty.

"Are you staying the full year?" asked Doodle, sitting down. I hesitated. "With Sarah, I mean."

"Maybe not the *full* nine months."

He stood up.

"How about a sauna?"

"Sarah?" I redirected his question to her, then turned to him with religious sincerity. "Me, I don't think so."

"Best thing in the world for you," Doodle assured us. "Constipated? Irritable bowel syndrome? Gall bladder pain? Got a pinch of the gout? Suffering a bad complexion?" He snapped his fingers. "Cures you like that!" he said earnestly. "Bingo! It's like an inoculation! I'm telling you, these people have all the answers. Do you ever see them groaning and moaning?" *Moaning*? Good god, I thought, all the time! Does not iciness as a national trait come under the psychosis of complaint? Sarah chose not to bother with the sauna but, not wanting to offend Doodle, I accepted. Not only moaning! Sourness like a truckload of bitter lemons, I reflected, as I disrobed, entered the tiny sauna-stall, and sat there in steam, as the temperature rose, naked and pink and almost scalded on a red-hot fireboard, humming with bemused impatience and repeatedly ladling cold water onto the hissing pile of faux coals like a wretched sinner in Sheol.

Doodle not only had his flag, an early collectible *Kalevipoeg*, his college beanies, his local tipple of White Diamond, and that sauna in his flat which gave him his bonafides, he went out of his way to shop with a net bag, mail home tins of Tartu *küpsis* — small raisin biscuits — and tried every chance he could to go mushrooming out in the woods with a big sickle, and his passion for the country extended even to eating things like *sylt* and *flikta* and *grunk!* "Want to go on that Põlva outing next Thursday, big guy?" he once asked me. "Amaaazing stuff." I graciously demurred, explaining that I was going to be ill that day. Doodle attended college banquets *(sööming)* and played with his little boy *(poiss)* and promised me that one day over mugs of beer we would sit down in a paradise of sweet nostalgia and analyze *(eritlema)* our Estonian experience when he got back to Rhode Island, which, when he did he enthusiastically assured me, much as he loved the U.S.A., would never be as exciting as Estonia.

I immediately forgot directly upon meeting them virtually all of the Fulbrights, although one did stand out. He was a Virginian of middling height with eyeglasses whose odd, blunt-muzzled head was shaped exactly like a capybara's. (I never did ascertain whether he had slightly webbed feet.) He had devil eyebrows — several scolding hairs came out of his eyebrows like Mark Twain's — and invariably when he spoke an avuncular forefinger was raised vertically above his closed fist to the level of his face. He wore a watch fob. His surname was Nosewheel. American students there frankly disliked him on the spot, even charitable Doodle, as the guy was a fractious, disdainful, and impossible know-it-all. The Village Explainer! Although he was officially connected to the University of Tartu as a sub-lecturer, for his lordly self-estimate he was one of those objectionable people, altogether too knowing, whose air of pretentious smartness, of cocksure superciliousness, was unbearable. The smug way that he shook out a sugar packet before pouring it alone made me want to shoot him. He spoke with a layer of aggressive concern and that kind of loathsome piety of speech almost always adopted by lessoning or hectoring types. As Goethe once remarked after meeting a fellow he did not like, "I thank thee Almighty God, that thou hast produced no second edition of this man." I could only wonder what he taught that others needed to hear. Stephen King in *Danse Macabre*, one of his feeble attempts at non-fiction, asininely refers to "the loonies who preach in Hyde Park" — George Bernard Shaw not only spoke at Speaker's Corner, that venerable spot in London where passionate intellectuals still voice their opinions in the open air, but it was frequented by such giants as Karl Marx, Vladimir Lenin, George Orwell, Friedrich Engels, C. L. R. James, Ben Tillett, Marcus Garvey, Sir Oswald Mosley, Kwame Nkrumah, William Morris, and Lord Bertrand Russell, among others

— when at the time up at the rustic University of Maine King himself was teaching a "lit" class entitled Themes of the Supernatural, as if the existence of such an infantile course in *college*, never mind "teaching" it, were *not* loony.

Nosewheel predicted the weather. He told people what to eat. He told them how to dress. He smugly corrected their schoolbook Estonian. He pontificated about the customs of the country and eagerly clarified the national rubrics of their odd behavior and remained generally dogmatic about the specific way everything was done there and, in the way it was not done and who was not doing it, an unbridled sower of calumny. He was self-invented like Felix Krull, with the same odd dodges and aspects of comical farce. He belonged to an epistemic community of exactly one, smugly manifesting an air of sheer cognitive privilege, identified by a cold, complacent, knowing smirk that never seemed to disappear, for he dismissed any and everyone who disagreed with him not only as poor unfortunates who were too blind or benighted to see the truth but also as unwitting dupes of secret, sinister interests. It gave his countenance a supremo's awfulness. Was not St. Evrémond correct when he insightfully wrote that affectation is a greater enemy to the face than smallpox? I was immediately reminded in Nosewheel of that hugely annoying, positively revolting, if farcically dismissible mannerbereft of a character that Mark Twain complained of in his *Innocents Abroad,* the shipboard nitwit on that *Quaker City* cruise to Europe in 1867 whom he derisively dubbed the "Oracle,"

...who eats for four and looks wiser than the whole Academy of France would have any right to look, and never uses a one-syllable word when he can think of a longer one, and never by any possible chance knows the meaning of any long word he uses, or ever gets it in the right place; yet he will serenely venture an opinion on the most abstruse subject, and back it up complacently with quotations from authors who never existed, and finally when cornered will slide to the other side of the question, say he has been there all the time, and come back at you with your own spoken arguments, only with the big words all tangled, and play them in your very teeth as original with himself. He reads a chapter in the guide-books, mixes the facts all up, with his bad memory, and then goes off to inflict the whole mess on somebody as wisdom which has been festering in his brain for years, and which he gathered in college from erudite authors who are dead now and out of print.

I believe that Nosewheel only spoke to me because he had heard I had a doctorate, that and the fact that one rainy afternoon I had once bought him a cup of cider and some gingersnaps (*piparkook*). As Harpo Marx once cattily said of his friend Oscar Levant, he never sponged off anybody he didn't admire. The aloof disregard Nosewheel's long-suffering colleagues held for him culminated in one of the more memorable if nasty remarks I heard someone make. "Tell me, if this guy is here, then who is running Hell?" I noticed within a very short time in Estonia that Capy — my eventual name for him — was quickly "otherized," since everyone began to avoid him. It was my dubious lot to see him everywhere. I saw him alone by the river. I saw him alone in the streets. I saw him, ass-wide, bustling busily about the tiny cobblestoned streets.

I mention Capy's negativity, an attitude he shared with other arrogant churls who in always taking fascistic refuge in an inordinate national pride are simply reimbursing themselves for their own obvious inferiority, because he reminded me in his arbitrary sourness and anti-intellectual contempt of gruesome old Moses Maimonides who held to a strictly apophatic theology in which only negative statements toward a description of God may be considered correct — you know, don't say "God is one," say "God is not multiple." The fact is, Maimonides who was an atheist personally believed in exactly *nothing*. Neither did Capy. For all of us poor souls who happened to be associated with peculiar herberts, thrusting buffoons, and pain-in-the-ass faux-arbiters like No-No-Nanette Nosewheel or Mo Maimonides the Mocker, life would never be easy. It was the great philosopher Maimonides who not only held that the crucifixion of Jesus, that "detestable Nazarene heretic" whose name, he insisted, should always be spat with a curse, was one of the supreme achievements of the Jewish elders, a treasonous rebel who, beyond that, should be boiled in excrement for all eternity! Maimonides was also a racist as brutal to his contemporaries, insisting that the Northern Turks and certain "extreme southern peoples near the equator" were non-human[80] and that aboriginals were lower than apes.

It turned out that Capy collected Nazi memorabilia and knew all the small shops in Tallinn that sold such stuff. He once directed me to a shop on narrow Pikk St. There I saw high on the wall lots of pastel portraits of the Romanov family, Czarist memorabilia with double-headed eagle, along with boxes of old Third Reich-related postcards which sold for about $40 each. There were many World War II medals (Axis) under glass. I saw Hitler Youth knives (HJ Fahrtenmessers); replicas of Knights Cross of the Iron Cross; Nazi fields caps. They also had a lot of guns, swords, pennants, clocks, many of them with "vintage" decals of Adolf Hitler glued on to them, all being palmed off as authentic. I even saw an old grey-blue tin of Zyklon-B, a little less than a two-gallon can. (The poison was provided in the form of pellets, which turned to gas when exposed to the air.) I dropped by the shop one early afternoon, which of course could have been midnight in Estonia, and who did I happen to spy there pedantically sorting out — fondling — whole handfuls of sleek black-and-red medals from Nazi Germany? You guessed it. I watched with shock the feathery runs that Capy made down several of the red-and-black ribbons and saw how priapically he squeezed the bronze medallions, and I heard his earnest questions as to the prices. He did not see me, as I stood back behind other customers. Capy began idly sorting through a pile of red Nuremberg armbands with swastikas, slipping several over his arm, holding up with great admiration. A World War II M40 German helmet with an SA Rune/Eagle decal took his attention. He fondly picked up a woolen M43 woolen field cap, tried it on, then put it down. I then heard a sudden exclamation. Even a blind squirrel eventually finds a nut. Suddenly he was holding high a mint shiny black Walther P38 pistol, the essential service firearm of the Wehrmacht, the very first locked-breech pistol to use a double-action trigger. Capy who was ecstatic tried weakly joking with the clerk, exclaiming with a loud hoot, "*Taaselustuma? Taaselustuma?* Revive? Will it revive?" (I effortfully wrote the word down in order to check it later.) I hated to conclude that this knuckle-dragging sub-monkey was a good little Bundist, but I must say I did seriously wonder walking home if the poet Fernando Pessoa was not correct when he once wrote, "Progress is the least noble of unnecessary lies."

I was Reynaldo in Estonia. I admit it. Remember him? He was the coy confidential servant — that may be too kind — in Shakespeare's *Hamlet* whom wily Polonius sends to spy on Laertes. As I wandered about the country, I made notes. I can hear the charge: you are a truculent traveler, just like your brother Paul, who for the record I benevolently consider nothing less than a realist. I am well aware of the "every-ship-is-a-romantic-object-except-the-one-we-sail-in" bit, as Emerson said, but I must say even moderating my hopes and lowering my expectations seemed to make my observations no sunnier or, not to put too fine a point on it, the people less dark. Tobias Smollett in his *Travels through France and Italy* irked Laurence Sterne who deftly dubbed him "the learned Smelfungus," an intrepid fellow who, traveling from Boulogne to Paris and from Paris to Boulogne, in Sterne's words, miserably "set out with the spleen and jaundice, and every object he pass'd by was discolored or distorted." What Smollett told to the world, as Laurence sarcastically had it, he should tell to his physician. All I can do in my defense is to quote from that peerless contemporary of Sterne, the Great Cham, Dr. Samuel Johnson, and repeat that I have found you an argument; I am not obliged to find you an understanding.

All the Fulbrights met his or her little exile in different ways, as is always the case. The advantage of consciousness can prove a disadvantage when the society you meet, the culture you confront, is almost imperious in its strangeness and the fealty it exacts of you in merely coming for a visit. I saw sad students trying not to show it, wistful students smiling, students on many of those doom-dark days courageously putting up a good front but feeling in their inner heart of hearts the certain crushing oppression of a cheerless, unending winter — most I think — trying far too hard to be happy. The delight of my little medal man! Pessoa again: "Evil is everywhere on earth, and one of its forms is happiness." I do not insist that my perceptions are correct. If you look fixedly at a pattern of bright red and then look at a piece of white paper, you continue to be aware of the pattern but as a pattern in green! What does that tell you?

Surely Pessoa is too cynical. But Ned Rorem in his *Knowing When to Stop* insists, "Happiness is blindness." He argues strongly that Tolstoy in *War and Peace* got it wrong. It is Rorem's belief that unhappy families are all unhappy in the *same* way, while happy families are happy in different ways. "Unhappiness renders virtually anyone undifferentiated and flat, and is the norm," he says, adding,

Happiness is rare, and should be; to be happy is to be unaware, a negative target in an unjust world. Happiness is blindness. Paradoxically, most people are blind, yet most people are miserable. I say people, not families, since even in America families are made up of divergent, unmolded parts.

Stone-faced

Speaking of unhappiness — or joylessness — I began to wonder in my stay abroad if this joylessness, this brusqueness, and the stone-faced mode in general also applied to the Estonian living abroad. Walking around Tallinn in the early 1950s with her partner Jean Paul Sartre, Simone de Beauvoir mentions in her later memoir, *Toute compte fait*, that she was surprised to find a number of shop windows displaying posters of Australian scenes — indeed, Australia, Sweden, and Canada became the new home countries for many. The further, the better, it seemed. During the thirty-year period from 1881 to 1910, over a million Russian Jews came to America. Several hundred thousand more arrived during 1911-1914. But what about our Estonian immigrants? They are not even mentioned as an ethnic group in Louis Adamic's rather well-known and often consulted book on immigrants, *A Nation of Nations*, a somewhat simple-minded book, at least in my opinion, which purports to celebrate diversity but does little more than *reinforce* the stereotype of every ethnic group that ever came to these shores. Adamic repeatedly relies on stock figures, for one thing, and for another, he writes poorly. The fact of the matter is: Estonians are well-represented in the United States. The largest wave of immigration took place after the Soviet annexation of Estonia in 1940. Surprisingly, there are more Estonian speakers in this country than there are in the city of Tallinn. (Are we as insular as most Europeans insist we are? It may be entirely the opposite. Were you aware that 100,000 people in the United States read a Cambodian newspaper? That there are over a million people here who speak Polish? When it comes down to that, the United States has more Jews than all of Europe combined!) The largest Estonian communities in the United States are in the New

York metropolitan area; in Lakewood, New Jersey; in Chicago; in Cleveland, Ohio; and in Los Angeles. One can also find the presence of many Estonians in and around Toronto and Vancouver. New York City was of course the most common and obvious port of entry into the States by ship both in the early-20th century and after World War II. Lakewood, New Jersey got its start as a large and growing Estonian center in the late 1940s and the early 1950s because many immigrant Estonians took jobs as farm workers — word-of-mouth — on all those New Jersey chicken, dairy, and vegetable farms. One particularly large employer of Estonians in the 1950s was Seabrook Farms in southern New Jersey. As I say, Chicago, Cleveland, and Los Angeles were also attractive cities with many economic opportunities for immigrants.

Many emigrating Estonians found work on big farms in or near Cucamonga, California, which old radio buffs will remember as a town memorable for being a stop in the comical train announcement on the Jack Benny Show: "Train leaving on Track 5 for Anaheim, Azusa, and *Cuuuuu-ca-mon-gaa!*" After repeated announcements the train announcer would continue, "Look, we're not asking much. Two of ya, or even one of ya…just somebody to keep the engineer company!" One might have taken the skit as a tourist ad for Estonia! In any case, it is interesting to speculate on how transmigration affects personalities.

There exist in the world those naturally malicious people we have read about, citizens and societies from the cultureless backwaters — those who are pleased to see a person fall, who rejoice in a neighbor's reversals, who delight in a competitor's failure — and we hesitate to believe it. But anyone who has read Carlo Levi's *Christ Stopped At Eboli* or Colin Turnbull's *The Mountain People* will get a glimpse by dint of the uncaring behavior of strange, merciless societies of Original Sin. I have heard the same of the Cayua, roughly translated as "the ones from the forest," in Paraguay, another xenophobic, landlocked country with an insular mentality where slavery and serfdom flourished long after it was abolished elsewhere and which not only has no tradition of political protest, but, as if languishing in a time warp, has made no attempt to woo the outside world — it maintains not a single tourist office abroad — nor shown the slightest interest in democracy.[81] *Trés étrange*, as they say in France. The fact of the matter is, sociologically, there do exist cultures that are by nature militantly unkind, ethically depraved, brutally cruel, enviously hateful. To author Levi, the villagers of Aliano were like people from another planet. He even says so in those words. He viewed them as rude, rustic, aboriginals, "Italic" people. In any case, peasants in my experience are only colorful superficially, anyway, and really do inhabit another world with different rules, which is not to say they are any worse or any better than their more advantaged classes. As the old Chinese peasant saying goes, "What is the greatest sound in the world? Your neighbor falling off his roof." What a charitable world! Sarah and I once saw a shop-lifting suspect being mercilessly shaken down in public by a policeman in the grocery store called Konsum, a hapless old man who looked as if he had not two kroon to rub together, while other shoppers walked by him without so much as a change of expression, and that included fussy Ron Currants and Dick Queel — we often saw the two of them shopping together, coursing the aisles with a kind of dithyrambic delight, fastidiously smelling knobs of cheese and testing gourds for freshness and squeezing tomatoes and fact-checking the ingredients of various bottled drinks — who were far more interested in the ecotones of produce and meat, bakery goods and delicatessen, frozen foods and candy in Estonian supermarts than questioning the treatment of a poor soul.

But how explain Estonians?

Mewshaw — "Quackwatch" —hadn't a clue, we knew.

I wonder if even the earnest Butterheads could.

Sympathizers explain them by pointing out that that they have unduly suffered. The Soviet boot. Stalinism. Bolshevik cruelty. Hitler and the Nazi threats. Occupation. Exploitation. Humiliation. Was my crass, if energetic, Americanism too much for them? Had too many sacrifices been asked of them? According to the writer Iris Murdoch, "The bereaved have no language for speaking to the unbereaved." If I was not the source of their glumness I saw, what was it? Provincial insularity? A refusal to wander widely? Is there an envious fear of a dancing intellect in others? Beavering away in the dark? What is the key to the pinched unforthcomingness? Is it not fair to ask? Does the cause come from within, from the depths of a remote, combative, weatherbeaten, wounded people who, in spite of themselves, somehow have come to identify more with surliness than with sunshine? The famous architect Le Corbusier memorably declared that design should proceed "from within to without," that "the exterior is the result of an interior." It perforce became the guiding principle of modern architecture. Why should it not apply to humans? Poverty is also cited to defend these dark Balts. (Avo Trumm in *Poverty in Estonia* shockingly declares that the average poverty rate in the republic in 2002 was "a little less than 20%," that for young people it was 40%, and for one-person households, as high as 35%.) How about country manners? Could that possibly explain them? The result of fifty years of the collectivized mind. Economic lassitude. All that. Salaries are small. One hears of course the notorious commonplace, "Once you get to know them, Estonians are the nicest people on earth." "They're all good-hearted underneath." You believe this, right?

I have to admit I relegated that to fantasy, to be filed in the same unique compartment as "I'm from the government, and I'm here to help you," "Don't worry, he's never bitten anyone," and "It's not the money, it's the principle of the thing."

I have also heard it commonly repeated, culturally accepted — a tired cliché, of course — that one first needs to take a sauna with an Estonian before he or she can ever become your friend. Nakedness as common denominator? As they do not eat much fish, maybe one can chalk up their misanthropy to a lack of omega-3 fatty acids from wild-caught seafood. Low brainpower! The human brain is 60% fat and what kind of fat one eats determines what one's brain cells are made of. Could that be it? I believe it was Voltaire who advanced the credible notion that very few men even know how to take a walk, and indeed it is sadly true that few men can take a walk with a prospect of any other pleasure than the same company would have afforded them at home.

I will not assert that I detected such indolence in Estonians, but who would deny that there is such a thing as psychic indolence? Mental analgesia? Diminished flex? Loss of pluck? The pioneer valiance that Americans used to possess — in my lifetime I have seen it ebb, even fully degenerate — was borne not only of opportunity but also of not being interfered with.

It made for joy and success. As you go about your business in Estonia, however, you rarely see a sign of brio or delight, nothing antic, not even pedagogical enthusiasm, only a peevish silence that amounts to a confession of vexation, an abraded temperament, excavating not even the possibility of good-will. On a dark and forbidding day such a thing can actually take on the distinct aura of malice, not because it is a raging, re-echoing imposition, but rather because it is precisely a *small* thing, I daresay a way of operating that most people accept and many will criticize me harping on.

Nun kenn' ich deine würd'gen Pflichten!
Du jannst im Grossen nichts vernichten
Und fängst es nun im Kleinen an,[82]

Faust insightfully tells Mephistopheles after the devil in *Faust (Part One)* boasts of how he upsets this clumsy world. I have to say I really do believe there is something to that.

The fact is there is a kind of person who can cope with coldness. What forces one mind to nurse aversions, fume over evils, collect injustices and act on them, another does not — or will not — reckon with. He takes sanctuary in or finds employment in his reserve with no chimerical wishes, no ardor, no sorrow to incapacitate, but then also no dreams, the sort of person that the screeching and paradoxically dictatorial reactionary dwarfette Ayn Rand was always attacking. Who knows, it is perhaps to have had insight into the brutal and terrible consequences of what passion might do. "Every desire is a viper in the bosom, who, while he was chill, was harmless; but when a warmth gave him strength, exerted it in poison," wrote Dr. Johnson to James Boswell on July 14, 1763. Is it a coping mechanism? What does it matter? "*Inter se convenit ursis,*" wrote Juvenal[83]. Beasts of each kind their fellows spare: bear lives in amity with bear.

"May Your Face Be As Ice!"

One of the nice things about living in Estonia is that you do not have to be polite — it is not expected of you. Good manners take time, extra effort, work. Here nobody expects greetings, salutations, waves. I was just going to write hugs. *Hugs?* Forget hugs! Not even close. A simple warm hug in Estonia is tantamount to fucking. It sounds crazy, but it is true. If you don't believe me, says Maldoror, go see for yourself. There are no exchanges: no thank yous, no you're welcomes, no have a good days. It is superfluous for you to reach into your heart for a bit of banter in a shop. There is no eye contact in the streets and never even the mild look of curiosity, only perhaps a quick glance that usually contains a surveying air. Several times I tried to broach the subject. One cold morning at the *kohvik*, a young Estonian college professor who had a bladed nose like the breastbone of a bird sat down near me with his breakfast tray, and after a smile or two we introduced ourselves and it was not long before we began talking about our respective countries. I complained, maybe too stridently, that Estonians seemed impervious to the concept of common etiquette. I could see by his hasty nod that he had often heard the objection, but that seemed to be the end of it. He seemed to feel, typically I thought, that Americans were all wealthy and probably, being impertinent, ill-mannered, and primitive themselves, fully deserved to be ignored. I argued some but concluded *these people don't listen — "Inimesed ei kuule."* (I went to the trouble of memorizing the phrase.) He had no sympathy. He dispatched his pancakes, smiled coldly, murmured something I missed, and breezed out of the room. I thought: Bugger off, you *kratt!* So much for my resolve to try to understand foreigners. When Nicholas Mosley wrote in his novel, *Hopeful Monsters*, "If we are to survive in the environment we have made for ourselves, may we have to be monstrous enough to greet our predicament?" he somehow seems to be answering his own question. I once bothered to mail to Jhumpa Lahiri, writer to writer, a striking book photograph of her I happened to come across, asking if she would inscribe it, which she snippily refused to do, returning it and saying haughtily she did not sign pictures. No problem, except that her not doing this in a happy kind of ocular redominance or perspective shift made me no longer want it. I disposed of it by leaving it on a table in a local library. I felt a refreshing relief in forgoing any care for her, and a new and sudden objectivity equally allowed me to see how mediocre her writing actually is. I mention this only because it was like that in Estonia. Their hyperborean indifference to small kindnesses let

one dispense with them. You surrender your freedom when you incur obligation. To our desires we are always victims. An argument can distinctly
be made that many of the hidebound Balts there are quite resolved *not*
to arrange the self, by faith or fortune or force, in order to be happy. It
seems extraordinarily to be something many throughout their entire lives
refuse. In *Black Lamb and Grey Falcon* Rebecca West perceptively noted,
"There is nothing rarer than a man who can be trusted never to throw
away happiness."

I refer to Estonians greeting their predicament. The phrase, "white
ship" (*valge laev*), has long been a proverbial Estonian expression for
hopeless expectation, inspired by an 1861 episode of Estonian religious
sectarians vainly waiting near Tallinn for a "White Ship" to take them to
the Promised Land. In 1854, a former Estonian farmer, miller, and bar-
keeper named Juhan Leinberg (1812-1885), calling himself the "Prophet
Maltsvet," began preaching in northern Estonia. Adjuring people to give
up amassing wealth, he created the sect of "Maltsvetians." A short im-
prisonment in 1858 increased the prophet's popularity, and the number
of his followers reached as many as 200-300 families. In 1860 he began
urging his followers to resettle in the Crimea in southern Russia, going
there himself in February 1861. The most fanatical of the Maltsvetians
gathered to wait in May and June 1861 at Lasnamäe beach near Tallinn
for the coming of the "White Ship" that was to take them to the Promised Land. The followers of Maltsvet also had an important part in the
peasant rebels in Albu and Ahula in November 1861. By the mid-1860,
Maltsvet's influence had begun to wear off. After returning to Estonia in
1865, he started in business again.

I have already mentioned the novelist, Eduard Vilde. He actually
treated the Maltsvetian in his novel, *Prophet Maltsvet*. Published in 1908,
it was the third book of a trilogy that established him as a major Estonian
writer. Like the other volumes, it mixed fact and fiction but was based
on letters and notes of interviews with Crimean Estonians. Other Estonian writers have also written about both the Maltsvet movement and
the "White Ship" episode in prose and poetry. Incidentally, Vilde's novel
also inspired the Finnish novelist, Aino Kallas, in her novel, *Lasnamäen
valkea laiva*, "The White Ship of Lasnamäe" (1913). In 1900 Kallas (neé
Krohn) married Oskar Kallas (b. 1868), an Estonian scholar, doctor of

folklore and later diplomat. The couple lived in Saint Petersburg and had five children. In 1904 they moved to Tartu. Aino became interested in the history and culture of her new homeland and she joined Noor-Eesti, a sociocultural society which campaigned for the independence of Estonia. Although she continuing to write in Finnish, she still addressed Estonian subjects. She lived in London from 1922 to 1934, while her husband was Estonia's ambassador to the United Kingdom. She published her diaries for the period 1897-1931 in the 1950s. A recurring theme in Aino's novellas is what she termed "the slaying Eros," a love that often leads to death, especially prominent in her trilogy of *Sudenmorsian* (The Wolf's Bride), *Reigin Pappi* (The Pastor of Reigi), and *Barbara von Tisenhusen. The Language of Sudenmorsian*, her most famous work, a story of werewolves set in 17th century Hiiumaa, is rich with archaic, romantic, colorful prose, something of a Kallas trademark.

Was it Kallas' treatment of the Maltsvetians and the "White Ship" that helped suggest the "Flying Ark" to the oddball Finnish "prophet" Toivo Korpela, the self-proclaimed Laestadian evangelist who traveled through Finland in the late 1920s preaching latitudinarian doctrines that allowed heavy drinking and unconventional sexual activities? Incidentally, in 1924 *The White Ship* was published in English with a foreword by John Galsworthy.

Reading about that Finnish religious sect reminded me of that Estonian movement expecting a "White Ship" to convey believers to the Promised Land. Both Finns and Estonians came under the heavy influence of Swedish pietistic religious sects in the 19th century, and there may be some kind of historical connection. Mid-19th-century Estonia, in the wake of Tsarist Russia's abolition of serfdom not only experienced a peasant revolt in 1858 but, with it, large-scale religious conversions and a mass exodus of peasants to Russia. To be waiting hopefully for something like a mythical White Ship fit the zeitgeist. This widespread motif with its diverse meanings in later Estonian literature originated from a sectarian religious movement in 1861, whose adherents were promised a better life if they emigrated to the Crimea in southern Russia; the White Ship, which crowds of people near Tallinn vainly awaited, was redemptive. So, the 19th-century Estonian White Ship cult fizzled out, but the concept of the White Ship — *valge laev* — remained and became a proverbial

Estonian metaphor for messianic or utopian expectation and became a favorite perennial theme in Estonian literature. An Estonian movie, *Valge Laev* was made in 1970. Tallinn has a Valge Laev Hotel. During the early days of the Soviet occupation in World War II, moreover, it is an indisputable fact that Estonians who vainly waited for a Western rescue from the Russians actually described themselves as waiting for an American or British "White Ship."

One wonders if things like messianic or millennial-like expectations can in the psychology of a people destroy a compulsion for self-reliance. Did it somehow snuff the urge to cope with the complexities of work-a-day life with things such as manners and etiquette? Could such fantasies mitigate the need to try? I think of a line from *The Duchess of Malfi*, "We are merely the stars' tennis balls, struck and banded which way please them." It sums up, at least for me, Estonian despair.

For, as I say, they do not try hard there — no gifts of fruit, no cakes, no offers for rides, no accommodating handshakes even. No bounty, no lavishness. It was a place custom-made for people like the tightfisted Mr. Belk whose default mode was not to have to spend *anything*. Laughter is not a big option. Gratuities are gratuitous. There is simply no scope for accommodating kindness. It is not that this is considered dumb or stupid. Simply, it is not considered. They count out coins during a transaction like funeral merchants after a corpse has been lowered. Sad struggle is built into their motioning hands, red conflicted eyes, crowbar voices. "May your face be as ice," goes a national saying. It is true. I am not making this up. I suspect that the subtext of all this — what they are saying — is, "Be balanced." You know, maintain objectivity. Disinterestedness is all. That sort of thing. W. B. Yeats in his poem, "An Irish Airman Foresees His Death," in a far more poetic and elegant kind of way makes the same point. An aesthetic balance, an unemotional and graceful objectivity, is seen by the poet to be an aristocratic trait of the World War I ace he writes about: "Those that I fight I do not hate/Those I defend I do not love."[84] I wonder what psychologists would make of a nation of ice faces.

No *bella figura* is required.

Völkisch suspicion will do, thank you.

As time passes while you are living over there, slowly, increasingly, imperceptibly you become the churl you have to become, finding a strange comfort in being saved from having to take the time to have good manners. A horrible truth intrudes; you realize: *suddenly you are saved time!* Grimly you begin to see good manners take effort, attention, style, but rudeness takes none.

The Estonian word for smile is *naeratus.*

Their word for turnip is *naeris.*

Revealing?

Rumble Strips On the Road

An Estonian will rarely offer things twice. (Oddly enough, in Korea it is actually polite to *refuse* any offering *three times* before one accepts it.) One morning in the small village of Räpina, after taking a very long bus ride from Tartu well before breakfast, Sarah and I were very hungry. Getting off the bus, we walked along one of those roads that was a long hump of packed dirt to make a visit. Farm country. Ramshackle outbuildings. The cold, dead air was full of animal noises: barking, crowing, chirping. I remember a sky grey as *galena,* the Latin word for lead ore. We knocked on a door and were let in. An acquaintance of ours named Opu tentatively offered us breakfast of some sort — it was not yet prepared — which out of graciousness we hesitated to accept, fearing that he might be put to a lot of trouble. His offer was made but once, only once, as is the Estonian way, but not again. We spent the next couple of hours sitting there starving, while Opu and his girlfriend, Õilme, who had silently appeared, proceeded leisurely to eat their breakfast in front of us, jam, *keefir,* a kind of yogurt, as well as *kurgid* sandwiches — they sliced each cucumber with finicky expertise — which without a word they scarfed down happily as we looked on. A complete silence held. There was no more of a smile to them than there was to a smoked pork-butt. A variety of thoughts, all of them negative, crossed my mind as I sat there about the nature of selfishness, remoteness, and disobligation — the self-defeat of removing oneself from the grace of sharing — not the least of which, among many, was one of the more significant lines from Goethe's *Faust*: "*Wer nicht für andre thut, thut nichts für sich.*"[85] Opu and Õilme both expressed vague interest in how we were going to get back to Tartu that night, for we had typically managed to miss the last bus. Standing there in the dark in the middle of a dirt road in central Estonia in the frozen dead of winter, I recalled what a frustrated Barack Obama had told his strategists, David Axelrod, at one particularly low point in their 2008 campaign: "This shit would be really interesting if we weren't in the middle of it." We spent the night at a small wooden hotel. I wanted to tell our breakfast companions what Groucho Marx, upon leaving a party, once told his host: "I've had a perfectly wonderful evening, but this wasn't it."

I was grumpy. I was not as charitable as dear Sarah, who was forgiving at all times. It was also not *my* Fulbright year. "I'm getting fed up," I would grizzle, feeling a close chest-squeezing histaminic attack coming on. "Katerina the Crank. Benny Profane. Currants and Queel. The noxious Butterheads. Sairey 'Is That Your Nose or Are You Eating a Banana' Golomb who in a discussion we recently had actually thought the Ottoman Empire was a chain of furniture stores. The notoriously cheese-paring Belk, the miser. And how about Capybara?" Nosewheel who was always sliding into my mind swam in my wake like the tick-tocking crocodile that stalked Captain Hook in *Peter Pan*. "Then those insufferable dorks at the American Embassy that refused to help you with your art brochure or bother to give you any assistance with transporting your paintings. And now we run up against Opu and Õilme, the Bubble Twins." Sarah grew quiet. "You like Waystacks," she encouraged. I said nothing. "You helped Esther Oyster and Alice Klamm when they needed you to move." I shrugged. "And you are nice to Doodle," she meekly offered, generously considering the glass half-full. "He's our neighbor," I granted. "And —" "And?" I tapped her on the nose. "Do you recall how Dr. Johnson defended himself when he refused to comment on the plot of Shakespeare's *Cymbeline*? He declared, 'It is impossible to criticize unresisting imbecility.'"

In any case, I apologized.

Estonians never apologize. They cannot say, "I am sorry." Or if they do say it, it kills them. They simply say nothing. It saves complexity. It saves face. It saves bonding, commitment, an unnatural emotion of obligation. I knew a young woman student who had depended on a studio being prepared for her months ahead of time, and she had gone out of her way to pre-arrange it. After she had arrived in Põlva, the woman who had promised her the studio simply shrugged, said it was not ready, and just stood there. It was an astonishing — and expensive — inconvenience. But tough shit. Not a word of contrition. When in another circumstance I was left high and dry regarding a promised deal that fell through, a little *hitlerlik* proceeded to tell me, "You no like, you go." *Anyway I can get you to French kiss the third rail?* I was going to say. But I stifled the remark. I had seen that trait in Katerina the squirrel-voiced virago, throw in this studio lady, add that insufferable dipshit manager at Ecolines, and it was beginning to add up. Apologize? Tear out his eyes! Apologize? Tear out his eyes!

I would frequently drop by to browse in a small used-book shop in Tartu and often asked the proprietress who worked there, Leirion, a dark, compact, friendly half-Russian/half-Estonian woman, a lot of questions about the country. She was very curious about my country, as well. On one of my first days there upon setting myself the difficult task of learning to read Estonian I had purchased a cheap copy of *Vahe Tera* — a translation of Somerset Maugham's *The Razor's Edge* — and we talked some. She was characteristically frank. Russians tend to be so. She immediately demanded to know why the oblivious and incompetent Secretary of State Condoleezza Rice — I along with several friends always referred to her as "September 10th" — instead of being immediately arrested, had *instead* been given one of the most important jobs in the United States government after being flatly proven so woefully and even criminally inept as National Security Advisor on September 11, 2001 when three planes were not only openly hjacked but two of them were suicidally flown into the Twin Towers in New York City at the cost of more than 3,000 lives. I could not defend that glaring incompetence — who could?[86] It was a small, dusty shop with lots of pamphlets, stacks of magazines, maps and atlases, old lexicons, boxes of old flavescent snapshots, a large section off to one side for Russian books and translations of Twain, Conrad, Poe. I also noticed the works of Cooper, Whitman, Frank Norris, Kipling, O. Henry, and even Thoreau who has always had a certain popularity among extremists. I saw a copy of Blaise Cendrars' *L'or*, a book that Stalin always kept on his night table. If books, as we are told, are a half-millennium-old commodity on the cusp of being swept away forever by technological innovations, one would not have known it there in this dusty little bookshop that seemed right out of a 19ᵗʰ-century lane in Charles Dickens' London. On one wall were tacked-up cheap photos of Jack London, Upton Sinclair, and even Edna Ferber, a stubby dwarf of a woman who looked about two-feet tall and was mostly nose — it was hard to imagine such an unprepossessing little grig had come up with such (faux) aristocratic names in her novels as Gaylord Ravenel and Yancey Cravat and McAlestar Couch. Yet maybe that is why she did. I browsed about the shop, sorting through piles. I was looking for a good detailed map of the country, an updated pull-out job, and never found one. G.I. Gurdjieff notes in *Meetings With Remarkable Men,* which sounds right:

> Good maps may perhaps exist for some localities, but with all I have had to do with them in my life, from ancient Chinese maps to special military topographic maps of many countries, I was never able to find one that was of practical use when it was really needed.

The woman behind a messy desk looked at me. "*Slovenska?*" (I am dark.) I shook my head. "*Magyarorszag?*" (I am tall.) I shook my head. She gave a quick once-over to my shoes and declared, "*Amireeklane.*" "Yes," I said. "*Ahhhhhh!*" I nodded to her and said, "Eesti?" She chuckled, said yes, and asked, "You speak?" She was pouring tea from a small steaming kettle and offered me a cup, which I was happy to accept. It was hot and as black as your hat. "These Bush fool! Iraag, like um, um, um, an illusion! *Meelepete!*" She tapped her temple. "Bang, shoot, attacks, but vhy?"

"Almost million Iraq — dead!"

"I know. And almost 6,000 American soldiers."

"*Vhy?*"

"I don't know."

"Innocent bipple, most."

"I can't explain it either."

"Sticky — *kleepuv* — bolitics, yes? You must know."

Leirion plaintively shook her head and, like spitting out an indigestible soursop seed, pronounced "Bush!"

A pinwheel of some of the factually challenged ex-president's remarks whirled in front of my eyes: "I know that the human beings and fish can coexist peacefully." "Families is where our nation finds hope, where wings take dream." "Rarely is the question asked: Is our children learning?" "There's an old saying in Tennessee — I know it's in Texas, probably in Tennessee — that says, fool me once, shame on — shame on you. Fool me twice — you can't get fooled again." (I watched the video clip of this, uttered in Nashville, Tennessee on Sept. 17, 2002, just to be certain I hadn't dreamt it.) "I just want you to know that, when we talk about war, we're really talking about peace." "Nobody likes to see dead people on their television screens." "I don't think America can stand by and hope the best from a madman." "I believe that people whose skins aren't necessarily — are a different color than white can self-govern." "In my judgment, when the United States says there will be serious consequences, and if there isn't serious consequences, it creates adverse consequences." "I know how hard it is for you to put food on your family." And his golden-tongued remark when asked how he thought history would judge the Iraq war? "We won't know. We'll all be dead." The great joke going around our premises in Estonia in 2008 involved Defense Secretary Donald Rumsfeld giving Bush his daily briefing and concluding by saying, "Yesterday, three Brazilian soldiers were killed." "Oh no," exclaimed Bush, "that's terrible." His staff sat stunned at this display of emotion, nervously watching as the President sat with his head in his hands. Finally, George Bush looked up and asked, "How many is a brazillion?"

As President Bush, Heckle, once memorably told Senator Joe Biden, Jeckle, "I don't do nuance."

How could I explain the cruel fate I foresaw for the those lying, thieving deviants and war-mongering criminals, Bush, Cheney, Rumsfeld, Wolfowitz, Tenant, Condoleezza Rice who, with barefaced lies, falsely claimed that Iraq possessed "Weapons of Mass Destruction" — making dire speeches fashioned out of total rubbish, utter bullshit. Things that made sense about the war in Iraq: nothing. Rice spoke prophetically of impending atomic mushroom clouds over the U.S. — and, committing us to a pointless and savage seven-year war on the basis of nothing but lies wantonly sacrificed not only thousands of young American lives but those of 600,000 Iraqis? I felt that such wanton and indiscriminate evil condemned the lot of them to a lake of boiling pitch, where, clawing each other and bobbing up and down with tar in their hair like bits of fat in a hideously roiling black stew, they would join other base malefactors of their kind like Malacoda, Scarmiglione, Alichino, Calcabrina, and dogscratching Graffiacane in the fifth bolgia[87] of Dante's *Inferno*!

"Bush!" I lifted my hands to stretch and waggle both of my ears — Disney's Dopey, Snap-Crackle-and-Pop, Fufluns, the Etruscan god of delight — and said in Russian, "*Shootka.*" Joke.

She burst out laughing. "In Estonian joke is *naljand.*"

I took out my pen and wrote it down.

She pointed. "Teacher?"

"I'm a writer."

"*Nüü York Times? Ajaleht?* Noospeppers?"

I shook my head, shrugged, and picked up a novel that was handy. "Like Jan Kross. *Romaani-kieranik.*" I was trying. "Or is it — *kirjutaja?*"

"*Jaa, jaa, jaa,*" said she, smiling. *Kirjutaja!*" She clapped her hands. "*Suurepärane! Eeskujulik!* I am say to you: kood! Kood!"

"Thank you. *Tänan.*"

"You, um, are liking this place?"

"*Jaa.* Yes," I said.

"But are not homesick, yes? *Kas Sul on kodu igatsus?*"

I shook my head. "*Ei, ei, ei.*"

"Nebraksa? Ohyyo? Washingtown?

I offered, "Massachusetts."

"*Naftatööstus?*" she asked, giggling, apparently in on a joke that I managed to miss, and kept repeating. "*Naftatööstus? Naftatööstus?*" Looking it up in a dictionary at hand, we had a good laugh together. *Naftatööstus* in Estonian means "the oil industry."

We chatted in a bumpy, affectionate way. She basically saw the people of the United States as resourceful, simple-minded, arrogant, generous, blustering, rich, vulgar, often downright comic people. A country of loud, hustling, crew-cut-haired, pink-skinned, overweight, deal-making, TV-watching, handshake-wagging, basically unimaginative businessmen and politicians in blue suits and red ties who have rarely read a novel or a word of poetry, merely books on management and systems-analysis. In the end, she took our measurement as a nation as profligate and caring, rapacious and generous, greedy and imperialistic, and, when Americans make up their minds to it, a people capable of endless invention, which in her lexicon would have included dissembling and lies.

I finished my cup of tea and thanked her. I bought paperback translations in Estonian of *Peyton Place*, *The Sun Also Rises*, and *Lolita* to try with a dictionary at hand to give them a go. I also bought a copy of *Hamlet* in Estonian ("*Hamlet, Hamlet, ma olen Su isa vaim!*" — "Hamlet, Hamlet, I am thy father's ghost!"), but it all proved too difficult. I soon gave up. Another woman worked in the shop on alternate afternoons, a big humorless drone whom I called, punning, Yvonne the Terrible, with her brittle-hard hair done up in a basketry of braids. She was a tartar. At first I tried to ignore the woman, and then began avoiding going there entirely the several days that she worked there. It was a white-lipped Yvonne who bluntly told me, "Russia may be the mafia, but the United States is the world's policeman, shoving everybody around." She despised President George W. Bush almost as much as I did. "We have kept you safe since 9/11," was his smug boast for years — but what about *September 11, 2001*? (After the disaster, as an anodyne, Bush encouraged us to *go shopping*[!] — and his wife told us to read to our children!) I would see the man on television walking forward like a rodeo rube out of Cut and Shoot, Texas, bowlegged, arms akimbo, the rictus of an idiotic smirk on his face, speaking like some callow fraternity dirtball, and never fail to wonder how in a country of almost 315 million people a churl like this ever got to be President. Money cannot buy merit, however. And it always goes back to the old dictum: when all else fails, lower your standards.

I could never explain, never mind defend — as what person could? — the deviousness and evil of that administration who hyped and manipulated threats from Iraq, cooked information, spread false reports and outright lies about WMD, politicized the CIA, instituted warrantless wire-tapping, shred civil liberties, maintained secret prisons, covered up the sadism at Abu Ghraib, arbitrarily sanctioned indefinite detention for Muslims without trial — one innocent ex-detainee Muhammad Saad Iqbal, 31, a professional reader of the Qur'an from Pakistan, was incarcerated for six years, five in a cage at the military prison at Guantánamo Bay although he was never convicted of any crime or ever charged with one and was then quietly released with the routine explanation that he was no longer considered an enemy combatant — and, worst of all, set policies of torture, savage, medieval, brutal! When is the war crimes trial to begin? I often called the White House loudly to complain and still remember the number: (202) 456-1111. It was a war that many pundits insist would involve us in an occupation there for decades to come. Aside from the anger and shame that any thinking American felt for these outrages, along with a war costing almost a *trillion* dollars in which, to say nothing of our own 6,000 dead and almost 35,000 wounded, we have also slaughtered as many as a million Iraqis (the arrogant U.S. military, in order not to look bad, has consistently refused to release body counts) — then wasted another $117 billion of taxpayers' money to rebuild the entire country — it was the source of no small discomfort to me to have to find myself in complete accord with that crazy braided cluck who always looked like she was rushing from a burning building, Yvonne, one of the biggest pains in the ass in the entire Baltic world!

The trillion dollars spent at war is, by the way, roughly the sum that the Bush tax cuts have bestowed on the top richest two percent of us. Who cares in the United States? No one has been drafted, for the first time in a century. America is fighting two long wars, each longer than our participation in both World Wars put together, without conscription. It is all of it hard fully to comprehend.

Who could have ever imagined the government of the United States of America, a smirking half-wit of a president and that old, wheezing, rusted-out, barely functioning body of Congress, a broken machinery of corrupt self-serving slobs, officially allowing the torture of *human beings* — euphemistically called by the CIA "rendition," a meat-slaughtering term! — *abattoirisme* in the way of masked, perverted, diabolical medieval inquisitors with knives and pincers and tongs and iron-maidens? Water-boarding! Freezing prisoners wet! Depriving captives of sleep for *months!* Open-faced slapping! Making them stand for whole days! Exercising them to the point of murderous exhaustion with a hessian bag pulled over their heads (a practice taken over from Israel's conscienceless Mossad)! Locking men in cells six feet by four feet! Prodding them with electric shocks! Threatening them with slavering dogs! Forcing them to take drugs! Piling as many as fifteen naked prisoners on top of each other with women's panties jammed over their heads! Duct-taping their mouths! Chaining them to the floor hand and foot in fetal positions for 18 hours or more, then watching while they urinated and defecated on themselves. Subjecting them to extremes of temperatures until they were literally pulling out their hair! Meanwhile, the public, slumbering away as usual, was kept ignorant. ("Treat 'em like mushrooms! Keep 'em in the dark"). Imagine, with a nod to George Orwell, having the effrontery to refer to this euphemistically as "extraordinary rendition" or "enhanced interrogation techniques"? What a horrid karma is the brute's. Have you ever truly pondered what punishment is likely to be meted out to torturers in the next world? I am convinced they will be put in a position not unlike that of the victims that they once abused.

In the end, ironically, Khalid Sheikh Mohammed — al Mukhtar, or "The Chosen One" — who at 24, by the way, had come to America to attend Chowan College in Murfreesboro, North Carolina and then later studied at North Carolina Agricultural & Technical State University in Greensboro where he graduated with an engineering degree but was often mocked and bullied as an Arab by racist fellow students during the period of the Iranian hostage crisis — told interrogators who also threatened to kill his two young sons if there were any further attacks on the U.S., that he lied when he was tortured and told the truth on other occasions.

What to me is the greatest mystery of September 11, 2001? The fact that the reasons for that attack, the savagery of such extremist hate, no matter how heinous the collective act was, is never, never discussed in the United States, not on television, radio, in magazines, in colleges, never by a politician, not by a candidate. The topic is avoided as if by fiat! To ask why is simply to be charged with treason, for any possible reason given, no matter how true, would be to blame ourselves and our allies, never mind by polemic but simply by explanation, for a fault.[88] The United States is fully innocent, of course. We have done not a thing to provoke anybody. The blood of martyrs has been the seed of the church, however, of holy causes, of just wars, for millennia. Those who die for what they believe surely give final proof of what reality is for them. It is an incontestable fact of history. Abraham, Sts. Paul and Peter, Iphigenia, John Brown. Is ours not a form of vanity, false pride, classic denial — how about national suicide? — a refusal, even as we commemorate the 3,000 deaths in the Twin Towers, to recognize that there was far more to it than an unprovoked attack? It is gospel that no attack through history has *ever* been unprovoked.

How could I begin to tell Leirion or for that matter any concerned European precisely when America's mad rush to military adventurism began? When LBJ signed the Civil Rights Bill (commonly known as the Fair Housing Act, or as *CRA '68*), which was meant as a follow-up to the Civil Rights Act of 1964, he secretly muttered to his friends, "We have lost the South for the next 30 years." His was a far-seeing insight. A political sea-change that took place across the country, still being felt, brought in the mad rising tide of intemperate, nativist, Islamophobic reaction: "Red States," "Yellow Dog Democrats," a wave of wanton, boomist, right-wing aggression fathering Vietnam, the Gulf War, Iraq, and now Afghanistan, the graveyard of empires, a raging orgy of us gratifying ourselves with insane world-wide aggression! It is also, only once again, another wrong war being fought in another wrong place, for, although we tend to think of the jihadists and al-Qaeda as associated with Afghanistan, it is really a Pakistan-based movement, precisely the country — the city Peshawar — in which the attack on the World Trade Center was devised. The focus is on the remote moonscape of the country of Afghanistan, but all the things that keep this movement fluid are in Pakistan.

I do have to say, however, that there was and is nothing that cannot be forgiven or understood in the Estonian mind-set, no matter how big a cloud of morosity hung over that country, for the brutality, the deprivation, they suffered at the hands of totalitarian regimes, whether Soviet or Nazi. For the many complaints I had there, when so many days created in me a resolve to just get up and leave, I figured I had come there, so why not make the most of it. I wanted to know the place. As Colonel Parker always declared, "If you want to see Elvis Presley, you buy a ticket."

Good manners — extraordinary manners — were at times in evidence, but rarely. After a showing in a public theater of the very moving documentary, *The Singing Revolution*, on March 5, 2008, a bunch of students, many of them Fulbrights, retired to an upstairs banquet room in the *kohvik* at the University of Tartu with tables set up with spanking white linen to discuss the ins and outs of that very moving film. (It was a unique experience, to say the least, to witness a documentary of goose-stepping Nazi storm-troopers and, then later, armed Soviet troops marching down the dark rainy streets of the city of Tallinn — Luise, Gonsiori, Tuukri — or of Tartu — Vanemuise, Fortuuna, Tiigi — and, then upon leaving the theater, to step out onto those very same streets!) When we arrived, food orders and drinks were taken by waitresses. This was the way things were done there, very formal and European. I looked around me. The room passed what Patrick Leigh Fermor called "the stern Mitford test" ("All nice rooms are a bit shabby"). Many of the Estonian "students" in attendance, several of them middle-aged women studying English, gracefully waited for everyone to be served before they began to eat. Suddenly, one attendee — a fat, self-regarding slob, a priggish American Fulbright who had ordered paprika soup — refusing to wait for others to be served, took up a roll and like Dickens' Barkis popped it at one gulp, exactly like an elephant, which made no more of an impression on his big face than it would have done on an elephant's, and then hunched over, elbows out, while he began loudly slurping from a large bowl he had the rodent's habit of looking sideways for predators with shifting eyes and rarely focused on what he ate. Who was it? You guessed it — Capybara. Nosewheel! I took that cue thereafter, I have to say, to avoid the company of most of the Fulbrights there and pretty much all Americans in general in Estonia for the same reason that poet Elizabeth Bishop refused to appear in all-women poetry anthologies — the anti-parochial factor. (Was it not the pithy Francis Bacon who adjured the traveler abroad that "… when he stayeth in one city or town, let him change his lodging from one end and part of town to another, which is a great adamant of acquaintance; [and] let him sequester himself from the company of his countrymen…"?)[89] I may carry the idea of combat in my person, I truly hope I do not, but that evening seemed to point me toward a major direction. In any case, *extending* themselves to you is not the Estonian way.

An old joke, among many such old jokes about them, is told that speaks to the Estonian way. A large party was thrown to which all the Baltic people are invited, and so everyone comes. All the Lithuanians who come, never leave. The Latvians who come, never leave, but say goodbye. The Estonians come, leave — but never say goodbye!

It is my conviction that people threatened by insignificance develop strange angles. Look at Waystacks and his bats. Doodle the Magnificent. Capybara the Nazi Rodent. I am certain I'm a candidate myself. Good god in heaven, I thought, had I become a Nosewheel? Once, a peasant, who was probably amused by my face and seeing I was a foreigner, brazenly tore off his shirt right there in public in the desperate cold, bare-chested and crazy, simply to show me how hardy he was. At first I thought he was a half-wit, a mere loon, one bottle short of a crate. Then I realized that the man was only a braggart — or was just frankly threatened, the way braggarts often are. "A brave man is never so peremptory as when he fears that he is afraid," Samuel Taylor Coleridge once observed. In any case, I misunderestimated him, as G.W. Bush once so chrysostomically put it. Weirdly, the fellow insisted on comparing his *thumb* to mine — a first for me. I thought with some apprehension that it was one of those "It's a dog-eat-dog world, and I'm wearing Milk Bone underwear" moments as tubby, beleaguered Norm on the TV sit-com *Cheers* once put it. Was the guy making a metaphorical comparison of the sort one need not go into? I thought maybe he was a Mason. I have been told that their gymnastic handshake involves nothing more than, when shaking hands with another Mason — am I out of line making this public and will I be punished? — one adept does little more with another than press hard with the thumb.

It is in many ways a wounded country. People have been *hurt*. Were you aware that neither the Marshall Plan nor the Truman Doctrine was ever extended to Estonia in any way? Could that have been the reason that, if a revolution began against the Soviet Union, they felt they would not receive American support? In the end, the question of whether a country is hurt or neglected or marginalized may best be answered by its own people. If their eyes say "we have been deserted," has not a verdict already been rendered? The fear they have felt! The brutishness of it all against a stomped-on people! I am reminded of a line of Hendrik Norbrandt's[90] which goes, "No matter where we go, we always arrive too late to experience what we left for." The people seem so isolated.

Fishermen in deep waders along the banks of the Emajõgi River running through Tartu always — only — fish alone. I would walk for endless miles along the banks of that muddy old river and never once notice one of those guys speak to another but rather like dubious sparrows feeding

241

on the ground remain always five feet from each other. Maybe that is the way with fishermen. But Estonian fisherman? Solitaries. There is never any small talk among them, no easy chatting or palaver.[91] I can state that. I watched, often, I never saw one of them catch a fish either. When I lived there and went on my morning walk to the gym, I always saw a tall dredging crane sucking up mud working loudly nearby rucking up the waters, yet it never deterred the fishermen, sweaty, hearty, red-faced, tut-mouthed men, their eyes soberly fixed upon the water, although the noise clearly scared the fish. It was not exactly as serenely bucolic as Izaak Walton fly-casting in the river Lea in the neighborhood of Ware or the Thames when Edmund Spenser long ago wrote lovingly of it when salmon-fishing was still a popular sport on its Westminster reaches. Was fishing in Estonia merely an existence assertion, a statement of freedom only? Those men to me were Estonia in small. They reminded me, as in a sense the whole country did, of the bewildered 12-year-old tomboy adolescent Frankie Adams in Carson McCuller's *A Member of the Wedding*, an "unjoined person," who suffers acute loneliness because she is not a *member* of anything. Her mother is dead, her father is too busy to spend time with her, and so she belongs to nothing. Her fantasies have been destroyed. The action springs from her desire to identify herself with something outside of herself. I often felt that Estonia in its isolation has long yearned for the chance to belong to the world it for so long has sought to embrace, right up to the present day, crucially unable to see and to feel and to know with certainty — and with good reason, after all that the pain they have been through — "We are all members of each other," as G.B. Shaw puts it in his play *Major Barbara*.

I have been told nevertheless that Estonians actually enjoy living far away from each other. Statistics have proven this. They tended to become irritable and upset when they were proximate, it seemed to me, which may even include the fellowship of going through the same door. Intimacy, closeness, bonding, and togetherness may kick in for community singing, but I do not see Estonians going in for jumble sales, buy-a-brick fundraisers, or convivially joining Moose clubs. A satiric strain runs through the culture. Irony is big there, as I say. I detect subversion. Others insist that as a foreigner once you somehow manage to pass magically into their acceptance — through a process of time or patience or graciousness or clubbability I myself cannot say — they can be truly friendly and even quite affectionate. A word they have, *tolgud*, denotes the act of community involved when someone invites friends and acquaintances over to his or her house, bringing everyone together, when a common job or activity is to be undertaken, a sort of communal Amish-like gathering, as Americans understand it, in order to, say, put up a fence or harvest vegetables or pick berries or paint a room or raise a barn by ensemble. I have been told Estonians love to do this in order to socialize. They may actually *need* to have such a word to establish a law or principle precisely because of native glumness, a fortress word invented the way a law is passed to stop a crime.

Pass Me the Crayon!

There is a disconcerting amount of graffiti in Estonia. It is a national disgrace — *häbiplekk* — a sign of disaffected youth, an indication in its huge anti-social compulsion of savagery, an endless rebus everywhere of bizarre spray-paint on brick walls, shutters, street signs, and on old buildings like that done by the Gogo people of Central Tanzania on rock walls near Dodona. Disturbed people commonly write on themselves. I wonder if it all indicates a future turn in Estonian fiction? Buses are also popular scribble-sites. Trains, as well. "For taggers attempting to win notoriety," noted Chris Faraone in *The Boston Phoenix*, "a moving train is the equivalent, visibility-wise, of securing a spot for your work in the Louvre." The contemporary genius of this genre is of course Banksy, the pseudonym of the British graffiti artist, political activist and painter. But there are many well-known "taggers" (as graffiti mavens and freakazoids are called) in the United States, ikons like the outlaws "Spek," "Floe," and "Utah," a New York graffiti queen, now doing time, who actually believe that what they do is art, but the law stalks them, comes down hard on them — the city of Boston earmarked $250,000 for graffiti removal in 2008 — and nails them as trophy kills. One international crew, "Dirty 30," goes globe-trotting about with spray cans and may even have reached Estonia. Agitprop finds the queerest outlets, like tagging. *Sunt lacrimae rerum*[92].

A distinct Civil War-period look clings to Estonian rivers and riverbanks, even in the city, that water flowing along the mud banks — no fences, old hanging trees, earth flowers — and the old troll-houses built along those banks with that familiar "roof hang" end, dull yellow or sickly-green clapboards of thick wooden planks (solid planks, not, as in America, long thin shells of cheap wood) evoking an older time. Einstein's was not just a theory; his riddle had come true. I also saw in many Estonian houses rawly plastered walls and rooms with wide crude old floorboards, like those of sour brown that one finds in so many of Lucian Freud's paintings. ("My world is fairly floorboardish," Freud once declared.) The further I moved through space, the slower I moved through time. I saw many log cabins, which were also used for saunas, which seemed as if they could be free-standing at Shiloh or Murfreesboro or Gettysburg. Vistas there recalled 19th-century paintings. Bierstadt. Constable. You could smell mud. I remember once looking at the dung-brown river coursing by as we sat along those banks and saying to Sarah as she painted a couple of small watercolors, "You should do what Paul Klee did the year he died — painting his raw *Death and Fire* with tempera on *burlap!*" Nothing modern adhibited to those sienna scenes. I sensed a specific time warp as we walked the brown banks and felt the quartering wind, slanting and cold, coming off the Emajõgi when and where over and over again I could hear the shivering lines of poet Theodore Roethke: "Saginaw, Saginaw, where the wind blows up your leg!" Was this solitude and calculated removal the way that they meditated, isolation bringing out the Carthusian in them? What do I know?

Much of living in Estonia in winter is about staying warm. The main source of heat for Sarah in the isolated country-studio she occupied in Mooste — the first time I went there with her I saw in the grim little place what looked like the Jo Mielziner reality-condensation set for *Death of a Salesman* — was an odd, tall, kiln-like chimney dominating one corner in a large rustic room with 15-foot ceilings. (The first lodging she had been shown when she first visited Mooste was a dark cavity at the back forty of a pig farm, and not cheap, a futile, stoveless hovel, virtually spelunkable, in which I believe she would have had to burn pine-knots for illumination.) There was an earthiness almost baked into the walls, an odor of wet wheat with something like the musty smell of ginseng. A metal door to a tiny oven opened into the stove-belly. Sarah had to pile oven-sized logs into the oven mouth — never too many as that might badly crack the stove — and then after loading it, fire it up, adjusting logs with a long metal poker. A safety grill had to be cocked at different widths to measure the amount of oxygen that she wanted. A routine was involved. She had to wait for the flames to burn out to get to the red-hot burning coals but could never shut the vent before all the wood burned down, for that move could prove fatal. The trick was to try to close the grate, lock the cast-iron door, and then simultaneously reach up high with the poker to hit the high latch that effectively closed the vent. With six or so logs, she was able to heat her full studio for 24 hours. On any day below freezing, Sarah was forced to keep to her room to work — she painted from her window — and when it was dark she could do little but read. She woke in the morning, cooked modest meals for breakfast of hot farina with butter or lingonberry jam. At noon she chastely had a bowl of soup with a slice of toast and cheese and sweet mustard and instant coffee with some powdered cocoa to make it more palatable. Sarah would then paint, read, doze, listen to music and the BBC news broadcasts by way of the Internet.

I reminded Sarah several times in order to buck her up that Descartes once inhabited such a small heated room in Germany in which he experienced a series of three powerful dreams or visions that he later claimed profoundly influenced his life and of which, in his *Discourse on the Method for Conducting One's Reason Well and for Seeking Truth in the Sciences,* he bravely remarked, "I was completely free to converse with myself about my thoughts." I concluded wisely, however, to omit any details about the brutal winter the philosopher spent in 1649 in Stockholm whither he had been invited as a teacher for Queen Christina — "It seems to me that men's thoughts freeze here during winter just as does the water," he wrote — and where he caught pneumonia and died.

On days that were not bitterly cold she headed out bundled up like a Christmas-card snowman to paint outdoors — her *métier* — where the need for woolen mittens or heavy gloves became frankly irksome. There were many paintable sites around the manor grounds there, one of the many German-owned properties that were destroyed and burnt in just over a week in December 1905 when, according to history, the Estonian peasantry ran riot. Seven hundred years of political and economic oppression exploded at the time, and Russian administrators, acting for German interests, sent in twenty thousand troops of the kind of brought on to attack Father Gapon and his striking workers in St. Petersburg on January 22, 1905 ("Bloody Sunday") and thousands and hundreds of Estonians were shot, sentenced to death, sent to Siberia. When she worked outside at her easel, Sarah was generally left alone, however, for unlike Americans who have not the slightest qualm about barging right up loudly to comment, "Can I see?" Estonians are not at all the type of people who would bother a *plein air* painter. The vast grounds of the impressive but slightly crumbling yellow-stucco manor were quite extensive. It was an estate obviously once run by a group of stewards, and simply walking around the extensive grounds, set off by ancient outlying barns and hedges, gave me something of a picture of the way things once were. I could feel the presence of old tenant holdings, lot-meadows, pastures, strips of arable fields, beast and hay pastures, cottagers and villeins who had to dig down to pay things like tithes and ditchsilver and, if it held there as it did in old England, that special service called "bederepe," reaping carried out for the lord of the manor by his tenants, a job originally understood as boonwork, but later made compulsory.

Sarah's room there, while close and warm, had all of the solitude of a Trappist cell but was not half as comfortable. A group of local workmen rehabbing a building connected to the studio who left doors open to the cold freely came and went to use the single bathroom, and gawked at her. "One word sums up probably the responsibility of any Governor, and that one word is 'to be prepared,'" as President George W. Bush once brilliantly declared. "'The future will be better tomorrow.'"

I invariably thought of bewildered Leirion, my bookstore friend in Tartu, whenever I heard in my head the echo of another nonsensical George W. Bushism. "The Axis of Evil?" Get real! The terrorist Osama bin Laden himself even had a better speech-writer. Osama referred to Palestine as "the Prophet's Night Travel Land." He told the world, "The effort was never: Determine which individuals we ought to roll up." "A swimmer in the ocean does not fear the rain," is truly memorable.

It was understandable that Sarah, alone at the time, sought out company and chose to spend Christmas with a couple she knew in the tiny but faraway little town of Oulu in Finland. She took a ferry to Helsinki and then wended her way north on a seven-hour train ride up the western coast, almost to Lapland, where she spent time painting, and several times biked to town, about three miles, on packed snow in 10-degrees-below-zero weather. It was romantically the period of "blue nights" there, when the evening sky overhead in an astonishing and mysterious epiphany manifested an eerie glowing blue, and it was then, she told me, that she could understand why Scandinavians have such welcoming home-stuffs, linens, bedding, couches, pillows, and rugs in those tidy little homes, clean and cozy, warmed by fires and soft lights everywhere and with lots of candles to combat the overwhelming cold and darkness of winter. Do not waste time waiting for Spring. Far more likely you'll get snow. *"Pluves hiemes"* ("more winters") as Horace said in his great *Ode I.* Whatever Jupiter grants! Estonia is located on the 59th Parallel North, one should not forget. The line passes through the Bering Sea! Alaska! Okhotsk! We are not talking Cuba here. It is even colder up in caribou country. Sarah had meals of salmon baked with mayonnaise, reindeer, honey and slices of pickle; went skiing in Ruka, near the Arctic Circle, up near the Russian border; and even visited the town of Suomussalmi — something to write home about on a postcard — which has the distinction of having the highest suicide rate in Finland, not an insignificant fact in a country that is known for them.

The long shadow of the Kremlin is still thrown across Estonia. "What we call history is really just the luxury of afterwards," I recall the sanguine widow declared in Allan Gurganus' *The Oldest Living Confederate Widow Tells All.* "Honey, history ain't so historical. It's just us breaking even, just us trying. Darling, you know what history is? History is lunch." Not in Estonia. They have a long memory of long crimes committed against them for a long time. Soviet crimes. Estonians are irreducibly yoked to that buggering fact. They see Russians around them everyday "The most accomplished exiles are and always have been Russians. They're tutors in it practically," notes Alan Bennett in his play, *Single Spies.* There is a small Russian Orthodox cathedral in downtown Tartu, on Magazin Street, just off the Old Town Square. It is a church, significantly, unlisted on any tourist map but one unalterably in sight. The phenomenon is it is cartographically ignored for simply being a Russian. If this noteworthy old church were located in Hyannis, Massachusetts, there is no question it would be one of, if not the, stellar tourist attraction of Cape Cod. In Tartu, it is simply snubbed. Just ain't there. Non-existent.

Sarah and I attended an Easter service in that church on Sunday, March 23, 2008. We had to seek it out. No one would tell us where it was, if they even knew in the first place. Church attendance was small, no children, mostly potato-faced old ladies in fat, insulated coats with turnip-sized handbags, all Russians. A bearded priest was presiding, in a heavy gold-sewn cope and alb. I began thinking of the recent world-wide scandal of pedophile priests in the Roman Catholic Church: it is so depressingly symmetrical that, all in grotesque concert but seemingly unaware and indifferent to each other, the priest in California was behaving the same way as the priest in Ireland and the priest in Buenos Aires. Is it the power that a priest has, the aura of authority, the conduit from God, that allows him this license? A new Savonarola is needed to scour the church clean.

I must say that, growing up, I tended to fear priests to a degree but never quite dared hate them; yet they always seemed to me in too many instances to be acting, hamming it up — and I think a good many of them were. Let me clarify something, though. I never went so far as to sink into a state of cranky, fat-witted, self-indulgent, or intellectually lazy faithlessness — a state of discontent almost always expressed in the form of bourgeois, puerile, exhibitionistic, and endless arias of complaint — such as those of shallow and maleducated Woody Allen's ("To me, there's no real difference between a fortune teller or a fortune cookie and any of the organized religions"[93]) or facile and faithless Christopher Hitchens' ("What can be asserted without proof can be dismissed without proof"[94]) or the utterly dunderheaded fascist Ayn Rand's ("God…a being whose only definition is that he is beyond man's power to conceive"[95]) or big, bad, busy, bumptious, bloviating Robert ("I defy God to strike me dead") Ingersoll's ("Christianity did not come with tidings of great joy, but with a message of eternal grief. It came with the threat of everlasting torture on its lips. It meant war on earth and perdition hereafter."[96]).

The writer Flannery O'Connor, who always had an unerring eye for the smugness of "virtuous" people, knew as well that grace was also possible in — and available to — every one of us in whom "good was something under construction."[97] I believe one of the most hopeful sentences in the Gospel is "God so loved the *world* that he gave His only begotten Son, that whosoever believeth in him should not perish, but have everlasting life" (John 3:16, my italics) It is a wide embrace. I have no doubt that this was the fond hope of Pope John Paul II when he visited Estonia on September 10, 1993, bringing benediction to a people sorely in need of it.

Our Father Zossima that Easter Sunday morning looked intent and devoted. Women in Russian churches still cover their heads, as they did in the United States way back in the 1950s. I counted only four old men in attendance — if you could give such a term to three figures slumped dolefully back into chairs and another, a century-old skeezix, looking incontinent and staring bewilderedly at the floor. People at a postcard-counter at the rear of the church were talking rather loudly throughout much of the service, ignoring the service going on at the altar. People were buying candles and various knick-knacks throughout the Mass. Going to a church does not make you a Christian — a paraprosdokian not to forget — any more than standing in a garage makes you a car, but I must say I had to remind myself as I stood there that it is one of the best places to start. We had to stand up through the service. There were no pews. Dark icons hung on the high walls. One can at least assert that a religious service was being held there, that this church was not merely an old dusty museum. I took heart that the faith of these worshipers, in spite of the irregularities, held. It crossed my mind that when Marx declared that the aim of Communism was to "realize the essence of man" in the classless society, he was, even if inadvertently, proclaiming the real aim of Christianity itself.

For Christ is truly the Perfect Man in whom all the potentialities of human nature coalesce and it is by membership of his Body that we become part of a social organism in which all the conflicts of class and race and religion are transcended. We are part of the Mystical Body of Christ. Talk about the blissful replenishing dream of perfect Communism![98] A tall blackened painting of the Savior recalled for me lines from Charles Causley's poem, "Christ at the Cheesewring:"

O will you drink my body deep
And wash my five wounds dry
That shot with snow now gravely grow
As scarlet as the sky?

All down, he said, the drowning day
And down the damaged sky
God's naked son his fingers won
About my thieving eye,

And like a bough about my brow
Planted a hand of horn
That men may see mirrored in me
The image of the thorn.

Ours was in all probability the only religious service given in Tartu that morning. Christianity very much resembles a cult in modern Estonia. There were no signs of celebration or of Easter or of palms or bells or resurrection in the city of Tartu. The Sunday squares were completely deserted. The sea of faith has visibly ebbed there. I believe the bold and scarifying lines from "The Scattered Congregation" by the Swedish poet Tomas Tranströmer (b. 1931) aptly apply:

Inside the church, pillars and vaulting
white as plaster, like the cast
round the broken arm of faith...
But the church bells have gone underground.
They're hanging in the sewage pipes
Whenever we take a step, they ring.

I remember reading years ago about a "religious" sect or order in Ursula Le Guin's *The Left Hand of Darkness* called the Handaratta who feel they are serving or honoring God by adamantly refusing to speculate one way or the other about His existence or attributes, rather like honoring the great chefs Auguste Escoffier or Jean Anthelme Brillat-Savarin by going on a fast! Were these Handaratta?

"The Lord gets His best soldiers out of the highlands of affliction," wrote C. H. Spurgeon, but no signs of such soldiery have surfaced there. The occupation of Estonia seems to have bred no notable saints, nor any holy protestors like Simone Weil or Hans Von Dohnanyi or Dietrich Bonhoeffer, the German Lutheran pastor and theologian who was a participant in the German Resistance movement against Nazism and founding member of the Confessing Church. Why is this?

Did Estonia throw off the yoke totalitarian regime only to collapse into a moral void or founder in a world of hedonism?

A weird paradox may be aborning. There is an inevitable void in a life without God, a point Dostoevsky raises all through *The Brothers Karamazov*. Making a case for the futility of political power when compared to that of faith, Evelyn Waugh wrote to a dying George Orwell[99] in the Cranham Sanatorium about his just-published novel, *Nineteen Eighty-Four*, to explain to his friend and fellow writer, an atheist, that he found a haplessness, a modern *délire* — a folly — in his character Winston Smith's private revolt against Big Brother and the repressive state as he seeks a mystical union with the proles by the ultimately false and morally insufficient means of sex as an expression of individuality, even if it is aligned with Julia and human love. "I think that in 1984 we shall be living in conditions rather like those you show," Waugh writes, yet then needs to explain:

> But what makes your version spurious to me is the disappearance of the Church…
> I believe it is inextinguishable, though of course it can be extinguished in a certain place for a certain time. The descendants of Xavier's converts in Japan kept their faith going for three hundred years and were found saying 'Ave Marias' and 'Pater Nosters' when the country was opened in the last century…The Brotherhood which can confound the [totalitarian] Party is one of love — not adultery in Berkshire, still less throwing vitriol in children's faces. And men who love a crucified God need never think of torture as all-powerful.

Waugh's point is clear. The dreaded "Room 101" is never the ultimate desolation for a person of faith.

I have mentioned that in Tallinn or Tartu I heard no bells, "the living voices of past centuries," in the words of A. N. Whitehead, something of an oddity in an Old World city, although a friend of mine assures me that on Sunday morning now in Tartu they are rung in some churches. I remember the Russian poet Andrei Voznesensky who, staying at my house for several days when I was teaching at Phillips Academy in Andover in the early 1980s, once happily remarking on the bright peal of bells from the school's bell-tower but also saying, enigmatically, "American bells are different from Russian bells" and adding with some sense of being scandalized that bells seem to have gone out of fashion in the United States. His incantatory poem, "Master Craftsmen," which celebrates the ringing of bells, he passionately recited one night to a packed auditorium of students and townsfolk, all the while raising his voice, revolving his right arm like a windmill. It was one of the most powerful recitations I have ever heard, showing how histrionic young poets held large Russian audience in the grip of a communal art that has a good deal in it of a dramatic performance.

Painting Easter eggs seems to be the essential pastime for Estonians during this holy day. They boil the eggs in onions and/or coffee-grounds which turns them brown and tan. Playfully, they then crack each other's eggs in games. A traditional Easter pudding, *pasha*, a pressed milk-curd dessert with raisins — the name is of Greek origin by way of Russian — is popular. But that is the extent of the Easter equation. Tinted eggs in profusion. Bunnytown.

Carmen Secularae

I was struck by the fact of how secular Estonia is. Churches for the most part have become museums there, such as Tallinn's majestic but strangely anomalous St. Nicholas, which is situated at Harjumägi at the foot of Toompea Hill. Originally built in the 13th century, it was partially destroyed in Soviet bombing of Tallinn in World War II. After restoration it is in use as an art museum and concert hall. One cannot picture pilgrimages made to this church, in spite of its imposing beauty. It is a tour venue in which visitors walk around and rubberneck. Booths at the back of significant churches in Estonia all sell postcards, offer tours, charge for pamphlets. What was it that the American political pundit Patrick Buchanan once said, "Every great cause begins as a movement, becomes a business, and eventually degenerates into a racket"? (Making the same point as Charles Péguy who declared, writing of the cynical exploitation of the idealism of the Dreyfus affair by French politicians: "*Tout commence en mystique et finit en politique.*"[100]) After spending time in Tallinn and Tartu, taking it in as I tried, I slowly began to wonder if I had not entered one of those weird, doomed, unrepentant Biblical cities of old such as those recalcitrant outbacks mentioned in Matthew 20 like Chorazin, Bethsaida, and Capernaum. I saw nothing touching of faith or Christian fellowship as I traveled about, and I must add that I had one or two worthy predecessors in the quest, for we learn from the Old English chronicles of Paulus Orosius, specifically in his *Seven Books of Histories Against the Pagans* that, along with Irish holy men, pilgrims, and scholars, Wulfstan of Hedeby, the 9th-century merchantman and traveler who famously traveled to the court of King Alfred the Great, also voyaged to the eastern Baltic — and visited Estonia! Why not also throw in the "Quackwatch" Chronicles — all those Mewshavian insights — in the department of deft explorers?

Most Estonians are too cynical and too dubious to fall for all of those transparently fraudulent TV evangelists and simonists, hawking God for cash, whom gullible, uneducated, and beef-witted Americans have made hugely rich. The very *names* of these sinful rogues alone — tricky Jack Van Impe, profane Jimmy Swaggart, smarmy Benny Hinn, roiling Rex Humbard, mouthy goofball Rod Parsley, haggling Tim Haggard, bloviating Oral Roberts, rubbery Robert Schuller, and, of course, the bulbous Catholic-hating fat-pants John ("God's beachball") Hagee — suggest chicanery. A truly skin-crawling oleaginous cracker with a forked devil's goatee from Lake Charles, Louisiana named Mike Murdock, a purveyor of "name-it-and-claim-it" theology who virtually lives on television, boasts with an almost licentious idiocy of how many suits he owns and cars he drives, and then for his finale always closes in toward the camera to whisper with a sidewinder's guile that if you mail him money God will automatically fill your coffers. ("All we're trying to do is seed the Kingdom of God here, folks! Call now! Don't wait! Go to the phones!") All are trolling for money. All have sham doctorates. All claim God speaks to them, a deity around which they cluster like sycophants around a dictator. All are Chaucerian frauds and transparently butterfingered media carnival barkers, swindlers, and mountebanks. Christopher Hitchens is surely correct when he declared, "If you gave [the late Jerry] Falwell an enema, he could be buried in a matchbox." Billy Graham who has been described by Marshall Frady in his fair-minded and disinterested biography as a "marceled Tupperware Isaiah" has all his life shamelessly shilled for the Republican Party and was actually awarded — and I might add fawningly accepted — a star on the *Hollywood "Walk of Fame!"*[101] As C.S. Lewis assures us in *Reflections on the Psalms*, "Of all bad men, religious bad men are the worst."

Needless to say, there are other ways to come to God than through the agency of such slick and treacherously cunning crocodiles, many ways. At times I wanted to shout out to Estonians with all the astringency I could muster Baudelaire's *"Dieu est le seul être qui, pour régner, n'ait même pas besoin d'exister."*[102]

Sadly, in the United States, any fool on television, no matter why or in what contemptible capacity, becomes an instant celebrity — a repulsive starboard-leaning, putty-white, racist glove-puppet named Glenn Beck; the disquietingly untalented jughead named Simon Cowell, a multi-millionaire I'm told, whose fame on a show called *American Idol* has been built on nothing more than his nasty hemorrhoidal opinions made with slouching disdain for amateur singers; the spectacularly ordinary daytime TV icon/blimp Oprah Winfrey, heroine to a million-woman army of servile, desperate, half-crazed house-bound women, all come to mind. The power of Winfrey's opinions and endorsement to influence public opinion, especially consumer purchasing choices, has been dubbed "The Oprah Effect." Television is all — only — about money.

Faith — churches, sacramentals, etc. — did not seem to take hold in the way of rule or reference, as say in Paris or Rome or Berlin. I see most educated citizens in Estonia as basically non-aligned, trans-religious progressives who, when they even bother to look, find orthodox religion as too demanding, specific, and probably even retrograde. (I find it somewhat revealing in retrospect by way of parallel that the eccentric Estonian-born architect Louis I. Kahn over a lifetime of energetic creativity never once designed a church, although at one point in his life had supposedly drawn up plans for a synagogue in Jerusalem, a schema that was never realized in stone.) It may be noted here that Estonia, uniquely, has retained a pagan religion centered on a deity called "Tharapita" a war-god in Estonian mythology believed by many researchers to be a variant of the famous Norse god, Thor. The name Therapita or Taaripita has been interpreted as "Thor, help!" which is *Taara a(v)ita* in Estonian. The *Chronicle of Henry of Livonia* mentions Tharapita as the superior god of Oeselians (inhabitants of Saaremaa island), also well known to Vironian tribes in northern Estonia. According to the chronicle, when the crusaders invaded Vironia in 1220, there was a strangely beautiful wooded hill in Virumaa where, so locals believe, the Oeselian god Tharapita was born and from where he flew to Saaremaa. The hill is believed to be the Ebavere Hill (*Ebavere mägi*) in modern Lääne-Viru County, one of 15 counties in Estonia. There are also Taarausk, an ethnographically-inspired modern "New Age" religion of a god, Taara, derived from Tharapita, worshipped in forest groves, and Maausk, which translates as "faith of the earth." Estonian folk who seem to be drawn to natural magic and druidical-like nature-mysticism seem easily to submit to the beckoning lure of the many animistic religions that preceded Christianity. When the German crusaders and knights invaded the far reaches of Estland in the 12th and 13th centuries, many of the priests who followed in the armies' wake, when they were brutally and mindlessly martyred, were burnt as offerings to the likes of Perun the Sun God and the Lord of Horses.

Speaking of nature mysticism, there once existed an ancient meteorite cult in Estonia. Somewhere between 7,500 and 4,000 years ago a meteorite fragmented over the island of Saaremaa, striking it with a force comparable to Hiroshima, leaving nine craters, including the 110-meter Kaalui crater, a gentle sloping bowl almost perfectly round and now filled with stagnant, murky water. There is archaeological evidence that this location may well have been a place of ritual sacrifice, as well. It was, and still is, considered a sacred lake by many Estonians.

It can be argued that what is a stumbling block to happiness in Estonia, on a personal level, with implications of course on its national face, is, in my humble opinion, the stumbling block — the actual *scandalon*, if you will — of sourness, a suspicion that joy is mere mystical twaddle.

There is in resolute immanence that which flatly refuses flight. The earthly sphere is of the *sarx,* not just flesh as such, but what St. Paul would call a lifestyle ungoverned by the spirit, and to fail to feel, never mind see, "God's wondrous works in glory that excel" is to miss out, to forego, almost categorically to refuse — it is not for me to say the chance of one's own salvation — but surely the joy of mystical growth. T.S. Eliot believed that the disappearance of the belief in Original Sin meant the eclipse or departure of true feeling, of the honest process of moral struggle. Vision departs.

I would spend hours on many days in Tartu simply sitting alone in the semi-dark in a wooden pew in the early 14th-century church of St. John's, ruminating, looking up the groins to the toplofty ceiling, surveying the long stone ribs, floating up there on high, saying prayers sometimes, reading pamphlets I borrowed from a chancel table, or day-dreaming, splayed there with my arms out reviewing the mended nave and transepts and broken terra-cotta sculptures, reconstructed pillars and pilasters. I almost always felt a quiet peace in that echo-haunted church, a huge stone mole with its oratories and side-altars, and when feeling that way in a dark church with its spectral presences I tend to hear within me over and over again for some reason the exquisite strains of Ralph Vaughan Williams' lovely *Five Variants of Dives and Lazarus.* Once or twice in the church I actually fell asleep right in the pew, drowsing, then nodding off on certain days after having gone on epically long walks, reminding me that when young Eutychus fell asleep on a window sill at Troas while St. Paul was preaching and fell out of a third story window, St. Paul brought him back to life![103] Would that for all my sins I can hope for the same.

The church of St. John's had been badly bombed in August 1944, and its structure seemed almost as fragile as the equally well-known remnant of the 15th-century Tartutoomkirik on the hill, its broken shell open to the heavens, that had been destroyed in the Northern Seven Years' War. I was struck by how transitory everything was, vanishing like Ozymandias, even the most seemingly indestructible things, and my thoughts would revert to the mysterious words of Mark 9:1: "And he said to them, "I tell you the truth, *some who are standing here will not taste death* before they see the kingdom of God come with power," [my italics]. Are then some of us, selected ones — and why — never to die? Who? Me? Will those chosen to see the kingdom of God in all its power remain *here*? Are not such places as these crumbling old brick churches filled with lost echoes and the shadows of ghosts made for the thoughts of such people as I, crouched there in pew? I would have reveries, even hallucinate, and on the cusp of some moon-dream or other yearn to rise like an eagle past the nave to soar through the ever-expanding, accelerating multiverse of quark masses, atomic nuclei, and black holes radiating energy into the photon-rich, neutrino-filled, wildly fluctuating, and dimensionless fields where there is no time, only space, and look directly into the eye of God.

I have just hunted down my copy of Peter Matthiessen's *The Snow Leopard,* in order to check a particular passage that suddenly came knocking on my forehead, one that I had once underlined, of an entry that he made up in the canyons of the black Himalayas with its rare beasts and scimitar-winged raptors all around:

> Also, I love the common miracles — the murmur of my friends at evening, the clay fires of smudgy juniper, the coarse dull food, the hardship and simplicity, the contentment of doing one thing at a time: when I take my blue tin cup into my hand, that is all I do.

Why didn't I feel that way myself? Was my sensibility so stunted, so soured, my heart so constricted, that I was immune to the subjective bliss any kind of existential moment or possibility of epiphany?

Maybe living abroad in such a marginalized country made me self-consciously fearful that I personally did not signify on this planet. But surely no one is insignificant in the ontological sense that no one is ordinary. Take, for example, the uncommonly strange and seemingly indifferent names Salmon, Zerah, Jothan, Azar, Asa, Hezron, Uzziah, Joram, Jeconiah, Shealtiel, and Zadok. Total nobodies, right? Wrong! They were each of them direct ancestors of Jesus Christ as listed in the genealogy of Matthew (1-16)[104]. Who that has lived could possibly be more distinguished, yet how many of us recognize those innocuous names today? No, in the matter of Christianity even sparrows count! Neither is any country insignificant. All places, as all people, are salvageable. Who remembers that right after the Satanic temptations in the desert, Jesus specifically travels — it is clearly a peculiar trip — to "the land of Zebulon and the land of Napthali by way of the sea, beyond the Jordan"? What was the purpose of this seemingly pointless journey or visit? It was precisely to bring hope "to those people *who sat in darkness* [my italics]," and in blessed consequence those benighted people come to see "a great light:" "upon those who sat in the region and shadow of the dead Light has dawned" (Matthew 4:16). I had this reflection in that church on a dark snowy day that in the spiritual realm no place is an outback just as no person is merely ordinary.

Did the people in remote Estonia, I wondered, feel the advantages of their faith or only the asperity of it?

When I thought of the secularism of Estonians, it occurred to me, as I sat there in the pews of St. John's, at the door of my tent, so to speak, like Abraham by the oaks of Mamre, except it was not during the heat of the day but on icy cold of the Estonian dark — and although I saw not the Lord, I felt Him — that secularism might be the renegade way that such abused and afflicted people alone can cope, beleaguered souls in the kind of desperate flux Hugo von Hoffmansthal wrote of with his "*manche freilich müssen drunten sterben/Wo die schweren Ruder der Schiffe streiben.*"[105] The country has actually *organized* itself beyond a need for God. I began to wonder if commonly pursued religious practices such as prayer, services, fasting, even if they provided the scaffolding on which to build a holy life, did not in some paradoxical way *exhaust* the meaning of holiness.

Estonians, as with anyone forced to believe, perhaps rejected such belief systems pushed on them over the centuries by every religion from Catholicism to Lutheranism to old Russian Orthodoxy — Soviet atheism included. But then, "what takes the place of empty heavens and its hymns?" as Wallace Stevens famously asked. (Poetry, it turns out, was the secular and aesthetic substitute for that great poet.) What a fund of other options, an endless supply of what Ralph Waldo Emerson referred to as "Rat-revelation," with posturing mediums charging a pistareen a spasm and nine dollars for a fit, a gospel that comes by taps in the wall and thumps in the table-drawer. Jehovah's Witnesses refuse blood transfusions, consider the United Nations diabolical, and believe that the number of Christians going to heaven is limited to exactly 144,000. Mormon theology — whose main text plagiarized of the King James English of at least 25,000 words — teaches that God was once a man, that every planet (of which there an infinite number) has its own gods, supports polygamy, condemns tea and coffee, and encourages the wearing of sacred underwear. Scientology, which I have always thought of as "Mensa for Idiots," panders to the minds of credulous dodos — many of its celebrated top co-religionists were high school dropouts — with a spate of technical jargon touching on Thetans and electropschyometers and Walls of Fire. In T.S. Eliot's "Gerontion," what replaced true faith was the actual creepy aesthetic of art worship, magic and séances, the emptiness of collecting antiques:

Among whispers; by Mr. Silvero
With caressing hands, at Limoges
Who walked all night in the next room;
By Hakagawa, bowing among the Titians;
By Madame de Tornquist, in the dark room
Shifting the candles; Fräulein von Kulp
Who turned in the hall, one hand on the door. Vacant shuttles
Weave the wind.

For the Estonian people the general alternative was ancient beliefs, as much as anything. Such old beliefs for many who are still seen as medieval peasants have survived in the form of folk tales and fables. I don't know why it is any worse or say stupider than the "faith" I heard sometime writer/director/and sometime cook Nora Ephron inanely announce to an NPR interviewer (August 7, 2009): "You can never have too much butter. If I have a religion, that's it." Estonians are far less blasé or decadent but soulfully credulous. They talk earnestly about wood-elves, centuries' old curses, wolves, ravens, leech-gathering, the uses of healing herbs and minerals, bark and fresh water. I rarely passed a dense forest in that country, especially in the deeper interior, without picturing in my mind's eye hirsute men wearing antlers living in crazy Jorvik mud-love or madly risible trolls doing cartwheels with pagan intent or groups of stark-naked, phenomenologically unashamed, melanin-deprived virgins with flowers in their hair traipsing about in the moonlight and playing kantele standing on their toes while ululating ancient *regilaulud*[106].

Certain locations have remained mysterious and magical for them. A well-known spot dubbed the "Witch's Well of Tuhala" which shoots up hot water and great white puffs of vapor for days on end attracts pilgrims from all over the country. Ellen Barry in the *New York Times* writes that the geyser "is believed to be 3000 years old and sits on Estonia's largest field of porous karst where 15 underground rivers flow through a maze of caverns, audible but unseen by human inhabitants."[107] The extra-natural has always fascinated Estonians, forming even in the abstract something of a faith, not perhaps by way of any recognizable orthodoxy, but rather through things like the ancient study of dreams or uncanny natural phenomena — there are strange and mysterious sinkholes all over the country — or, I don't know, stories of magic white stags in the sky or wild hairy boars that appear in the moonlight wearing golden crowns.

The peasantry — *talurahvas* — has been open for centuries to various superstitions. It extended even into the 1920s when many shamanic elements came together to form the strange cult of Tassi, an outlandish neo-pagan religion along the lines of modern Wicca, which fused supposedly ancient beliefs with a nationalist, right-wing agenda and which was crushed as counter-revolutionary in Soviet times, as James Palmer points out in *The Bloody White Baron*, his fascinating account of the sadistic, sinister anti-Semite, Baron Ungern-Sternberg, who, born to an Estonian father of German blood, with his burning hatred of communists as well as a penchant for Eastern mysticism, conquered Mongolia in 1919 and went further. It was Ungern-Sternberg with his mad and insistent obsessions and the kind of genocidal violence that foreshadowed the Nazis — he organized the only massacre of Jews in Mongolian history — who sought with his own crazy horse-borne army of native Mongolians, White Russians, Siberians, and Japanese to invade — and retake — Moscow. The warlord was tried and sentenced to execution by firing squad for his counter-revolutionary involvement in Bolshevik Russia.

There is in the ongoing psychosocial dynamics of that country, from what I experienced in my very limited way, far less to do with faith than forest minstrelsy. It is an alternative, secular ontology that has eclipsed, if not supplanted, faith. "Most men are scantily nourished on a modicum of happiness and a number of empty thoughts which life lays on their plates," writes Albert Schweitzer in *The Philosophy of Civilization*." "They are kept in the road of life through stern necessity by elemental duties which they cannot avoid... Dreadful discords only allow them to hear a confused noise, as before, where they had thought to catch the strains of glorious music. The beauty of nature is obscured by the suffering which they discover in every direction." The pessimism of the world, even to a degree in Christianity as we doggedly try to live it, Schweitzer insists can be transformed by faith in Christ, no matter how difficult the struggle for truth. In Estonia, at least from my viewpoint, one had scant glimpses of the process. The hoofprint of old-shoe Communism seems imprinted in the very stones. I noticed even upon arrival a sense of timidity, the kind of self-consciousness where intellect right off impresses sooner than the heart.

I do not mean to sound insufferably judgmental. I am sure I brought my own prejudices abroad from what I have seen with growing impatience for the kind of insouciant, increasingly indifferent secularism one now sees everywhere in the United States. It is now literally considered in *bad taste* in the United States to say, "Merry Christmas," an offense, I gather, against Jews and Muslims who make up, respectively, 2.2 percent and 0.8 percent of the national population. I was scolded at a T.J. Maxx shopping one Christmas night by a bulb-nosed clerk, a middle-aged dragon with a black scowl, snapping, "You're not supposed to *say* that!"

I remember after our wedding cordially introducing a friend of mine to the priest who presided at the Mass. The reception was small but filled with witty and intelligent guests. At one quiet moment, my friend inquired if the priest belonged to a particular religious order. "No, I'm just a diocesan," he answered, whereupon the priest asked my friend, who was then a fairly prominent face in Boston news, if he himself was religiously affiliated, and he smugly replied, "Oh, I follow Emerson." "No, I mean your faith," corrected the priest. An awkward silence briefly held. My friend smiled and in a slightly condescending way reiterated, "Emerson." The Sage of Concord has always been a solid name in the intellectual milieu of Cambridge and environs, certainly an intellectually chic one, but what he had to do with God and faith and salvation one is hard-pressed to say. The priest missed not a beat. "The Unitarian, you say? Trust yourself? Being is flux? Follow your own inner promptings? There is a crack in everything God has made? Nothing can bring you peace but yourself? The fellow who dogmatically proclaimed 'Make your own Bible' and who praised his wife Lidian's remark that, 'it is wicked to go to church Sundays,' and who himself declared, 'It is not certain that God exists, but that he does not is a most bewildering and improbable chimera'?" My friend squirmed with sudden embarrassment. "Do you know the joke of what the Ku Klux Klan did to the Unitarian prelate?" the priest asked him. "They burnt a question mark on his lawn." I had to laugh. I know very well the humanistic milieu at Harvard, the arseless latitudinarianism, and more than anything pitied it. I will always insist that any so-called Christian church that fails to preach the resurrected Savior and the need for faith should be turned into a Dairy Queen.

But Europe itself, spiritually speaking, is an empty shell. It has as an aggregate one of the least religious populations in the world. Ancient churches, religious shrines, the notion of all of those pilgrimages? Empty, gone, depleted, all of it. Religious vocations, church attendance, love of sacramentals? Through, finito, *ausgespielt.* "In Britain, France, Germany, Holland, and Belgium, fewer than 10 percent of the population attend church as often as once a month," observes T.R. Reid in *The United States of Europe.* "Only 12 percent of Britons describe themselves as 'active' members of the Anglican Church. In Scandinavia, the handsome high-steepled churches that mark every city and village attract less than 3 percent of the people." And so it goes with Estonia, Russia — as few as 2% of Russians attend church, although as many as 80% are Orthodox Christians — and Scandinavia. As one of the most secular nations in the world, Estonia is not unique. According to statistics, it does have the highest level of irreligious individuals of any polled country, with over 75% of the entire population stating no specific religious affiliation whatsoever. Less than one third of the population defines itself as believers, and of those the majority are Lutheran, whereas the Russian minority is Eastern Orthodox. Today, about 25% of its native population are members of a church or a religious group. Is it any surprise that tree-worship or frenzied Odinic rituals or ancient equinoctial traditions there are held in high regard? It was a perfect place for Johnny Jump-Up the Actor, as well as for Currants and Queel and their wingnuts along with Putzel and her holy skinfood!

Since Estonia is a country pagan in many ways, almost prelapsarian in its woody whims, should we then censor them ("we live in a world plainly plain," laments Wallace Stevens, "everything is as you see it") and do nothing but grieve over a world where

> The houses are haunted
> By white night-gowns.
> None are green,
> Or purple with green rings,
> Or green with yellow rings,
> Or yellow with blue rings.
> None of them are strange,
> With socks of lace
> And beaded ceintures.
> People are not going
> To dream of baboons and periwinkles.
> Only, here and there, an old sailor,
> Drunk and asleep in his boots,
> Catches tigers
> In red weather.[108]

Indeed, no! We should bless those funny ghouls and ghosts! Celebrate the places where they gather! Honor their intrusions! Estonians need the redemption of *flare* and *fire* and *fable!* Colorate the palette! In a country that too often tends to ignore what it does not state, too often states what it would do much better to sing, although song is something they pride themselves in, what heartless and self-righteous beadle, proctoring their lives, would scold them for their lack of orthodox faith or proscribe the bright fables they tell that interact with their cold realities? I have often reflected on how for centuries, in direct contraposition to secular Estonia, religion for American negroes has taken the place of their history. The Negro, uprooted by slavery and robbed of his African history, lacks knowledge of his ancient past and after 400 years of cruel and crushing servitude in the Americas, was prevented from exploring, and so taking solace in, those feelings of identity and pride which almost all other émigrés, just about every other ethnic group, have had the opportunity to know regarding their own cultural origins. In the end, however, for Estonians, merely to love fables and bonfires, folk-tales and natural magic, is to miss the singular comfort of a deep religious faith. You can have love for the forest or for mountain peaks and show *amicitia* or brotherly love, but, no matter the passion, nothing can touch — or compare to — the love of God.

One more word on this matter of the past. The old wistful songs of the American Negro, whose aggregate racial pain certainly qualifies them to pine for the comforts and consolations of the Heaven they acknowledge in so many songs — "Blow, Gabriel, Blow," "Lift Every Voice and Sing," "Swing Low, Sweet Chariot," "Deep River," "Cabin in the Sky," etc. — invariably all seek by theme the sanctuary of a better world. No Heaven, in my opinion, however, should exclude our lives on this earth, the knowledge gathered, the experiences met. Are they of no consequence? Of negligible import? Why then have we lived? The very *details* of our lives must surely never be forgotten. Eternity in short should incorporate time, in my view. Our earthly lives, our personal histories, fit into any true, comprehensive and blessed Heaven, at least that I can conceive. Our dreams, the sunsets we have seen, camping out, kisses given and taken, our marriage, children, nights when we pondered the moon, the crash of ocean waves on us when we were small, the sweet taste of lobster, carnival rides, a walk through the woods, the scent of flowers, even our very names! Shall none of this *matter*? Why, the sad times should be included, as well. Robert Frost had my opposite worry, positing the possibility of the kind of merciful Heaven that erases life on earth. Addressing God in *A Masque of Reason,* Job declares,

> You perhaps will tell us
> If that is all there is to be of Heaven,
> Escape from so great pains of life on earth
> It gives a sense of let-up calculated
> To last a fellow to Eternity.

Walking around Estonia, reflecting on the point of the lives we lead, I often thought that Eternity (*igavik*) should incorporate Time (*aeg*), as both of those big words in the language, comic and guttural, seem to call up the other. Literally, in some inexplicable but charming parallel, the word *igavik* seemed to *include* the word *aeg*. Paradoxically, the word *igavene* is also used in that country as a mild semi-blasphemous swear-word in the sense of "damned," "doggone," "darn" or "goddam," almost as if the curser (in time) still petulantly — even if in a spiteful, angry moment — still doggedly insisted on keeping his sacred goal (eternity) in mind! Let us chalk that up to only another Estonian irony.

A small aside on cursing? I have noticed that universal expressions like "Fuck you" in almost all languages seem brainlessly sturdy and concise. It goes *"Haista vittu!"* in Finnish. In Estonian, one hears *"Mine!"* or *"Perse!"* — "Go in [your] asshole!" The actual phrase, "Fuck you!" would be literally *"Nussi ennast! Or "Nussi ise ennast!"* — "Fuck your [own] self!" but that is not the idiom in Estonia and is rarely if ever used. Europeans do not curse the way Americans do. *"Grenadenscheiss,"* a German will say ("Grenade shit.") *"Arschloh!"* Finns snap, *"Saatanan runkkari!* ("Satan is a wanker!") So many of phrases sound corny and totally out of it. Estonians say *"Laksa Kotte"* — "slap your balls!" It just sounds goofy! Remember the Czechoslovakian brothers on TV's *Saturday Night Live*, Jorge (Steve Martin) and Yortuk (Dan Aykroyd) Festrunk, try to pick up a pair of women? *That* kind of uncool. Cussing properly is an act of linguistic panache — consider some of the peppery profanities of people like Martin Luther, General George S. Patton, Harry Truman, Carole Lombard, etc. — and those with particular finesse can raise it to an art form. "I'll wring the bastard fucker's bleeding blasted fucking windpipe" — found in Joyce's *Ulysses* — at least rhythm-wise is almost poetry. I once heard a warthog-type in Canada, missing a cab, blasphemously scream, *"Tabernâcle de trois étages!"* obviously the spiteful locution of a bad Catholic. *"Calisse,"* you will hear ("Chalice!") *"Maudit bloke!"* ("Bad guy!") Long gone are all those old, semi-medieval etymonic curses such as "egad," "'zounds," "gadzooks," "odds bodkins" and, at least in the West, floral execrations like "May wild pigs defile the grave of your grandmother!" "It's a load of old cambronne" is a quaint phrase that used to be heard in the tea rooms and coffee houses of 19th-century England when someone doubted the veracity of some idea or opinion. Cursing in many countries takes the form of blasphemy, but then again in what country is taking the name of Our Lord in vain not a common imprecation? Taboos about religion have served profanity in most European countries since the Middle

Ages. In Europe to this very day the most improper and sinful "oaths" are those invoking a sacred figure like the Italian *Pote di Abramo!* ("Abraham's cunt!") Rabelais loved the dysphemism "rumpswab." In the scatological epic, *Gargantua and Pantagruel*, we read, "Christ, look ye, it's *Mère de ... merde ...* shit, Mother of God." I have an almost comically pusillanimous brother-in-law who in the heat of anger — it is as daring as this diffident person gets — actually says, "*H-e-double hockeysticks!*"

What about cursing in the Psalms? Malice. Pettiness. Hatred. Calling down vengeance. *Adjuring,* if you will. Look at Psalm 109[109] which is filled with imprecations of a sort culminating in the bold assertion that the Lord will "make thy enemies thy footstool" and will "crush the heads in the land of the many." The profane is everywhere in the Psalter. After eleven verses of gentle pleas and pious supplication in Psalm 142, the Psalmist adds in the twelfth, almost as a cheeky and presumptuous afterthought, "and in thy mercy thou wilt destroy my enemies." Why, even in the much-quoted and venerable Psalm 23, after following a sober profession of simple faith, we suddenly slam up against "Thou shalt prepare a table for me *against them that trouble me.*" Finally, in the otherwise beautiful Psalm 136, a poetic lamentation of the Hebrews in exile and a paean on hymn-singing, a blessing is pronounced on anyone who will snatch up a Babylonian baby and dash out its brains against a rock!

The ancient Hebrews, at least as far as the Sadducees went, were as secular, let us say terrestrially bound, as the Estonians, which is why the Psalms for all their occasional festal poetry and dancing lyricism are so often muscularly non-transcendental. "Remember what my substance is: for has thou made all the children of men in vain?"(Psalm 88: 48) "What profit is there in my blood whilst I go down to corruption? Shall dust confess to thee, or declare thy truth?" (Psalm 29: 10) "For there is no one in death, that is mindful of thee: and who shall confess to thee in hell?" (Psalm 6:6) "He shall go the generations of his fathers: and he shall never see light." (Psalm 48:20) It is the gloomy portent of the Psalms that we all come to nothing in the end which is why C.S. Lewis writes, "It seems quite clear that in most parts of the Old Testament there is little or no belief in a future life; certainly no belief that is of any religious importance." David who danced before the Ark with such abandon that his wives thought he was making a fool of himself did so simply because

— when there is no thought of resurrection — song and dance, frolic and fun, is a deep requirement. Or was it a desperate jittery dance to try to stamp out the murderous memory of his having sent his rival, Uriah the Hittite, back to Joab, the commander, at the siege of Rabbah with a message instruction that he be abandoned on the battlefield "that he may be struck down, and die"?

Songfests and Suicide

Christmas is celebrated, of course, in Estonia but the greatest celebration there is held on St. John's Day — *Jaanipäev* — which falls on the 24th of June. On St. John's Night, the shortest night of the year — midsummer — which, by the way, is celebrated on the night between the 23rd and 24th, people all across the country gather to make massive bonfires to jump over, to dance about, to frolic, to flirt, to drink, and to sing, abdicating normal behavior and in their wildness enacting, I gather, the freewheeling kind of *jubilation nue*, or naked jubilation, that poet Stéphane Mallarmé extols in his poem, *"Petit Air."* The high fantasticalities will recall for any literate people Nikolai Gogol's famous fable, "St. John's Eve," his very first story, as a matter of fact, which evokes demonic men, old crones, big black dogs turning into cats, all sorts of curses and wizards and loony pigs. This is their biggest day. The day is also called *Jaaniuss* — St. John's Worm — because the glow-worm begins appearing then. "On Midsummer Eve, by Midsummer fire, the old Viking blood of Estonians, defiant of all fetters, will curiously stir," as an old 1937 travel book, *Picturesque Estonia* puts it. I believe Estonians sing more than the Welsh do. They love to sing and live to do so and virtually look for any public occasion to burst into communal song, linking hands and arms. On this special day people also go about searching for fern blossoms. Ferns blossom once a year, and then only for a few seconds, and so folk head for the forest like wood-trolls to make wishes which are all supposed to be fulfilled. It is believed that any young maiden who has the luck to find such a fern-flower and eat it will find the young man of her dreams, a faithful companion for life.

As I say, on St. John's Day, there is no end of singing — singing is at the heart of virtually every serious public enterprise in the country — and heavy drinking, of course, imbibing with both hands, and please let it not be said an Estonian cannot knock back a brew! Estonians supposedly have made the world's only 195-proof vodka fit for human consumption: according to report the drink is said to be so dry, so remorselessly sec, that it literally sucks moisture from the air, a killer quaff leaving the stomach "full of galvanic batteries, yellow hornets, pepper sauce and vitriol," as Mark Twain said of the brandy that was known as Washoe, Minie Rifle, or Chain Lightning that he drank in Virginia City Flare, fire, and fable. An Estonian never sees an oak tree without seeing a Dryad.

Song as celebration needs, of course, neither explanation nor discourse. It is worthwhile simply to note that to some people it indicates a form of faith and in instances may actually constitute it, the kind of worship that reaches as far back as the "dithyramb," the ancient Greek hymn sung and danced in honor of Dionysus, the god of wine, theater, and fertility. Walt Whitman's "song" has all the connotations of such, for the trope of joining is faith and there is no question that God is in his music. ("And I know that the hand of God is the promise of my own,/ And I know that the spirit of God is the brother of my own") Remember, as well, how Emily Dickinson cites the *music* of Orpheus' song — his "warbling truths" — as being more efficacious in bringing people to God than the hectoring polemics, the finger-wagging condemnations, of grim Scripture:

> The Bible is an antique Volume —
> Written by faded Men
> At the suggestion of Holy Spectres —
> Subjects — Bethlehem —
> Eden — the ancient Homestead
> Satan — the Brigadier —
> Judas — the Great Defaulter —
> David — the Troubadour —
> Sin — a distinguished Precipice —
> Others must resist —

Boys that 'believe' are very Lonesome —
Other boys are 'lost' —
Had but the tale a warbling Teller —
All the boys would come —
Orpheus' Sermon captivated —
It did not condemn.

Judith Farr in *The Passion of Emily Dickinson* points out that Dickinson, who tirelessly revised her work, significantly, chose the word "warbling" over 13 other adjectives: "typic," "thrilling," "hearty," "bonnie," "breathless," "spacious," "tropic," "ardent," "friendly," "magic," "pungent," "winning," and "mellow." Song is chosen over stricture, in short. After all, as St. Augustine assured us, "He who sings, prays twice."

I mention the word *viking*. I understand that the word has no exact or fully identifiable meaning in any of the Scandinavian languages. Scholar Hillary Bird has comically suggested that it may simply be a corruption of the word *vee-king*, meaning "water shoe" in Estonian, in reference to a shoe-shaped hull of a boat, from *vee*, genitive or possessive case of *vesi* ("water") and *king* ("shoe"). The common derivation of "Viking" is from Old Norse *vikingr*, "going on an overseas raid or expedition." Whether Estonians themselves sailed such boats or suffered as the result of their intrusive and unwelcome Viking visits I cannot say.

Estonian *vesi–vee*, by the way, is derived from Proto-Uralic *wete* ("water") found in various forms in all the Uralic languages, and strongly suggestive of an ancient Uralic-Indo-European affinity — it is obviously the same word as English *water*, German *wasser*, Swedish *vaten*, Greek *hüdor*, Russian *vodá*, Lithuanian *vanduo*, Sanskrit *vatura*, Hittite *wetur-wetenaš*, all reflecting a Proto-Indo-European *wedor–wodor*. This *wedor* form co-existed in Proto-Indo-European with another "water" word, *akwa*, reflected in Latin *aqua* — and of literally world-wide distribution, found in recognizable form as the word for "water," "drink," "river," or "rain" in languages all over our planet, reflecting a "Proto-World" form *akwa*. Perhaps in a majority of Native American languages, the word for either "water," "drink," or "river" is something like *ak, aka, akwa, ukwa, oka, uka, ug, ogo*, etc., echoed for instance by forms like *ok* in New Guinea and *koko, gogo, gugu* in Aboriginal Australia. "Proto-World" *akwa* ("water, drink, river") must be at least 60,000 or 70,000 years old!

St. Paul's Day (*paavlipäev*), January 25, is another big day — but no different for value or reverence, let it be noted, than the very popular Cabbage Lady Day (*kapsauramaarjapäev*) which takes place on March 25, the day, tradition holds, on which Jesus was conceived through Mary by the Holy Spirit. On St. Catherine's Day — to make a last observation on Estonia's rather remarkable secularity — in the eastern part of the country there is a custom, not to pray, or to light vigil lights, but of "bleating." That is correct — children *bleat* and are summarily handed out treats, as if they were servile pups, treats of food, like pepper biscuits, barley, porridge, and flummery. Santa Claus, in Estonia called *Jõuluvana* ("Old Man Yule"), has a wild, ragged weirdness about him and might as well be a Grimm figure. (Santa Claus in the Finnish Christmas tradition used to be a wild boar that would eat children!) Barley and porridge are not odd treats there. Estonians are porridge people. *Kaerakile!* We had several great rib-sticking breakfasts of rolled oats (*kaerahelbed*) and oatmeal (*kaerajahu*) over the course of several particularly brutal winter days. It is needless to say a perfect anodyne to the bone-eroding cold of a winter's day. A bowl of *tatrahelbed* (salty porridge) — yum! To me since, strangely, brutal cold often — always? — conglobes with misery, depression, and sternness, I decided to check on the suicide rate in one of the world's most futile countries. What did I find? Russia and the Baltic countries — with Lithuania the highest (75, mostly males, out of 100,000) — have *the highest suicide rates in the world!* Finland has the highest teenage suicide rate in the world. In Mexico only 5 out of 100,000 kill themselves. China has the highest suicide rate for women, about 150,000 a year, one every four minutes. Virtually no one in the Dominican Republic commits suicide. I am quite certain it is the same in Puerto Rico, Costa Rica, and sunny Uruguay! The statistics are revealing. A survey taken in December 2009 of the "happiest" and "unhappiest" of the United States regarding general quality of life listed the top five happiest as Louisiana, Hawaii, Florida, Tennessee, and Arizona. At the very bottom were Indiana, Michigan, New Jersey, Connecticut, and New York, not one of them, unsurprisingly, identifiably sun states.

The jaw-twisting Estonian for "sunny" is *päikesepaisteline*, a word as rarely used as it is unpronounceable.

Laplanders and peoples of Fennoscandia smear the lintels of their front doors with butter in order to nourish Beiwe, sun goddess of fertility, before she continues on her journey. A young woman in Sweden on St. Lucy's Day (December 13) wearing a crown of lit candles leads a solemn procession as a sign of rebirth. The Aztecs of Mezoamerica who believed that the heart embodied solar power sacrificed victims to Huitzilopochtli, the personification of the sun and of war, tearing out their hearts, so releasing the "divine sun fragments" entrapped by the body and its desires in order to ensure continued favor. To plead for light, to evade darkness is truly elemental. Thomas Hardy wrote in *The Return of the Native*, "To light a fire is the instinctive and resistant act of men when, at the winter ingress, the curfew is sounded throughout nature. It indicates a spontaneous, Promethean rebelliousness against the fiat that this recurrent season shall bring foul times, cold darkness, misery and death. Black chaos comes, and the fettered gods of the earth say, 'Let there be light.'"

I have never quite felt the importance of the sun, the *heat* of the sun, its glorious light, until I spent day after day after day in the occlusive and penetrating darkness of an Estonia winter. Is not sun redemptive on the most elemental level, a blessing, a benison, even if it does nothing more than scotch the surges of dimness and darkness, salvific in terms of point-of-view alone? Philip Larkin was surely correct when in his poem, "The Whitsun Weddings" he notes "the sun destroys/The interest of what's happening in shade." I would have waking dreams of flying on a speeding platinum-bright train through the reaches of the sunny American far west where crystal wine-glasses tinkled, silver cutlery danced on starched white linen tablecloths, bud-vases sprouted with a single red rose, and one looked out across the shining desert floor of a blessed land filled with blazing sunshine. I recall reading that a dying sperm whale will always turn toward the sun. I can understand why. It becomes a kind of viaticum, redemptive in the comfort of its uplifting light. Tell me that darkness — lack of *sun* — has no influence on the psyche. Argue that ghosts inhabit a cherry orchard in sunlight. Convince me that faith — spiritual light — has no import in happiness! It brings forth nothing less than life itself in its sacred warmth and energy. Didn't Osiris swallow the sun and excrete it, bringing about the redemption of creation, the timeless present of eternity?

It may be argued among funny apologeticists that the act of suicide being a sin against God does no longer hold in a doggedly secular world, but "it is an illness that grows the more attention paid to it," as the character Blue astutely insists in Orhan Pamuk's *Snow* in the light of a suicide epidemic in that novel.

> The whole race is a poet that writes down
> The eccentric proposition of its fate,

writes Wallace Stevens,

> By the terrible incantations of defeats
> And by the fear that defeats and dreams are one.[110]

The oldest painting in Tallinn is the famous *"Danse Macabre"* ("Dance of Death") by the Lubeck master, Bernt Notke. This astonishing giant medieval work done in the 15th century and nearly thirty meters (98.4 ft.) in length — only the initial fragment of the original 30 meters is extant — depicts the transience of life, the skeletal figures of the Grim Reaper harvesting the mighty as well as the feeble in a truly scary pavanne of frightening dark skeletons and red-robed clergy, the Pope, the Empress, the Cardinal, the King, and other figures. A scroll of didactic text warning of the brevity of life runs along the complete length of this masterpiece, which to me subjectively represents Estonia at its most medieval, somehow an evocation of this old country when it was denominated on all old maps as the quaint "Esthonia." This great painting hangs in the St. Anthony Chapel of the venerable St. Nicholas (*Niguliste*) Church which stands in the heart of the city, an imposing church/museum of which Sarah did a brilliant painting from a window of ours in that temporary flat, our first, we had in Tallinn. This was the dimly-lit, unprepossessing flat to which we would return after lunch around two in the already lowering winter dark, threading up the black staircase rising up and circular like the newel of a snail's shell. The solid and depressive darkness of those unrelenting, unsparing Estonian winter days was not quite the terrifying darkness of Revelations 16:10 where the afflicted "gnawed their tongues for pain," but I have to say that the way the night came down at day made it a perfect backdrop for the uncompromising dread evoked in Notke's masterpiece.

Heidegger in A Paper Hat

"I betook myself to linking/Fancy unto fancy, thinking what this ominous bird of yore,/What this grim, ungainly, ghastly, gaunt, and ominous bird of yore/Meant in creaking 'Nevermore,'" writes Edgar Allan Poe in his sinister poem, "The Raven." Superstition is always on the rise when religious faith falters.[111] To pagan Balts the sky was a mountain. And why not? One can forgive that. There is no end of Estonian superstitions. Estonian women customarily drink red wine on March 25, the "Day of Mary," in the hope that they will gain rosy cheeks for the entire year. Expectant mothers traditionally change shoes daily in order to confound the spirit of sickness. When the frying pan gets rusty, they say, the mistress will die. All sons who look like their mothers and daughters who look like their fathers are considered lucky. In Estonia, Monday and Wednesday and Friday are considered unlucky and one should avoid doing significant things that day. Whistling indoors is considered bad luck in Estonia. Spitting over one's left shoulder three times is the equivalent there of Americans knocking on wood. One must always kiss the bread that one has inadvertently dropped. Whoever uses the cooking pot for washing up will have a drip at the tip of his nose for the rest of his life. If you see a lilac flower with five petals, instead of four, it will bring you happiness and you must eat it. Show your wallet to the new moon — never the old moon — and it will become full. You hear and read and come across this kind of thing all the time. It all seems to be right out of the medieval Livonian handbook, circa 1386. Fabliau-culture. Chaucerian lore. Never send yellow flowers to someone, as there is a superstition in Estonia which says that they are a sign of a coming loss of a loved one. It is also a taboo to give the gift of a dozen roses — one must always give odd numbers of flowers. (I believe this custom exists in the West, as well, where, if it is done for an aesthetic reason, as some suggest, I am hard-pressed to say why. Is symmetry considered tasteless?) Even-numbered offerings are reserved for sorrowful occasions. Red is the color of the dead. (Latvians, I learned, always erase their footprints from the sand or dirt around a grave after every cemetery visit lest the ghosts of the dead follow them home.) A bride in Estonia traditionally casts money on the fire when she enters her new home for the first time, and the spirit of flame, *Tule-ema*, the fire-mother, is specifically evoked by name in this ceremony. Another widespread lingering belief, I have heard, is that in all churches on mysterious All Soul's Eve, congregations of ghosts assemble while the service is being celebrated by ghostly priests or ministers.

According to legend, every year on New Year's Eve, a grey little man rises out of the depths of grey Lake Ülemiste, which lies high above the town — and which I could see at a serene and foggy distance from the window of the Ülamiste Hotell where I stayed on my very last night in that country — and that gimp little fellow always hobbles down the road to ask the town-watchman whether the town of Tallinn is at last completed. The question is invariably answered in the negative. The man then disappears for another year. If the answer should ever be answered in the affirmative, or so goes the fable, the town will be quickly destroyed. The building of Tallinn, in short, must never be finished. It is an ongoing project. The lake itself was formed of — and by — the bitter tears of Kalev's wife, Linda, the royal widow who is the mother of the fearless and undaunted Estonian hero, Kalevipoeg, who, being pregnant and dropping a stone, had not the strength to build a monument to her husband after the great king died. She wept until her tears formed a pool, which then changed into a pond, and ultimately into a lake that placidly sits there still.[112]

Savored also and retold are real mysteries. The tragic sinking of the cruise ferry *Estonia* in 1994, which, claiming 852, lives made it one of the very worst maritime disasters of the 20th century — the Baltic Sea is one of the world's busiest shipping areas with 2,000 vessels at sea at any time — not only touched the heart of nearly every Estonian but has become something of a fireside tale since, one recounted late at night, along the lines of the doomed Donner Party in the Old West, for many rumors surround the tragedy. Speculations abound as to the reasons the ship sank. Was it a Russian mine and was its Secret Service involved? Was military equipment being transported? What about the strange disappearance of Captain Arvo Pihti? Had UFOs spirited him away? According to ghostly legend, it is whispered that victims who went down with the ship are reported to have telephoned relatives on their mobile phones. A famous national actor, Urmas Alender, the most well-known passenger and best-loved by Estonians, is reported to have been singing as the ship was going down. The national disaster soon took on the dimensions of folklore, approximating, say, the terrible sinking of the *RMS Titanic* on April 15, 1912.

I noticed that a good many proverbs in Estonia are misogynistic: "The pipe is nearer than the wife," "Who weds a widow with three children takes four thieves into the house," "Young maidens and white bread age quickly," "One cannot make soup out of beauty," and so on. There is a distinct partnership between the proverb and the European mind, a sort of homestake in the universal truth of them.

Estonia is a country strongly given over to folklorish or natural wisdom and cautionary tales. A lot of what is located in the rustic mind takes the place of religion or worship. I found many of them to be forest fables. I recall reading about Heidegger wearing a paper hat whilst living alone in the Black Forest in Germany. A nutty sage in a wild-boar fur vest in the woods remains my image of that dark fabulous world even if it was in another country. An old-world Estonian mother might quote lessoning proverbs or *sententiae* to her children from such popular stories as *Pipi Pikksukk* (Pippi Longstocking), for example — it would be a high operatic treat to hear the heroine's full name, Pippilotta Provisionia Gaberdina Dandeliona Ephraimsdaughter Longstocking, rattled off in Estonian: *Pippilotta Viktualia Rullgardina Krusmynta Efraimsdotter Långstrump* — or *Reinuvader Rebane* (Reynard the Fox) simply to amuse them but also to warn them against clever, roguish little picaros who might assail them or put dark curses on them or try to wangle money out of them with topoi right out of the Grimm fairy tales, one example of which is *Kaval Ants ja Vanapagan* ("Clever Hans and Old Nick"), a collection of dozens of folk tales about a ponderous, dim-witted farmer and the wily young farmhand who works for him. Estonians seem to love tales of cheeky, young tricksters, animal or young man, subverting bullish authority. A popular tale in Estonia tells of such a farmhand who is asked by a brutish farmer to churn some cream (*koor*) into butter. Instead, he mischievously churns a bushel of birch bark (*koor* = bark, as well as cream) into a kind of mush. When his master expresses shock and horror, the farmhand feigns innocent naïveté, protesting, "But you never specified just what kind of *koor* you wanted me to use!" Estonian fables are peopled by the same colorful cast of characters so familiar to kids all over the world. Wily red foxes. Trolls under bridges. Elves. Giants. Forest imps. Tree spirits. Crafty brothers. Tricky impudent fools who are wise in a topsy-turvy sort of way and who are always one step ahead of the law. We all know about King Lear's sagacious fool. His prankish offshoot or type of bedlam figure, Pickleherring — an archetypal simpleton — has always been a hugely popular figure in Europe. Some scholars believe that it was this legendary goose that was alone responsible for the wide dissemination of Shakespeare's plays on the continent, by the way. King Lear's Fool of course easily surpasses all constituted Pickleherrings by the subtlety of his wit and the acuity of his perceptions, but this fellow — for his irony, his anti-authority, his irreverent cheekiness, even his odd disappearance[113] — thrills most Balts, indeed most Europeans. The word for fool or dolt or booby in Estonian is *loll* or *tola,* and one would hear it used quite often.

There are many tales of magic and remote places. Strange and secret gardens. ("Don't go into Mr. McGregor's garden; your father had an accident there," we read in Beatrix Potter's *The Tale of Peter Rabbit.* "He was put in a pie by Mrs. McGregor.") I saw ornately illustrated copies of *Saabastegakass* (*Puss in Boots*) in bookshops. Popular in Estonia are also tales of pretty young maidens gazing fondly at their reflections in ponds or bowls of water to try to discern the face of their future husbands or boyfriends. I also heard the recitation of a brief prayer Estonian peasants would commonly use to whisper into the mouth of the pig they were slaughtering, sort of like the prayerful Ainu apologizing to a bear they were about to kill. Going near outdoor wells is a taboo in Estonia, I have heard, for this is a spot where water-monsters dangerously lurk. Of course, the four seasons figure in many Estonian proverbs which is typical of rustic old world cultures. It was not kind, but I remember that H. L. Mencken in his excoriating but seminal essay on ignorance, "The Sahara of the Bozart" specifically went out of his way to say that the

American South was about "as devoid of high culture as Montenegro or Estonia!"

Weather Or Not

So we know Estonia is a cold, isolated place. Wind sometimes seems sharp enough to tear a roof off. And I do remember one or two nights that cold and wind combined, when, tramping home late outside, I believed I was heading toward the undiscovered country from whose bourn no traveler returns. Rain comes in short, sharp bursts all the time. Is it because it is on the water like England and Ireland? It seemed always to be raining hard, viciously, like a pissing cow, as the French say. The rain was as thunderous as it is in Domenica, but faster and blacker. The winter nights can be gelid, inviting what I call the Voods! What exactly are the Voods? *Voodririie* ("lining"); *voodiriided* ("bed clothes"); *voodipesu* ("bed linen"); *voodilina* ("bed sheet"); *voodikate* ("bed spread")! And if you are lucky, don't forget the *voolumõõtja* ("electric meter")! It seems like a perpetual dusk — *eha* — every morning. There is not much snow in Estonia, not often a white world, none of that "feathers from the Scythian sky so thickly that people can neither see nor travel."[114] From January to March, yes, it can snow frequently, but for the most part much of Estonia has no lasting snow at all through winter. Severe weather, such as tempestuous winds and massive blizzards, are rare. The last hurricane raged through the country in 1969. Snowfalls, I have been told, are actually yearned for in Estonia in the dead of winter to bring in some cheerful *light* and to put an end to the crepuscular dark and the terrible nocturnalizing drabness. Chionomaniacs — people obsessed with snow — dance in delight in a blizzard there, even if it is howling into eternal nothingness. "My native land, my joy, my delight," goes the non-ironic opening lines of the Estonian national Anthem, "*How fair thou art and bright* [my italics]."

Mu isamaa, mu õnn ja rõõm
Kui kaunia oled sa!

I saw the Old Towns in both Tartu and Tallinn in the grip of mid-winter without snow, and they were little more than icy cobblestones and a gloomy pocket of old buildings. But at night after snowfall the places virtually lit up. The Old City or Vanalinn in Tallinn is breathtakingly beautiful covered with white powder, with all those medieval guildhalls, quaint hotels, curious old houses with chocolate-box exteriors and roofs with turrets and finials, and strange cobbled streets but a few paces wide, twisting and improbably narrow, with odd names like Cheese Lane and The Street of the Fishing Cat and Zinc Street that seemed to evoke the quaint settings and backgrounds of old prints and story-books I loved in childhood with Maxfield Parrish illustrations of rotund millers, funny-looking piemen, long-nosed pastry cooks with clipped Dutchboy haircuts, and chefs in white doublets wearing toques, holding big shiny spoons and pots presiding over thick wooden tables. Am I — was I — thinking of *The Knave of Hearts* by Louise Saunders? With all the lights on the Town Hall in Tartu aglow, the Old Town positively sings. Pure fantasy! Snow blowing down by the river enchants the lights of the bridge which are changing colors every few seconds, blinking on and off, and the glowing powder crowns the Kissing Student statue in the middle of the square in the composition of a winter paradise, and one sparkling evening Sarah and I danced about there in a snow-scene almost as unapologetically romantic as Gene Kelly and Leslie Caron in *An American in Paris* intertwined on the Greutert fountain as a magical *fumata* plays around them. As to cold, it is revealing to read as I did in *Baltic Holidays*, if you can overlook the oxymoron,

> The frozen sea often makes access to the smaller islands [Saarema and Hiiumaa] easier in winter than in summer since roadways are marked on the ice.

By midsummer at the end of June, the relentless daylight lasts as long as 18 hours a day. It is briefly warm during this welcoming interval. In December and January there are that many hours of darkness. Heatwaves of 90 degrees (F) can occasionally take hold in Estonia, when the country will warm up so because of the Gulf Stream. Heat, however, never lasts long in Estonia. Where can you fight it? Go to Lake Peipsi. Or head down to the refreshing Gulf of Riga and to the city if Pärnu — or, for that

matter, neighboring Pootsi or Munalaiu Port — which is Estonia's summer party capital. What about the bat caves of Piusa in Põlva country?
Or the Meenikunno bog? As I say, in Estonia generally the sunniest of all
months — only one of many anomalies — is March.

In the dead of winter, noon is meteorologically dark. The city of
Tallinn shares a bitter latitude (48°) with Igaluit, the capital of the Canadian Arctic territory of Nuravut. We felt on one particular night that we
needed a good dinner, a feast, to reward ourselves for having survived the
winter. The Holy Saints themselves legendarily knew the importance of
indulgenza as a balancing factor. "There is a time for penance and a time
for partridge," as the mystic St. Teresa of Avila wrote. (She was reportedly
a very beautiful woman and might not only have been used to but possibly cherished any pampering that came her way.) When he was on his
deathbed and asked if he had any regrets in his life, St. Francis of Assisi
supposedly nodded and replied, "I have been too harsh on Brother Don-
key," his term for his own fleshly body, meaning that, while he also came
to see the value of having a partridge or two, and maybe a tipple — life
not being all penance — he had puritanically ignored doing so for much
of his life. (At the end even Hitler himself was eating two pounds of pra-
lines a day.[115]) So one bright night with stars twinkling though a skylight
Sarah and I sat down like hedonists to a bottomless golden pie with tomatoes, a side-dish of *rosolje* — pink beet salad — a delicious homemade
spongy strawberry roulade for dessert, and two stalwart bottles of a very
smart Burgundy.

I went to bed that night, smiling, with warm feet, dreaming of rho-
dodendrons in Myanmar. Spring can be lovely. It is as though the countryside has been given a fresh coat of paint, and every heart awakens to
dreams that seem to lift all the burdens of life. One is no longer thinking
of going cross-country skiing in Otepää or ice-fishing in Lake Vagula or
snow-kiting in Halinga but suddenly begins in the language of Schubert's
song, to have *Frühlingsglaube,* and to sing with the poet Ludwig Uhland,
"*Die Linden Lüfte sind erwacht, sie sauseln und weben Tag und Nacht.*"
Winter dress is discarded, green stems shyly peep out, rivers are glassing,
and warm breezes gently riffling the fields and meadows unexpectedly
awaken the primitive longings and feelings in people that have been hibernating half a year. "There is a distinct — and brightening — change of

mood in late Spring," Sarah explained to me after I left when she began traveling around alone. Motoring. She borrowed a friend's faded blue 1983 Volkswagen, used the official license connected to the car, bought insurance coverage (for about $30 a month), and then drove around the country pretty much everywhere, out to the islands, Saarema, Hiiumaa, and even stayed awhile on the island of Muhu. Sometimes if she thought she would not be bothered she stopped to paint, bringing her easel into meadows filled with yellow mustard, tufts of white birch, stalwart forests — Estonia is almost 50% forest — and Queen Anne's Lace. Hiiumaa is the most forested county in Estonia, where more than two-thirds of all the plant species native to the country can be found. Curiously, by patristically preventing access to the island for over 50 years, the Soviets unwittingly preserved not only many rare plants and animal species but also the island's traditional way of life. Sarah's paintings became larger, richer, more colorful. What she could do with her Winsor & Newton filbert, her natural badger fan, that round Kolinsky Red Sable #6 brush of hers was astonishing to me. She also managed fairly well with her car, in spite of the fact that a red warning light repeatedly flashing on the dashboard of the car for several weeks, indicating a need for water confused her! Many of the long back country roads of Estonia are stone-covered or just mud-covered. How could that be in the year 2008 A.D.? Would it cost so much to tar them? The pygmies in the deep Ituri Forest of the Mountains of the Moon had roads as good. As to petrol, it cost about $70 (700 kroon) to fill the diesel tank at the time, more than for the rent Sarah was paying in the old Soviet flat she occupied in the rural crossroads of Mooste. True, there was very little traffic out in the country. A car would bump by every half hour or so. For hours at a time Sarah saw no other cars. Side roads in Estonia can seem very remote, almost haunted with the whin, the foggy mists, the vista of land as endlessly flat as it is in Oklahoma, oh yes very much American Midwest, with the singular and heartwarming exception that out there in the American Midwest everyone is armed! I remember on dusty buses in Estonia, boring along for endless hours, a nosy beobachter staring out past flat potato fields and red-brick barns, riding through the lone, level countryside and seeing farmers and field-hands and lumbermen, just as I often would driving in the United States, and pondering the question: *why do all places with wide open spaces breed narrow minds?*

Driving about in her car, Sarah saw long-vacated Soviet barracks and old ammunition sheds completely deserted and eerie. Distances in Estonia by definition seem remote. For the roughly 180 miles between Tallinn and Tartu, about the same distance between Cape Cod and New Haven, Ct., it is virtually all spreading forest and farms — no malls, no eateries, no amusement parks, no washeterias — and this is between the two largest cities in the nation. But the sense of peace, the beauty, are comforting. On the west coast of Hiiumaa, Sarah observed certain seaside plants and wild flowers she had never seen on earth before. I felt anxious for her but comforted by thoughts of what gender re-assigned Jan Morris — and who should know better than someone who has traveled both as a man and a woman? — once said:

> The general run of hazard is exactly the same for men as for women, and the treatment that a woman gets when traveling is, by and large, better. People are less frightened of you. They tend to trust you more. The relationship between women, between one woman and another, is a much closer one than the relationship between men. Wherever a woman travels in the world she's got a few million friends waiting to help her.

All this may be true if you are a burly, ham-handed, unprepossessing figure as long in the tooth as Ms. Morris is, or at least was when I met her a decade ago, but what about younger, waifish women?

"People are kindlier in Spring, hearts are lighter, flowers abound. I saw guys on buses naked from their waists up, their shirts in hand," Sarah told me. "A psychic change takes place there from the end of May through mid-July. It is hard to believe! You see smiles, you hear music, you find much less strain in the people in general. There seems to be an uplift everywhere. The streets of Tallinn are jam-packed; all outdoor cafés come alive with laughter and bonhomie. I never saw so much gardening being done. It is an entirely different place than in winter." On the island of Muhu, Sarah and her friend, Karin, used to go outside to hear the nightingales singing and flitting among the wild juniper bushes, of which there are many in Estonia[116]. She drove out to the town of Rõuge and did some paintings of the lakes there — one of them the deepest in

Estonia — in a spot also known as the "Valley of 1,000 Nightingales."
I have mentioned white storks. Driving along, Sarah would see storks,
white bill-clattering wading birds with black wings, clacking away, "talking Egyptian," as Hans Christian Andersen would have it, making their
fat nests of straw on top of the square concrete telephone poles on roads.
Devices — bird excluders that are basically a wire mesh ball — can be
purchased or even made to protect the tops of chimneys from their suf-
focating nests, but storks of course famously not only bring good luck
but are symbols of fertility. I should mention that Estonia is a paradise
of migratory birds, for it forms a link in a well-known migratory track
of Arctic water birds. Walking the soft sphagnum bogs and oozy, mud-
rutted marshes along the many precarious boardwalks laid out, trail-wise,
for hikers amid forests of spruces, firs, and junipers, I saw white-backed
woodpeckers, common swifts, Eurasian jackdaws — *hakk* is the suitable
Estonian name for them — and of course many barn swallows, their
national bird. It is comforting to know that almost half of Estonia —
47 percent, in fact — is forest, marsh, woodlands, and bogs, rich bird-
sanctuaries. Beyond that, as much as 10 percent of the country is nature
reserve and conservation land.

I would often hear in my mind the limpid and richly dramatic music
of Arvo Pärt — his "*Te Deum*," the "*Festina Lente*" for String Orchestra,"
his "*Salve Regina*," the "*Cantiques des degrés*," the now famous "Tabula
Rasa," his choral "Beatitudes," the "Consolation," his "Credo for Piano
Solo," say — as I looked off at the deep, silent, mysterious forests of Estonia and rude, hardscrabble land. Pärt's still, sad, limpidly clear music,
hauntingly spiritual, melodic sounds that seem to float through the crys-
tallized air like virga, is sylvan in spirit and very much evokes the spirit
of the woods with its spare, repetitive textures. The woods there are not
the same as the thrusting green American forests or its seemingly limitless
flat fields, with occasional rolling meadows and wild beauty, quite like
American land. Their forests are spare and chaste with nothing like our
bold American woods or the golden waving sandcastle plains of central
Nebraska, sunny and hopeful, of which in "The Prairies" William Cullen
Bryant wrote:

These are the gardens of the Desert, these

The unshorn fields, boundless and beautiful
For which the speech of England has no name

or the dark green forests of Maine or Missouri or West Virginia, and I
must say that I saw there nothing whatsoever that came close to the eerily,
mysterious, silent, wind-swept, God-drenched, Edenic, eternal rolling
green hills of, say, Wind Cave National Park in the Black Hills of South
Dakota — which for me, regarding nature, is the most beautiful place on
the face of the earth, a temple of nature, a region too sacredly enchanting for words in a way — no, the Estonians forests are tight, unfussified,
scarcely lush with sudden ravines and somber trails.

I was told that the old broadleaf forests below the chalk cliffs between
Saka and Ontika, with its famous frozen waterfalls in winter, as well as
the pine forests of Nõmme and the Mustamäe juniper dunes are all magnificent to see, which I never had the chance to do. I did however see
working deep in the woods actual *metsatööline* ("lumberjacks") — a word
I managed to remember because it sounded so much, with a jiggle, like
the Italian *mezza luna*, or half-moon, under which the men probably often labored, cutting, as well as the well-known kitchen utensil, the curved
steel blade, often with a vertical handle at each end, used to chop food.

About those people gardening in bikinis or in their underwear, could
it be a way to get some vitamin D? Along with respectable people on
city buses or public transportation appearing shirtless, Sarah saw many
people with untanned bodies sunning themselves virtually naked along
the banks of the Emajõgi, and a human is never more naked than when
fish-belly white! She was also shown around properties when she was
looking for painting possibilities by good-hearted but clueless men who
were virtually nude or wearing Speedos and nothing else. I think it may
speak to a sauna-culture. Nude mixed-sex sauna baths are uncommon.
Sarah heard many "sauna stories" from the string of residents that came
and went each month at the Estonian residency that she lived in for
awhile. People would habitually join in what is a sacred Estonian practice
and, from what she was told, bonding took place there in just about every
sense. In one village where she stayed a sauna festival was held, including a smoke sauna, a cooking sauna, even a sauna in a bus — but in
all saunas typically the sexes were kept separate. Saunas are traditionally

once-a-week events with families. Generally one sex goes first, then the other. In old traditional houses, often a small compound with out-lying huts, there is always a sauna hut, a smoke sauna heated with wood. Sarah and I once visited one and were amazed to see the entire ceiling charred black from smoke. There are even shops devoted solely to sauna paraphernalia, with items like scented oils, all sorts of scrubbers, brushes and birch leaves to promote blood circulation, strange oversize bonnets in funny character shapes (paper boats, milk maid, dwarf, ogre, etc,) made of hemp and offered to protect the head!

In Finland, with the exception of families, men and women never take saunas together. *Saunahenki,* the code of the sauna, holds the sauna as an almost sacred place — no sex, no violence, no crude behavior. It is considered especially rude to curse in sauna, even in company not shy of swearing, and conversation is not only relaxed but arguments and controversial topics are avoided. It is also rare to use titles or other honorifics in the sauna. It has often been said that there are only two times when Finns are normal: when they are drunk and when they are naked. Drunk and naked together? Why, even better. The same truth may hold for Estonians. To the formal person, both are a relief.

The Giant Kalevipoeg

I have made reference to the classic Estonian national epic, the *Kalevipoeg,* very much a saga of the physical. Friedrich Reinhold Kreutzswald compiled the poem — wrote it, if you will — with the hope of interpreting it as the reconstruction of an absolute *oral* epic. In 1839, Friedrich Robert Faehlmann chose to read a paper at the Learned Estonian Society about the legends of a rugged, muscular country giant named Kalevipoeg — he was first mentioned by Heinrich Stahl in the 17th century — and in doing so began sketching out the plot of a national epic-poem. This particular reading had a major effect on Kreutzwald. After Faehlmann's death in 1850, in an attempt to give these fluid and unharnessed legends some national identity Kreutzwald with extreme care and national concern patiently gathered and unified the texts, gathering fables here and there. Such are the origins of the specious. The first version of the *Kalevipoeg* (or Kalev's son), which was censored, by the way — it was eventually anglicized as *The Kalevide* — appeared in 1853. It consisted of 13,817 verses. A second version, which grew to 19,087 verses, was published between 1857 and 1861. The third version, an abridged edition of 19,025 verses — XX Cantos — which was completed in 1862 and printed in Kuopio, Finland is the one most popular with common readers today.

Curiously, only one-eighth of those verses in the epic are considered to be "authentic," with the rest literary imitations made to sound older, evocative, antique. It is all of it *manufactured* folklore, pure and simple. But must that matter? The Psalms themselves were written or composed by many poets. Although a few go back to the reign of David, most were written at different later dates. Scholars allow that Psalm 18 (of which a slightly different version occurs in I Samuel 22) might actually be by David himself. But many are later than the "captivity," or the deportation to Babylon. There is no denying that this national work lies in the rich, fabulous tradition of such national fables as Lönnrot's *Kalevala*, Longfellow's *Hiawatha*, and McPherson's *Ossian*. Most Estonians regard it these days, however, more as a monument of the 19th-century Estonian cultural revival than as a strictly literary work of vast importance.

My American-Estonian friend, T. Peter, told me, "My father much preferred reading the novelist, August Gailit. More 20th-century Estonians read Gailit than they do the *Kalevipoeg*. You might even say he is the equivalent in Estonia of F. Scott Fitzgerald, Ernest Hemingway, D.H. Lawrence, or even James Joyce. He was half-Latvian — his surname, *gailiits*, means 'cock, rooster' — and his most famous novel is *Toomas Nipernaadi* which was published in 1928 and tells the story of a vagabond." In the final analysis, however, probably the real super-giant of early 20th-century Estonian literature — Estonian's answer to Henry James — is the brilliant imaginative novelist to whom I have already referred in my taxonomy of Estonian writers, Anton Hansen Tammsaare (1878-1940), whose pentalogy, *Tõde ja õigus* ("Truth and Justice" [1926-1933]), is generally considered to be one of the major works of all Estonian literature. You will not be surprised to learn that *Truth and Justice*, scandalously, has never been translated into English, but there are two complete translations that have been made into German and one into French.

The *Kalevipoeg* is neither a unique nor idiosyncratic Estonian cultural artifact. It is a rather typical 19th- or early 20th-century nationalistic production of what some historians and sociologists call the "invention of tradition," of which the now-institutionalized African-American holiday, Kwanzaa, is a good example. Although there is no Lithuanian national epic, the neighboring Latvians do have their own *Kalevipoeg*-type artificially created 19th-century faux-archaic national hero-epos. It is called *Lacplesis* (pronounced "*lahts*-play-sis" — "The Bear-Slayer") and was compiled from Latvian folk-tales and folk-songs by the 19th-century poet, Andrejs Pumpurs, who wrote it between 1872 and 1887. (Lacplesis Day, honoring the legendary hero — at one point he actually battles with the giant Kalapuisis (*Kalevipoeg* in Estonian) — is celebrated in Latvia every November 11.) For that matter, even Virgil's *Aeneid* could be seen as a very early prototype of this sort of manufacture, a conscious attempt to bolster Roman imperial and cultural pride (and to flatter Augustus at the same time) by deliberately providing the Romans with their own answer to Homer. As I say, Lithuania, whose language is the oldest Indo-European tongue, comparable in age to Sanskrit, oddly enough, has no national epic.

Kalevipoeg — his real name is John (*Soini* in Estonian) — is the son of Kalev and Linda. The poem, which recounts his many strange adventures, documents an enchanting medieval world in which predictably we encounter sorcerers, dwarves, maidens, hunting, journeys, islands, fir trees, swords, castles, wolves, plowing and planting. Many of the hero's deeds are oversized, such as building towns, wading through oceans. He carries stones and throws them at enemies and uses planks as weapons. He follows the advice of a hedgehog. He dies after his feet are cut off by his own sword. Mythic topoi predominate in the epic, for example, the idea of Estonian *Tagurpari-taat*, which is based on a favorite notion that everything (and everyone) in the nether world is backwards, or reversed, or opposite in relation to the world of light, rather as in *Alice in Wonderland*. The book presents a pagan world. Before the 13th century, Estonia had not been systematically Christianized. Much of the *Kalevipoeg* is also anti-clerical. The word for jackdaw, *kirikuhakk* has long been a popular — and, needless to say, blackly derisive — name for clergymen. I have browsed through the *Kalevipoeg* several times. It is a fund of quibbles and complaints. Part of the virtue of the epic is the essentially elemental, bare, unadorned, quality of the writing. It is a raw and raucous bundle, unchamfered, so to speak, with as much concern about style as a pig has about asparagus.

Where the Fugawi?

I am constantly struck at how insignificant a role Estonia plays as a place of reference in books in general. It rarely appears. References to the country in books in general are rare. I have seen it misspelled in old school geographic books and of course ridiculed even today when it is satirically rendered as Boneraniia, Stonia, Stanistan, Setomaa, e-Stonia, Elbonia, Estoina, Iceland, I'm stoned, and even Hesteralia. Leg-pullers love to claim that the name Estonia comes from what is known from an ancient place that turns people into stone and that for that reason travelers have always spookily avoided going to Estonia. I see Estonia figuratively as a tiny, self-sacrificing, hard-working wife to her husband, Russia, slaving away always to appease him, doomed to spend years appeasing her demanding spouse but asking meekly for nothing. I mean by this that she stays at home rinsing vegetables while the big man goes out to party. There is a stereotype about people in Scotland being incredibly mean: A man in Dundee says to his wife, "I'm going to the pub, get your coat on." Astonished, she hopefully replies, "Oh, does that mean you're taking me with you?" To which he replies, "No, I am turning the heating off while I'm away."

I have mentioned how Graham Greene planned to use Tallinn in a book title but then did not. F. Van Wyck Mason in one of the sixty-five novels he published, *Himalayan Assignment* (1952) — what person inditing that many books could possibly be accurate? — gives us an Estonian princess (!) named Princess Atossa as minor character, although there were never any princesses in Estonia, and Atossa is not and never was an Estonian name. (Readers of Herodotus will recall Atossa was the name of the ambitious wife of King Darius the Persian King and we see her in the *Histories* in her husband's bed in one of the first royal bedroom-scenes in world literature!) Science-fiction writer, Theodore Sturgeon, for whom Sturgeon's Law is named ("Ninety percent of SF [science fiction] is crud, but then, ninety percent of *everything* is crud"), in an excoriating story called "The Comedian's Children," references a victim from Estonia, a small girl in this case. A greedy showbiz celebrity and comedian named Heri Gonza (from the Spanish word for "grimace" or "awful joke") runs fund-raising telethons for sick or dying children — an obvious satirical attack on Jerry Lewis' Annual Muscular Dystrophy Telethons — which are of course nothing but scams, and one of the victims he exploits turns out to be little crippled Koska who is flown in from "Esthonia." ("She is a little Esthonian girl, from the far north. She doesn't speak very much English, so she won't mind if we talk about her.") Then, in one of the books of the prolific Arthur C. Clarke, *The Hammer of God*, he writes about American and Soviet agents who try to get hold of designs for a super-weapon created by an Estonian physicist, a lot of that standard 1950s and 1960s sci-fi hoodoo, and I can add that I once managed to find a copy of the book but, after reading two or three pages of it which put me to sleep, I left it in a swap-shop.

I came across another gratuitous literary/cinematic allusion to Estonia recently — witchiness and weirdness always seems inevitably evoked in such references to the country, an "exotic signifier" — reading about the 2009 horror movie, *Orphan*, about an evil child. After the death of an unborn child, a couple adopts a 9-year-old Russian girl, Esther, from an orphanage. The creature turns out to be a cold-blooded serial killer reminiscent of little Rhoda Penmark in William March's *The Bad Seed*. After some anxious investigation, Kate, the adoptive mother, learns that Esther had been housed at a mental institution in Estonia called the Saarne Institute. Kate later gets a call from the Institute's director, Dr. Värava (Karel Rioden) who reveals that Esther is not 9 years old at all, but (yes!) a 33-year-old woman named Leena Klammer. It is explained that she suffers from hypopituitarism, a disorder that stunted her physical growth, and that she has spent most of her guileful life posing as a little girl! The doctor tells Kate that Esther is dangerously psychotic and has killed dozens of people. I can easily picture the boxing of the child's biography. "Where should such a weirdo come from? Somewhere in Chile? Hoboken? *Maine?*" asks the screenwriter, conferencing with the director. The director hastily grabs a nearby world-map which he quickly surveys, moving his fat thumb into the upper, outer, more remote regions of the world. "I got it! *Estonia!*"

No movie title exists with the word Estonia in its title. *None.*[117] The place just does not figure as a world reference. Check the rolling indices of any book, travel or otherwise. Investigate cruise-ships. Go to the travel magazines to look for articles. No country, no locale, is wanting in ads. Come to Somalia! Visit the Dordogne! Virginia is for lovers! *We are worth it.* Or so the tocsin sounds. Most nations wear themselves to a shadow trying to state as much. One understands fluctuating modes of fashion. I remember in the mid-sixties everyone trendily wanting to visit Greece. A place that one likes, another will not. And who would deny that taste is largely whim? But Estonia is a realm apart. It is not mentioned in Hans. J. Morgenthau's *Politics Among Nations.* Churchill skips by it in *The World Crisis.* It makes no appearance in the elegant *Relais & Châteaux,* the essential annual European guide for the best and most charming hotels in the world. I saw no reference to it in *The Adventures of Marco Polo* or Milan Kundera's essays in *The Curtain* or in any of the works of Dostoevsky. It seems to have been bypassed in just about every travel book that ever was. I looked for it, in vain, in Amy Axelrod's *Pigs on the Move: Fun with Math and Travel.* I checked out Peter Parley's *Balloon Travels of Robert Merry and His Young Friends in Europe over Various Countries in Europe* and found nothing. I even went so far as to go haphazardly flipping through a library copy of Howard R. Garis' *Dick Hamilton's Airship, or, a Young Millionaire in the Clouds* — zip on Estonia. We are talking obscure here.

One comes across historical figures in Estonia that one has never heard of elsewhere. Take the money. In France you see Descartes and Molière and Balzac on the currency. In Britain, you see the Queen, of course, but British notes also celebrate historical figures such as Charles Darwin, Robert Burns, Elizabeth Fry, and, needless to say, Shakespeare — inexplicably, golfer Jack Nicklaus also showed up a few years ago! But in Estonia? It called to mind comedian Artie Lange's crude assessment of "funny Canadian money" in his gonzo memoir, *Too Fat to Fish,* when he writes, "There were no pictures of presidents to stare you down. There was shit like geese and bacon looking back at you from a backdrop of weird Monopoly paper." On the grey-blue two-kroon bill can be seen staring out a dour, munch-mouthed fellow, stranger to all the world, named K.E. von Baer (1792-1876). Prof. Karl Ernst von Baer *was* the founder of modern embryology, as much a pioneer of modern biology as Darwin, Mendel, Pasteur, and Watson and Crick. You can see Paul Keres (1916-1975), an Estonian chessmaster, on the five-kroon note who looks like a young version of the actor Herbert Marshall.[118] On the ten-kroon note, there is Jakob Hurt (1839-1907), a sort of cross between orchestra conductor Mitch Miller and the traveling wizard, cherry-cheeked Professor Marvel, played by Frank Morgan that young Judy Garland as Dorothy in *The Wizard of Oz* encounters when she runs away from home! (Perhaps the weakened U.S. dollar I found there still diminishes my sense of their money.) Whereas once the Estonian kroon returned for a dollar 14.38 EEK, in 2008 a dollar was worth only seven! Eeeek! (Get it?) The lovely national poet, Lydia Koidula (1843-86), Estonia's first lady of literature, can be seen portrayed on the 100-kroon note with her bountiful hair, deep-set eyes, and a firm beautiful chin set for destiny. She was born Lydia Jannsen, but the soubriquet *koidula* — *koidulaulik* means "singer of the dawn" — she adopted for obvious poetical reasons. A founder of the Estonian theater, Koidula married one Eduard Michelsen, a Latvian army surgeon, and then moved to Russia, near St. Petersburg, and lived in Kronstadt for 13 years, where she was supposedly very homesick for her native land. Although much of her poetry is shot through with pastoral romanticism and themes of home, family, religion, and scenes of rural life, sort of delicate proto-Beidermeier melodies, she can raise her voice in political dudgeon to sound the cry for freedom. Her most important work is generally held to be her *Emajõe Ööbik* (1867), the "Nightingale of the Emajõgi." Her last poem was *Enne Surma — Eestimaale!* ("Before Death, To Estonia!") Her dramatic and heart-stirring song, *Mu isamaa on minu arm* ("My Country is My Love") always finishes every song festival in Estonia, with or without permission, a tradition that persists to this very day. It was this kind of ritual that always made me feel, when I considered the secularism of Estonia, that the good people there regard music as *ancilla theologiae* — a servant of theology, the way that composer

Adrian Leverkühn did in Thomas Mann's *Doctor Faustus*.

There is a lovely statue of Lydia Koidula in flower-rich Koidula Park in Pärnu, the town of her youth. The sculpture done by Amandus Adamson is also the last work of the sculptor. Most statues in Tallinn and Tartu, with a few exceptions, seem to be of impish little men. Some with big heads. Tall green-bronze statues of men holding top hats. Big beaver-faced loons. Be-whiskered scientists. A popular statue in Tartu [that I mentioned before], the locus classicus of nutty if memorable statues and always the cynosure of all eyes, memorializes in dark bronze two notably stark-naked figures, a bearded man and his fat oversize son, who is bigger than the father, both with — disturbingly — the same size penis, holding hands. This statue was sculpted by Ülo Õun. It is a popular meeting-place, I am told. And why not?

There is an unforgettable statue of a giant pig — a bronze sow — right in front of the Tartu Torg, a market building, the *Lühikirjeldus*, a wonderful sculpture, like a primitive idol. I have seen people deck flowers around her clean neck and ears. (I am certain that it is pigeon-proofed by a small admixture of gallium in the bronze.) One can see a series of cement turtles on the streets in Tartu, blocking off any car access. Is it art — or barriers? In the village of Viinistu, one can also see a gathering of some 100 suitcases, all white, with name tags yet, sitting in parking lot. It is *sculpture*, in fact — created by an important Estonian artist named Kaido Ole — and represents the Estonian diaspora, I am told. It is quite amazing to come across. There is a narrow lane in Tallinn called Katrina Kaik — St. Catherine's Passage — that is replete with art shops and studios, where you can watch ceramicists, weavers and even bookmakers at work, in fact the narrow lanes in a very real way constitute a sort of art.

It was the infinitely kind Kaido Ole who not only drove us, helped us move, from Tallinn to Tartu — and became something of a mentor to Sarah in Estonia, her main affiliation there and head of the painting department of the Estonian Academy of Art, the pre-eminent art school in Estonia, helping her hang several important shows, along with giving her a teaching job on the island of Muhu — but also was a fund of information about the ways and means of his country. His daringly avant-garde paintings and sculpture are some of the best work being done in Europe.

Art in Estonia, which is high-priority interest, is more than healthy.

I was lucky enough to witness some splendid original work being done there, in colleges, in galleries, in shows, in museums. I honestly believe that talent in this country may be matchless. The Estonian Academy of the Arts is ground zero for splendid work being done, with many examples of genius. The faculty, stressing both the traditional and the avant-garde, must be a great source of inspiration. I have looked through the art catalogues for the last four or five years and cannot believe the creative potential there and the high-quality of the art being turned out: painting, photography, granite sculpture, minimalist jewelry, tile art, set design, sign-making, posters, exposition boxes, book illustration, tapestries, Chinese costume, fashion-design, scenography, glass and leather art, even futuristic sportswear, mobile huts, silk-screens, Plexiglas high heels, therapeutic environment solutions — a very Estonian concept — and all sorts of public "installations." Abstract talent is highly convincing there. I saw designs for a fictitious travel agency. Brilliant original wine-bottle labels. Original playing-card art. Gravestone designs. A car created for Arctic voyaging. Woman's shoes inspired by Hans Christian Andersen. Concept lighting for Alexander's Church in Narva. I saw hotels being designed, bedspreads woven, handbags fashioned out of elegant glass, barbecue grill-plates being forged. I never saw such variety of work being done in the United States. Maybe Le Corbusier was correct when in the 1960s he pointedly declared, "Because of its financial control, the U.S. is the last country to awaken artistically."

As I say, much of the art being done there is postmodern, if one wants to rely on that overused term — "Today's interpretation of yesterday's vision of tomorrow" is one of my favorite definitions. Artists there, especially young ones, are subversive and with a demystifying and debunking candor work from the kind of antic side of Estonian irony already mentioned as a national trait, having plugged into that still popular postmodern fascination with the idea of shifting interest from the what to the how of art, from the things represented in a painting to the business of representation itself. It is young art, cheeky, dangerous, and new. I saw no examples of "crudely painted, not so funny, plywood, cut-out folk art," to quote a memorable episode of television's satire, *Family Guy* — no fat Amish ladies, bum upwards, watering their plants!

I went to several art exhibits in Tallinn. There were examples of amazing cast-iron sculpture that I would have bought on the spot. One young woman student was "inventorising," as she put it, "and cataloguing the Painted Beam Ceilings in the Old Town of Tallinn." Fans and fan-design as cultural phenomena was another subject of art. Crackle-glazing is popular. Another keen student was designing postage stamp models, another porcelain and ceramic figures.

Performance art is very popular there. One young student's concentration was videos of spinning. ("Spin is an act of movement. The head turns around, first in an even circle, transfers after awhile to an irrational swing and reaches a point of joy. It is made by combining long time exposure photos with stop motion technique.") Another student performed trapeze acts in Old Town. I saw living collages. Several women revolving a network of colored brooches mimicked the solar system, or so they claimed. A woman walked around shopping with a pair of glove bags. The aim of another project was to create a modular clothing kit. Another collection was inspired by totalitarian garments, clothing "that has oppressed the human body throughout history — corsets, straitjackets, high starched collars, etc." I saw one particular music video of an electric woman windmilling her arms. I was grateful not to see (raised claws!) mimes.

Clothing, let me add here parenthetically, is a not inconsequential subject in Estonia, neither a random one. It is nothing less than a preoccupation. (An old Norwegian proverb goes, "There is no bad weather, only bad clothing.") Strong parkas, wool hats, good boots, the Eastern Mountain Sports bit. I never saw an Estonian looking or acting cold or indeed complaining about it. I would see people ice-skating or watch pick-up games of "pond" — or what I call "firewagon" — hockey and witnessed nothing but hearty hooping. The weather suits their clothes, as the old song line has it. Dancer becomes dance, in short.

Much art in that country, not surprisingly, revolves around folk activity — stringing trees in the woods, donning costumes more colorful than a wood-duck's, hurling axes, tittuping about in tall pointed hats, rolling balls, frog-hopping in twos at midnight before tall blazing fires while singing inexplicable chants. I have mentioned that Estonians love bonfires. I have never known a people or any country, however, so enamored of *huge* bonfires! Heath folk out gathering furze, in the old *Return of the Native* way! Piling high crude slats of fir, oak, apple, hazel and roman wood for fodder! Brightness on Rainbarrow! The fairy magic of flame! The dynamic draw of huge smoking balefires lighting up the night! Mummers painted with passion dancing, gamboling and playing pipes and zithers and whipping in crazy circles like bumming-tops! The "Tallinn Light Festival" is held every year, when high school and university students build these towers of wood — fire sculptures — tall constructions composed of logs, old Christmas trees, leaves, straw, grass, and hay. The festival took its cue from Helsinki's "Forces of Light Festival." In Tromsö, a large northern city in Norway, a huge municipal party is also held each year on January 21, when around noon-time the sun squeaks above the horizon for about 10 or 15 minutes, a weak promise of a summer that never seems to come! Latvians, by the way, are also maniacs for fire. They decorate their Christmas trees with real candles. Candles are lit on birthday cakes, at funerals, in windows, for worship, during graduation ceremonies, at the traditional midnight wedding ritual of *micǒšana*. Bonfires, since 1991, have lighted the "Days of the Barricades" celebration which led to the restoration of Latvia's independence. Light-therapy. It has been medically proven that light cuts down depression. According to Estonian statistics as many as one in four people in that country — strangely, 80 percent of them are women — suffer from S.A.D. (Seasonal Affective Disorder), a disorder linked to a lack of sunlight. On lighted nights, traditional wind instruments, derived from those used by old shepherds, are still used. In Estonia, on Mother Tongue Day or Lady Cabbage Day or St. John's Day or Nationality Holiday — February 24 — which marks the Independence Day of Estonia, which is also a day of rest, I have no doubt that you can still find folk in the woods playing fiddles and fifes and concertinas and kannels, after which they will often gather in smoky huts to guzzle beer and wolf lingonberry fritters.

It is an old English rhyme, but one can quite easily imagine young Estonians with bunches of flowers — *lillekimp* — and passementerie ornamental headbands traipsing through the dense woods in the warm mud of delicious spring, chanting,

Hooray! Hooray! The Seventh of May
Outdoor screwing begins today!

It is light alone that opens a struggling heart. "Only by virtue of light, i.e., through brightness, can what shines show itself, that is, radiate," wrote Heidegger in *On Time and Being*. "But brightness in its turn rests upon something open, something free which might illuminate it here and there, now and then. Brightness plays in the open and wars there with darkness… Only this openness grants to the movement of speculative thinking the passage through that which it thinks." The philosopher brilliantly aligns the idea of light to the concept of openness.

> The forest clearing (opening) is experienced in contrast to dense forest, called 'density' (*Dickung*) in older language. The substantive 'opening' goes back to the verb 'to open.' The adjective *licht* 'open' is the same word as 'light.' To open something means: To make something light, free, and open, e.g., to make the forest free of trees at one place. The openness thus originating is the clearing. What is light in the sense of being free and open has nothing in common with the adjective 'light,' meaning 'bright' — neither linguistically nor factually. This is to be observed for the difference between openness and light. Still, it is possible that a factual relation between the two exists. Light can stream into the clearing, into its openness, and let brightness play with darkness in it. But light never first creates openness. Rather, light presupposes openness. However, the clearing, the opening, is not only free for brightness and darkness, but also for resonance and echo, for sounding and diminishing of sound. The clearing is the open for everything that is present and absent.

Did not the light that was given to us on the first day alone allow for the space to be found in order that we might live?

Cold Pork

Estonian cuisine is something of an oxymoron. Their food is heavily dependent on the seasons and simple peasant food. Estonians eat mainly potatoes, cabbage, pork, dairy products, and black bread. They are fanatics for dill. Berries are very popular, as they are all through the Baltics and Scandinavia. Traditionally, in winter, jams, preserves, and a variety of pickles are brought to the table. I have heard farming in Estonia referred to as "nitwit agriculture." The country has been through rough times in the past and gathering and conserving fruits, mushrooms, and vegetables for winter has always been essential. A sea-facing country, its people do not seem to be big fish-eaters — and when they eat fish, it is for the most part smoked. (This more or less answered for me the epistemological question I constantly pondered there as to whether Estonia is an outward or an inward-facing country. I would vote: the latter. Neighboring Norway, with its long history of seafaring, shipbuilding, fish-eating is, in stark contrast, clearly — vital, unselfconscious, comparatively young, non-neurasthenic — an *outward*-facing country.[119]) The fish that Estonians do eat is mainly cod and herring from the sea. Estonians also seem to crave sprats. You see stacks of tinned sprats at the Targ. I will always think of the place as "Spratville." I saw sprats everywhere. Like James Joyce's gastronomically peculiar Leopold Bloom, most Estonians also love tongue, liver (*maks*), the lights, wursts, guts — *sisikond* — lungs, relishing "the inner organs of beasts and fowls." That goes for other tastes and odd appetites that we read Bloom had in the Calypso episode in *Ulysses*, such as "thick giblet soup, nutty gizzards, a stuffed roast heart, liver slices fried with breadcrumbs, fried hen-cods' roes." Most of all Poldy savored — even craved — grilled mutton kidneys which gave to his palate "a fine tang of faintly scented urine." *Sült* or head-cheese (from the German *Sülze*) has always been a big Estonian favorite. They love ham and give it as gifts. (Were you aware that a left ham is more tender than the right ham because pigs specifically use only their right leg to scratch themselves?!) A person can also enjoy eating pig's ears there. Pig's ear cookery — eaten warm or cold — is found in a number of cuisines around the world, notably Filipino, Japanese, and Chinese. When cooked, the outer texture is gelatinous, akin to tofu, and the center cartilage is crunchy. Pig's jowls. And of course the full pig's head. You haven't lived until you have had Pig's Head Torchon, where the cloth — laundry cookery! — actually shapes the meat. No wonder they raise statues to pigs. I saw farm after farm of swine, all grist for the groaning board, pot-bellied pigs, sows, barrows, gilts, hogs, piglets. "Estonians use everything from the pig, except its tears" as an old Estonian saying goes. One sees great gouts and hanks of fresh pork in all the food shops. I once rhymed out of satirical disdain:

Estonia
Is filled with cretonia.
Show me a churl
Wolfing platters of pork
And I will show you
— although nothing new —
A typical Baltic dork.

Cold pork is a huge favorite with them. *Cold pork*: I began to feel those two words summed up my aversion to the Baltics. But pork at any temperature is a favorite. An Estonian consumes 71 kilograms of meat per person per year, half of which is pork. They will devour knobs of *pure fat!* I once mistakenly bought a roll of meat (*rubiroll*), which looked good at the shop but which turned out to be nothing but a raw knob of inedible fat, flecked with tidbits of dead carrot — not a trace of meat! Are you surprised that the name for ham there is *sink*? A favorite comestible of theirs is *kats* which is made by boiling pig's feet into a gelatin and then poured into a mold. As Brendan Behan exclaimed of the prison food in *Borstal Boy*, "Jesus judge the food that could be worse." Another jellied meat thing in Estonia is called *sylt* or *sult*, a sort of Meat Jell-O. Who eats this stuff and why? To fight the cold in winter? To stave off cutting winds? To explate past sins? To save money? I have no shame in confessing that in preference, flying even in the face of Acts 10:15, I would rather head to the seaside and gnaw tiny barnacles off a wet rock! Every culture with a pig-based economy has a version of jellied meat. In England it is called "brawn" and is made of the meat of a pig's head — actually it is a terrine — with trotters to provide the jelly. Mouthwatering! I remember an Estonian proverb that goes, "A poor beggar always begs without a bag." A good variation of it in the Baltics might be, "A poor fellow never eats without a snout." Words that scare Estonians off food are "diet," "healthy," "spices," "vegetable." (It is an established fact that Estonia ranks a scandalous 5th in the world for both coronary and arteriosclerotic heart disease — Ukraine, Bulgaria, and Russia head the list — with as high as 715.6 deaths for every 100,000 people.) No better example presents itself, I think, than the obesagenic Estonian diet to justify George Orwell's elemental remark in *The Road to Wigan Pier* that

"A human being is primarily a bag for putting food into; the other functions and faculties may be more godlike, but in point of time they come afterwards."

Blood is also huge in Estonian food. At Christmas, sausages are made from fresh blood and festively wrapped in pig's intestines. God rest ye merry, gentlemen, let *nothing[!]* you dismay! *Terimaks!* A favorite food of theirs is *verikäkk*, which is essentially balls of pork blood — *blecch!* — rolled in flour and eggs with added bits of pig's fat thrown in for taste. Sometimes blood balls are coated in chili jam and/or rolled in anything from wheat grain to chopped peanuts to cilantro, then sliced, fried, and served. I just heard Sairey Golomb squawk, "*Nedugehdach!*" Blood sausage or *verivorstid* is popular in all seasons but is especially cherished as a Christmas staple and often homemade. Intestines are washed with water and salt, then filled with some meat, oats, onions, cooked barley, allspice and marjoram (an herb in Estonia that grows everywhere), and blood let from a pig. Blood is of course highly perishable and must be cooked right away, so fresh blood sausage is straight-away taken and boiled, frozen and saved as a treat for Christmas Eve and the following festive days. For later use it is often treated with salt in a cauldron and left outside in winter. All I have to say is: *Rõõmsaid ja õnnistatud jõulupühi ja Head uut Aastat!* "A Merry and Blessed Christmas and a Happy New Year!" Blood is Estonian fuel! Even *Mäkdonald's* serves bloodburgers and extra-big bloodburgers. You can actually buy blood in supermarkets, where it is sold in small packages like juice.[120] They even have a blood bread — *verileib!* Curiously, however, they all seem to prefer *pekk* (the fat of pork) over *liha* (red meat). I think I will sign off on this paragraph with what Jimmy Durante proclaims in *On An Island With You* (1948), "And a delicious charlotte rooster to you!"

"In the north we give a great mythological importance to the pig," declared Isak Dinesen — Danish Baroness Karen Christentze Blixen-Finecke — to a *Paris Review* interviewer, in spite of the fact that in most Western and Eastern traditions pig symbolism is negative. (Mary Lennox in *The Secret Garden* spitefully calls an Indian servant, "Pig! Pig! Daughter of pigs!") Not so for Dinesen, who declares, "He is a kind of minion of the sun. I suppose because his sweet fat helps to keep us warm in the darkest and coldest time. Very intelligent animal." Have a stubbled pig's-trotter on me! Saltiness is big with Estonians, in almost all cases. Porcupines which are said to adore salty food in any grub they eat would love it there! So is cold food a delight. The Estonian penchant for cold food warrants further study — a doctoral dissertation, surely, for some young future scholar. Alfred Knopf, who was of course a publisher but also a gourmand, recommended to the venerable Wine and Food Society to which he belonged that if anyone ever vilely served them a cold plate from which hot food was to be eaten, or served a warm plate on which was offered cold food, they throw the offending dishes *on the floor!* One may wonder what Alfie would have done with *verikkäk* on a plate of any temperature! I fought my rising gorge and simply thought of Horace and the lines from his *Epode III:*

> *O dura messorum ilia*
> *Quid hoc veneni saevit in praecordiis.*[121]

Although Estonia has an extensive coastline, fish do not seem to take pride of place in Estonian "cuisine." (St. Nicholas, a hovering saint there, is Patron Saint of Fisherman yet.) I cannot understand it. Look at a map of Estonia and you can see how much the bountiful coastline graces, virtually surrounds, this country — the Baltic Sea, the Gulf of Riga to the south, the Gulf of Finland to the north, all those thousands of inlets of the eastern islands, and Lake Peipsi on the eastern border. The names are different — no body of water on earth, curiously, bears the name of Estonia — but they are all part of the dark, tempestuous Atlantic Ocean. I have always found arresting playwright Arthur Miller's reflection in *Timebends:* "There was always something listless, almost forlorn, about the lazy Pacific, unlike the sharp and cold and saltier Atlantic that was so full of anger and ideas." I have been told that, for some reason, these are all "young seas" [sic], whatever that indicates, presumably that they are not as fish-full as the vast and open oceans and are maybe even wanting in sustaining food for fish. The sea itself, on the other hand, where no ancient Jew incidentally ever willingly went — the Hebrews, *pace* Sts. Peter and Paul, never looked toward the ocean — may terrify them as it did Jonah You see some fishing boats being worked everywhere, I saw them everywhere in the Gulf of Finland, but whenever I thought of the national appetite for pork over fish, I would inevitably recall the warning of Job 41:22: "He shall make the deep to boil like a pot, and shall make it as when ointments boil."

I asked one angler squatting under a mutton-chop hat what he had caught. Someone told me the most common catch for fly fishermen in Estonia is brown trout, which inhabit more than 90 rivers, most fast-running streams, even slower clear creeks there. Most effective time for trout-fishing is from late April to mid-September. "I fly fishing. I go to coast of Kola Peninsula every spring autumnal for one, two veeks. Now I preferred big 15-17 feet rodpoles and click-pawl reels like Hardys [?}. I love sound of that reels. It's a music best, um, for me. Me home river joy makes salmon in Narova. Is big river like Tana in Norway!"

I can assert that Estonians, however, do love sprats, pickled herring, smelts, crayfish, a variety of dried fish, and of course while they did not seem to eat much seafood, at least from what I saw, they do relish smoked fish — *suitsukala* — and especially the smoked fish from Lake Peipsi. *Schnitzel*, a breaded, fried pork fillet, like most cheap Estonian cuisine, they often douse with sour cream and is a big favorite there. *Seljanka* — meat stews — are a big item. So is maksapasteet, liver paste. And *pelmenid* (dumplings). Cheese (*juust*) when I lived in Estonia was more expensive than it is in the USA. Too many cheeses in Estonia, by the way, are are bland and plasticky. I once noticed in a supermarket the chumless Fulbright miser Belk — our dear friend, the blinking Mr. C.D.E. Floptz with his haptic bias — coldly walk over and imperially, impatiently, snatch from his poor wife's hand a small knob of curd cheese, disdainfully smell it, toss it back into the bin, pirouette about for a minute, and then pompously squawk, "Let's go with celery." I can say I once enjoyed eating elk sausages. You are welcome to the *keel* (tongue) I happily passed over — all of it. Same with *angerjalised* — eel — which was often smothered in cream, and also *metssiga* — boar — which proved far too gamy for me. Baltic chili, which is unidentifiable to any American, is eaten unseasoned — I tried a bowl of it with a piece of *karask*, a cake-like barley bread — and it tasted like wallpaper paste.

They Love Knob Food

They love wet salads. I believe beet salad (*rosolje*) is the top favorite in that department, a potpourri of diced beets, potatoes, hard-boiled eggs, diced apples, dill pickles, sour cream, deviled eggs, and sauerkraut braised in dark beer. I love their red cabbage salad, the simple recipe for which goes:

¼ head of red cabbage
½ onion
1 large celery stalk
1 Granny Smith apple thinly sliced
2 tbsp. vegetable oil
1 tbsp. lemon juice
¼ tsp. salt
¼ tsp pepper
pinch of sugar

Cheese, simple cheese, is expensive there. I will never understand why. A wedge of cheese costs more in Tallinn than on Martha's Vineyard. Soy sauce and Tabasco sauce are also far too pricey, when you can even find them. Fully unavailable in Estonia are cornmeal, molasses, chocolate chips, and a serious cook when shopping can face an afternoon of fungible disenchantment. Estonians enjoy raclettes of meat, cheese, and potato. I enjoyed a *cepelinae* once, which originated I'm told in Vilnius — blimp-shaped dumplings named after Zeppelins. I have to say I also loved the *pirukad*, or pierogi, that are made there. *Nami nami* — which is to say yummy! Dumplings, chunks of pork, blocks of cheese, a sheep's head! Do you see a trend? The fact of the matter is they love *knob* food in Estonia, unlike most other people on earth who eat what can generally be described as flat food — why not? — food close to the plate, that is, like veal cutlets and filet of sole and omelettes and mushrooms. But in Estonia it is oncological knobs! I'm talking dirigibles! Big, assertive, lumpy, bumpy, clock-sized, muscular, bone-in, knob food! There are 400 edible species of fungi in Estonia, by the way. It is a great place for ceps. Mushrooming is a favorite activity for many of them, and you will often see hunters traipsing into the dense forests after a heavy drenching rain with a bucket, a knife, and safe shoes looking everywhere for ceps, especially the most prized ones. Chanterelles. Morels. The large, thick Boletus. I wondered how often, if ever, mycophagists skimming the fields there came across the lethal Death Cap (*Amanaita phalloides*), which originated in and are still found all over Europe. *Seenakaste* (mushroom gravy) with potatoes and kurgid is a popular Estonian dish, eaten at any time of the day. "Have you *seen*?" you can shout at them. "Seen? Seen what?" "Mushrooms! Mushrooms!" *Seen* is the Eesti word for mushrooms. It's a joke. A feeble one, to say the least. Wordplay for idiots. I apologize. Despair will make anyone a comedian.

Did they also hunt mandrakes? Wild ginseng? Truffles? All those jewels in the earth that make people rich? Don't half of these tubers and roots actually *look* like little humans? Ginseng, with its odd branchiness, is Cantonese for "image of man." Mandrakes supposedly shriek when pulled up. ("Go and catch a falling star/Get with child a mandrake root!" wrote John Donne.) The mandrake, a plant of the nightshade family and an ancient anesthetic, was used to numb or sedate patients before various operations, typically inhaled. It has long been a folk theory among diggers that nature can help cure their counterpart in the human body. The brain looks like a walnut, so what's good for it? Walnuts! Tomato juice, red as blood? A perfect tonic for tired plasma! Heartfood is everywhere.

Where Mark Twain in *A Tramp Abroad* said that meat served on the Continent was "as overdone as a martyr," I found in Estonia that almost all meat was usually undercooked and fatty. Mind you, we were most always eating at home or in poor restaurants. On their family trip abroad in 1878, fondly looking back at America, Twain expressly began to miss "hot biscuits, *real* coffee with *real* cream…fried chicken, corn bread, *real* butter, *real* beefsteak, *good* roast beef with taste to it," and I soon joined with him in his reveries. I began using bread with everything.

Bread there is delicious. They have a wide variety. My favorite was Eesti Pagar Jassi Seemneleib (*valgud* 110 g., *süsivesikud* 30.8 g., *rasvad* 14.3 g.) I used to buy huge, moist, earthy Estonian sourdough loaves so dense that each one weighed as much as four pounds that slathered with butter made a perfect meal. There is no corn in it. Stalin tried to introduce corn, but Russia was too far north for corn to do well in the cold fields. Most of the breads are dark and dense. I have also eaten thick black breads that tasted like wool blankets. Along with blood employed in bread, Estonians also use parsnips (*pastinaak*) in bread, and potato (*kartul*) in bread. Bread is the Estonian staple, as sacred as anything in that country. I have already mentioned it, but I'll say it again: *Jätku leiba!* May your bread last!

I am mildly surprised no cabbage bread exists in Estonia. (Parsnip bread does!) Koreans crave kimchi, no matter the variety. Italians love yellow risotto with saffron which definitely reeks of iodine. Irish love carrageen, a flat, cartilaginous, pale-green, bavaroise-like jelly made of seaweed. Mongolians far from home miss the all-pervasive smell of rancid mutton fat. The Balt loves his cabbage, even if, in the words of Victorian prudery, it embarrassingly tends to repeat. (A popular proverb there goes, "Meat unites, cabbage divides.") There are certain sensations, I've come to see, whose banality does not exclude intensity. Cabbage to an Estonian means far more than it should, in the way, I would say, a good male dancer to certain women represents reproductive potential. "Rice is communism," declared Kim Il-Sung. For Estonians? "Cabbage is us."

It is the Russian habit to have cabbage parties at the time of the Great Fast, about the middle of February, according to the Orthodox Church seven weeks during Lent of prayer and fasting. Constantin Stanislavsky's *My Life in Art* (1924) devotes a whole chapter to the custom.

I have already alluded to the tins of Tartu *küpsis* — small raisin biscuits — that Doodle loved to munch and sent back as gifts to America. I almost suffered heart-seizure when I saw the flint-skinning niggard Belk ostentatiously bring a gift of such a tin to the host of one of the few parties we attended there, a good example of left-handed — *vasakukäeline* — generosity, bought for a few kroon. Estonia has no signature dessert like the illustrious Sacher torte, the pride of Austrian coffeehouses, or those Sprüngli chocolate cakes, found in the famous sweet shop in Zurich, which are well-known all over Switzerland or, say, Turkish baklava. There is the *sokolaaditort,* a classic light layer cake, but it's essentially the same recipe as a jelly-roll cake and reaches to nothing like fabled dimensions.

There is no *street food* of any kind, hot or cold, in Estonia. Not in Tallinn, not in Tartu or Narva or Pärnu, Maardu or Kohtla-Järve. It is something found more or less in just about every major city on earth, every city that I've been in — Berlin, Paris, Warsaw, Rome, Edinburgh, Bangkok, London, New York, Cairo, etc — but not in Estonia. (Why has not some entrepreneurial soul thought to cook up bunches of *pirukad* to hawk in the streets? Or homemade *kotletid*? Or *kringel*, those tasty pretzel-shaped coffee-rings covered with nuts and powdered sugar? Or how about simple delicious wursts — *like a hot-dog stand!?*) I have to admit that I well-suspected before I traveled east that, food-wise, I was not exactly visiting Paris or Vienna or Berlin, although I had not resorted to the kind of ludicrous extremes that Truman Capote was driven to before he went off to the far reaches of rural Kansas to investigate the murder of the Clutter family when, fearful that there would be no discernible (or palatable) cuisine in the Midwest, he had fussily and rather laboriously carted out with him along with all of his luggage a full footlocker stuffed with provisions as if he were heading down the Zambesi with bearers and a pith helmet! To many — most — young Estonians, gourmet food is fast food. There is, as I have mentioned, the McDonald's chain there: one can be found in Tallinn, right downtown. There is also a very busy one located in Tartu.

One day Sarah and I had a yearning for Chinese food. We looked up a Chinese restaurant in the telephone book and paid a visit to a small unprepossessing place on a backstreet, but the meal we ordered proved to be nothing but an uncomplicated dish of rice served with a few wilted vegetables on the side. (As to ethnic food, a chalkboard at the Pool Kuus restaurant off Raekoja plats, where we lived for a spell, boasted "Est-Mex food here.") The cheapest meals in Tallinn can be found at Dietsöökla on Dunkri, a cafeteria with its fare based on dairy products. Things are pretty basic over there. (I have even heard that there is an Estonian tradition to have picnics over relatives' graves!) I occasionally went for breakfast at the closeted little *kohvik*, a couple of wooden rooms, in the University of Tartu student union reserved for eating buffet-style: scrambled eggs, baked beans, bacon, tea. That is standard American. The usual Estonian *Hommikueine* or "morning meal" — *Hommikusöök* means "morning food" (the suffix *eine* is perhaps a bit more "high-toned" than *söök*) — consists of all or a combination of rye bread, eggs, cheese, pastries, sandwiches and/or porridge, usually with a pot of coffee. (Estonians love their coffee, although their passion cannot compare with the people of Finland, the #1 coffee-drinking country in the entire world in which, according to statistics, the average person drinks 1681 cups annually — 24 lbs. 11 oz. per capita! (Finnish coffee, which is strong, has a red tinge to it and something of as bitter aftertaste.) I very much liked Estonian yogurt, porridges, and jams. Sarah and I used to call our jars of jam Currants and Queel. "I need something sweet," I'd say. "Where is that delicious jar of Currants and Queel?"

My friend T. Peter's mother who was born in Rasina in eastern Estonia, near Lake Peipsi — his father was born near Kodavere in Pala township — used to make him dishes of *roosa-manna*, a cream of wheat both flavored and made pinkish with cranberries or cranberry juice. The main Estonian meal, incidentally, is traditionally eaten at midday and is generally made up of three courses: soup, a main dish of meat or fish or potatoes, and dessert, which is often fruit or fruit preserves, in keeping with the dessert of Shakespeare's time ("My news shall be the fruit to that great feast," as Polonius tells Claudius in *Hamlet* (II, ii)). Common soups for lunch include bouillon, cabbage, and pea. Dinner in Estonia is commonly a lighter meal, most often eaten at about six p.m. It invariably consists of basic, solid, essential, peasant food, a cuisine that rarely involves major flourishes — *volants et s'épanouit*[122] — calling to mind, touching on the secularism of the people, if A.N. Whitehead was not wrong when he once curiously remarked, "Cooking is one of those arts which most requires to be done by persons of religious nature." Among the many and various walks I took in Tartu involved strolls down and around the hilly old streets adjacent to the college there, and as I rambled along the hilly streets I could often smell the rich odor of proletarian food coming from what I assumed were students' rooms in old wooden houses that, to me, evoked a brief passage from Thomas Pynchon's *Gravity's Rainbow*:

> In the Studentenheim there's no heat, not much light, millions of roaches. A small of cabbage, old Second Reich, grandmothers' cabbage of lard smoke that has found, over the years, some détente with the air that seeks to break it down, smells of long illness and terminal occupation stir the crumbling walls.

Berries figure very largely in Estonian consumption. Lingonberries are very popular in the Baltics. They put them in and on anything. *Pannkoogid*, pancakes with lingonberries, is tasty and popular and became one of Sarah's favorite foods. She also loved the taste of reindeer stew in Finland. "And *platt panna*," she added. "Berries on oatmeal, cold or hot. I remember before bedtime one night, after visiting some friends — quite late, I mean — we had tea and jam with bread, when I was also treated to four kinds of homemade preserved berries in jars. Raspberry and currant jam. Arctic cloudberry jam on thin pancakes. Apple and whortleberries. Blueberries. Wild cranberries kept in water. Then gooseberries baked and sweetened in sugar and colored with blackcurrants." I never heard Sarah ask for *salmiakki*. Ammonium chloride, or *salmiakii,* is a mysteriously popular Finnish candy that tastes something like oversalted black licorice. Nor did I hear her cry, "*Lisää karhunpaistia!*" More bear steak!

I would loved to have wandered up along the *calotte* of Finland, northern Sweden, Norway, and the Kola Peninsula of Russia to the land of the Sami people — they regard the terms "Lap", "*Lapp*", or "Laplanders" as pejorative — and share with the folks in four-cornered hats and gákti of heavy woolen jackets a platter of roast reindeer, which I am told includes the viscera, minced and cooked udder, hooves, even the brain (as an ingredient in bread), not excluding reindeer cheese which, along with the tongue, heart. and even reindeer milk (mixed with angelica and sorrel), are considered delicacies. I can add it would be a thrill to see waving the Sami national flag which may be the world's most impressive.

As to berry picking, I have mentioned, throughout the Baltic countries one can walk across long crude wooden boardwalks laid out in old forests, over wet marsh and grimpen, maybe, and one can go threading, squelching, along the gently rising and falling planks to pluck berries or sniff flowers or cut ferns or find mushrooms.

Sarah and I ate a lot of spaghetti, potatoes and red wursts in our Estonian flat. The wursts we ate were small hot dogs (*viiner*) that came in blister packs and were soft as puppy shit. I liked them fried. We ate these tidy meals hunched like gypsies over a small table. "Better is a dinner of herbs where love is than a stalled ox and hatred withal" goes Proverbs 15:17. We seemed always to be hungry. We became stove lizards and often talked about food. Was it the darkness, the cold, the dislocation

— *nihestus?* It became our habit to shop at the Maxima foodshop, and sometimes a large supermarket called Konsum in Tartu. There are highly visible store-police, uniformed and armed, in all the supermarkets there. (We stuck out. Was it because married couples in Estonia wear wedding rings on their *right* hands, as we did not? The store-police with pulled faces seem to have strong foreigner-radar and walking the aisles scowlingly tend to eye anyone with a flare in a coat or a bright scarf or new shoes and especially anyone laughing.) There are potatoes of all kinds available, some cut for you to see the kind, violet, yellow, pink, etc., and in the Farmer's Market behind the bus station in Tartu fat farmers of both sexes stand at the stalls with burlap bags of potatoes holding a spading fork or a knife to cut them for you. Fingerlings. Russets. Finnish *peruna*. Round reds. Pink Eyes. Spunta. Waxy whites. Gold ones. Men will often take up a sample to chew a piece before they buy. In Estonia potatoes are fried, baked, boiled. Lord Bertrand Russell in his Nobel Prize Acceptance Speech said,

> I once befriended two little girls from Esthonia [sic], who had narrowly escaped death from starvation in a famine. They lived in my family, and of course had plenty to eat. But they spent all their leisure visiting neighboring farms and stealing potatoes, which they hoarded. Rockefeller, who in his infancy had experienced great poverty, spent his adult life in a similar manner.

I would see in the market a lot of grubby little boys lugging bags of potatoes and feel bad for them, hearkening back in my mind to the nearly word perfect portrait of childhood, maybe the best ever written, in the early chapters of George Eliot's *The Mill on the Floss* and could not help but compare luck and lucklessness. No, potatoes are the staff of life in Estonia, and any Spudulike, a fast-food chain in the UK specializing in potatoes, would do very well in that country, pushing it, say, as an *adaptogen*, a word from Chinese medicine referring to plants that help the body with its daily adjustments. I recall years ago reading that in Ireland, where potatoes are a big comestible, there is very little prostate cancer, and some scientists think there is a connection. Tomatoes, no surprise, were very expensive, especially in the winter in Estonia. I love both but especially love potatoes, the number one-selling vegetable in the USA. I could not help but reflect on the so-called historic "Columbian Exchange," when commodities were swapped, mainly food, following the conquest of the New World. The Old World got potatoes, tomatoes, chocolate, squash, corn and peppers. The New World — was it a fair exchange? — was the comparatively deprived recipient of little but coffee, sugar cane and cotton, and, while we are at it, why not throw in smallpox, measles and a few other exotic contagious diseases brought in that decimated the native population! The beautiful Arawaks in what is now Barbados, hard upon Columbus' visit in 1492, were literally wiped out by that dread disease. Whenever I got upset in Estonia, I pondered the idea of hurling potatoes at them, that is, until I realized that by default I was but implementing the Columbian Exchange and that, to boot, the buggers would only take them home and fry them up!

Live From the Grill-O-Mat Snack Bar

Americans, fatter than ever, love potatoes. The potato centers a good deal of native obesity in this country. Our bad diet heavy in fat, sugar and salt is killing us. "Eatertainment," it is called. Wily companies do craveability studies and pitch food as fun. Every occasion is now a *food* occasion — sports, dating, movies, watching television, parties, even our school corridors are filled with soft-drink and junk-food machines! (Soft drinks, presently the number one food consumed in our diet, have more or less replaced drinking water.) "Mass culture is a machine for showing desire," wrote Roland Barthes. Youngsters sitting around playing video games and dickering around with computers never exercise and can no longer do push-ups. It has been proven that conditioned hypereating is in the very same category of stimulus-response disorders as compulsive gambling and substance abuse. Served food in the USA is quite commonly *stacked* — as in the 980-calorie Burger King Quad Stacker: four beef patties, four pieces of bacon, and four slices of cheese for $4.99! The United States — LDLville — is the home of hydrogenated fats and oils. These oils are widely recognized as being a major cause of not only obesity and degenerative diseases such as heart disease and cancer, contributing to impaired cellular function and nervous system disorders, but also premature aging. When shopping, know that in the United States the food label can read "zero grams trans-fat" if it contains less than .5 grams of trans fat per serving. So, the more you eat of these items, the more trans-fats you're consuming though you may think you are in the clear because of that "zero grams" label.

A currently popular American cable TV show, "Man vs. Food" on the Travel Channel (54) features a cretin named Adam Richman — a ravenous, hollow-eyed, homely, grotesquely fat perspiring widebody — whose "talent," while people, fans I gather, jump up and scream and applaud, is wolfing down stacks of food, beef, pork, fistwiches, hot pepper platters, pizzas the size of manhole covers. It is a sad but unintentional reiteration of Monty Python's "Live from the Grill-O-Mat Snack Bar." I watched during a so-called "Carnivore Edition" when in a typical fit of gluttonous lust Richman bore into the chankings of a pig sawn in half in The Pit in Raleigh, North Carolina; and at the Coyote Bluff restaurant in Amarillo, Texas wolfed several "Hell Burgers" stuffed with jalapeño peppers.

Every third American is a chubster with a wide ass and double chin and an almost gibbering yen for slabs of ground meat and sweet mus tardy dressings and fries. "More than twelve million Americans now have a body-mass index greater than forty, which, for someone who is five feet nine, entails weighing more than two hundred and seventy pounds," wrote Elizabeth Kolbert in her essay, "XXXL"[123]. Surprisingly, the United States does not top the world list of fattitude or even weight gain. In their book, *Globesity*, authors Delpeuch, Maire, Monnier and Holdsworth point out that "current data reveal that in Cyprus, the Czech Republic, Finland, Germany, Greece, Malta and Slovakia, the proportion of overweight adults is actually higher than in the United States."

Always alert, my dear Sarah insisted, while invoking a theory along the lines of Gresham's Law or some variation of it, that if one failed to shop in the morning for food, pastries, fruit, meat, and potatoes, one would not get fresh food, or in extremis even find edible food. I well remember many cold mornings when we went poking through the meat department of the Targ and in what looked like scenes in that house from the *Texas Chain Saw Massacre* seeing skinned pigs hanging snout-down from hooks, piles of cow brains under glass, great gouts and shanks of goat meat and even an ante-room nearby with wide tin tables where customers were either dining or tasting certain foods that they had just purchased.

I would reflect with amusement on fussy eaters, exacting types whose delicacy in dining brooked no compromise, people like snobbish and disgustable Mrs. Frances Trollope who was horrified during her regrettable sojourn in the United States in the relatively rude 1820s to find herself dining upon cornbread and a glass of rainwater at a common table with a passel of other guests, tradesmen, ditch-diggers and farmers, while seated directly across from her servant, William. Picture her gnawing an aitch-bone or with a beaten-tin spoon tucking into a bowl of *hapukapsa!* Or that prim character Waldo Lydecker, in the words of the witty Florence King "the kind of overcivilized epicene male known in the South as 'an old maid in britches'" — he was played to perfection in the movie by the just as elaborately fey Clifton Webb — whom Vera Caspary describes in her 1941 novel, *Laura*, as fastidiously demanding to have

> his plate arranged just so, pork on this side, duck over there, noodles under the chicken-almond, sweet and pungent spare-ribs next to the lobster, Chinese ravioli on a separate plate because there might be a conflict in sauces. Until he had tried each dish with and without beetle juice, there was no more talk at our table.... He snapped his fingers. Two waiters came running. It seems they had forgotten the fried rice. There was no more talk than necessary, and he had to rearrange his plate. Between giving orders to the Chinese and moaning because the ritual (his word) of his dinner was upset, he talked about well-known murder cases.

St. Anthony the Hermit eating acorns in the wilderness — St. John Cassian munching black radishes — they were not!

I have alluded to Mrs. Trollope having socially to drink glasses of rainwater in 19th-century America. Sarah and I drank lots of water in Estonia when at times we were skint. "Water!" says spluttering Frank Morgan with disgust, sipping a glass of it at a family dinner in the movie, *Summer Holiday* (1948). "What will they think of next?" Thin milk in Estonia is derisively called "Peipsi water" *(Peipsi vesi)* — not only another Leida

Peips allusion but a reference to the fact that Lake Peipsi, the fifth largest lake in Europe, is located half in Estonia, half in Russia.

Leonardo da Vinci actually wrote in his *Notebooks*, "Wine is good, but water is preferable at table."

Eating in Estonia was almost always an adventure. Blood sausage? Cold marinated eel? Headcheese? Cow brains? Liver paste? Jellied meats — *lihaželee*? *Harakas*? Magpie? (Don't laugh. A dish of baked doves was a time-honored gift in northern Italy four hundred years ago — see *The Merchant of Venice*[124]). Smoked something or other in a pile of flesh? Beetroot and horseradish with an eye-watering punch form the basis of many dishes, as they do in Poland. I could not help but notice that sourness figured quite a bit in tastes there. *Hapu* food! Sauerkraut soup. Sour beer even. *Hapukapsas* and *hapukurk*, which literally mean "sour cabbage" and "sour cucumber," are the specific terms there for sauerkraut and pickles. *Hapupiim*, literally sour milk, is often used for buttermilk. It is a favorite drink in the country. Milk gone off, especially when mixed with flour from different grains, called *kama*, is a favorite. Goat milk is another Estonian staple, lending itself to the old adage, "Better a goat that can give milk than a cow who cannot." They also love old sour porridge, *kaerakile*. *Hapukoor* — sour cream — is liberally dolloped on virtually everything.

Winter butters, pale and ripe, often hydrolytically rancid, are greatly to their liking, not the mild factory kind we know in the United States, sweet, newly risen, and pasteurized with a mild lactic acid. Theirs is in fact a butterophagous society: butter and milk durably keep in the cold — potatoes and onions also last a long time before they sprout — for they need the vitamin A. "Butter divides the people of northern Europe as radically from the oil-loving southerners as beer and cider distinguishes them from wine drinkers," notes Margaret Visser in her splendid book, *Much Depends on Dinner*. Standard "rotten" cheeses like Stilton, Pont l'Evèque, and Roquefort intrigue them. Estonian cheese biscuits made pungent with caraway seeds (*Köömnesõbra juustuküpsised*) was one of my favorite comestibles there. Are you surprised to hear they're feet-shaped?

Sourness, in short, the taste that detects acidity, excites the Estonian palate. The vinegary, the acidic, the acrid. Its warheads, shooting to the hydronium ions that are formed from acids and water, explode taste receptor PKD2L1! Of the four flavors the tongue can taste, sweet, salty, bitter, and sour, they predominantly favor, savor, biting "off-flavored foods." Rancidity, pungency, tartness, tang.

Tang seems to be a requirement. They eat tang. They love tang. Tang is irony. Tang is attitude. Tang is daring. Tang is taking the mickey out of dumb, dopey, loud Americans with crew cuts, and cameras and bland shiny faces who with blundering good-will go around saying things like "How de doo!" or "Sorry, I'm fresh out" or "You betcha!" or "Ya wanna nother Coke, hon? How about Jimmy Bob?" Tang is ignoring you. *Tang is not saying thanks!* Tang is walking through the door you hold for them without so much as a fart of acknowledgement, never mind gratitude. Tang is the secret of the country I never cared to learn.

Regarding food, Estonians are accomplished generalists, like crows, and will devour pretty much anything: corn, oats, edible flowers, potatoes, grapes, sardines, aspic, tripe, beans, stubwort, beets — the most beloved root vegetable of the Russian people — bunny meat, *blaukraut*, mosses and lichens from the fog forest, I've heard, wild boar stew, gelatins and what-all in brine, innards, offal, no end of berries from sea buckthorn to cloudberries to black crowberries, lungwort and mugwort and no end of green "beggary baggage" from rootland, Latvian pickle, pigs' ears and tails, nuts, and cabbage pies as full of nutmeg as Connecticut! What is not on the credenza there? There is on *YouTube* a "30-second Vegetarian Nightmare" showing, to the accompaniment of a bright cheery incantation of girls chanting, "*Kana, kana, kana, hakkliha*" ("Chicken, chicken, chicken, minced meat"), glops of beige chicken-meat being exuded from a grinder, an old (satirical? vicious?) Soviet television ad from 1986. But Estonians who can also laugh at themselves must also find this quite funny.

I will always insist that one of the best meals I ever had in my life was an Estonian buckwheat-mushroom oven pie (*tatra seemevorm*) that chef de cuisine Escoffier himself could not duplicate. It was the ant's pants! The gnu's shoes! The pig's wings!

Name Your Poison

Tap water is dodgy in Estonia. People drink bottled water. All of the carbonated mineral water in Estonia is particularly salty. Wine — *veinid* (veins! blood!) — is good. I found their native white wines a little hard and calcareous. Was it strained through a filter of schist? My favorite drink in Estonia was Cido ("*citrona nektars*"), a beverage with a ferocious belt of lemon and grapefruit that comes in a paper carton, the kind of fruit juice that is called *mitz* in Israel where, unlike Estonia, the drinking water does not taste so good. You do not see the vast quantities of soda water called *gazoz* in Israel that is gulped in that country. (Another parallel with the Republic of Estonia and Israel is the practice of tipping: both countries have managed to institute a notable antipathy towards tipping. Is it pride or parsimony?) Vodka as a tipple is probably the best buy for the money in Estonia. Good vodka is cheap, White Diamond Latvian Vodka is considered the best — drunk chilled and neat. We also drank a Polish vodka called Zubrowka, an aromatic drink whose name and flavor is derived from a single blade of buffalo grass placed in each bottle. Boozers down on the brown banks of the Emajõgi gather to drink near the market, and I've seen rummies as white-faced as patient livestock sleeping off their fantasies face down in the mud there on some of the coldest days of winter.

It was often so brainlessly gelid, the cold would gather water in my eyes. White cold, infecundity, of the sterile sort that Jean-Paul Sartre writes of when discussing in his book on Baudelaire his cult of frigidity, where he explains that the coldness stood for himself — "sterile, gratuitous, and pure." "He wanted to be sure of killing the warm germs of sympathy...[and] deliberately surrounded himself with a no man's land where none could penetrate and he saw his own coldness reflected in the face of his fellows." I used to sit on a bench along the Emajõgi, across from the dispiritingly austere white-and-red Atlantic Hotell, munching a bar of Kalev *komm* and reading *The Baltic Times* — the only English language print newspaper covering all three Baltic states — sometimes sipping a tasty Le Coq Pilsner chased with a plum tart, and occasionally trying to write the odd poem or two, blow-drying my thumbs at intervals and recalling lines from John Crowe Ransom's "Winter Remembered:"

A cry of Absence, Absence, in the heart,
And in the wood the furious winter blowing...
And where I walked, the murderous winter blast
Would have this body bowed, these eyeballs streaming,
And though I think this heart's blood froze not fast
It ran too small to spare one drop for dreaming.

Thomas Merton felt that all truly valid poetry, good poetry, is a kind of recovery of paradise. Not that the poet has found his way back to Eden, merely that in and through his work he is trying to summon it anew in whatever small way he or she labors, for the act involves hope, is grounded in renewal, seeks beginnings, define it any way you want. It was in spite of the drab world in which I found myself not because of it that I was reminded of this and in doing so found some comfort. In the Bible there is no mention the sky is blue — we yet locate heaven there.

I sometimes sought out a bar where I could write. Occasionally I ferreted out a big empty classroom at the University of Tartu in which to work. In a hall there I once heard a pianist playing what I recognized as a movement from the great Ukrainian composer Valentin Silvestrov's "Symphony No. 5." "I do not write new music," he once said. "My music is a response to an echo of what already exists." Once I found a small tea-shop where I talked with an Ossetian waitress who recommended a delicious Ossetian potato-cheese bread khachapuri. Mostly when not in the apartment, I went down by the river and chose a bench. Mallarmé maintained that the poet should live like a hermit — how about with a hermit's inconveniences? My hands were Pepsi Cola purple from the cold. The pen I held, costive from the cold, might not flow. I would always have my grey grammar at hand, my *Eesti-Inglise Sõnaraamat Kooli dele* by C. Parts (1969) — or Car Parts, as I thought of him — my nearly whitflawed fingers often frozen "like parsnips hanging in the weather." I associate drinking in Estonia with studying the quiddities of that crabbed language and writing my poems there. It was an activity for which I ask no credit and seek no special praise, for I was of one mind with Boris

Pasternak who observed in *Doctor Zhivago*, "Writing poetry is no more a vocation than good health." Estonia became enough of the "real world" to me — false because faulty (they are cognate words!) — that I poetically wanted to correct, for I was convinced of what Fernando Pessoa paradoxically believed, that the true poet to be true must be an artificer giving not what is but rather what should be:

> The poet is a faker
> Who is so good at his act
> He even fakes the pain
> Of pain he feels in fact.
> And those who read his words
> Will feel in what he wrote
> Neither of the pains he has
> But just the one they don't.

When I first landed in that country, Sarah and I in our flat in Tallinn, with grammars and dictionaries, would both stay up real late drinking beer — "evening beakers," so to speak — while Sarah nibbled her favorite grilled-onion potato chips and I ate popcorn, and in all earnestness we tried to learn the language. Thomas Carlyle said that he who knows only his own language knows none, and we took him seriously. I figured that if George Orwell could learn Burmese, Samuel Beckett French, Unity Mitford German, Julia Child Norwegian ("Soon my Norsk was good enough so that I could read the newspaper and go shopping"), and the resourceful and ingenious Thomas Jefferson Spanish — a polyglot, he also learned Latin, Greek, Italian, French of course, and more than twelve Native American dialects — I should do my best to try to learn Estonian. Those little "seminars" of ours invariably became Q and A sessions: "What is dandruff?"

"*Kõõm*. Like comb!"

"Right. How about train?"

"*Voor*."

"All right, then, what is *kõrvarõngas*?"

"I give up."

"Wrong! Earrings."

"No, no, no, I mean I said I give up in the sense that I don't know! Bugger it!"

"All right, count from zero to ten!"

"*Null, üks, kaks, kolm, kuus, seitse —*"

"Ongwray, you missed four — *neli!*"

I got to the point where I made some headway reading, trying to read, *Üheksu Juttu* by one Jeerum Taavet Sälindzher but ultimately, fumblingly, giving up. (I even tried with intrepidity to read the same book in Finnish, *Yhdeksan Kertomusta!* with no better results.) Have you guessed the title? *Nine Stories* by J.D. Salinger. We soon packed it in. Elias Canetti wrote, "In the play of language, death disappears," but he was wrong — I wanted to shoot myself! I remember once reading that the novelist Rebecca West who wanted to write a book about Finland bothered enough to learn enough Finnish to be able to read entire novels in that language. (Her obsession possibly began with her coming across what is far and away one of the most pleasant sounding sentences in any language in the world: *Aja hiljaa sillalla* — "Drive quietly on the bridge.") Where West was impressed, however, I have to say I fell short. Alcohol, I am afraid, brought neither the looseness of lucidity to either of us, nor, even sadder to say, that wonderfully comforting crocked feeling that it did not matter. I simply continued to ask over and over again in my desperation what insane illogico-linguist in Estonia had managed to cook up all those eye-chart-killing words they loved like *murdlaineliugleja* for "surfer" or *hommikusöök* or *hommikueine* for "breakfast" or that pointlessly tricky word *suusasidemed* for "ski bindings"? At one point, equipped with an endless supply of supportive bottles of Saku Originaal and Presidendi Pilsner, I attempted over the course of a few weeks what I thought might be the somewhat easier study of Janis (Latvia) and Jonines (Lithuania) but found that the grammar of even those impenetrable Indo-European languages — the torturous declensions and thorny conjugations — precipitately fell out of my head within an hour or two. Was not Thomas Mann classically wrong when he said, "Only the exhaustive is truly interesting"?

Eesti Kali is a flat, sweet, dark beverage, Estonia's answer to Coca-Cola. (One brand, in fact, *Linnuse Kali*, is actually a product of the Coca-Cola Company.) It is made of fermented bread and contains no alcohol. A bland drink, it is really a shot of liquid mouth-feel that has a sub-taste of molasses, gentian, wax. There is nothing of bitterness in it or the tang of American Moxie, which it aspires to be. Russian *kvas* — with water, raisins, yeast, and sugar — is also made from black bread. A word on Coca-Cola, a foreigner's staple: it is of course sold in Estonia but is expensive and can cost as much as a quarter to a third of the price of your main meal, and yet the soft drink there comes either in unsatisfactorily small 250 ml. glass bottles, in amplitude roughly that of an A-size bra, or in unnecessarily large half-liter plastic bottles, but not — why? — in standard, fist-friendly 355 ml. cans.[125] Beer in Estonia is good. We drank a lot of it. Estonian Saku — it sounds like a Japanese name but it is pure Estonian — and A. LeCoq beer which is made in a factory right there in Tartu are first-rate beers. (There are six breweries in Estonia, for the record.) Whenever Sarah and I went out at night to buy beer we would often stop at one of the small street kiosks — dinerettes with Edward Hopper *Nighthawks*-light — to purchase potato chips, invariably having to point to the bag-rack and simply say "Lay's" — for the proprietress knew the brand as the product — which for us was a great deal easier to say than "*kartuliviilud.*" Was it a figment of my imagination or did I also see on the shelves tiny packs of old-brand cigarettes like Sweet Caporals, Helmars, Spuds, Murads, and Fatimas? Sometimes late at night on the crazy modern stove in our digs in Tartu we made our own popcorn — *röstitud maistiterad* — shaking a pan over a tiny unpredictable electric grid. I have already mentioned the potent "Hammer and Sickle," Vana Tallinn with sparkling Russian wine, which one evening toward the end of my stay I tried — oddly enough with a wedge of *piparkoogid* (gingerbread) — and found delicious, especially when the two are taken together.

A favorite Estonian drink is a vodka and cranberry juice called "The Rolling Estonian," made from *klukva,* the word for large juicy cranberries. Bright drinks have always intrigued me — the notorious "Green Fairy" not excluded. One can actually buy absinthe in certain shops in Estonia, the real thing, I mean, not merely Pernod, absinthe's legal, wormwood-free descendant: absinthe with wormwood *(Artemisia absinthium)*, the ingredient containing thujone, a terpene that falls into the sub-class of ketone that is able to cause brain damage or convulsuions, as Hamlet bitterly knew who when the Player Queen declaims about murder and adultery mutters, "Wormwood, wormwood."

We drank bottles of black balsam (Rīgas Melnais Balsams), the classic herbal liqueur mixed with pure vodka which comes from Riga. It has 45% alcohol, and, along with a sharp, very bitter, smoky, creosote-like kick, more exotic ingredients than is used by the Evil Queen in Walt Disney's *Snow White and the Seven Dwarfs* to concoct her magic potion in order to transmogrify into the old crone. The traditional recipe, created by Abraham Kunze, a Latvian pharmacist living in Riga, is composed of as many as 24 different ingredients, including roots, buds, herbals, plants, seeds, flowers, juices, oils, and berries prepared in oak barrels. Sold in sleek, hand-made ceramic flagons, it is not only drunk straight but used in mixed drinks, as an ice-cream topping, with tea or coffee, and even taken even as a cold remedy, for digestive problems, and in cases of dyspepsia. I love it. I noticed in the spirits, liquor, and beer sections — in Estonia they take up a large corner of supermarkets — a lot of bottles of the "pick-me-up" variety, tonics or miracle medicine drinks along the lines of H.G. Wells' Tono Bungay or "Buck-U-Uppo" ("acts directly on the red corpuscles…a slightly pungent flavour, rather like old boot soles beaten up in sherry") sold in P. G. Wodehouse's *Meet Mr. Mulliner.* "One teaspoon of the Buck-U-Uppo 'B' administered in the morning bran-mash," it is explained in the novel, "will cause the most timid elephant to trumpet loudly and charge the fiercest tiger without a qualm." (May I humbly suggest that many, if not most, people in countries wanting in religious faith tend to be gullible about things that supplant it?) As I say, black balsam is only one of a number of such drinks. Balts love concoctions — remedies of the patent-medicine/panacea variety, I mean. I called to mind all those 19th-century elixirs, bitters, herb medicines, peptics, flukums, oils, colas, deep blood-enriching drinks, nostrums, compounds, extracts, syrups, and iron tonics, so popular in the United States hundreds of years ago, that were advertised in magazines, newspapers, and on the bunkum circuit: Pluto Water, Fletcher's Castoria, Electric Bitters, Telephone Headache tablets, Radam's Microbe Killer, Edison's Polyform, Vegetine Blood Purifier, Nuxated Iron and Gout Poison, Hamlin's Wizard Oil, Dr. Williams' Pink Pills for Pale People, and of course the world famous Lydia E. Pinkham's Vegetable Compound ("18% alcohol added solely as a solvent and preservative") introduced in 1875 and which (with less alcohol) can still be found in the American market. I could picture on any street in Estonia and Lithuania and Latvia an enterprising salesman, street barker, or drummer with a dusty derby opening up his "keister" — the name for all those old satchels which open out to make a case — and, hawking magic bottles and curatives, making a small fortune.

Kisel, more a dessert than a drink, is made from sour fruits. As I say, Estonians love sour and notably sour buttermilk, often waking up of a morning and simply cutting a cup of whole milk with vinegar. Do you find that strange? In India today, cow urine presently is being launched as a soft drink! The bovine brew — mainly cow urine, mixed with a few medicinal and ayurvedic herbals — is now in the final stages of development by the Cow Protection Department of the Rashtriya Swayamseval Sangh (RSS), India's largest and oldest Hindu nationalist group. Om Prakash, head of the department, said the drink, called *gau jal* (or "cow water") in Sanskrit, will be good for mankind and promises it will be exported. "Don't worry," he said, "it won't smell like urine and will be tasty, too. Its USP will be that it is going to be very healthy. It won't be like carbonated drinks and would be devoid of any toxins." Why am I reminded of the bottles back in college we grabbed off the window-sill for quick "expiration chugs"?

What Did I Hate About Estonia?

I hated the pointless cold. I hated the fact that most people are sour but consider that normal. I hated the ungrammatical "5, 2 litre" alcohol-content comma, when it should be a period (5.2 lit.)! I hated the endless array of buildings everywhere of hideous white brick and what it did to my bowels. (It never fails that I also feel equally nauseous when passing on Huntington Ave. in Boston those huge repellent white-brick buildings of Northeastern University, a tightening tension that approximates both sorrow and depression.) I hated that bridges there are given dumb names like "Angel Bridge," "Devil's Bridge," etc. I hated the fact that doors all abnormally opened *outward!* I hated the fact that there is no national cuisine except for what potatoes and cabbage can offer — fart food. I hated the fact that the whole place is secular, cold, too dark, then — insanely — too light, too flat, snowy, and has no national costume. I began to hate a lot of those truly goofy Estonian first names, like Ants, Mall, Tiit, Ott, Väino, Egerti, Maire, Henno, Yrje, Ain, Uba — it means *bean!* — Hardo, Horgist, and, if you can believe it, even the name Haarm! I hated the awful brown hexagonal industrial bars of soap they use. I hated the canopy of homogeneity that, shadowing everybody, prevented people from emerging as individuals. I hated that the country tried to fob off as literature its faux-national epic, the *Kalevipoeg*. I hated the national retro fascinations with The 5ᵗʰ Dimension and Chic and Stevie Wonder that are still being inflicted on everybody as late as 2009! I hated the fact that their national airline, Estonian Airways, is composed of nothing but creaky old Aeroflot airplanes. I hated the bizarre symmetry in their language of that irreducible spate of hysterical umlauts and double-vowels and tildes. I hated the fixed, scowling, imprecise faces of people who breezed by me without so much as a by-your-leave whenever, out of slavish good manners, I foolishly bothered to hold the door for them like the pratboy I assume they thought I was. I hated their idea of their naïve, simpleminded singing like the Whos in Whoville as a sole defense against the guile of black-hearted totalitarianism. I hated their little drab mud hills and the lack of bookshops outside of cities and the damp, empty soulless churches that were only employed as museums and the dirty windows of their buses as well as the high cost of cheese. I hated that I had eaten only one Ossetian potato-cheese bread khachapuri of the many I could have had. I hated their odd twi-colored crows which are half black and half grey. I hated that while I was eating a veal cutlet in that country I was eating a thing called *snitsel* and hated myself for that. I hated the fact that to buy an Arvo Pärt CD there cost almost as much as buying a house, added to which scandal this great Estonian composer chose to live in *Berlin!* I hated the sight in every supermarket of the maleficent presence of fully-armed policemen and the depressing implication that a good many shoppers are nothing but maniacal shoplifters. I hated the fact that in shops the choice of meats was pork, pork, pork and more pork. I hated the salty McDonald's cheeseburgers they served. I hated the barking incongruity between the felicitous title — indeed, opening lines — of the Estonian national anthem, *"Mu isamaa, mu õnn ja rõõm"* ("My

Fatherland, My Happiness and Joy") and the sour, poker-up-their-arsed black frowns they never put away! I hated the pleading desolation of the old German manor houses and the lost aura of them. ("Nothing is emptier than an empty swimming pool," wrote Raymond Chandler.) I hated the tubes of meat-paste (*pasteet*), for no better reasons than that meat is neither a paste nor should come in a goddam tube! I hated the fact that instead of assuming positions of friendliness and accommodation, even if they did not mean it, they were perfectly prepared to pass on all sorts of cornball lore like how to keep unwanted bunnies out of your garden by breaking an egg in water or in milk and spreading it around the plants. I hated the rude-tasting *gaffalbitar* (herring tidbits), the Ryvita husks, the ham and jam combos, the brown cheese, the soot-tasting mutton, the imported Icelandic Hákarl which is half-dry, half-rotten shark. I hated not merely that Z is not the final letter of the Estonian alphabet — *üü* is — but that foreigners looking up words in an Estonian dictionary were always confounded because words with diacritical marks (cute carons, ugly umlauts, inverted hats!) — the word *kruus* ("gravel"), for example, precedes the word *kõrb* ("desert") — seem so arbitrarily slotted. I hated the pitiless supermarket checkers who always rushed me and mocked my currency ignorance. I especially hated having to look into the hard human eyes there, dure and cold as pebbles — I often discerned suffering in them but too often fury. I hated the withering intolerance I thought was aimed at me alone. I hated the insidious way so many restaurants in Tallinn and Tartu were set back from the street in dark, covert alcoves which always made it seem one was entering the dangerous ramparts of a noir movie or a James M. Cain story or even a brothel. I came to hate the relentless slabs of Soviet-bloc apartments that rose like a bad dream of Kafka which all seemed to be painted nausea green, barf purple, catlap yellow, and even a garish swimming pool, post-Chernobyl blue, as if they had somehow been growing out of a morass of unnaturally infected soil. They were phylansteries of Cherneyshevskyian gloom, just rising, strictly utilitarian rectangles with no visible marks of style — no spandrels or arches, no mouchettes or tracery, no corbels or molding, no quoins or acroteria, no stringcourses or brise-soleils (*soleils?*), no pergolas or pavilions. E.E. Cummings had glimpses of this kind of architecture, "Shortage Conformation," I call it, unimaginative dearth coupled with ratty lack, when traveling through Soviet Russia in 1933: "a rigid pyramidal composition of blocks; an impurely mathematical game of edges: not quite cruelly a cubic cerebration — equally glamourless and emphatic, withal childish…perhaps the architectural equivalent for 'boo! — I scared you that time."[126] I could never walk past one of those soulless, compressed, deeply dehumanizing, granoblasted monstrosities, tackily functional and built at a minimum cost, without thinking of the rancorous remark tossed off by the British architect, Sir James Stirling when, in 1984, the commission for the Getty Center in Los Angeles chose Richard Meier in preference over him: "They'll get another washing machine." If windows are the eyes of a building, the glimps in those moribund flats had long closed and seem perilopusly dead. I found only cavernous holocaust stares. I acknowledge that there are cases of aesthetic conversion when eyes, accustomed to traditional styles, are accorded a revelation, and can find beauty, even significance, in what because it is different, has previously seemed ugly and chaotic, but in these hulks something had truly perished, if it were ever alive or vital, and they had the effect on me of sad, undraped, melancholy Rothko paintings, unredeemed and unredeemable. As film director Michelangelo Antonioni said to him upon meeting Rothko, "I film nothing, and you paint nothing."

Was all the meretricious uniformity and soulless brutality of Soviet-bloc buildings the upshot of Viennese architect Adolf Loos' pronouncement that "ornament is crime"?[127] Or is function itself ornamental, as Otto Wagner once insisted?

I came to understand how one could contrive to make up out of Estonia's dystopian oddities the rarest fiction, for the stark reality of the place lent itself almost imponderably to dream. The late Canadian novelist Robertson Davies was surely correct when he astutely observed, wrote, "Fiction is not photography, it is oil painting."

It should be pointed out perhaps that there are some first-rate restaurants in the city of Tallinn, but then again why would there not be? The restaurant Balthasar, the very first Estonian garlic restaurant which opened in 1999 — garlic plays a main role in many of their meals — can be found in a medieval building of the Town Hall Apothecary in the center of Old Town. The elegant Tchaikovsky, which can be found in the Hotel Telegraph, recreates the recipes of forgotten masters. I have already mentioned the Püssirohukelder where I ate potato skins, drank beer, and commiserated with poor, depressed Waystacks who with that family of fat, evil sisters went haphazardly wandering off to look at bat life in southern Estonia. Bocca is ranked by Britain's *Restaurant* magazine as number 15 among the 50 most prestigious and valued restaurants in the entire world, which is no small thing. We were too insolvent to eat in such high-end Estonian restaurants. I remember one doomful evening, after a disagreement with my wife when I wanted to be alone[128], going out to a fashionable restaurant and having a salmon dinner, a meal that reminded me of the title of a René Crevel novel, *Les Pieds dans le Plat* ("Your Feet Are in the Plate"), and it cost about $45! The menu boasted of the chef's talent, but let us just cut to the chase and say Jacques Pépin he was not and leave it at that. Recalling that evening, I ruefully thought of a letter that Graham Greene wrote to his wife, Vivien, in 1934 and so I looked it up only to find with surprise that he wrote, "It is amazingly cheap here. We had dinner, the two of us, 6 vodkas, a delicious hors d'oeuvres, 2 Vienna schnitzel with fried potatoes, & two glasses of tea. Total bill in one of the swell restaurants 3/6d." *Autre temps…*

I soon wanted to be on the move. Whenever my father finished a project, he always cheerfully (and eccentrically) exclaimed by way of a blessing, "And the child's name is Anthony!" I heard that echo.

Katabasis

I decided to leave. I chose to make the country smaller and move myself to the left. I have to say I was content in leaving Estonia. I left on impulse, took the three-hour bus ride up the long rural road from Tartu to Tallinn one late afternoon — I happened to see Esther Oyster on board, alone, a mortise without tenon, so to speak, lugubriously staring out of the window and heading god knows where — and stayed a night at the Ülamiste Hotell by the airport before I made a "wet exit," as a kayaker might put it, in a snowstorm. It was a Thursday, that particular weekday on which Abraham Lincoln in sorrow would never eat because that was the day that his son, Willie, died. (He wanted to make all Thursdays a day of national mourning for the boys who lost their lives in the war.) I reflected that Estonians, who were so often on the bottom, needed to be on top, as any nation would. I reflected that we all of us in our own polemical beings are both masters and always, always at loggerheads. (Dr. Jekyll knows Mr. Hyde — such is man's private battle — but my question is: does Mr. Hyde ever acknowledge Dr. Jekyll?) I reflected that in their silent and cold, if nerdish, self-consciousness Estonians struggled bravely with their need for identity, for singularity, for "face," that in their tight-arsedness and impervious rigidity they were also — and commendably — always obviously striving for mastery, of self, of society, of country. Estonians whose history has been so unthinkingly brutal, so unreasoningly invaded, know both the striving and the servitude. Ball and peen. Bash and pull. Heat and blister. A favorite short poem of mine, Kingsley Amis' "Mastery" which begins:

> That horse whose rider fears to jump will fall,
> Riflemen miss if orders sound unsure;
> They only are secure who seem secure;
> Who lose their voice, lose all

paradoxically concludes:

> By yielding mastery the will is freed,
> For it is by surrender that we live,
> And we are taken if we wish to give,
> Are needed if we need.

I also reflected that although I had spent too much money, regretted that the American dollar was toilet-paper weak, and resented that for too many days I felt at sixes and sevens, I had spent time with Sarah and had seen my assignment through, knowing at bottom that I was going to write something about my time there, paying my devoirs, as it were, to my time spent there and to my craft and sullen art. I only wondered if I was going to put a button on the foil. I cannot honestly state that it was a vacation, not in any sense of holidaying, I gotta say. As the French essayist

Michel de Montaigne wrote in 1580, "There are triumphant defeats that rival victories." It was a remark I pondered as I walked to the airport from the hotel across a stony stubblefield, bag in hand, muttering — sunniness having been thin on the ground there — "Goodbye, Bagpuss! Goodbye, Grumpball! Goodbye, Twistedknickers! Goodbye Snarksters! Goodbye, Sulkqueens! Goodbye, Mr. Peevey! Goodbye, Sourslop!"

Suddenly, I felt free as a finch.

Boarding, I flew out sans incident, glancing down at the rooftops while thinking of some lines of a Rilke sonnet

Be ahead of all Departure, as if it were
behind you like the winter that's just passed...

Be — and at the same time know the implication
of non-being, the endless ground of your inner vibration,
so you can fulfill it fully just this once[129]

and arriving in frozen Warsaw, where in a mediocre airport restaurant, rushing, I tried to pay for a late breakfast with Estonian money. At the cash register a nettled woman who looked like Wallace Beery, bewilderedly appraising me, exasperatedly began slap reversing the ten-kroon note I had temeritously offered her, turning it upside down, flipping it, raising it to the light, and then hind-side-to again. She did not recognize the currency. I wondered: did no Estonians ever come *through* the damned place? I re-paid in American currency — $35 for two eggs, an English muffin, bacon, and coffee, no lie. In 1969, when in my student days I was traveling by train through East Germany to Warsaw on my way to the then Soviet Union, I literally could have purchased a small *car* for such a sum. I remember back then being approached by a young, well-dressed college student in a bold tie outside the Polish hotel lobby who, ascertaining I was an American student, wanted to swap 10 *zloty* for one U.S. dollar. "What if you're a Soviet agent?" I asked. He laughed and heartily replied, "No way, not!" I rashly gave him a dollar, not without apprehension. He handed me ten times that. So I gave him $10. He promptly returned ten times that, and after some halting discussion, being flush, I asked him if he wanted to join me for lunch. We ended up sitting at a table in the elegant, high-ceilinged main restaurant of the Orbis Europejsk, the oldest hotel in the city, where we leisurely enjoyed (on my tab) a lavish three-course dinner: sweet butterflied stuffed pork chops, kolduny, Brussels sprouts, mounds of roasted potatoes, a dish of pelmeni, a small dish of golonka, smoked kielbasa, poppy-seed pastries, several bottles of wine, topping it off with a porcelain pot of caviar, while a smiling violinist at intervals occasioned by to play for our entertainment, one of the tunes being "Cherry Pink and Apple-Blossom White." I must say, that seems like a lifetime ago, when not only the American dollar had clout but also at a time when two men dining together were not necessarily assumed to be married!

But here I was in 2008. I finished my *petit dejeuner extorsionnaire* and, bag in hand, boarded a flight to New York on LOT Airlines — the airline was given its name (*lot* means "flight") the same way Holly Golightly named her cat "Cat" — which was filled to overflowing with what seemed to me like middle-class and even working-class Poles, all vigorous and apple-cheeked and carrying fat lunch-bags, gaily flying off to the New World to take advantage of the stark buying power of the comparatively healthy Euro and shop 'til they dropped. As we lifted off, in leaving Estonia, I have to say that while part of me was if not sad at least wistful that it had all come to an end, part of me felt like light-hearted Bobby Van in saddle shoes dancing and singing, "I'm Through With Love" in *The Affairs of Dobie Gillis*. When we landed in the States, everybody — something new to me — broke out in an explosion of vulgar applause!

It is not necessary to be in a country long to be able to see into it, in fact it may be argued that fresh eyes can more readily find a "figure in the carpet" than seasoned eyes. Not every writer was Lafcadio Hearn who spent 24 years in Japan. D. H. Lawrence went to Sardinia for a week — and wrote a 200-page book about it. Graham Greene was in Liberia all of eighteen days and proceeded to write a well-known book about that place called *Journey Without Maps*. How long was Bruce Chatwin in Patagonia, one week? V.S. Naipaul in the American South? D.H. Lawrence in Australia? Six weeks. Geoffrey Moorhouse in the Sahara? Five months. Herman Melville spent but a month in Typee Valley yet grandly claimed it was four months. How long was Ryszard Kapuscinski in Angola? Not even long enough to count. Henry Thoreau was on Cape Cod for three weeks and only one on the Concord and Merrimac. (No chap loved to be home more than Thoreau and whenever away badly missed it.) Was Darwin longer than a month in the Galapagos? I don't think so. Joseph Conrad was in the Congo for 6 months, including 29 days on the Congo River. So, you see, time spent in a place has no bearing on the worth of a book — it's true. By the way, Rudyard Kipling who wrote about Mandalay *never* even went there.

"Being there" names that which should first of all be thought of as a place — the location of the truth of Being. "The 'essence' of being there lies in its existence," says Heidegger in *Being and Time* (*"Das 'Wesen' des Daseins leigt in seiner Existenz"*). I want but to say, I stood in that place and can assert without care of scorn or obloquy I stayed as long as I wanted. Here witness is made.

Valedictory

There is no question that Estonia is elliptical. That is not a bad thing. It is part of the dynamic of the place and if it adds to the enigma of the country, it nevertheless also enriches it. I have alluded to *Hamlet* several times in my discourse, the Dane who lived more or less across the way. Shakespeare, the richest of writers, is also the most elliptical. I have heard Prof. Harold Bloom say so a hundred times when I was teaching at Yale in the late 1980s, and I agree. You always have to follow what it is that he is leaving out by intention — *omitting* as much by dramatic stealth as creative genius — what he expects you to figure out. It is the reason that Bloom particularly singles out Falstaff, Iago, Cleopatra, and, indeed, Hamlet out of many other wonderful characters of the Bard for singular acclaim. They are elliptical. There is that in mysterious and muddled Estonia that compels us, again and again, to try to solve it. In an enthymeme, part of the argument is missing because it is assumed. You have to find it. I discern upon looking over my travel notes that I am also something of a didactician, or at least a moralizer. I ask you to overlook if they prove irksome my satirical observations, to forgive my impieties. *Sermones* was, after all, the title Horace did give his satires.

He also prudently foresaw the inevitability of provincialism, writing, "*Caelum non animum mutant qui trans mare currunt.*"[130] I do not want to lay open to the charge of being provincial. An old joke explains the failures of a certain egoistic citizen from England to profit from travel by the fact that "he took himself along for company."

I remember a book from my childhood from which my parents used to read to us, *Adventures in Toyland* by Edith King Hall and specifically a chapter in it that always took my attention entitled, "How I Went to Why." A finger-post stood where three roads met, I recall, that confounded the young traveler. One arm was a sign that stated, "To Nowhere." Another one was inscribed, "To Somewhere," which was decidedly a little better, the narrative pointed out. But the third one said, "To Everywhere Else." It seems to me that in Estonia I was like the earnest young traveler going to visit the King in the Valley of Why, craning my neck to try to figure out enigmas as abstract and bewildering as those fabled signs.

George Orwell who was fixed on the failures of society and the misuses of power in a well-known essay on him knocked Charles Dickens in his novels for "always pointing to a change of spirit rather than a change of structure," arguing that any purely moral critique of society has far less of force than political power — *realpolitik* — and even revolution. I would humbly assert that the reverse is true for Estonia, that what the country needs more than anything is a national sense of uplift, an optimistic destruction, so to speak, of its insistent and terrible past, a new mystique, a sort of "forgetting" that would let them rise above their deprivations and by doing so allow them to replenish their national soul.

Memory is long in Estonia, however. People *remember*. After the Tarquin Dynasty was expelled about 500 B.C., the untrusting Roman people never once allowed themselves again to have a king. Although Julius Caesar publicly thrice refused a "kingly crown" he was nevertheless stabbed to death for merely giving hint of such an ambition.

"I have a left shoulder blade that is a miracle of loveliness. People come miles to see it. My right elbow has a fascination few can resist," declares Katisha in *The Mikado*. A right elbow, a left shoulder blade, nothing big and in spite of the boast nothing memorable. This travel book may not feature enough of a roadmap for people to walk miles to buy, but who would deny that, even in small but vigorous exertions, virtues can be found? I do hope that, by scope if not by splendor, by effort if not by excellence, this book of mine might one day occupy a shelf with Lawrence's Sardinia and Canetti's Marrakesh and Theodore Cook's Old Provence. What the book does leave out I would like to think might somehow help underline the pertinence of what it includes, or, failing that, may by simple default throw some light on the subjects I have been proven too incompetent, or too ignorant, properly to address. "There may always be another reality," wrote Christopher Fry in *A Yard of Sun*. "To make fiction of the truth we think we've arrived at." I daresay my Estonia is as much about me and my crotchets as it is about anything else, but as Thoreau pointed out in *Walden*, "I should not talk so much about myself if there were anybody else whom I knew as well." I wanted disinterestedly to present, on the one hand, neither a pointlessly grue-some nor, on the other hand, a misleadingly overly-superlative picture of a place where I had unexpectedly found myself and which when I ultimately looked up saw to be, simultaneously, as foreign as some of my own perceptions of myself, made visible — I do not necessarily say at-tractive — if only by my being there. The message of the tale, for I have to say it does not pretend not to have a message, is that traveling about in such a strange, unlooked-for place at the back of beyond is perhaps made as worthwhile for the fascination of its strangeness, its elliptical presentations, its eccentricities, its odd confounding facts, as it is for the record one could make of those. Other accounts will differ, I daresay. I have already mentioned, paranomasiacally, I left no Estonian unturned. Those who are less charitable may even insist that I left no turn unstoned. What report of anything is definitive? Of that singular moment of the two angels in white at Christ's tomb, every report of it gives a differ-ent description of what took place. "Then there we are!" says Lambert Strether in *The Ambassadors*, conclusively, if not triumphantly, summing up his experience. It is a cumulating remark I echo. I had had resolution if I had not had rhapsodies. I was a pupil there, not a person looking to administrate. I could have stayed there longer and written a profounder book, but there are other countries to visit and other books to be written, and, as it is said, night is coming and the woods decay, and after many a summer dies the swan.

"We all go from thing to thing and back again, depending on our individual cycles," as James Thurber wittily put it. I saw I had come to what that humorist also referred to as an embraceable impasse, which as an oxymoron has all of the ambiguity I felt about Estonia — a stalemate, so to speak, one can settle for.

A parade walks by in all my dreams, but the defatigable fact is it always disappears over the hill, enough to make me want to refuse my sleep. Allow my sangfroid therefore to join with my love of rarity. An injury can always be avoided by foregoing a reprise. I confess I will always love a thing that will never be seen a second time.

Endnotes

1. Rose, oh pure contradiction, joy

   Of being no one's sleep under so many lids

2. *The World Within the Word* (Alfred A. Knopf, 1978)

3. *Dialogues of Alfred North Whitehead* as recorded by Lucien Price, 1954

4. Condors, which have the most protracted period of helplessness of any North American bird, do not nest every year, and lay a single egg every second year, each requires six weeks to hatch. A condor chick takes five months to fledge and are dependent on their parents for several months after leaving their nest.

5. According to recent statistics, the population of Estonia, which also has a high mortality rate, with 10 births and 15 deaths per 1000 people, could be reduced by 46% by 2050 if the current low rate of fertility persists. The trend in immigration which saw an increase of 10,000 migrants every year for 50 years, mainly Russians, has dramatically reversed since 1990, when the flow has gone the other way and people have returned to the Ukraine, Belorus, Georgia, etc. Illegal immigration is negligible, by the way. As few as 134 illegal immigrants entered Estonia in 2009.

6. A nuclear power plant is being considered, as I write, with potential locations for the reactor being on the country's northern coast, notably Suur Pakri and Keibu Bay as the best locations for obtaining cooling water.

7. *What Am I Doing Here* (Penguin Books, 1989)

8. *Hopscotch* (Random House, 1966) chapter 52, p. 307

9. See his *Bloodlands: Europe Between Hitler and Stalin* (Basic Books, 2010)

10. Since the era of Stalin, Soviet propagandists have been making counterfactual assertions that the original Erna team participated in the mass murder of Soviet political activists. There have long been rumors that the letter E was vengefully cut onto the backs of the victims. These claims were reinvigorated in the 1980s, it has been charged, as a way of distracting historians from once more recalling the Kautla massacre, and have been repeated in the Russian media in 2000s. The Russian Federation's original position incorrectly classifies the members as "Nazis". However, Russian authorities continue to regard the commemorative Erna Retk as a "Nazi orgy". The Battle of Kautla, a pitched battle between Soviet destruction battalions and the famed Estonian "Forest Brothers," took place in Kautla, Estonia in July 1941. It involved a series of murders of civilians known as the "Kautla Massacre." For the people of Estonia this tragic event which sticks deep in their collective memory will never be forgotten. On 24th July 1941, an extermination battalion murdered Gustav and Rosalie

Viljamaa of Simisalu farm and set their farm on fire. In subsequent days, the systematic murder of all civilians in the region took place, along with the wholesale burning of their farms. The Kautla farm was burned down by the Red Army with all the family and staff inside, killing Johannes Lindemann, Oskar Mallene, Ida Hallorava, Arnold Kivipõld, Alfred Kukk and Johannes Ummus. More than twenty people in total, all civilians, were murdered — many of them after bring tortured — with countless farms destroyed. The low toll of human deaths in comparison with the number of burned farms is due to the Erna long-range reconnaissance group breaking the Red Army blockade on the area, allowing many civilians to escape.

11. The Nuremberg Trials, in declaring the Waffen SS a criminal organization, explicitly excluded conscripts in the following terms. The Tribunal declared to be criminal within the meaning of the Charter the group composed of those persons who had been officially accepted as members of the SS who became or remained members of the organization with knowledge that it was being used for the commission of acts declared criminal by Article 6 of the Charter or who were personally implicated as members of the organization in the commission of such crimes, excluding, however, those who were drafted into membership by the State in such a way as to give them no choice in the matter, and who had committed no such crimes.

12. *Sochineniia* (XXIV, 122)

13. *New York Times* January 7, 2011

14. "Where do we come from? What are we? Where are we going?"

15. Exodus 10:21-29

16. Why was Heisenberg's wife unsatisfied? When he had the time, he didn't have the energy, and when he had the position, he didn't have the momentum.

17. "Self Reliance"(1841)

18. "Graham Greene's Chance Encounter With a Model Spy" March 1, 2006

19. There are brilliant talents in the country. Sigrid Kuulmann, a splendid Estonian violinist, for example, has performed as a soloist with most Estonian orchestras as well as Kuopio City Orchestra, and has appeared as a soloist with conductors Neeme Järvi, Andres Mustonen, Andrei Chistyakov, Gregory Rose, Nicholas Smith etc. She has given recitals in England, Germany, Scandinavia, and Estonia, and has participated as a soloist in Europäisches Musikfest Münsterland and Internationales Klassikfestival im Allgäu Oberstdorfis in Germany, as well as many Estonian music festivals.

20. Possibly the strangest, most anomalous statue in all of Tallin is the oversized bronze bust of the actor Sean Connery, created by Estonia's most famous sculptor Tiiu Kirsipuu and unveiled on January 27, 2011 outside the capitol's Scottish Club, an organization for Scottish expatriates. Weirdly, the bald head and grim, unsmiling visage of this actor with its mustache and beard most resembles — Lenin!

21. The listed figures are, respectively, Governor. James M. Curley, Boston Celtics coach Arnold ("Red") Auerbach; Boston Red Sox left-slugger, Ted Williams; and Leonard P. Zakim.

22. In the end, however, Picasso did think enough of them to name his daughter, Paloma. John Richardson, "How Political Was Picasso?" *New York Review of Books*, November 25, 2010

23. As for *fuck, shit, piss, cunt, prick*, and *asshole*, the usual "vulgar" grouping, I am told that the commonest, most popular Estonian terms are respectively *nussima* (verb), *sitt, kusi. puts, munn*, and *perse* (ass) or *perseauk* (asshole, with the word *auk* for "hole"). Estonians rarely if ever curse with the classic perennial in English, "Fuck you!" or "Go fuck yourself!" literally, with forms of the verb *nussima* "to fuck," but instead generally prefer to say *"Mine perse!"* ("Go into your asshole!" — the equivalent of the popular Italian vulgarism, *"Va' fa' un culo!"*) The most common term of insult and popular curse word in Estonia is *munn* ("prick.") Likewise, "damn," "damned" or "goddamn" are rarely if ever expressed by the literal theological terms *needud* ("cursed, damned, accursed") or *Jumala-needud* ("God-damned, cursed by God;") rather, Estonians usually say *"Sa kuradi siga!"* ("You devil's pig!") or just simply — oddly — *Kuradi!* ("the devil's!" that is, "[You are] the devil's [own spawn]!") Curiously, for such a secular society as that of Estonia seems to be, the word *kurat* ("the devil") also seems to be the familiar all-purpose curse or oath.

24. One of the many strictures demanded by the AFL-CIO after the R.M.S. *Titanic* disaster on April 10, 1912 drowning 1,517 people was that legislation should immediately be passed banning any doors opening inward. Strangely enough, entrance doors to most private homes open inward, while in most public buildings the entry doors open outward.

25. No other country has as many spas per capita as there are in Estonia — more than 49 official spas for 1.3 million people. Kuressaare, a town on the island of Saaremaa, has only 15,170 permanent inhabitants, while the official count of beds in its spas comes to 1,230, making Kuressaare probably the most spa-dense town in the world.

26. *New York Times* December 15, 2010

27. Estonia has compiled one of the largest collections of folk songs in the world, with written records of as many as 133,000 folk songs.

28. There is a myth that while Moses was parting the Red Sea, this poor creature — Israelis apparently love to eat it — was caught in the middle and was split in half.

29. *Vanity Fair* Sept. 1998

30. "A Cloud in Trousers," III. 21, Translation by Herbert Marshall in *Mayakovsky* (Hill & Wang, 1965)

31. "Water: Our Thirsty World.: A Special Issue." *National Geographic* (April 2009)

32. *The Disengagement Plan and Its Repercussions on the Right to Health in the Gaza Strip* (Physicians for Human Rights-Israel, 2005, p. 9)

33. Vintage Books, 2001, p. 341. See also the searing indictment of Israeli oppression in Noam Chomsky, *Failed States*, especially Chapter 5, "Supporting Evidence" (The Middle East, 2006)

34. *History of Friedrich of Prussia called Frederick the Great* (Merrill and Baker, N.Y.) Vol. III, Book 16, Chapter VII, p. 127

35. The Shasu who appear on the Merneptah Stele of 1200 B.C. are a separate entity from the later Israelites or ethnonymic Hebrews since they wore different clothing, hairstyles, and were long ago determined differently by Egyptian scribes.

36. No amount of praise is sufficient enough for the fearless, resolute, and valiant Israeli journalists, Gideon Levy, Dov Alfon, and Ms. Amira Hass, among others, who have fought so hard for the Arab cause and justice for the Palestinians. "Blessed are the merciful, for they will be shown mercy," Christ assures us. "Blessed are the peacemakers, for they will be called sons of God."

37. These are all indisputable facts. Confer for fuller details John J. Mearsheimer and Stephen M. Walt's, *The Israel Lobby and U.S. Foreign Policy* (Farrar, Straus & Giroux, 2007).

38. The senator's name was Giorgio Turbiglio (1845-1918). He was a politician, lawyer, and professor at the University of Ferrara. In 1882, he was elected to the National Government in Rome and served in the Senate until his death at the age of 74 on March 13, 1918. His notable brother, Sebastiano was the author of several books — still in print — on the subject of philosophy, specifically on Spinoza.

39. Compare it with the ancient Paionian, a language spoken in Illyria (or possibly southwestern Thrace) some 2,200 years ago which has survived merely as fragments. Linguist Kevin Hodges has pointed out (*Smithsonian*, November 2010) that the language, as we know it, is composed solely of three words: *monapos* (bull); *talon*, the name of a fish that once lived in Lake Prasias, Macedonia, and *paprax*, another fish in that lake. Memorize them and you know every word of Paionian! Hodges suggests you can use it to swell your résumé — "Fluent in Paionian."

40. The semi-autobiographical, misogynistic novel *Moravagine* ("Death to the Vagina") —the *Naked Lunch* of 1926 — follows the trail of a grotesque dwarf-madman, a descendant of the last King of Hungary, and a young doctor on their worldwide adventures from the Russian Revolution to the First World War. He is a monster, a man in pursuit of a theorem that will justify his every desire. Moravigne's madness becomes a metaphor for the dissolution of the world and the chaotic disorder of life. "There is no truth. There's only action, action obeying a million different impulses, ephemeral action, action subjected to every possible imaginable contingency and contradiction. Life." Moravigne died in an asylum and the manuscript of the story finds it way to Cendrars, one of the characters in it.

41. In English: "There is reason (or cause) for getting together. March 10-15 is (or will be) the 90th anniversary of the TTU in Tartu." "Orders [are] inside (or enclosed)." "Services offered by us." "Lot (plot, ground) for sale" and "Discus throwing!"

42. There is no verb "to be" in Turkish, nor is there a verb "to have." As with Estonian, no gender distinctions are made in Turkish, and there is also only one word for "he, she, or it." It is an agglutinative language, as Maureen Freely, translator of Orhan Pamuk points out in her "Translator's Afterword" of *The Black Book*, which means that root nouns in even the simplest sentences can carry five or six suffixes. ("Apparently, they were inside their houses" is a single word!)

43.   Language is a ford across the river of Time.

It leads us to the dwelling place of those who are gone;

But he will not be able to come to this place

   who fears deep water.

Quoted and translated by Rimma Bulatova, "Illič-Svityč : A Biographical Sketch," in Vitaly Shevoroshkin, ed., *Reconstructing Languages and Cultures* (Bochum, Germany: Studienverlag Dr. Norbert Brockenmeyer, 1989)

44. "Analysis of a Theme" from *Collected Poetry and Prose*

45. "Notes Toward a Supreme Fiction", ibid.

46. "One language never suffices."

47.   It is, of course, from Act III, Scene I:

To be or not to be — that is the question:

Whether 'tis nobler in the mind to suffer

The slings and arrows of outrageous fortune,

Or to take arms against a sea of troubles

And, by opposing, end them. To die, to sleep

No more — and by a sleep to say we end

The heartache and the thousand natural shocks

That flesh is heir to — 'tis a consummation

Devoutly to be wished.

(translated in *The Klingon Khamlet*, 2000)

Although, like Turkish, the Klingon language lacks any form of the verb "to be," so that famous opening line is rendered as "It either continues, or it doesn't continue. Now, I must consider this sentence."

48. *Walden* was a moderate success when it was first published in 1854. It sold well and was received favorably among reviewers.

49. See *A Yankee in Canada, with Anti-Slavery and Reform Papers* (1866), edited by his sister Sophia Thoreau and Ellery Channing. The volume contains a five-part description of Thoreau's 1850 trip to Canada, and to that excursion are added ten additional essays.

50. David Foster Wallace, in his essay "E Unibus Pluram," offers a possible explanation for this when he writes, "I'm not saying that television is vulgar and dumb because the people who compose the Audience are vulgar and dumb. Television is the way it is simply because people tend to be extremely similar in their vulgar and prurient and dumb interests and wildly different in their refined and aesthetic and noble interests." — *A Supposedly Fun Thing I'll Never Do Again* (Little, Brown and Co., 1997).

51. I had to memorize the entire Gettysburg Address in the 6th grade as an overnight assignment and ever since have found myself reciting the full speech in my mind about once a week.

52. John Hay, close friend and one of two secretaries to the President, who in his biography, A. Lincoln, A History (1890), co-written with John Nicolay, certainly not for lack of charity failed to see any overly noteworthy grandeur in his heartfelt words — and Hay was a literary man — writing of that notable day in only a handful of very succinct sentences, "In the morning I got a beast and rode out with the President and suite to the Cemetery in procession [which]....formed itself in an orphanly sort of way, and moved out with very little help from anybody....the President, in a firm, free way, with more grace than is his wont, said his half-dozen lines of consecration, — and the music wailed, and we went home through crowded and cheering streets."

53. *The Later Lectures of Ralph Waldo Emerson (1843-1871)* Volume 1 1843-1854, edited by Ronald A. Bosco & Joel Myerson, includes the entire speech.

54. 1 Timothy 5:23

55. At the Annual Wife-Carrying World Championship held in Sonkajärvi, Finland, Margo Uusorg has emerged victorious five out of the past seven years. His brother Madis won in 2004. The latest champions, winners in both 2009 and 2010 contests, are Taisto Miettinen and Kristiina Haapanen, both of Finland. Uusorg, however, is the only man to have won the contest with three different female partners (you don't have to carry your own wife, understand). Uusorg and his fellow Estonians are so dominant in the sport, which involves sprinting with one's "wife" across various surfaces and water obstacles, that their technique has become known as "The Estonian," which, as I have described in the main text, involves a spouse hanging upside down with her arms around her husband's waist while her legs are hooked up to and around his neck.

56. This is formally called Symphony No. 2, written between 1888 and 1894. Mahler devised a narrative program for the work, which he showed to a number of friends.

57. Peips was also seen as something of a Kremlin ass-kisser. One joke went that after attending a Communist Party Congress, she could no longer efficiently milk cows and had to give up her milkmaid job. The satirical explanation was that she could no longer move her hands up and down, as in milking, but only sideways, fawningly, as in applauding. In other words, she had crippled her hands from constantly applauding at a Party Congress.

58. It is also a brand in Russia of a soft drink known for its caramel taste.

59. Several homoerotic poems of Bayard Taylor's, notably "Hylas," "The Bath," and "To a Persian Boy" seem to support the poet's interest in the subject of male erotic love.

60. The Mel Brooks interview, *Playboy* (February 1975)

61. *Decision Points*, Bush's 2010 farcically unreliable and revisionist memoir, in which he neglects to mention that in his election of 2000 he lost the popular vote, only continued his big lies and was, in the words of the *New Yorker* not only "a tissue of omission and evasion" but also "records a notable lack of personal development other than the famous turn away from alcohol and toward evangelical Christianity."

62. George Orwell named the nefarious Room 101 after a conference room at BBC Broadcasting House where he had to sit through tedious meetings.

63. Just look at the "Frequently Asked Questions" on his website: http://www.alandershowitz.com/faq.php

64. "In Attica" from *Collected Poems 1928-1985* (1986)

65. Antiopholus of Syracuse asks, "Where America, the Indies?" (III, ii, l. 127)

66.   *In Lappland sind schmutzige Leute,*

   Plattkopfig, breit maulig und klein;

   Sie kavern ums Feuer, und backen

   Sich Fische, und quaken und shrein.

"*Abends am Strand*" (1840) lyrics by Heinrich Heine, music by Robert Schumann

67. See Hedda Hopper, *The Whole Truth and Nothing But,* 1963, p.132

68. Ironically, in this scene Katharine Hepburn's shiny, gorgeously rich auburn hair, perfectly matching for sheen the illustrious beauty of that sleek fur coat she is wearing, got its soft bounce and shine thanks to her protein-enriched shampoo for which she famously used six eggs.

69. "On a Fan That Belonged to the Marquise De Pompadour"

70. Many Estonians make the extraordinary claim that their "Christmas" (*Joulud*) has not the slightest connection whatsoever with Christianity as we know it, in spite of the fact that the decorations and customs they employ over the holidays look suspiciously traditional. One of the more important Estonian peasant customs involves the bringing home of an authentic "Christmas straw," which is supposed to symbolize the manger. My question: whose manger?

71. The Scandinavian countries are listed, along with Vietnam, as the top four non-churchgoing countries in the world. What is sociologically diagnostic in this matter, I will let you determine. In the United States, just for the record, however, Mississippians, according to a recent Gallup poll, were rated the most frequent churchgoers in the nation in 2009, with 63% of residents attending weekly or almost every week. Nine of the top 10 states in church attendance are in the South; the only non-Southern state is Utah, with 56% frequent attendance. At the other end of the spectrum, 23% of Vermont residents attend church frequently, putting it at the bottom of the list of churchgoing states. Other states at the bottom of the church attendance list are in either New England or the West.

72. Solzhenitsyn had befriended Arnold Susi, a lawyer and former Estonian Minister of Education in a Lubyanka Prison cell in 1945. After completion, Solzhenitsyn's original handwritten script of *The Gulag Archipelago* was kept hidden from the KGB in Estonia by Arnold Susi's daughter, Heli Susi, until the collapse of the Soviet Union.

73. "Graham Greene's Chance Encounter With a Model Spy" *The Times Literary Supplement,* March 1, 2006

74. "At last! The tyranny of the human face has disappeared, and now there will be no one but myself to make me suffer."

75. pp. 244-246, Farrar, Straus and Giroux, 1997

76. Answering Dante's question how she and Paolo Malatesta first realized that they were in love — the two were innocently reading aloud together about Lancelot and Guinevere — Francesca di Rimini passionately speaks the following words:

> *Quando leggemo il disiato riso*
> *esser baciato da cotanto amante,*
> *questi, che mai da me non fia diviso,*
> *la bocca mi bacio tutto tremante.*
> *Galeotto fu il libro e chi lo scrisse:*
> *Quel giorno più non vi leggemmo avante.*
>
> (Canto V, lines 133-138)

"'When we read that the smile so desired was kissed by so great a lover, this man, who will never be parted or taken from me, kissed my mouth, all trembling. A Galeotto [panderer, go-between] was that book and the man who wrote it; that day we read no more.'" [my translation]

Dante has Beatrice smile often in the *Paradiso*, however.

77. "Great lover, scholar, soldier, sailor, singer, toreador, tycoon, jockey, prizefighter, automobile racer, aviator, farmer. Mickey Mouse lives in a world in which space, time, and the law of physics are nil. He can reach inside of a bull's mouth, pull out his teeth and use them as castanets. He can lead a band or play violin solos; his ingenuity is limitless; he never fails." — *Time Magazine* (1931)

78. "A major catastrophe!" in Yiddish

79. The national flag, named after the colors of the bands, was originally the flag of the Estonian Students' Society at the University of Tartu, by the way, and was consecrated in the hall of the pastorate of Otepää on June 4, 1884. The original flag is preserved in the Estonian National Museum. The Danish flag, incidentally — dating back to the 13th century — is the world's oldest unchanged national flag.

80. See his *Guide for the Perplexed*, Book III, chapter 51, paragraph 3

81. While the term *Cayua* is sometimes still used to refer to settlements of indigenous peoples who have not well integrated into the dominant society in Paraguay, the modern usage of the particular name Guaraní — a Spanish word given them meaning "warrior" in the Tupi-Guaraní dialect spoken there — is generally extended to include all people of native origin regardless of social status.

82. "Now I know your worthy functions! You cannot destroy anything on a large scale, so you begin in a small way."

83. *Sat.* XV. 164

84. Major Robert Gregory (1881-1918) was not only a World War I hero but considered the definitive

gentleman by the poet W.B. Yeats, who not only compared him without hyperbole to the illustrious Sir Philip Sidney but also wrote as many as four poems about him, most notably "In Memory of Major Robert Gregory." An accomplished artist, Gregory also excelled at bowls, boxing, horse riding, and cricket. He was killed in Italy at the age of 36 when an Italian pilot mistakenly shot him down.

85. "He who does nothing for others does, by that very token, nothing for himself."

86. The testimony of former White House security advisor Richard Clarke to the 9/11 Commission has been thoroughly vindicated. In 2004, Clarke conscientiously told the Commission under oath that he had warned then-National Security Adviser Condoleezza Rice and the administration about the terrorist threat posed by Al Qaeda in early 2001. The alert was made on January 25, 2001: "Memorandum for Condoleezza Rice." It begins, "Condi, Steve asked today that we propose major Presidential policy reviews or initiatives. We urgently [underlined] need such a Principals level review on the al Qida [sic] network." For the record, that "principals" meeting finally took place on September 4, 2001, more than eight months after Clarke requested it, and exactly one week before 9/11. Obviously, the memo was completely ignored."

87. Cantos XXI and XXII

88. "Why the United States?" asked Abdul Hakim Murad, radical Islamist friend of masterminds, Khalid Sheikh Mohammed and his nephew Abdul Basit Abdul Karim who contrived the World Trade Center attacks. He explicitly told investigators, "I was working for my religion, because I feel that my Muslim brothers in Palestine are suffering. And, if you check the reason for the suffering, you will find that the U.S. is the reason for this. If you ask anybody, even if you ask children, they will tell you that the U.S. is supporting Israel, and Israel is killing our Muslim brothers in Palestine. The United States is acting like a terrorist, but nobody can see that."

89. *Essays, Civil and Moral*, XVIII: Of Travel

90. b. 1945, Denmark

91. Estonians, according to one Internet poll, have one of the strongest needs for personal space in the world — a good example of that being settlement density which is four times less compared to Denmark and 12 times less compared to The Netherlands.

92. "There are tears for things." The term comes from line 462 of Book I of Vergil's epic poem, the *Aeneid*. Weeping, Aeneas laments, "*sunt lacrimae rerum et mentem mortalia tangent*" while gazing at one of the murals found in a Carthaginian temple depicting battles of the Trojan War and the deaths of his friends and countrymen.

93. Interview with Dave Itzkoff, the *New York Times*, Sept. 15, 2010

94. *God is Not Great*

95. *For the New Intellectual*

96. *A Christmas Sermon*, 1891

97. "A Memoir of Mary Ann" in *Mystery and Manners*

98. St. Paul speaks of all Christians as members of Christ, so that with Him, they form one *Mystical Body* (Cf. 1 Cor 12:12-31; Col 1:18; 2:18-20; Eph. 1:22-23.) The Church, the Mystical Body, exists on this earth, and is called the Church Militant, because its members struggle against the world, the flesh and the devil. The Church Suffering means the souls in Purgatory. The Church Triumphant is the Church in heaven. The unity and cooperation of the members of the Church on earth, in Purgatory, in Heaven is also called the Communion of Saints.

I made something of a private study of St. Paul in Estonia as a kind of personal project, particularly *Romans*. I have gone back to that book in various and strange places over a span of years — in a Trappist monastery; in graduate school over Christmas vacation at the University of Virginia (I was all alone on the grounds, too busy with writing papers to go home to Boston); and, as I say, over a winter in Estonia. It is a book profoundly important for any seeker. His epistles are public letters, non-literary yet artistic, essays, in fact. I am always struck that Paul has many voices, moods, tempers, and modalities. Arguing. Heckling. Thundering. Pleading. He is excitable, often too busy to write, almost always dictates. He loves digressions — "It would not be St. Paul, if he did not digress," wrote Msgr. Ronald Knox — and sees the value of paradox and understands its force. He loves tree imagery, the language of potters, Socratic questioning, legal terminology. The man was taut as a tangent, a short-ruddy-haired Pharisee from Tarsus in Cilicia (now Turkey), a tent-maker, also a Roman citizen with privileged legal status that once saved him from a whipping in Jerusalem. No man on a mission was ever more intent than the dauntless St. Paul. If I were ever seeking to hide, he would be the very last person I would ever want pursuing me. The man never gave up. Is it any wonder that the heathen Galatians mistook him for the god, Mercury?

99. David Lebedoff's *The Same Man* (Random House, 2008) offers a brilliant analysis of the parallels between and relationship of Waugh and Orwell.

100. "Everything begins in mystery and ends in politics," it is a quote from Charles Peguy, the noted French poet, essayist, and editor who was a devout, but non-practicing, Roman Catholic.

101. As an inquisitive test of generosity years ago, something of an experiment, I sent books with requests for signatures to both President Jimmy Carter and the Rev. Billy Graham. Carter, not only a humble and, I believe, deeply spiritual man but a humanitarian, a peace ambassador, an author, a poet, and a dedicated Christian who for decades has been giving of his time and effort since 1984 with Habitat for Humanity, personally building houses for the poor — a U.S. President! — took time to inscribe my copy. The book that I sent to Graham predictably came back, unsigned, with a form letter of lordly corporate bullshit about the man being too busy to sign it. He was meant for larger things, it seems. I add this simply because a postcard exists showing Billy Graham large and in charge in a public square in Copenhagen actually autographing a Bible, an anomaly of such glaring and egregious delight — if you charitably choose to overlook the blasphemy — that the brilliant Flannery O'Connor, who typically savored irony, went so far as to keep one of these cards impishly tucked between the pages of her Bible — surely for comic relief! (See Brad Gooch, *Flannery* (Little Brown, 2009) p. 252)

102. "God is the only being who in order to reign does not even *need* to exist!" [my stress] — an imposingly paradoxical definition that can be found in Baudelaire's *Fusées*, 1867

103. Does that sound amazing? I find it equally if not more astonishing that, reluctantly, but to spare the feelings of a group Judeo-Christians whose company he shared, St. Paul actually rolled up his sleeves and literally — personally — circumcised Timothy, the young Greek born of Jewish mother whom he met in Galatia, and took him along for company on to Macedonia, Philippi, Thessalonia, and Athens.

104. Matthew's genealogy commences with Abraham and then from King David's son, Solomon, follows the legal line of the kings through Jeconiah, the king whose descendants were cursed, to Joseph, legal father of Jesus. Matthew's gospel, like Luke's, states that Jesus was begotten not by Joseph, but by the Holy Spirit, being born to Mary through a virgin birth.

105. "Some of course have to die down/Where the heavy oars of ships drag." Hugo von Hoffmansthal, "*Manche freilich...*" (1895-96) in: *Ausgewählte Werke in zwei Bänden*, vol. 1, p. 22

106. Saxo Grammaticus wrote of old Estonian warriors who, gathered together, sang at night while waiting for an epic battle to begin. Runic singing was not the polyphonic choral song that we know today but primarily monophonic chanting with a lead singer and a chorus, where, uniquely, curiously, the singing provides no opportunity for drawing a breath, only yet another Estonian anomaly.

107. "A Hole in the Ground Erupts, to Estonia's delight", December 9, 2008

108. "Disillusionment Of Ten O'clock" from *Collected Poetry and Prose*

109. We are following the Douay Rheims Version throughout

110. "Men Made Out of Words" from *Collected Poetry and Prose*

111. As many as one hundred or more witch trials were held in Estonia in the years 1610-1650, when it was recorded that as many as 29 women and 26 men were executed for sorcery. These were basically werewolf trials, not quite witchery, as it was understood back in the days of old Salem, Massachusetts. Although Christianity had been established by the end of the 13th century in Estonia, pagan ceremonies were common at the time. Superstitions rose of people being werewolves, and accusations followed. The most infamous case recorded in Estonia was probably that of "Hans the Werewolf." In 1651, accused of sorcery, Hans was brought before the court where he openly confessed that he had hunted as a werewolf for two years. The last trial of sorcery was performed as late as 1816 in the area of Harju County, which is located in northern Estonia on the south coast of the Gulf of Finland, when a certain farmer Jacob and his wife, Anna, along with four others, were accused of trying to track thieves by the use of magic. Jacob and Anna were given a public whipping, while the others were reprimanded for "fraud which appeals to superstitions and ignorance."

112. Regarding lakes and superstition — or faith, if you will — Lake Pühajärv in Otepää, a town in southern Estonia, is regarded as holy.

113. The Fool is a big mystery: what happens to him? He disappears after Act III, Scene 6, and nobody ever explains where he has gone.

114. Herodotus' *Histories* (Book 4:7) translated by George Rawlinson

115. *The Hitler Book* edited by Henrik Eberle and Matthias Uhl, p. 294

116. Juniper berries, Estonians believe, can help cure 99 diseases, overcome witchcraft and the devil, as there is a cross on top of each berry.

117. The one exception that I ever came across, in this case only by my having blundered upon it, means of a blundering flash-through, can be found in a crapulous 1985 novel by one Benjamin Stein — now a TV shill — called *Her Only Sin* in which his character Susan-Marie Warmack, a movie-struck fan, is fixated on a film, "Estonia," a daffy sci-fi parable she has seen six times — she also worships the director — in which "a part of Russia that was separated from the mainland by a giant earthquake has become a kingdom that, even in 1939, is still living [sic] by courtly seventeenth-century folkways."

118. Estonian chess grandmaster Paul Keres (1916-1975), born in Narva, in his day was dubbed the "Crown Prince of Chess." He held many chess records, was the only player to beat nine undisputed world champions, and represented the Soviet Union in seven consecutive Olympiads, winning seven consecutive team gold medals, five board gold medals, and one bronze board medal. Estonia seems to be a breeding ground for chess geniuses. Lambert Oll, a recent grandmaster from Kohtla-Järve, won multiple European and World junior championships but then tragically committed suicide in 1999, at age 33, by leaping out of the window of his a fourth-floor apartment, exactly as did the protagonist in Vladimir Nabokov's novel, *The Defense*. No list of Estonian chess can be compiled without mention of the legendary Lionel Kieseritzky (1806-1853) who, strangely enough, became world famous for a defeat by the German Adolf Anderssen. Born in Tartu into a Baltic German family, he was not only vain, haughty, and narcissistic — he held himself up in a kind of megalomania to be the "Chess Messiah" — and yet his career was blighted by repeated misfortune and an endless series of unsound acts. On May 18, 1853, after an extended bout of mental illness, he died alone and was buried in a pauper's grave in Paris, a city he called home for most of his life. The eccentric Kieseritzky who gave sporadic chess lessons for income could often be found playing games for five francs an hour at the Café de la Régence in Paris, not only an important European centre for chess in the 18th and 19th centuries but also a meeting place for such celebrated thinkers as Diderot and Rousseau and, later, Marx and Engels. A show-off, Kieseritzky was known for intentionally handicapping himself and beating lesser players by ostentatiously playing games without his queen. Oddly enough, it was Kieseritzky himself, during his period as editor of *La Régence*, the chess journal that he launched in 1849, who recorded and published — as a penance? — the now legendary off-hand game in London that he so ignominiously lost against Anderssen and that has ever since so thrilled

generations of chess players that it has been dubbed "The Immortal Game". The game — an informal one — was played in London on June 21, 1851 at Simpson's-in-the-Strand during a break in a formal tournament. What characterized play in the main were the very bold sacrifices made by the daring Anderssen to secure victory, for he gave up both rooks and a bishop, then his powerful queen, checkmating his opponent with his three remaining minor pieces. It has been called an achievement "perhaps unparalleled in chess literature." The incongruously inspired Kieseritzky was so impressed when the game was over that he immediately telegraphed all the moves of the game to his Parisian chess club. The French chess magazine *La Régence* published the game in July 1851. It was later in 1855 that the Austrian Ernst Falkbeer nicknamed it "The Immortal Game." The town of Marostica in Italy has replayed the game with live players, dressed as chess pieces, every year since 1923. Further, the chess game that is played in the 1982 film, *Blade Runner*, is based on "The Immortal Game." On the album of the electronic band, Symbion Project, *Immortal Game*, released in 2003, the first and last tracks are titled after the first and last moves of the game for which the album is named ("Pawn to King 4", and "Bishop to King 7, Checkmate") Finally, the writer David Shenk went on to name his 2006 book documenting the history of chess after this same game, with a move-by-move description of the game appearing intermittently in the narrative. For further excitement, recreations of the game can be seen played out on *YouTube*.

119. I find it equally curious that such a demi-sea-girt country as Estonia has given the world so few ocean explorers and sea travelers, when, for example, Norway with only 4 million people produced such intrepid sailors as Fridtjof Nansen, Roald Amundsen, Helge Ingstad, Thor Heyerdahl, and many others. One can however point to Thaddeus Von Bellingshausen (1778-1852), the Arctic explorer, who was born in Osel, Estonia when it was part of the Russian Empire.

120. The Rakvere *Lihakombinaat*, or meat-processing plant, east of Tallinn, is the biggest manufacturer of meat products in the Baltic States, dating back to the year 1890 when the first slaughterhouse was opened in Rakvere. Back in 1987, a merger was made with the Finnish enterprise "Suomen Rakennusvienti," and it became the biggest, most modern meat-processing plant in the Baltic States, cranking out meat products of every possible kind: luncheon meats, wieners, wursts, frankfurters, minced meat products, smoked meats, smoked sausages, patés, jellied products, deep-frozen products, blood sausages and puddings, bacon, and sausages for the grill. Since 2004, the company commendably gives out food packages at Christmas to all families in Estonia with seven or more children. In 2008, 236 families received this charitable Christmas package.

121. "O you strong stomachs that cull it!
    What poison is this that is burning my entrails?"

122. Ruffles and flourishes

123. *New Yorker*, July 20, 2009

124. Act II, Scene II, Gobbo says: "I have here a dish of doves that I would bestow upon your worship,

and my suit is—"

In Shakespeare's time, the words *doves* and *pigeons* were used indifferently as regards to all members of the family *Columbidae,* and, to some extent, this is still the case. In general parlance the terms "dove" and "pigeon" are used somewhat interchangeably. In ornithological practice, however, there is a tendency for "dove" to be used for smaller species and "pigeon" for larger ones, although this is in no way consistently applied, and historically the common names for these birds involve a great deal of variation between the terms "dove" and "pigeon." Young doves and pigeons are called "squabs," probably from Scandinavian *skvabb,* meaning "loose, fat flesh." Squabs are raised to the age of roughly a month before being killed for eating, having reached adult size but having not yet flown.

125. Coca-Cola Hellenic Baltics (HBC), for business reasons, closed down its Estonian plant in April 2010 but kept the Baltic headquarters as well as warehousing and marketing facilities in Tallinn, The production of PET packages — food-grade recycled polyethylene terephthalate plastic for bottles — was transferred from Tallinn to the plant in Alytus in Lithuania. Glass bottles are commissioned by way of sub-contracting from Poland.

126. See *Eimi,* "Tuesday," p. 25 (Liverright Publishing Corp., New York, 2007)

127. Loos, who considered ornament even "immoral" and "degenerate," took as one of his examples the tattooing of the Papuan whose surface decorations he considered not to have evolved to the moral and civilized circumstances of "modern" man. Who knows, maybe it was his penchant for or, as he put it, "passion for smooth and precious surfaces" — all three brief marriages (and divorces) of his were to very young girls — that may have led to the notorious paedophilia scandal in 1928 in Vienna that finally disgraced him and rendered him penniless.

128. No murderous enfilades here, mind you. Not Wotan and Fricka. Cheek-to-jowl living can be stressful, that's all, especially in benighted circumstances. Returning to the flat after a cold day's exile I used to think of the place — in a mood both comic and rueful — as The House of Him Who Had His Sandal Pulled Off (cf. Deuteronomy 25:10)

129. Sonnet #13, Part II, "Sonnets to Orpheus" (translated by Alfred Poulin, Jr.)

130. "Those who run across the seas change the sky, not their souls. Heaven knows." Epistle 1.11

Index